Black
Americans

FIFTH EDITION

Black
Americans

ALPHONSO PINKNEY

Professor Emeritus, Hunter College
The City University of New York

PRENTICE HALL, Upper Saddle River, New Jersey 07458

Library of Congress Cataloging-in-Publication Data

PINKNEY, ALPHONSO.
   Black Americans/Alphonso Pinkney. — 5th ed.
      p.   cm.
   Includes bibliographical references and index.
   ISBN 0–13–082577–8 (alk. paper)
      1. Afro-Americans—History.   2. Afro-Americans.   I. Title.
   E185.P5   1999
   973′.0496073—dc21   99-19865
                                                                         CIP

Editorial director: Charlyce Jones Owen
Editor-in-chief: Nancy Roberts
Managing editor: Sharon Chambliss
Editorial/production supervision and interior design: Rob DeGeorge
Copyeditor: Virginia Rubens
Buyer: Mary Ann Gloriande
Marketing manager: Christopher DeJohn
Cover art director: Jayne Conte
Cover design: Jayne Kelly

This book was set in 10/12 Times Roman by DM Cradle Associates
and was printed and bound by Courier Companies, Inc.
The cover was printed by Phoenix Color Corp.

Printed in the United States of America

10   9   8   7   6   5   4   3   2

ISBN 0-13-082577-8

PRENTICE-HALL INTERNATIONAL (UK) LIMITED, *London*
PRENTICE-HALL OF AUSTRALIA PTY. LIMITED, *Sydney*
PRENTICE-HALL CANADA INC., *Toronto*
PRENTICE-HALL HISPANOAMERICANA, S.A., *Mexico*
PRENTICE-HALL OF INDIA PRIVATE LIMITED, *New Delhi*
PRENTICE-HALL OF JAPAN, INC., *Tokyo*
PEARSON EDUCATION ASIA PTE. LTD., *Singapore*
EDITORA PRENTICE-HALL DO BRASIL, LTDA., *Rio de Janeiro*

For My People

The American Negro is a unique creation;
he has no counterpart anywhere and no
predecessors.

James Baldwin

Contents

Preface

When this book was first published in 1969, African-Americans faced a serious crisis arising from the assassination of Martin Luther King, Jr. Angered by this act, blacks took to the streets in cities around the country, demonstrating their outrage by massive acts of property destruction. In general, white individuals and institutions responded to the tragedy of the assassination by attempting to make some amends for past injustices. Colleges and universities recruited black students in greater numbers than ever before, and programs of African-American and African studies were organized on a wide scale. It appeared that equality for blacks had finally become an issue of critical importance.

However, by the time the second edition appeared in 1975, little change in the status of African-American people relative to that of white people had come about, but many changes in the mind and mood of African-American people had occurred, mainly in the ascendancy of nationalist sentiment in the black community. Black nationalist organizations thrived until the Federal Bureau of Investigation and other government agencies commenced a systematic campaign to destroy this movement. Because of this campaign and the inevitable internal dissension within these organizations, the movement virtually collapsed. Nevertheless, with the advent of affirmative action, some progress was made in the status of African-Americans in the United States. For a brief time there was an official commitment to racial equality.

With the third edition in 1987, the mood of the country had changed, and conservatism had become the dominant ethos of American politics and of the country as a whole. The right-wing administration of Ronald Reagan and the egocentricity of the American people combined to mount a serious attack on compensatory justice. They were joined in this effort by black conservatives who opposed affirmative action and other measures to improve the lot of African-Americans, insisting that blacks must rely on individual initiative and self-help rather than government assistance. These forces succeeded in reversing some of the gains that African-Americans and others had made through intensive struggle.

The fourth edition in 1993 found African-Americans facing additional challenges of major proportions: acquired immune deficiency syndrome (AIDS), adolescent pregnancy and childbearing, crack cocaine and other substance abuse, homelessness, and widespread homicide, among others. By promoting and condoning racial oppression through the years, the government must bear major responsibility for the impact of these problems on African-Americans.

In this, the fifth edition of the book, it should be noted that there has been little, if any, change in the problems enumerated in the fourth edition. In addition, there has been an intensified effort to end affirmative action, thereby impeding an important avenue to black progress. Because of this, a chapter on the subject has been added, along with some other changes, including a chapter on crime and justice.

Although this book is a sociological study of African-Americans, it addresses the general reader as well as the professional student of society. It is hoped that sociological perspective and analysis have not been sacrificed.

I would like to thank the following reviewers for their helpful suggestions: Darnell F. Hawkins, University of Illinois at Chicago; and Robert L. Carter, Hunter College, CUNY.

Several people assisted in preparing this edition, including my editor, Sharon Chambliss, and my production editor, Rob DeGeorge, at Prentice Hall; and Mark Schwartz and Denise Garland of the U.S. Department of Education. I am grateful to them for their contributions to whatever virtues this edition may have, but its shortcomings are mine alone.

Alphonso Pinkney

Black
Americans

CHAPTER ONE

Historical Background

Historians insist that a knowledge of the past is essential for understanding the present. This axiom is especially relevant insofar as black Americans are concerned, for theirs is a unique history. Virtually all aspects of their history are without parallel when compared with those of other minority groups in the United States. The very circumstances that led to their departure from their homeland, to the Middle Passage between Africa and the New World, and to the institution of slavery that developed on their arrival in what is now the United States are unique to black Americans out of all U.S. minority groups. The institution of slavery, with all its peculiarities, has left a legacy that continues to play a dominant role in the life of Americans. After nearly three and a half centuries, white Americans continue to react to African-Americans with a mass irrationality that precludes the complete entrance of blacks into the larger society. Yet it would be difficult to imagine members of a group putting forth more diligent and persistent efforts for acceptance than those put forth by black Americans. A variety of approaches has been attempted throughout the years, and some gains have been made; but a series of historical circumstances has preserved the low status of African-Americans in the society.

The history of black people in the United States is complex, and no attempt to record this detailed sequence of events in one chapter can succeed. However, certain occurrences have a greater bearing on the present status of black people in American society than others.

SLAVERY

Black people were among the earliest participants in the Spanish explorations of what is now the United States, but the first Africans to settle on its shores arrived in 1619. In that year a Dutch vessel landed in Jamestown, and the captain sold twenty blacks to the Virginia settlers. This was twelve years after the establishment in

Virginia of the first permanent British colony in America and one year before the Pilgrims landed on the *Mayflower* at Plymouth Rock (Massachusetts). Inasmuch as there was no precedent for slavery in English law, these blacks and those who followed for some time after that had the same legal status as white indentured servants. Their term of service was prescribed by local laws. Throughout much of the seventeenth century, the status of blacks was not at all clearly defined, and the institution of chattel slavery gradually evolved into one in which black people, in part because of their physical differences, held a caste position in society. Like white indentured servants, they had a chance to gain their freedom after working for a specified number of years or after converting to Christianity. The ambiguity of this status as indentured servant rather than slave, combined with the uncertainties attached to the Indian and white indentured servant supply, led to the ultimate relegation of black people to a status of perpetual servitude.[1]

Slavery as practiced in North America was a complex institution. In some respects the practices varied by state, region (Deep South versus Border South), size of plantation, number of slaves involved, season of the year, and, of course, the convictions of the individual slaveholder. However, many practices were common throughout the slaveholding states. Furthermore, many of the restrictions imposed on the slaves were also applicable to "free" blacks in the United States, both in the South and elsewhere in the country. In addition to the general characteristics of slavery in the South, of special relevance to the present discussion are the slaves' loss of their native culture, the attitude of white people toward slaves, the reaction of slaves to their status, and the status of black people who technically were not slaves.

General Characteristics of Slavery

The first statutory recognition of slavery in North America occurred in Virginia in 1661. This lead was soon followed by the other colonies, and by the time the colonies gained independence, chattel slavery and a body of law defining the status of slaves had become institutionalized. These laws covered every aspect of a slave's life. In general, slavery in North America developed into the harshest form of social relations ever to exist. Slaves received none of the protections of organized society because they were not considered to be persons; rather, they were considered to be property, and only to the extent that a citizen's property must be protected could the slave expect society's consideration. Slaveholders maintained absolute power over their property. They were endowed by law with rights over the slave and in return were expected to assume certain obligations toward the slave. "The law required that masters be humane to their slaves, furnish them with adequate food and clothing, and provide care for them during sickness and old age."[2] Therefore slaves were at one and the same time human beings and property, and "throughout the antebellum South the cold language of statutes and judicial decisions made it evident that, legally, the slave was less a person than a thing."[3] In such a status the slaves were denied virtually all rights, both civil and political. Perhaps the most important element in defining the status of slaves was the perpetual nature of slavery; slaves were destined to occupy this status throughout their lives and to transmit it to their children, who in turn transmitted their inherited status to their children. Slave and African-American became synonymous, and because slaves were defined as innately inferior, blacks were defined as inferior beings.

Because slaves were forbidden by law to enter into contractual arrangements, their marriages were not legally binding relationships. Husbands, wives, and children could be separated at the discretion of the slaveholder, as happened frequently. Thus it was impossible to maintain a stable family system. The slave family had little importance with regard to the traditional functions that marriage was expected to perform for those who entered into the relationship. Parents had little to say or do about rearing children or controlling other forces leading to cohesion in family life. The nature of the institution of slavery was such that no family in the usual sense can be said to have existed. Children derived their condition from the status of the mother. The father " . . . was not the head of the family, the holder of the property, the provider, the protector."[4] His wife could be undressed and either whipped or violated by the slaveholder or overseer in his presence and in the presence of the children.

Slaves were property that could be sold, traded, or given as gifts, and slave families were frequently dissolved for economic reasons. As Stampp has written, "They were awarded as prizes in lotteries and raffles; they were wagered at gambling tables and horse races. They were, in short, property in fact as well as in law."[5] Female slaves were encouraged to engage in promiscuous relations with other slaves. Although these relations occasionally developed into stable ones, they were more often associations entered into for the express purpose of reproduction. In the words of Frazier: "To the slave trader, who had only an economic interest in the slave, the Negro was a mere utility."[6] Clearly no stable family system could develop under such circumstances. The permanency of marriage depended on those rare opportunities slaves had to live and work together within a situation of common experiences and trust.

According to the laws of the antebellum South, slaves had no civil or property rights. "A slave might not make a will, and he could not, by will, inherit anything. Slaves were not to hire themselves out, locate their employment, establish their own residence, or make contracts for any purpose."[7] They could not be a party to suits involving free persons. Strict interpretations of laws regulated every aspect of their lives, and the enforcement machinery was such that violations rarely went unpunished. These strict laws were geared toward the behavior of the slaves, but they also clearly regulated the behavior of whites who might interfere with slave discipline. To slaves who were found guilty of violating the slave codes, a variety of punishments were meted out, the most frequent being whipping for minor crimes and harsher forms of punishment, including burnings and mutilation, for more serious crimes. The death penalty was common and resulted from such offenses as striking whites.

Stampp views the rigidity of the codes and the harshness of the punishments as serving to instill fear in the slaves. This atmosphere of fear, he maintains, was accomplished through a series of steps designed by the slaveholders to preserve absolute control over their "human property": "accustom him to rigid discipline,

demand from him unconditional submission, impress upon him his innate inferiority, train him to adopt the master's code of good behavior, and instill in him a sense
of complete dependence."[8]

The work performed by the slaves depended on whether they were on a large
plantation or a small farm; whether they were rural or urban; whether the slaveholder
specialized in cotton, tobacco, rice, sugar cane, hemp, or other agricultural products;
whether they were male or female; whether they were assigned to the slaveholder's
house or to the fields; and, of course, what the season of the year was. Regardless of
the foregoing conditions, however, slaves were generally required to work from sun-
rise until dusk. They usually worked under the supervision of a white overseer whose
job it was to maintain strict discipline. All slaves were required to work, and the
slaveholder decided at what age children should go into the fields. In general, by the
age of five or six children were expected to follow their parents into the fields. When
a slave woman was too old to work in the fields, she was expected to perform domestic tasks for the other slaves, such as caring for small children and preparing food.
Old men tended gardens and cared for the animals.

On larger plantations an elaborate division of labor developed. There were
skilled craftsmen, such as carpenters, mechanics, and blacksmiths; a variety of
domestic servants, such as coachmen, housemaids, butlers, cooks, and laundresses;
and, of course, there were field hands who cultivated and harvested the crops. In the
cities slaves worked in construction and maintenance work, in domestic work, at various crafts such as carpentry and cabinetmaking, in laundries, and in cotton presses.[9]
There were few occupational tasks in the antebellum South that slaves did not perform, and, although some slaves managed to evade the 14- to 16-hour day by malin-
gering, the system was such that most of them were forced into a rigorous routine of
hard labor.

Because of the division of labor among slaves, status distinctions developed.
Status was frequently derived from the wealth and extent of holdings of the slaveholder, but the most important distinctions were those between domestic slaves and
those relegated to field work. The "house slaves" enjoyed higher status than the
"field slaves," and they jealously guarded their superior positions. Slaveholders
tended to attach greater significance to the appearance of these slaves. Being around
the slaveholder's family afforded house slaves the opportunity to assimilate the
external forms of behavior that they observed.[10] Slaveholders and their families, who
usually preferred mulatto house servants, encouraged the division between house
slaves and field slaves as a means of maintaining control.[11]

The living conditions of the slaves were generally in keeping with their almost
total lack of status. Most of them lived in small, crude huts without the most elementary provisions for sanitation and safety, such as floors, windows, and interior
walls. Whole families were frequently crammed into one-room cabins. According to
Stampp, "The common run of slaves cabins were cramped, crudely built, scantily
furnished, unpainted, and dirty."[12] Cabins were generally without stoves, beds, or
other essentials. Writing about his childhood as a plantation slave, Booker T.
Washington recalled: "I cannot remember having slept in a bed until after our fam-

ily was declared free by the Emancipation Proclamation. Three children—John, my older brother, Amanda, my sister, and myself—had a pallet on the dirty floor, or, to be more correct, we slept in and on a bundle of filthy rags laid upon the dirt floor."[13] He reports that his mother, the plantation cook, prepared food for all the slaves and whites on the plantation on an open fire in their small cabin. The crowded conditions under which slaves were forced to live were a constant threat to health and sanity. "One Mississippi planter had 24 huts, each measuring 16 feet by 14 feet, for his 150 slaves."[14]

On some of the larger plantations, slaveholders maintained communal kitchens for all slaves, but in general the food provided was the least expensive possible, and no consideration was given to its nutritional value. "A peck of cornmeal and three or four pounds of salt pork or bacon comprised the basic weekly allowance of the great majority of adult slaves."[15]

Because they lived under such adverse conditions, the morbidity and mortality rates among slaves were high. Malaria, yellow fever, cholera, pneumonia, tuberculosis, and tetanus were widespread. Infant and maternal mortality were commonplace. Some of the larger plantations maintained medical doctors for the care of the slaves, but folk medical practices were usually resorted to. Even when doctors were available, the practice of medicine among the slaves was something short of scientific. The doctors frequently complained that they were unable to administer treatment because the slaves were not amenable to the same medical treatment as white patients. Frances Kemble summarized the conditions in a slave infirmary on one plantation: "In all, filth, disorder, and misery abounded; the floor was the only bed, and scanty begrimed rags of blankets the only covering."[16]

Loss of Native Culture

The Africans who arrived in North America represented many cultures. Contrary to popular belief, they were representative of a variety of highly advanced civilizations.[17] These slaves carried with them to North America a knowledge of the complex cultures they left behind. How much of these original cultures was able to survive the brutality of antebellum slavery has been disputed by scholars. There is general agreement, however, that systematic attempts were made to strip these people of their culture. In the first place, slaves were widely scattered on plantations, small farms, and cities throughout the colonies and later throughout the United States. Second, slaves arriving in North America were from a diversity of cultural backgrounds. These cultures might have contained many common elements, but they contained even more distinctive characteristics. Furthermore, since young male slaves predominated in the earliest importations, it was virtually impossible for the slaves to recreate the cultures they knew. Frazier summarizes the impact of slavery on the slaves as follows:

> The African family system was destroyed, and the slave was separated from his kinsmen and friends. Moreover, in the United States there was little chance that he could reknit the ties of friendship and old associations. If by chance he encountered fellow

slaves with whom he could communicate in his native tongue, he was separated from them. From the very beginning he was forced to learn English in order to obey the commands of his white masters. Whatever memories he might have retained of his native land and native customs became meaningless in the New World.[18]

It is not surprising, therefore, that much of the Old World culture failed to survive. However, the circumstances under which slaves lived did not preclude their retaining some cultural characteristics. For example, Franklin sees African survivals in language, folk tales, music, social organization, and aesthetic endeavors.[19] Other scholars maintain that many other survivals of African culture were so pervasive that they have remained to the present day.[20]

Clearly, some aspects of African cultures survived in the antebellum South, but the adjustments these new arrivals were required to make were of such a magnitude that an essentially new way of life developed. Whatever a slave's occupation had been in Africa, he or she was usually forced to enter farming or domestic service in North America. Slaves were forbidden to practice their traditional religions and were required to practice the religion of their oppressors. Although they were denied formal instruction, they had to learn English. The foods they had eaten in Africa were unavailable on southern plantations. Family patterns they had practiced were not permitted. Given these circumstances, and denied participation in the culture of the South, the slaves somehow had to survive in a world that was both hostile and strange. This struggle for survival forced them to create their own patterns of culture, which represented a mixture of elements brought from Africa and those created by their life experiences in the New World.

Attitudes of White People toward Slaves

Although the first Africans to arrive in North America were not treated differently from white indentured servants, as the institution of slavery developed, it became exclusively African-American. The process was gradual, and some historians attribute it to economic forces,[21] although others see race as the primary motivating factor.[22] Regardless of whether the precipitating factor was economic or racist, the attitudes that ultimately developed toward the slaves, and the behavioral component of these attitudes, led to a system of human bondage without parallel in human history.[23] As Tannenbaum has noted, slavery in North America differed from other systems of human slavery, especially those practiced in Latin America, in that the North American slaves were denied, in law and in practice, moral personalities. He writes:

> While the impact of the law did not and could not completely wipe out the fact that the Negro slave was human, it raised a sufficient barrier to make the humanity of the Negro difficult to recognize and legally almost impossible to provide for. This legal definition carried its own moral consequences and made the ultimate redefinition of the Negro as a moral person most difficult.[24]

Hence, rather than being reacted to as human beings possessing moral personalities, slaves in North America were considered simply "beasts of the field."

Not all attitudes toward slaves were strongly negative; however, throughout most of the period of slavery the blacks were considered uniquely suited for human slavery as a result of certain racial traits that, it was thought, made it impossible for them to adjust to the "civilized" world of the Anglo-Saxons.[25] Hence they were "destined by God" to serve Caucasians. This attitude became dominant and governed the behavior directed toward them. Racial inferiority thus became *the* justification for the institution of slavery in North America. Furthermore, the "free" blacks were responded to in similar fashion. Throughout the slave era black people were accorded different treatment from whites, regardless of degree of achievement. Black status was based on ascribed, that is, racial, characteristics.

During the antebellum period slaves came into contact with a variety of white people: slaveholders and their families; overseers, who were usually poor and landless whites; and religious leaders. Although slaveholders differed in their treatment of slaves, they were in general convinced of the innate inferiority of the slaves and treated them accordingly. If the slaves disobeyed orders, they were to be whipped. According to Franklin, "Some planters went so far as to specify the size and type of lash to be used and the number of lashes to be given for specific offenses. Almost none disclaimed whipping as an effective form of punishment, and the excessive use of the lash was one of the most flagrant abuses of the institution."[26]

Slaveholders maintained absolute control over their slaves. As a means of social control, punishment was felt to be most effective. Violation of the norms set by the slaveholder was met with a variety of forms of punishment. Stampp describes some of the more ingenious methods:

> A Maryland tobacco grower forced a hand to eat the worms he failed to pick off the tobacco leaves. A Mississippian gave a runaway a wretched time by requiring him to sit at the table and eat his evening meal with the white family. A Louisiana planter humiliated disobedient male field hands by giving them "women's work" such as washing clothes, by dressing them in women's clothing, and by exhibiting them on a scaffold wearing a red flannel cap.[27]

Frederick Douglass, an ex-slave who became an Abolitionist, a writer, and a minister to Haiti, recalled that the first slaveholder on whose plantation he lived frequently engaged in acts of cruelty toward his slaves. For example,

> I have often been awakened at the dawn of day by the most heart-rending shrieks of an own aunt of mine, whom he used to tie up to a joist, and whip upon her naked back till she was literally covered with blood. No words, no tears, no prayers, from his gory victim, seemed to move his iron heart from its bloody purpose. The louder she screamed, the harder he whipped and where the blood ran the fastest, there he whipped the longest. He would whip her to make her scream, and whip her to make her hush; and not until overcome by fatigue, would he cease to swing the blood-clotted cowskin.[28]

Stampp cites many examples of psychopathic slaveholders who thoroughly enjoyed the practice of inflicting extreme brutality on their slaves.[29]

Because slaves represented an important capital investment in the plantation economy, slaveholders naturally protected their investments, and some reports of the relations between the slaves and the slaveholders indicate ambivalent feelings on the part of the latter. Many of them developed affectionate relations toward their slaves—an affection always tempered by antipathy.

On small plantations slaves had direct contact with the slaveholders. On larger plantations overseers, generally recruited from among the poorer whites, maintained discipline among the slaves. Their treatment of slaves was indicative of the low esteem in which they held these people. On plantations where overseers were employed, cruelty and brutality were institutionalized. Reports of the treatment of slaves by overseers are filled with instances of torture. The overseers were in a peculiar position because they felt exploited by the system, and they tended to displace their frustration onto the slaves. It is reported that fights between slaves and overseers were common, and slaves frequently forced overseers to leave plantations.[30] The brutality of the overseers was indeed widespread, and relations between them and the slaves were rarely amicable.

Although many religious leaders ultimately adopted antislavery positions, most of them perceived slavery as being divinely sanctioned and thereby a natural condition. Most slaveholders approved of religious training for their slaves, but a series of codes developed whereby religious services were rigidly regulated. One of the most universal of these practices was that blacks were prohibited from becoming ministers. Services were conducted by white ministers, who interpreted their function as one of teaching the slaves to adjust to their condition of servitude. Frequently, slaves were required to attend the church of the slaveholder. Through the medium of the church, slaveholders sought to maintain slavery intact. As Franklin has written, compelling the slaves to attend church with the slaveholder was "the method the whites employed to keep a closer eye on the slaves."[31] Slaveholders employed ministers who instructed slaves to be obedient and subservient. Bishops and other religious leaders themselves frequently owned slaves; for example, an Episcopal bishop in Louisiana owned four hundred slaves.[32] Although slaveholders were generally responsible for the religious life of their slaves and the selection of clergymen to preach to them, they had little difficulty finding allies among the clergy. The Scriptures were employed to justify slavery, and many books were written in its defense.[33] In general, the clergymen with whom the slaves came into contact were men who used their religion as a means of maintaining the status quo.

Reactions of Slaves

Owners of slaves, supporters of slavery, and believers in the innate inferiority of the African-American justified slavery on a variety of grounds. One such ground was that the slaves, being docile and childlike, approved of their status. Slavery advocates cited the infrequency and failure of serious insurrections to support their contention that the slaves were indeed happy with their lot in life. Evidence that failed to support their contention was generally ignored. That their beliefs were not rooted in reality is evidenced by the extreme measures they were forced to resort to in order to maintain slavery. Slave revolts occurred in the earliest records of the period and continued throughout the era. Indeed, evidence indicates that the slave traders in Africa experienced both constant resistance to capture from the slaves and numerous revolts during the Middle Passage between Africa and the New World.[34] In addition, many thousands of slaves managed, often against extraordinary odds, to escape from chattel slavery. That slaves reacted to their status with constant attempts to alter it meant that throughout the period they managed to be "a troublesome property" for slaveholders. Attempts to gain freedom took many forms, two of which were insurrections and flights from captivity.

Altogether some 250 slave insurrections and conspiracies are reported to have occurred in the history of African-American slavery, and although some of these were more serious than others, the history of slavery in North America is not without widespread popular revolts on the part of slaves.[35] The first such revolt occurred as early as 1663, and such uprisings continued throughout the slavery era. Some revolts were well planned and organized, and others were haphazardly planned.[36] The 250 revolts reported involved numbers estimated as ranging from ten to fifty thousand slaves.

Three of the many slave revolts stand out because of the seriousness of the attempts, the number of slaves involved, and the reaction they generated throughout slaveholding North America. In 1800 a slave named Gabriel, a worker on a plantation near Richmond, Virginia, who perceived of himself as having a divine mission, organized the first major slave insurrection in North America. Gabriel is said to have possessed unusual intelligence.[37] For weeks he met on Sundays with fellow slaves at parties and dances. On these occasions he selected special slaves to serve as assistants to work on plans with him. Gabriel picked what he felt to be the most advantageous date for the insurrection. The plan called for the use of few weapons. They were to murder the slaveholders and their families on the nearby plantations. Initially, all whites were to be killed, but as the revolt spread, landless whites were to be recruited to fight against wealthy landowners. Strategy was mapped for the spread of the revolt and the enlistment of additional slaves into Gabriel's army. Gabriel had been inspired to insurrection by reading the Bible and by the French Revolution. It is reported that " . . . he was said to have planned to buy a piece of silk cloth to have the egalitarian slogan 'Liberty or Death' printed on it."[38] The revolt never materialized because two fellow slaves on the plantation informed on the slave rebels, and the organizers and other participants were killed.

The second major plan for a slave insurrection occurred in Charleston, South Carolina, in 1822. Denmark Vesey, an ex-slave who had purchased his freedom with money won in a lottery, planned this insurrection. He was a gifted carpenter and, like Gabriel, was said to have been endowed with exceptional intelligence.[39] In his early years in Charleston he used his shop as a meeting place for black people, and he spent much of his time attempting to strengthen his feelings of self-confidence. He was irritated by complacency among both slaves and free blacks. He became a member of the African Methodist Episcopal Church and later a preacher, for the purpose of recruiting prospects for the rebellion he was planning. Altogether he spent four years planning his revolt, and slowly he selected those in whom to confide. This insurrection, like Gabriel's, failed because a "faithful" house servant informed on his fellow slaves. The planners were rounded up; 35 of them were killed, and 34 were deported.

The third and probably the best-known slave revolt occurred in Southampton County, Virginia, in 1831. The leader of this outbreak was Nat Turner, also an intelligent and talented man.[40] Turner had escaped from slavery but had voluntarily returned because of religious convictions. He became a mystic and frequently buried himself in prayer. Through visions he became convinced that he had been divinely ordained to lead his people out of bondage. Because of his mysticism, little time and effort went into planning the revolt. Therefore it involved fewer participants than previous revolts; but it became the biggest slave uprising in North America. Armed with an ax and clubs, six men first murdered the plantation owner and his family and then proceeded to nearby houses, killing all through the night. Altogether they murdered 55 whites. By the time the rebellion had been quelled, Turner's troops numbered more than sixty. The Army of the United States was finally called to put down the rebellion, and the soldiers were joined by other whites, who attacked the slaves indiscriminately.

The attack on Harpers Ferry by John Brown, a white man, was an important uprising and no doubt played a major role in the abolition of slavery. However, few slaves joined Brown in his attempt to liberate the slaves. Brown devoted his entire life to the elimination of slavery; once he became convinced that moral appeals were of no avail with slaveholders, he concentrated on armed revolt. As with Nat Turner's revolt, John Brown's raid on Harpers Ferry was subdued by the armed militia.

Although there were many revolts by the slaves in North America, few of them gained significant momentum, and all failed. In no case did they succeed in improving the status of the slaves; rather, they generally brought forth repressive measures. Some reasons for the failure of the slave revolts may be advanced. The very nature of slavery and its effects on the slave were such that successful insurrection was impossible. As Elkins has written, "American slavery operated as a 'closed' system—one in which, for the generality of slaves in their nature as men and women, *sub specie aeternitatis,* contacts with free society could occur only on the most narrowly circumscribed of terms."[41] Such a system had a demoralizing effect on the slaves' personalities, thereby rendering widespread participation in revolts unlikely and, in many cases, unthinkable. As has been mentioned, slaveholders encouraged status differences among slaves as a means of dividing and conquering them. Revolts were most often betrayed by that category of slaves most closely allied to the owner—the house slaves. Because the plantation was a closed system, communication among slaves on the various plantations was impossible. Whenever slaves met, for whatever reason, they were under the constant surveillance of whites. Finally, of crucial importance was the ratio of slaves to whites in North America. Slaves were usually outnumbered, and where they happened to be in a majority, any slaveholder had the full force of the military at his or her disposal for the purpose of maintaining order. This was the situation after the colonies gained independence, and it was during this period that organized slave revolts were common. Therefore the lack of success of slave revolts cannot be taken as an indication of blacks' acceptance of their status. As Stampp has written, "In truth, no slave uprising ever had a chance of ultimate success, even though it might have cost the master class heavy casualties. The great majority of the disarmed and outnumbered slaves, knowing the futility of rebellion, refused to join in any of the numerous plots. Most slaves had to express their desire for freedom in less dramatic ways."[42]

Recognizing the futility of organized rebellion, most slaves expressed their antipathy for slavery in individual acts. Most frequently these acts took the form of escape. From the very inception of the institution until its end, runaway slaves posed problems for the slaveholders. The newspapers of the period were full of advertisements in search of escaped slaves. The exact number of slaves who escaped is not known, but it is estimated that thousands fled each year. Estimates of the total number of escapees in the four decades between 1810 and 1850 run as high as one hundred thousand, with a value of more than $30 million.[43] So great was the number of runaway slaves that in 1793 Congress enacted the Fugitive Slave Law, which empowered a slaveholder to seize runaway slaves who had crossed state lines and ultimately return them to the state from which they had fled. The persistence of slaves in risking their lives to escape serves as dramatic evidence of their reaction to their status.

A significant proportion of the slaves who escaped were aided by free blacks and white Abolitionists. The Underground Railroad, an organized effort to assist slaves attempting to escape, is said to have been incorporated in 1804.[44] It was operated in defiance of federal fugitive slave laws, and thousands of slaves were able to escape to the North and to Canada through its utilization. So well organized was it that funds for its operation were solicited from philanthropists. Employing several thousand workers, the Underground Railroad operated hundreds of "stations" in the East and West. The number of slaves to escape through the Underground Railroad is not known, but estimates run into the hundreds of thousands, with an estimated forty thousand passing through Ohio alone.[45] There are recorded instances in which individual "conductors" on the Underground Railroad assisted thousands of black people in their escape from slavery.

Although some slaves successfully accommodated themselves to their status, the persistence of runaway slaves posed continuous problems for slaveholders. So widespread was this phenomenon that a southern doctor was convinced that blacks suffered from a "disease of the mind," which he called "drapethomania," which caused them to run away.[46] In reality, however, aside from the general harshness and degradation inherent in the institution of slavery, several of its special features served to motivate slaves to flee.[47] Arbitrary separation of slaves from their families induced many to escape. Other slaves resented being moved against their will. Still others reacted to such factors as attempts to work them too severely, fear of punishment, and fear of being sold into the Deep South. The major motivation, however, was a desire to escape from the inhumanity that the institution of slavery imposed. The constant fleeing of slaves is hardly compatible with the view of them held by a leading historian of slavery during the first three decades of the twentieth century. Ulrich B. Phillips saw the slaves as possessing "a readiness for loyalty of a feudal sort," and he viewed them as a people who were eager to please the slaveholders by working "sturdily for a hard boss."[48] He saw them as a people "who for the most part were by racial quality submissive rather than defiant."[49] The views expressed by Phillips were widely shared among slaveholders and writers of the period.

The "Free" Blacks

Not all black people in the United States were enslaved prior to the Civil War. Indeed, the population of the free blacks increased steadily from the middle of the seventeenth century until emancipation. Although they were generally referred to as "free," their status was only slightly higher than that of the slaves and was significantly lower than that of their white neighbors. And although their status resembled that of the slaves, they were in truth neither slave nor free. As one historian of the period has written, "Since the Constitution made no mention of race or color, the states and the federal government separately defined the legal status of free Negroes. Both generally agreed, however, that the Negro constituted an inferior race and that he should occupy a legal position commensurate with his degraded social and economic condition."[50] The population of free blacks in the United States numbered 59,557 at the time of the first census in 1790, and by the census of 1860 (the last before the Civil War), it had increased to 448,070.[51] They were, roughly, evenly divided between the South and non-South regions of the country.[52]

Several factors account for the steady increase in the population of free blacks:[53] (1) manumission of slaves, which had been practiced since the beginning of slavery, became a major factor in the increase in the free black population; (2) children born to free blacks inherited the status of their parents; (3) mulatto children born of free black mothers were free; (4) children of free black and Indian parentage were born free; (5) mulatto children born to white mothers were free; and (6) slaves continued to escape to freedom. Although the population of free blacks came from several sources, their African heritage still relegated them to a precarious position in society.

Perhaps the most difficult task for the free blacks was that of maintaining their freedom. Franklin describes this condition as follows:

> A white person could claim, however fraudulently, that a Negro was a slave, and there was little the Negro could do about it. There was, moreover, the danger of his being kidnapped, as often happened. The chances of being reduced to servitude or slavery by the courts were also great. A large majority of free Negroes lived in daily fear of losing what freedom they had. One slip or ignorance of the law would send them back into the ranks of slaves.[54]

Free blacks were denied many of the rights that white Americans enjoyed. The degree of freedom they enjoyed depended on whether they lived in the South or North, and within these regions it varied from state to state. Their movements were generally restricted, especially in the South, where they were required to carry passes. Most states enacted laws forbidding them to convene meetings unless whites were in attendance. It was especially difficult for them to earn a living. Several states restricted the occupations they could engage in. In spite of these restrictions, free blacks engaged in a number of skilled and professional pursuits; they became druggists, dentists, lawyers, teachers, tailors, carpenters, barbers, shopkeepers, salespeople, and cabinetmakers.

Southern states generally excluded free blacks from the franchise, and most northern states made it difficult for them to vote. Only one state (Georgia) forbade free blacks from owning property, and many of them amassed great wealth.[55] Indeed, many of the free blacks owned slaves. In general, however, black ownership of slaves differed from white ownership in that the free blacks usually also purchased their slaves' spouses, relatives, or friends. Although many of the free blacks attended religious services with whites, in segregated sections of the churches, several all-black congregations and denominations were established during this period. In the South, religious worship, except in the segregated white churches, was difficult for free blacks because it was feared that all-black services would be used to organize insurrections among slaves.

It was difficult for the free blacks to secure education. All southern states made it virtually impossible, and in the North segregated education was the norm. In spite of the difficulties involved, many blacks managed to achieve the highest levels of scholarship. Black people were graduated from college as early as 1827.[56] Before the Civil War, two colleges, Lincoln University in Pennsylvania and Wilberforce University in Ohio, were established for the education of free blacks.

In general, laws reinforced the low status of the free blacks, but where this was not the case, violence was resorted to. Between 1830 and 1850 race riots were widespread throughout the United States. Roaming bands of whites frequently invaded the black sections of cities, burning homes and churches and beating and killing the residents. Violence was resorted to when whites felt that free blacks were competing with them for jobs, and whites commonly drove free blacks from cities. Rarely were blacks protected from these acts of violence by law-enforcement officials.[57]

Although life for the free blacks was somewhat less circumscribed than for the slaves, they were forced to live within a set of rigid rules that made it virtually impossible for them to fulfill the obligations of citizenship. Yet the highest degree of civic responsibility was demanded of them, always at the risk of jail or slavery. In spite of the restrictions on their lives and the uncertainties of their status, many notable achievements were registered. Several free blacks distinguished themselves as Abolitionists; many emerged as educators, poets, playwrights, historians, and newspaper editors.

THE CIVIL WAR

By the middle of the nineteenth century, slavery had become a serious problem for the United States at home and in its relations with other countries. Antislavery sentiment within the country reached significant proportions, and, since the British government had already emancipated the slaves in its colonial possessions, relations between the two countries gradually deteriorated. Various proposals for dealing with slaves were discussed by federal officials, and intersectional strife had reached the point where a bloody confrontation seemed inevitable. The Abolitionists gained ground in their cause of freedom for the slaves, and the slaveholding states maintained their determination to perpetuate the institution. Antislavery societies mushroomed throughout the non-slaveholding states, and the supporters of slavery responded to the challenge by wide-spread acts of violence. Furthermore, at about this time slavery had ceased to be profitable as a system.[58] By the time the president-elect, Abraham Lincoln, arrived in Washington in 1861, he had become well acquainted with the institution of slavery through travels in the South. He had expressed opposition to slavery and vowed, on occasion, to put an end to it. At other times Lincoln expressed segregationist views. It appears that he was both opposed to the institution of slavery and opposed to racial integration. When he assumed the presidency, the country had already become divided on the issue, and since seven of the slaveholding states had already seceded from the Union, a civil war was imminent. The Civil War was an all-important development for the slaves, and of special significance were the participation of blacks in the war, the emancipation it brought about, and the destruction wrought by this armed conflict.

Participation by Blacks

At the beginning of the Civil War, blacks rushed to enlist in the Union army, but they were rejected. In several instances, after being rebuffed, they organized themselves and trained for service in the expectation that they would ultimately be permitted to participate in a war that they were convinced would end with the free-ing of the slaves. In the early stages of the war, they were rejected because it was believed that to permit them to fight would endow them with a status comparable to that of white soldiers. Furthermore, blacks were considered incapable of fighting wars. As Du Bois has pointed out, "Negroes on the whole were considered cowards and inferior beings whose very presence in America was unfortunate."[59] As the war developed, however, army commanders were permitted to use their own discretion about utilizing blacks. Some commanders insisted on returning runaway slaves to their owners, and others permitted them to fight. As the Union army moved South, where the war was being fought, blacks rushed to the Union lines.[60] When they were finally permitted to enlist in Union armies, blacks did so enthusiastically. By the end of the Civil War, approximately 186,000 black troops had been enrolled. These troops took part in 198 battles and suffered 68,000 casualties.[61] It is estimated that 300,000 blacks were involved in the war effort, including servants, laborers, and spies. The troops were organized into various regiments, including artillery, cavalry, infantry, and engineers. They fought in segregated units and were known as the United States Colored Troops. Most of the black troops served under white officers, but Woodson estimated that "Negroes held altogether about 75 commissions in the army during the Civil War."[62] In addition to being segregated, they were paid differ-entially for their services. "The Enlistment Act of 1862 provided that whites in the rank of private should receive $13 a month and $3.50 for clothing, but Negroes of the same rank were to receive only $7 and $3, respectively."[63] Such discrimination was protested by black troops and by their white commanding officers. During the Civil War blacks were engaged in combat in every major battle area and suffered significantly higher casualty rates than did white troops. It is generally conceded that they made significant contributions to the victory of the Union armies.

The Confederate armies, like those of the Union, at first denied blacks the right to fight in the Civil War, but unlike the Union armies, the Confederacy was afraid that if blacks were armed, they would rebel. Furthermore, few, if any, blacks expressed willingness to fight for the cause of the Confederacy. One of the major problems faced by this region was the widespread desertion of the slaves to join the ranks of the Union armies. Confederate army units utilized blacks for cooking and other menial tasks, and several Confederate soldiers took their black servants to war with them.[64] Toward the end of the Civil War, in 1865, the Confederate senate enacted a bill calling for the enlistment of 200,000 black troops who were to be freed if they remained loyal throughout the war. In addition, a bill calling for the conscription of 300,000 additional troops, including blacks, proved unsuccessful. Few blacks volunteered, and many fled to avoid conscription. Furthermore, by this time the Union armies were virtually assured of victory.

The role of the black soldiers in the Civil War has been deprecated. However, one historian of the period summarized their participation as follows: "Without their help, the North could not have won the war as soon as it did, and perhaps it could not have won at all. The Negro was crucial to the whole Union war effort."[65]

The Emancipation

In the midst of the Civil War, on January 1, 1863, President Lincoln proclaimed that "all persons held as slaves within any State, or designated part of the State, the people whereof shall be in rebellion against the United States, shall be then, thence-forward, and forever free." The president made it clear that this action was taken in order to preserve the Union and not to destroy slavery. The newly freed blacks were asked to refrain from violence and to seek employment at reasonable wages. The Emancipation Proclamation gave impetus to increasing black participation in the ongoing Civil War.

News of the Emancipation Proclamation was received by the slaves with bewilderment. There were nearly 4 million slaves in the South at that time, and few of them had ever expected to be set free. They did not know what to do. The state of illiteracy that had been perpetuated for most slaves served to complicate their new lives. In many instances they were powerless to protect themselves against the violence directed toward them by white persons. It is reported: "Many of the slaves immediately left the plantations when they learned that they were free. This was seen as natural since one of the tests of freedom was the ability to move around freely. On the other hand, the attitude of subordination was still strong in some slaves and they were afraid to assert their newly acquired rights."[66] It is perhaps fair to say that emancipation initially came as a shock to the slaves because they were unprepared for it. However, evidence indicates that by and large they welcomed their new status.

The slaveholders and other southern whites, on the other hand, were not pleased with the disruption of the way of life they had grown to cherish and upon which they were dependent. It was reported that "some planters held back their former slaves on the plantations by brute force. Armed bands of white men patrolled the country roads to drive back the Negroes wandering about. Dead bodies of murdered Negroes were found on or near highways and byways. . . . A veritable reign of terror prevailed in many parts of the South."[67] Some slaveholders accepted the change in status of the slaves without such vindictiveness but with reluctance, while others appeared to be relieved that they could now reject a system that had long ago become unpleasant for them.

Destruction Caused by the Civil War

Whatever the causes of the Civil War, the destruction wrought by the conflict was vast. When the Confederate army surrendered in 1865, it signaled the end to the costliest war in which the United States had ever engaged and, indeed, the bloodiest civil war in human history.[68] Its end marked a victory for the Abolitionists and for the blacks, for it ended a system of human slavery that had persisted for almost 250 years. However, since the war had been fought in the South, that area had suffered widespread destruction. With the end of the war came widespread social disorganization among the whites as well as among the slaves. This social disorganization was matched by massive physical destruction. "Fields were laid waste, cities burned, bridges and roads destroyed. Even most of the woefully inadequate factories were leveled. . . . And if the Union forces did not loot quite as many smokehouses and pantries as they were blamed for, what they did do emphasized the helplessness of the once proud Confederates."[69]

One reporter, traveling in the South immediately after the Civil War, recorded the physical destruction of that region. Arriving in Richmond, Virginia, he reported:

> All up and down, as far as the eye could reach, the business portion of the city bordering on the river lay in ruins. Beds of cinders, cellars half filled with bricks and rubbish, broken and blackened walls, impassable streets deluged with debris, here a granite-front still standing and there the iron fragments of crushed machinery—such was the scene which extended over 30 entire squares and parts of other squares.[70]

Of Atlanta, Georgia, he wrote:

> Every business block in Atlanta was burned, except one. The railroad machine shops, the foundries, the immense rolling mill, the tent, pistol, gun carriage, shot-and-shell factories and storehouses of the Confederacy had disappeared in flames and explosions. Half a mile of the principal street was destroyed.[71]

Such descriptions as these could be matched for each of the principal cities of the Confederacy, and loss of lives was staggering. The South had suffered a humiliating defeat by a superior power. Added to this military defeat was the destruction of a way of life, the most serious aspect of which was the liberation of the slaves, a situation that posed social, economic, and political problems of enormous magnitude. Although General Robert E. Lee accepted the terms of the surrender imposed by General Ulysses S. Grant, southerners were determined that defeat in battle would not significantly alter their relations with the newly freed ex-slaves. They considered the blacks to be free but were convinced of their inferiority, and they were also convinced that, given time, southerners would decide their status to their own satisfaction.

RECONSTRUCTION

The efforts to rehabilitate the South, and the role of black people in these efforts, loom as two of the most controversial aspects of American history. Since economic, political, and social life was disrupted by the Civil War, problems posed by Reconstruction were not limited to the South, nor was their outcome determined solely by the role played by the nearly 4 million ex-slaves. It is primarily to the role of the African-American in Reconstruction and to the effects of this period on the present status of black people in the United States that attention is now directed.

Presidential Reconstruction

The year following the Civil War was an especially difficult one for the newly freed blacks. President Lincoln had envisioned Reconstruction as a function of the office of the president, but his assassination in April 1865 put an end to the plans he had formulated. The South was in a state of almost total disorganization, and Lincoln's successor, President Andrew Johnson, appeared to be less concerned about African-American rights than about other aspects of Reconstruction.[72] Meanwhile, the condition of black people gradually deteriorated. Southern whites grew more violent, and as one historian has written, "It seems as though in 1866 every Southerner began to murder or beat Negroes."[73] The president was indifferent to the treatment of black people because his conception of democracy did not include the blacks. The southerners, who had waged a war to keep blacks enslaved, proceeded to pass a series of laws that became known as Black Codes. These laws were specifically designed to restrict the rights of blacks. As Du Bois has written, they represented an attempt ". . . on the part of the Southern states to make Negroes slaves in everything but name."[74] The Black Codes varied from state to state, but in general they dealt with virtually every aspect of the lives of ex-slaves and were designed to take advantage of their precarious position. These codes covered such diverse features as whether blacks could enter certain states, the conditions under which they were allowed to work, their rights to own and dispose of property, conditions under which they could hold public assemblies, the ownership of firearms, vagrancy, and a variety of other matters. In some states any white person could arrest an African-American. In Opelousas, Louisiana, one ordinance provided that "no Negro or freedman shall be allowed to come within the limits of the town of Opelousas without special permission from his employer, specifying the object of his visit and the time necessary for the accomplishment of the same." It continued, "Every Negro freedman who shall be found on the streets of Opelousas after ten o'clock at night without a written pass or permit from his employer, shall be imprisoned and compelled to work five days on the public streets or pay a fine of five dollars."[75]

The southern ex-slaveholders enacted such laws for a variety of reasons, one of them being their irritation at the presence of black troops with bayonets stationed in the South. This practice was only slightly more offensive to them than the establishment by Congress in 1865, over the veto of the president, of the Bureau of Refugees, Freedmen, and Abandoned Lands, commonly known as the Freedmen's Bureau. This agency had as its responsibility aiding refugees and freedmen by "furnishing supplies and medical services, establishing schools, supervising contracts between freedmen and their employers, and managing confiscated or abandoned lands."[76] The Freedmen's Bureau suspended the Black Codes before they became effective. Nevertheless, it became clear to northern observers, Abolitionists, and members of Congress that the president maintained little interest in protecting the rights of the freedmen. Violence directed against them became widespread. During the summer of 1866, for example, bloody race riots erupted throughout the South during which hundreds of black people were killed. Congress therefore voted itself responsibility for Reconstruction.

Radical Reconstruction

Congress established a procedure whereby the South was divided into military districts, and the freedmen became wards of the government. Military commanders of each of the five districts were empowered to suspend the functions of civil government when deemed necessary and to call constitutional conventions consisting of delegates selected without regard to race or previous condition of servitude. The South was finally moving toward democratic reconstruction. In 1865 the Thirteenth Amendment to the Constitution, which abolished slavery, was enacted and ratified, and in 1866 Congress passed, again over the president's veto, the Civil Rights Act of 1866, which made blacks citizens and gave them the same rights enjoyed by white Americans. This law ultimately became the Fourteenth Amendment to the Constitution, which prohibited states from depriving any person "of life, liberty, or property, without due process of the law," and forbade states from denying blacks "the equal protection of the laws."

Perhaps the most revolutionary aspect of Reconstruction was the participation by blacks in the political arena. In the former Confederate states black people registered to vote in greater numbers than whites. The series of Reconstruction Acts enacted by Congress between 1866 and 1868 and the Fifteenth Amendment, which became part of the Constitution in 1870, guaranteed them the right to vote. During the first registrations, when delegates were elected to state conventions in 1868, 703,000 black voters registered as compared with only 627,000 white voters.[77]

Blacks were in the majority in the South Carolina state convention and made up half of the delegates in Louisiana. In the other states they constituted minorities ranging from 10 percent of the delegates to 19 percent.[78]

During the period of Radical Reconstruction, black people participated in politics to a greater extent than in any other period in American history. The masses of blacks, however, were illiterate and depended on southern landowners for support. The landowning class capitalized on the traditional antiblack prejudices of the poor whites, with whom the blacks were in competition, and thereby sought to maintain their position of dominance. Ultimately the landowning class was successful in these efforts, but the blacks managed to play a significant role in the political life of the South. Although they made up numerical majorities in the population of several states, they never effectively controlled the affairs of any states. They often held important offices, but there was never a black governor. There were two lieutenant governors, and several blacks represented their states in the U.S. Congress.

Many of the black leaders in the South were well educated. For example, a black state treasurer in South Carolina had been educated in Glasgow and London; one of that state's black representatives in Congress had been educated at Eton College in England; and a black man who was a state supreme court justice held a law degree from the University of Pennsylvania. Florida's black secretary of state had graduated from Dartmouth College. According to one historian, "One of the really remarkable features of the Negro leadership was the small amount of vindictiveness in their words and their actions. There was no bully, no swagger, as they took their places in the state and federal governments traditionally occupied by white planters of the South. The spirit of conciliation pervaded most of the public utterances the Negroes made."[79] In the realm of social relations, black people gave no indication of serious interest in interpersonal relations with white people. Their chief concern was with being accorded a position of equality with southern whites.

In spite of the constant attempts at counterreconstruction, especially by such avowed white supremacy organizations as the Ku Klux Klan, the Red Shirts, and the Knights of the White Camelia, the newly freed slaves in the South enjoyed a kind and degree of freedom they had not known before and have not known since. Of paramount concern to them was the question of education. In five states black men were elected to the state superintendency of education, and throughout the South both the young and the old flocked to schools. They freely attended places of public accommodation, they voted in large numbers, and they elected intelligent and capable blacks to public office. In effect, they enjoyed a significant measure of political, economic, and social freedom.

The Compromise of 1877: Turn toward Slavery

Throughout the period of Radical Reconstruction, attempts were made by ex-Confederates to impede the progress being made toward racial democracy in the South. Conservatives frequently seized power in state governments, and by 1876 they had succeeded in coming to power and effectively destroying

Reconstruction programs in eight states.[80] Federal troops had been withdrawn from all but three states. Violence directed against blacks was widespread. It was clear that the South was determined to maintain white supremacy at any cost. It was effectively assisted in this endeavor by the outcome of the disputed presidential election of 1876, in which Rutherford B. Hayes was the Republican candidate and Samuel Tilden the Democratic candidate. This disputed election was settled in Congress by the Compromise of 1877, in which Hayes was finally declared the winner. In effect, the Compromise of 1877 saw the Republican party (the so-called Party of Emancipation) abandon the blacks to former slaveholders.[81] The party leaders believed that action was necessary to avert another civil war. Nevertheless, for all practical purposes, this compromise signaled a turning back toward slavery that was to characterize the relations between blacks and whites in the South for decades to follow. The remaining troops were withdrawn from the South, and the South was accorded complete home rule and other political favors. The most important favor to the southerners was the promise that the compromise brought in the realm of race relations: "It did assure the dominant whites political autonomy and nonintervention in matters of race and policy. . . ."[82]

The leaders of the South promised that the rights of blacks would be protected, and especially that the newly ratified amendments to the Constitution would be adhered to. Political leaders in Washington, who were aware of the course the South had been taking since emancipation, appeared to be more interested in political stability than in human rights. Thus virtually all the accomplishments of Radical Reconstruction were gradually overturned. Black people had been most effective in political life, and the southern whites were determined to disfranchise them. It was not long before they succeeded. For the blacks the South proceeded on a backward course. As summarized by Franklin, "Reconstruction was over. The South was back in the Union, with a leadership strikingly like that of the South which had seceded in 1860."[83]

INSTITUTIONALIZED WHITE SUPREMACY

From 1877 to 1954 virtually all the events pertaining to black people in the United States adversely affected their status. Although this period of more than seven decades saw profound changes in the society as a whole, the African-American's status remained relatively fixed. Americans persisted in their prejudiced attitudes toward blacks, and these attitudes were translated into acts of segregation and discrimination in virtually every aspect of life. Where segregation and discrimination were not required by law, they became deeply ingrained in the mores. Such behavior became part of the "American way of life," and few white Americans challenged these sacred practices. Black people, on the other hand, constantly challenged them, especially those that were enacted into law; but they were consistently rebuffed. They had been relegated to a caste position in society, and no black, no matter what his or her level of achievement, could expect to be accorded treatment equal to that of a white person.

The Emergence of "Jim Crow"

With the end of Reconstruction in the South, the restoration of white supremacy was underway. Race became the crucial factor in political, economic, and social life. Although the South was in the vanguard of this movement, it had many allies throughout the country. In 1883, for example, the Supreme Court declared the Civil Rights Act of 1875 unconstitutional. This act made it a crime for a person to deny any citizen equal access to accommodations in inns, public conveyances, theaters, and other places of amusement. Several other judicial rulings of the nation's highest court served to institutionalize white supremacy in the United States. Principal among these was the decision of the Court in the *Plessy v. Ferguson* case in 1896. In this case the Court ruled that separate (i.e., segregated) facilities for blacks and whites were not a violation of the constitutional guarantees of the Thirteenth and Fourteenth Amendments. "If one race be inferior to the other socially, the Constitution of the United States cannot put them upon the same plane," declared the majority opinion.[84] This ruling set the pattern for attitudes toward blacks and treatment of them in the United States that have persisted to the present. It became known as the "separate but equal" ruling of the Supreme Court, and southerners were more concerned with the separation of blacks than with equality. This decision had been foreshadowed by that in a previous case, *Hall v. de Ceur,* in 1877, which stated that "a state could not *prohibit* segregation on a common carrier," and in the case of *Louisville, New Orleans, and Texas Railroad v. Mississippi,* in 1880, when the Court ruled that "a state could constitutionally *require* segregation on carriers."[85]

Jim Crow laws had existed in the South since the fall of the Confederacy, but they were quickly repealed by Reconstruction legislatures. However, with the Compromise of 1877 they reappeared, gradually at first, and by 1890 they were mushrooming throughout the South. In the two decades between 1890 and 1910 these laws served to relegate black people to subordinate status in virtually all aspects of life.[86]

Added impetus to the institutionalization of white supremacy was given by the black educator Booker T. Washington, who advocated accommodation on the part of black people at a time when accommodation meant continued relegation to a subordinate position in society. He encouraged other blacks to accept, as he himself had done, the subordinate position of the African-American. "Cast down your bucket where you are," he admonished black people. Washington's position was clearly set forth in a speech he delivered at the Cotton States Exposition in Atlanta, Georgia, in 1895. Among other things, he told his predominantly white audience: "As we have proved our loyalty to you in the past, in nursing your children, watching by the sickbed of your mothers and fathers, and often following them with tear-dimmed eyes to their graves, so in the future, in our humble way, we shall stand by you. . . ." He continued, "In all things that are purely social we can be as separate as the fingers, yet one as the hand in all things essential to mutual progress."[87] Upon completion of his address it is reported that the white audience "came to its feet, yelling" approvingly, while the blacks in the audience wept.[88] The "Atlanta Compromise" speech, as it became known, assured Americans that the recently mushrooming Jim Crow laws defined the proper form of relations between blacks and whites. Washington was acknowledged as the "leader" of the black population of the United States. The outcome of Washington's program of accommodation to white supremacy was accurately predicted by his most formidable critic, William E. B. Du Bois.[89]

As a leader, Booker T. Washington enjoyed wide popularity among both black and white Americans. He was highly respected by white philanthropists and government officials. As adviser to two presidents (Theodore Roosevelt and William H. Taft), he is reported to have recommended virtually all the appointments of blacks to high office during their administrations. Washington achieved prominence at a time when relations between black and white Americans were deteriorating, and although many aspects of his self-help program might have seemed to improve the status of the freedmen, his lack of concern with equal rights for blacks did not represent an insightful long-range plan.[90]

A wave of terror, stemming from violence directed against blacks, spread throughout the South. As Frazier has noted, during Reconstruction blacks responded to violence by organized action, which often led to race riots, but because of the precariousness of their position at this time, organized action was rare. Hence whites resorted to lynching and terror as means of containing the blacks. Lynchings in the South increased between 1882 and 1890, and the last decade of the nineteenth century witnessed a sharp increase. This increase coincided with the many legislative acts in that region that institutionalized the subordinate status of the blacks.[91]

White Americans in the North had apparently lost interest in the welfare of black people. Indeed, many who had championed the cause of the blacks defended the southern view of race relations. Many periodicals, such as *The Nation, Harper's Weekly,* the *North American Review,* and the *Atlantic Monthly,* carried articles by "Northern liberals and former Abolitionists mouthing the shibboleths of white supremacy regarding the Negro's innate inferiority, shiftlessness, and hopeless unfitness for full participation in the white man's civilization."[92] Meanwhile, disfranchisement of black people proceeded rapidly, and the number of blacks holding elective offices declined. By the turn of the century, the last black congressman had left office, and virtually all black people in the South were disfranchised.

The Black Response

Because of their economic plight and the widespread violence directed against them, many black people sought to improve their status through migration. In 1900 nearly nine-tenths of the blacks in the United States were in the South, the vast majority of them living in rural areas. The migration took several forms: Rural blacks sought safety in the relative anonymity of cities; southern blacks moved North; and many blacks moved to countries in Africa. Because of their economic plight, the absence of skills, and discrimination elsewhere in the United States, however, most blacks remained in the rural South.

The campaign to prove that black people were innately inferior was under way. Southerners led the campaign, but they were by no means alone in this endeavor. Northern newspapers and magazines supported their efforts by running a steady stream of editorials in which blacks were caricatured as subhuman beings. Meanwhile, a talented group of black intellectuals, led by William E. B. Du Bois, challenged the leadership of Booker T. Washington and organized to protest the subordinate position to which black people had been relegated. Du Bois's response to Washington's teachings was stated as follows:

> . . . so far as Mr. Washington apologizes for injustice, North or South, does not rightly value the privilege of voting, belittles the emasculating effects of caste distinctions, and opposes the higher training of our brighter minds,—so far as he, the South, or the Nation does this,—we must increasingly and firmly oppose them. By every civilized and peaceful method we must strive for the rights which the world accords men.[93]

Despite the widespread campaign to prove the innate inferiority of black people, and despite the efforts of Booker T. Washington in counseling them to accommodate to the status quo, many blacks reached the highest realms of scholarship and organized to protest the many Jim Crow laws being enacted throughout the country. By that time disfranchisement in the South was virtually complete, and a system of rigid segregation had been enacted into law. In 1905 these intellectuals met and organized the Niagara Movement, an organization that demanded for blacks the same rights enjoyed by white Americans. This movement convinced numerous white Americans that many black people had rejected the leadership of Booker T. Washington. Furthermore, Washington's program of accommodation appeared to be ineffective in dealing with the widespread antiblack mob violence and other acts of white supremacy spreading throughout the United States. Consequently, a group of whites and blacks met in 1909 and organized the National Association for the Advancement of Colored People (NAACP). They adopted a platform calling for the abolition of segregation, equal educational opportunities, the right to vote, and the enforcement of the Fourteenth and Fifteenth Amendments.[94]

World War I and Its Aftermath

The participation by the United States in World War I did little to improve the status of black people. It did, however, influence their geographic distribution. From 1914 to 1920 an estimated 400,000 to 1 million black people left the South to work in industries of the North.[95] The steady stream of immigrants from Europe had virtually ceased, and blacks in the South were recruited by northern industries. In addition to economic opportunities, continued lynching and intimidation in the South stimulated the northward migration of blacks. As these migrants settled in northern cities, they were forced into segregated neighborhoods. Although continued southern violence had in part motivated this migration, violence also greeted them in their new locations. For example, a mob of whites in East St. Louis, Illinois, massacred and burned 125 blacks in 1917. While black troops fought abroad, their civilian counterparts were forced to defend themselves in the streets back home. Lynching continued in the South. A crowd of three thousand white spectators in Tennessee responded to a newspaper invitation to watch a black man being burned alive.[96] Violence directed against black people during this period was not limited to civilians; black soldiers in uniform were the subjects of continued violence, including lynching, especially in the South.

Meanwhile, nearly 400,000 blacks registered for military service in World War I. In characteristic American fashion, they were enrolled in segregated units and trained at segregated camps. They served mainly in the army, being barred from the marines, and were utilized in only the most menial capacities in the navy. In the army they served in nearly all branches except the Aviation Corps. Service in the army was difficult for blacks because they were constantly insulted by white officers. Throughout the war severe clashes between black and white soldiers erupted. Despite these difficulties, they remained loyal, and some 100,000 of them served on overseas duty. Those who served overseas, like those who remained in the United States, were subject to indignities from white soldiers. Nevertheless, many of them performed heroically in battle and received praise for their services from the French.[97]

The year following the end of World War I was also difficult for blacks. More than 70 black persons, including 10 servicemen in uniform, were lynched. The summer of 1919 was called the Red Summer because of the racial violence that took place. From June to September some 25 race riots erupted in American cities, and 14 blacks were publicly burned alive. The most serious outbreak occurred in Chicago, where 38 persons were killed, 23 of them blacks. The postwar antiblack violence convinced many blacks that it was necessary to defend themselves from these attacks; therefore armed self-defense was widespread, especially in cities.[98]

After the war many blacks remained in Europe, especially in France, where they experienced racial democracy for the first time. Those who returned expected to find changed attitudes in the United States but found instead that white supremacy was still the norm. There had been a deliberate effort to belittle their roles in the war effort, and their scores on the army intelligence tests were widely interpreted as proving their innate inferiority.

The widespread economic prosperity of the 1920s had little effect on the low status to which black people were relegated. By then much of the country was completely segregated along racial lines, and antiblack violence, including lynching, continued unchecked. In response to those conditions, scores of black people in the North and South rallied to the support of Marcus Garvey and the Universal Negro Improvement Association.[99] Garvey was able to build the largest mass movement among blacks in American history. The number of black people who actually became members of the organization is not known; however, estimates range up to 6 million.[100] Garvey's popularity was based on his nationalistic appeal to poorer blacks. He advocated pride in blackness and the eventual establishment of a black nation in Africa. Middle-class blacks, especially the leadership of the NAACP, were his strongest critics, for they envisioned the complete integration of black people in

American society. After a persistent stream of rebuffs, however, many black people maintained doubts about this eventuality. One historian has written in appraisal of Garvey's program: "Its significance lies in the fact that it was the first and only real mass movement among Negroes in the United States and that it indicates the extent to which Negroes entertained doubts concerning the hope for first-class citizenship in the only fatherland of which they knew."[101] The Universal Negro Improvement Association finally declined in 1923, when Garvey was convicted on a charge of using the mails to defraud in raising money for the shipping line that he founded. He was subsequently deported to the West Indies and eventually died in London in 1940.

The post–World War I decade witnessed, in addition to the phenomenal growth of the Universal Negro Improvement Association, what has been called a Negro renaissance. During the 1920s a number of blacks, especially those in Harlem, were active in publishing books, magazines, and newspapers. The theme of the writings and music of this period was an attack on the injustices imposed on blacks by the larger society. Although black authors had published books prior to this time, it was this period of extraordinary literary activity that convinced the owners of publishing companies that black people were capable of high-caliber literary achievement. Although most of their efforts may be termed social protest, the artistic merit of their work marked them as among the outstanding contributors to American literature and music.

The Depression, the New Deal, and World War II

The Great Depression of the 1930s virtually ended the massive migration of blacks from the South. Although most Americans suffered from the depression, it was especially difficult for those in low-status occupations, and the overwhelming majority of blacks fell within this category. By the mid-1930s great masses of blacks were receiving public assistance; in some sections of the country the figure was as high as 80 percent. When the unemployed and hungry blacks applied for public assistance, they again met with discrimination. In many sections of the country, there was a significant differential between the allocations they received and those received by white Americans.[102]

The government agencies created to deal with problems brought about by the depression were effective in aiding those poor people who were in greatest need, including a significant proportion of blacks. Whatever assistance was provided by the New Deal generally occurred within a framework of segregation. President Franklin D. Roosevelt appointed what became known as his Black Cabinet to advise him on matters pertaining to the welfare of black people. Many blacks held high (although primarily symbolic) positions in such agencies as the National Youth Administration and the Department of the Interior. Because of the interest of Roosevelt and of Eleanor Roosevelt in the general welfare of the poor, and of blacks in particular, black people began to shift in large numbers from the Republican party to the Democratic party. The northward migration and the residential segregation of blacks in large cities stimulated political rejuvenation for the first time since

Reconstruction. The New Deal policies of the Roosevelt administration ushered in a new conception of the role of government toward citizens. Many of the social welfare measures enacted during the period helped bring the country out of the depression and have since become firmly established social policy.

In many ways the New Deal signaled a turning point in attitudes toward blacks.[103] Many of the prominent politicians of this period expressed an interest in the plight of the black population as part of a broader humanitarian interest in the problem of poverty. For example, one individual who expressed great interest in the welfare of black people was Harold L. Ickes, secretary of the interior and a former president of a local chapter of the NAACP. In addition, black voting strength in northern cities reached a point at which blacks' welfare could not be easily ignored. Furthermore, blacks organized to protect their interests. In 1933 the Joint Committee on National Recovery, a coalition of black-rights organizations, was founded to fight discriminatory policies in federal works projects. One of its main accomplishments was exposing differential wages paid to black and white workers.

In general the New Deal benefited black people by creating a favorable climate of opinion for increased civil rights, by increasing the material benefits paid to the unemployed, and by reducing discrimination in employment. However, discrimination continued in federal works projects and in the policies of the Agricultural Adjustment Administration; moreover, segregation was maintained in public accommodations in the South and in housing financed by the Federal Housing Administration.[104]

The rise of industrial unionism, especially the formation of the Congress of Industrial Organizations (CIO), had its impact on race relations during the 1930s. Although separate locals were maintained in the South, the CIO made interracial trade unionism respectable. It gave black and white workers a sense of common interest, and for the first time black and white workers worked together, receiving equal pay for comparable jobs.[105]

As the United States became increasingly involved in the war in Europe, a period of widespread prosperity was enjoyed by most Americans, including blacks. Again the southern blacks migrated north by the millions. As they sought employment in the war industries, they were faced with characteristic acts of discrimination. It took the threat of a massive march on Washington by blacks to force President Roosevelt to issue an executive order barring discrimination against blacks in industries with government contracts. Since many black people had received technical training during the New Deal administration, they were well prepared to work in industries supporting the war effort.

More than a million black men and women served in the military service during World War II. Approximately 500,000 of them served overseas. As usual, the military services were rigidly segregated, although toward the end of the war a practice of integrating black platoons into white units overseas was established. Widespread violence and discrimination continued, causing black servicemen to question their participation in a war being fought for "four freedoms" by a country that denied them the very principles for which they were fighting on behalf of others. Servicemen in uniform were beaten and murdered by southern policemen and citizens. Attempts on their part to resist segregation and discrimination resulted in frequent clashes on military installations, both at home and abroad, that sometimes led to race riots. One of the more humiliating practices for black servicemen was that of restaurant owners' serving German prisoners of war in places of public accommodation in the United States while denying similar service to black servicemen.[106]

The continued adherence to white supremacy in the face of widespread participation by blacks in World War II, as well as the support of the war effort by black civilians, raised doubts in the minds of many black people about the seriousness of cultural pronouncements of such concepts as "freedom," "justice," and "equality." Meanwhile, as the war was being waged in Europe and Asia, European colonial powers were beginning to lose their black colonies in Africa. At the close of the war the United Nations was established, and the United States became increasingly concerned about its "image" abroad.

During the years immediately following World War II, because of the combination of increased black militancy and changing world conditions, several events occurred that gave black people some hope that their depressed status might somehow be altered. New York State enacted the first state Fair Employment Practices Law in 1945. President Harry S Truman created the first national committee on civil rights in 1946, and in 1948 he issued an executive order banning segregation and discrimination in the armed forces. Meanwhile, the Supreme Court, beginning in 1946, issued a series of decisions outlawing segregation in various aspects of American life, culminating in the decision in 1954 that prohibited racial segregation in public education.

•   •   •

This brief sketch of significant historical events in the lives of African-Americans since the first permanent black settlement in North America has focused on those circumstances that are responsible for the present state of race relations in the United States. Blacks were enslaved and subjected to a system of bondage with few parallels in human history. Formal slavery ended in a costly war, and a caste system developed that continued to relegate the former slaves and their descendants to a subordinate position in society. By the middle of the twentieth century, the oppressed status of black people had finally been recognized as a social problem of some magnitude, and there were attempts by both black and white Americans to deal with the problem. These approaches are discussed in the next chapter.

SELECTED BIBLIOGRAPHY

APTHEKER, HERBERT. *A Documentary History of the Negro People in the United States*. New York: Citadel Press, 1951.

———. *American Negro Slave Revolts*. New York: International Publishers Co., 1963.

ARMSTRONG, GEORGE D. *The Christian Doctrine of Slavery*. New York: Charles Scribner's Sons, 1857.

BENNETT, LERONE, JR. *Before the Mayflower*. Baltimore: Penguin Books, 1966.

BROWN, INA C. *The Story of the American Negro.* New York: Friendship Press, 1957.

BUCKMASTER, HENRIETTRA. *Let My People Go: The Story of the Underground Railroad and the Growth of the Abolition Movement.* New York: Harper & Brothers, 1941.

CRONON, EDMUND DAVID. *Black Moses: The Story of Marcus Garvey and the Universal Negro Improvement Association.* Madison: University of Wisconsin Press, 1955.

DAVIS, DAVID B. *The Problem of Slavery in Western Culture.* Ithaca, NY: Cornell University Press, 1966.

DEGLER, CARL N. *Out of Our Past.* New York: Harper & Row, Publishers, 1959.

DOUGLASS, FREDERICK. *Narrative of the Life of Frederick Douglass, An American Slave.* Edited by Benjamin Quarles. Cambridge, MA: Harvard University Press, 1960.

DOUNAN, ELIZABETH. *Documents Illustrative of the History of the Slave Trade to America.* Washington, DC: Carnegie Institution in Washington, 1935.

DU BOIS, W. E. B. *Black Folk, Then and Now.* New York: Henry Holt & Co., 1939.

————. *Black Reconstruction.* New York: Harcourt, Brace & Co., 1935.

————. *The Souls of Black Folk.* Chicago: A.C. McClurg & Co., 1903.

ELKINS, STANLEY. *Slavery: A Problem in American Institutional and Intellectual Life.* Chicago: University of Chicago Press, 1959.

EMBREE, EDWIN R. *Brown Americans.* New York: Viking Press, Inc., 1946.

FEHRENBACHER, DON. *Slavery, Law, and Politics: The Dred Scott Case in Historical Perspective.* New York: Oxford University Press, 1981.

FITZHUGH, GEORGE. *Cannibals All! Or Slaves Without Masters.* Richmond, VA: A. Morris, 1857.

FRANKLIN, JOHN HOPE. *From Slavery to Freedom.* New York: Alfred A. Knopf, 1948.

————. *Reconstruction after the Civil War.* Chicago: University of Chicago Press, 1961.

FRAZIER, E. FRANKLIN. *Black Bourgeoisie.* Glencoe, IL: Free Press, 1957.

————. *The Negro Family in the United States.* Chicago: University of Chicago Press, 1966.

————. *The Negro in the United States.* New York: Macmillan Co., 1957.

FREYRE, GILBERTO. *The Masters and the Slaves: A Study in the Development of Brazilian Civilization.* New York: Alfred A. Knopf, 1964.

GENOVESE, EUGENE D. *The Political Economy of Slavery: Studies in the Economy and Society of the Slave South.* New York: Pantheon Books, 1965.

GRANT, JOANNE. *Black Protest.* New York: Fawcett World Library, 1968.

GUTMAN, HERBERT. *The Black Family in Slavery and Freedom.* New York: Random House, 1977.

HALASZ, NICHOLAS. *The Rattling Chains: Slave Unrest and Revolt in the American South.* New York: David McKay Co., 1966.

HARLAN, LOUIS R. *Booker T. Washington: The Making of a Black Leader, 1865–1901.* New York: Oxford University Press, 1973.

HARRIS, MARVIN. *Patterns of Race in the Americas.* New York: Walker & Co., 1964.

HERSKOVITS, MELVILLE. *The Myth of the Negro Past.* New York: Harper & Brothers, 1941.

HIGGINBOTHAM, A. LEON. *In the Matter of Color: Race and the American Legal Process: The Colonial Period.* New York: Oxford University Press, 1978.

HUGHES, LANGSTON. *Fight for Freedom: The Story of the NAACP.* New York: Berkley Publishing Corp., 1962.

KEMBLE, FRANCES A. *Journal of a Residence on a Georgia Plantation in 1838–1839.* Edited by John A. Scott. New York: Alfred A. Knopf, 1961.

LITWACK, LEON F. *North of Slavery.* Chicago: University of Chicago Press, 1961.

LOGAN, RAYFORD W. *The Negro in the United States.* Princeton, NJ: D. Van Nostrand Co., 1957.

McPHERSON, JAMES M. *The Negro's Civil War.* New York: Random House, 1965.

MEIER, AUGUST, and RUDWICK, ELLIOT. *From Plantation to Ghetto.* New York: Hill and Wang, 1966.

MYRDAL, GUNNAR. *An American Dilemma: The Negro Problem and Modern Democracy.* New York: Harper & Brothers, 1944.

NOEL, DONALD L., ed. *The Origins of Slavery and American Racism.* Columbus, OH: Charles E. Merrill Co., 1972.

OLMSTED, FREDERICK L. *The Cotton Kingdom.* Edited by Arthur M. Schlesinger. New York: Alfred A. Knopf, 1953.

PHILLIPS, ULRICH B. *American Negro Slavery.* New York: D. Appleton & Co., 1918.

ROSS, FRED A. *Slavery Ordained by God.* Philadelphia: J.B. Lippincott Co., 1857.

SIEBERT, WILBUR H. *The Underground Railroad from Slavery to Freedom.* New York: Macmillan Co., 1898.

SIMKINS, FRANCIS B. *A History of the South.* New York: Alfred A. Knopf, 1959.

STAMPP, KENNETH M. *The Peculiar Institution: Slavery in the Ante-Bellum South.* New York: Alfred A. Knopf, 1965.

TANNENBAUM, FRANK. *Slave and Citizen: The Negro in the Americas.* New York: Alfred A. Knopf, 1946.

TROWBRIDGE, JOHN T. *The Desolate South.* New York: Meredith Press, 1956.

U.S. BUREAU OF THE CENSUS. *Negro Population 1790–1915.* Washington, DC, 1918.

WADE, RICHARD C. *Slavery in the Cities.* New York: Oxford University Press, 1964.

WASHINGTON, BOOKER T. *Up From Slavery.* New York: Doubleday & Company, 1900.

WOODSON, CARTER G. *The African Background Outlined.* Washington, DC: Association Press, 1936.

———. *The Negro in Our History.* Washington, DC: Associated Publishers, 1922.

WOODWARD, C. VANN. *Reunion and Reaction.* Boston: Little, Brown & Co., 1951.

———. *The Strange Career of Jim Crow.* New York: Oxford University Press, 1957.

NOTES

1. Joseph Boskin, "Race Relations in Seventeenth Century America: The Problem of the Origins of Negro Slavery," *Sociology and Social Research* 49 (July 1965), 446–55; John Hope Franklin, *From Slavery to Freedom* (New York: Knopf, 1948), pp. 70–71; Wilbert E. Moore, "Slave Law and the Social Structure," *Journal of Negro History* 26 (1941), 171–202.

2. Kenneth M. Stampp, *The Peculiar Institution* (New York: Knopf, 1956), p. 192.

3. Ibid., p. 193.

4. Ibid., p. 343.

5. Ibid., p. 201.

6. E. Franklin Frazier, *The Negro Family in the United States* (Chicago: University of Chicago Press, 1966), p. 360.

7. Arnold A. Sio, "Interpretations of Slavery," *Comparative Studies in Society and History,* 7 (1965), 294.

8. Stampp, *Peculiar Institution,* p. 148.

9. Richard C. Wade, *Slavery in the Cities* (New York: Oxford University Press, 1964), pp. 28–54.

10. E. Franklin Frazier, *The Negro in the United States* (New York: Macmillan, 1957), p. 55.

11. See Frederick L. Olmsted, *The Cotton Kingdom,* ed. Arthur M. Schlesinger (New York: Knopf, 1953), p. 184; Stampp, *Peculiar Institution,* pp. 151–53.

12. Stampp, *Peculiar Institution,* p. 294.

13. Booker T. Washington, *Up from Slavery* (New York: Doubleday, 1900), pp. 3–4.

14. Franklin, *From Slavery to Freedom,* p. 194.

15. Stampp, *Peculiar Institution,* p. 282.

16. Frances A. Kemble, *Journal of a Residence on a Georgia Plantation in 1838–1839,* ed. John A. Scott (New York: Knopf, 1961), p. 71.

17. See Lerone Bennett, Jr., *Before the Mayflower* (Baltimore: Penguin, 1966); Edwin R. Embree, *Brown Americans* (New York: Viking, 1946); Franklin, *From Slavery to Freedom;* Melville Herskovits, *The Myth of the Negro Past* (New York: Harper, 1941); August Meier and Elliott Rudwick, *From Plantation to Ghetto* (New York: Hill and Wang, 1966), pp. 4–22; Charles Silberman, *Crisis in Black and White* (New York: Random House, 1964), especially chap. 6.

18. E. Franklin Frazier, *Black Bourgeoisie* (Glencoe, IL: Free Press, 1957), p. 12.

19. Franklin, *From Slavery to Freedom,* p. 40.

20. Herskovits, *Myth of the Negro Past;* Carter G. Woodson, *The African Background Outlined* (Washington, DC: Association Press, 1936).

21. See, e.g., Stanley Elkins, *Slavery* (Chicago: University of Chicago Press, 1959); Eugene Genovese, *The Political Economy of Slavery: Studies in the Economy and Society of the Slave South* (New York: Pantheon, 1965); Rayford W. Logan, *The Negro in the United States* (Princeton, NJ: Van Nostrand, 1957); Stampp, *Peculiar Institution.* A recent anthology presents convincing evidence that American racism was more a product than a cause of slavery. See Donald L. Noel, ed., *The Origins of American Slavery and Racism* (Columbus, OH: Chas. E. Merrill, 1972).

22. Two of the chief proponents of this view are Frank Tannenbaum and Stanley Elkins. See Tannenbaum's *Slave and Citizen* (New York: Knopf, 1946); and Elkins, *Slavery,* pp. 52–89. In a recent work the author puts forth the thesis that slavery in Brazil was not radically different from slavery in North America. See Marwin Harris, *Patterns of Race in the Americas* (New York: Walker, 1964). See also David B. Davis, *The Problem of Slavery in Western Culture* (Ithaca, NY: Cornell University Press, 1966), pp. 223–61; Carl N. Degler, *Out of Our Past* (New York: Harper & Row, 1959).

23. See Nathan Glazer's introduction to Elkins, *Slavery;* David B. Davis, *Slavery in Western Culture,* p. 60.

24. Tannenbaum, *Slave and Citizen,* p. 103.

25. Ulrich B. Phillips, *American Negro Slavery* (New York: Appleton, 1918), pp. 342–43.

26. Franklin, *From Slavery to Freedom,* p. 192.

27. Cited in Stampp, *Peculiar Institution,* p. 172.

28. Frederick Douglass, *Narrative of the Life of Frederick Douglass, an American Slave,* ed. Benjamin Quarles (Cambridge, MA: Belknap Press of Harvard University Press, 1960), p. 29.

29. Stampp, *Peculiar Institution,* pp. 181–82.

30. Franklin, *From Slavery to Freedom,* pp. 192–93.

31. Ibid., p. 199.

32. Ibid., p. 200.

33. George D. Armstrong, *The Christian Doctrine of Slavery* (New York: Scribner, 1857); George Fitzhugh, *Cannibals All! Or Slaves Without Masters* (Richmond, VA: A. Morris, 1857); Fred A. Ross, *Slavery Ordained by God* (Philadelphia: Lippincott, 1857). Both Armstrong and Ross were ministers.

34. See Frazier, *Negro in the United States,* chap. 5; and Elizabeth Dounan, *Documents Illustrative of the History of the Slave Trade to America,* 4 vols. (Washington, DC: Carnegie Institution, 1935).

35. Herbert Aptheker, *American Negro Slave Revolts* (New York: International Publishers, 1963), p. 162.

36. For a typology of slave revolts see Marion D. deB. Kilson, "Towards Freedom: An Analysis of Slave Revolts in the United States," *Phylon* 25 (Summer 1964), pp. 175–87.

37. Nicholas Halasz, *The Rattling Chains* (New York: McKay, 1966), pp. 87–97.

38. Ibid., p. 91.

39. Ibid., pp. 116–38.

40. Ibid., chap. 8.

41. Elkins, *Slavery,* pp. 81–82.

42. Stampp, *Peculiar Institution,* p. 140.

43. Franklin, *From Slavery to Freedom,* pp. 255–56. See also Wilbur H. Siebert, *The Underground Railroad from Slavery to Freedom* (New York: Macmillan, 1898).

44. Henrietta Buckmaster, *Let My People Go* (New York: Harper, 1941).

45. Franklin, *From Slavery to Freedom,* p. 256.

46. Stampp, *Peculiar Institution,* p. 109.

47. Ibid., pp. 109–24.

48. Phillips, *American Negro Slavery,* pp. 291–92.

49. Ibid., pp. 341–42.

50. Leon F. Litwack, *North of Slavery* (Chicago: University of Chicago Press, 1961), p. 30.

51. U.S. Bureau of the Census, *Negro Population, 1790–1915* (Washington, DC, 1918).

52. Meier and Rudwick, *From Plantation to Ghetto,* p. 66.
53. Frazier, *Negro in the United States,* pp. 59ff.
54. Franklin, *From Slavery to Freedom,* pp. 215–16.
55. Ibid., pp. 221–23; Phillips, *American Negro Slavery,* pp. 432–36.
56. Logan, *Negro in the United States,* p. 14.
57. Franklin, *From Slavery to Freedom,* pp. 231–34.
58. See Carter G. Woodson, *The Negro in Our History* (Washington, DC: Associated Publishers, 1922), especially chap. 9.
59. W. E. B. Du Bois, *Black Reconstruction* (New York: Harcourt, Brace, 1935), p. 56.
60. Franklin, *From Slavery to Freedom,* p. 269.
61. See Logan, *Negro in the United States,* p. 22; James M. McPherson, *The Negro's Civil War* (New York: Random House, 1965), p. ix
62. Woodson, *Negro in Our History,* p. 374.
63. Franklin, *From Slavery to Freedom,* p. 287.
64. Ibid., p. 284.
65. McPherson, *The Negro's Civil War,* pp. ix-x. Copyright 1965, Random House, Inc.
66. Frazier, *Negro in the United States,* p. 111.
67. Quoted in Du Bois, *Black Reconstruction,* p. 671.
68. See Francis B. Simkins, *A History of the South* (New York: Knopf, 1959), p. 243.
69. John Hope Franklin, *Reconstruction after the Civil War* (Chicago: University of Chicago Press, 1961), p. 2.
70. John T. Trowbridge, *The Desolate South: 1865–1866* (New York: Meredith Press; and Boston: Little, Brown, 1956), pp. 84–85.
71. Ibid., p. 238.
72. Simkins, *History of the South,* especially chap. 17.
73. Ibid., p. 265.
74. Du Bois, *Black Reconstruction,* p. 167.
75. Ibid., p. 177.
76. Franklin, *Reconstruction after the Civil War,* pp. 36–37.
77. Simkins, *History of the South,* p. 271.
78. Frazier, *Negro in the United States,* p. 132.
79. Franklin, *Reconstruction after the Civil War,* pp. 89–90.
80. Ibid., p. 209.
81. C. Vann Woodward, *Reunion and Reaction* (Boston: Little, Brown, 1951), Chap. 11.
82. From p. 246 of *Reunion and Reaction* by C. Vann Woodward, copyright 1951, © 1966 by C. Vann Woodward, reprinted by permission of Little, Brown and Company, Publishers.
83. Franklin, *Reconstruction after the Civil War,* p. 226.
84. Logan, *Negro in the United States,* document no. 9A.
85. C. Vann Woodward, *The Strange Career of Jim Crow* (New York: Oxford University Press, 1957), p. 54.
86. Ibid., pp. 49–95.
87. Logan, *Negro in the United States,* document no. 8.
88. Bennett, *Before the Mayflower,* pp. 228–29.
89. W. E. B. Du Bois, *The Souls of Black Folk* (Chicago: A. C. McClurg, 1903), especially Chap. 3: "Of Mr. Booker T. Washington and Others."
90. A strong defense of Booker T. Washington's leadership is put forth in Howard Brotz, *The Black Jews of Harlem* (New York: Free Press, 1964), pp. 72–83. For a different appraisal see Louis R. Harlan, *Booker T. Washington: The Making of a Black Leader, 1865–1901* (New York: Oxford University Press, 1973); Meier and Rudwick, *From Plantation to Ghetto,* pp. 181–86.
91. Frazier, *Negro in the United States,* p. 159.

92. Woodward, *Strange Career of Jim Crow,* pp. 52–53.
93. Du Bois, *The Souls of Black Folk,* p. 59.
94. Langston Hughes, *Fight for Freedom* (New York: Berkley Publishing Corp., 1962).
95. Franklin, *From Slavery to Freedom,* p. 465; Logan, *Negro in the United States,* p. 70.
96. Franklin, *From Slavery to Freedom,* p. 467.
97. Woodson, *Negro in Our History,* pp. 526–27.
98. Franklin, *From Slavery to Freedom,* pp. 471–76.
99. See Edmund David Cronon, *Black Moses* (Madison: University of Wisconsin Press, 1955).
100. Ibid., pp. 205–7.
101. Franklin, *From Slavery to Freedom,* p. 483.
102. Ina C. Brown, *The Story of the American Negro* (New York: Friendship Press, 1957), p. 120; Franklin, *From Slavery to Freedom,* p. 488.
103. Meier and Rudwick, *From Plantation to Ghetto,* pp. 210–17; Gunnar Myrdal, *American Dilemma* (New York: Harper, 1944), pp. 1000–1001.
104. Meier and Rudwick, *From Plantation to Ghetto,* pp. 212–13; Myrdal, *American Dilemma,* pp. 464–66.
105. Meier and Rudwick, *From Plantation to Ghetto,* p. 213.
106. Franklin, *From Slavery to Freedom,* pp. 570–73.

CHAPTER TWO

The Persistence of Jim Crow and the Black Revolt

The post–World War II era has been a period of rapid change in the United States and in the world. Although changes affecting the status of black Americans have been neither rapid nor widespread, they have occurred and they have generated greater expectations. The resistance of white Americans to change has made blacks apprehensive about the willingness of society to accord them treatment equal to what its white citizens receive. The caution with which public officials have moved to make amends for what are rather widely regarded as past injustices has created greater black militancy. The depth of antiblack sentiment in society has frequently been indicated by the negative response of white Americans to increased black militancy. Because white Americans insist upon determining the pace with which changes in race relations occur, a crisis has resulted. Blacks have learned from experience that positive changes affecting their status are more likely to result from political pressures than from altruism. In the mid-1950s it appeared that increased civil rights for blacks might become one of the major tasks to which American society might address itself for the first time in a century.

BEGINNINGS OF THE REVOLT: BLACK PERSISTENCE AND WHITE RESISTANCE

The Supreme Court decision of May 1954 outlawing segregation in public education was welcomed by black Americans and their white supporters, who felt that somehow this act might signal the beginning of a new era in the relations between black and white Americans. The decision had been expected, and black Americans felt that it would afford white Americans, especially those in the South, the opportunity to share in the worldwide movement for greater human rights. White southerners responded to the desegregation ruling not with feelings of relief, but with the establishment, during the summer, of White Citizens' Councils, which had as their primary function massive resistance to the ruling of the Supreme Court. Since the Supreme Court did not indicate how its ruling was to be implemented, school districts that had either required or permitted segregation reopened in September on a segregated basis (except those in Washington, DC, and Baltimore, Maryland, where attempts were made to comply with the ruling of the Court). Throughout the South, plans were made to do whatever became necessary to maintain the long-standing practice of racial segregation in schools. Statements by public officials in that region (governors, senators, representatives) supported the notion of massive resistance.

When the Supreme Court finally issued its implementation decree—that desegregation in public education should proceed "with all deliberate speed"—in May 1955, the forces opposing integration in public education had already organized themselves throughout the South.[1] Southerners were determined to maintain separate schools for black and white pupils, regardless of the ruling of the Supreme Court. The extent of their opposition came as a surprise to blacks and their white supporters. It appeared that their hopes for a new era in race relations would not materialize. If a ruling of the highest court in the country could be met with such contempt by those responsible for maintaining the constitutional rights of citizens, how could black people ever expect to be accorded rights equal to those of white Americans?

Signs of growing unrest were evident among black Americans. African colonies were demanding and receiving independence from European colonial powers, and it appeared that all of Africa would achieve political freedom before black people in the United States would be able to assert the fundamental rights of service in places of public accommodation or attendance at schools supported by taxes imposed on them. Later in the summer of 1955, Emmett Till, a 14-year-old black boy from Chicago, visiting in Money, Mississippi, was kidnapped and lynched. He was accused of having whistled at a white woman, and, characteristically, those responsible for his murder were never apprehended. Feelings of disillusionment were widespread in black communities.

On December 1, 1955, a black seamstress, Rosa Parks, boarded a public bus in Montgomery, Alabama. She took a seat in the section set aside for blacks. Shortly thereafter she was ordered to vacate her seat so a white man could occupy it. She refused and was arrested. When word of the arrest spread through the black community, the Montgomery Bus Boycott was organized.[2] The bus boycott lasted for more than a year, ending in December 1956, when the Supreme Court upheld a lower-court ruling outlawing racial segregation on buses in Montgomery.

This massive demonstration of solidarity among blacks in opposition to long-standing practices of segregation and discrimination can be considered the first major act of resistance by blacks in modern times and signaled the birth of what might be called the black revolt.[3] The story of the Montgomery Bus Boycott spread throughout black communities in the United States and served as an impetus for similar acts in other cities. Tallahassee, Florida, and Birmingham, Alabama, followed with bus boycotts. Nonviolent resistance to what was considered an "evil" system composed of "unjust" laws became the official means of dealing with the caste system of the South. The philosophy of nonviolence, according to its principal spokesman, contains the following elements: (1) active resistance to "evil," (2) attempts to win over one's opponent through understanding, (3) directing one's attack against forces of "evil" rather than against persons performing such acts, (4) willingness to accept suffering, without retaliation, (5) refusal to hate one's opponent, and (6) the conviction that the universe is on the side of justice.[4]

As the nonviolent resistance movement spread, massive opposition to social change in the realm of race relations was intensified by white southerners. One hundred southern members of Congress signed the Southern Manifesto, opposing the Supreme Court decision of 1954. They vowed "to use all lawful means to bring about a reversal of this decision which is contrary to the Constitution." Accordingly, laws implementing massive resistance to desegregation were enacted in Alabama, Georgia, Louisiana, Mississippi, South Carolina, and Virginia. While the Southern Manifesto did not explicitly call for the use of violence as a means of preventing black pupils from attending schools with white pupils, its impact generated violence.

A federal court ordered officials at the University of Alabama to admit a black student in February 1956. Her appearance on campus was met by mob violence from white students and others who were determined to maintain an all-white student enrollment.[5] She was removed from campus when the rioting flared and was forced to sue for readmission. The university officials responded with permanent expulsion on the grounds that she had made unfair statements about the University of Alabama.

On the elementary- and secondary-school levels violence became the accepted means of preventing desegregation. In September 1956 a mob prevented black pupils from enrolling at the public high school in Mansfield, Texas. Mobs demonstrated against school integration in Clinton, Tennessee, and in Sturgis and Clay, Kentucky. In the latter cases it became necessary to deploy the National Guard to protect the black pupils. In the following years, when black parents attempted to enroll their children in schools with previously all-white enrollments, they were met with acts of violence, frequently directed at them by white women. One of the more highly publicized of these events occurred at Central High School in Little Rock, Arkansas, in 1957.[6] The courts had approved a desegregation plan, submitted by the Little Rock School Board, calling for the gradual desegregation of public schools beginning with the admission of nine black students to Central High School. The evening before they were scheduled to enroll, the governor announced that he would dispatch the National Guard to the school because of the possibility of violence. When the first black pupil appeared two days later, she was met by thousands of jeering white citizens, who barred her from entering the building, and by 270 National Guardsmen. Weeks later the National Guardsmen were withdrawn; nine black pupils entered the school, but local citizens forced them to withdraw. Mob violence in Little Rock continued to keep the black pupils from entering the school until the president ordered 1,000 paratroopers to Little Rock and federalized 10,000 members of the Arkansas

National Guard to ensure their enrollment. This action represented the first time since Reconstruction that federal troops had been sent into the South to protect the rights of black people. Finally, on September 25, the nine black students entered Central High School. Federal troops remained at Central High School throughout the school year. At the beginning of the following school year the governor of Arkansas ordered all high schools in the city closed for the school year 1958–1959. This was ostensibly done to prevent "impending violence and disorder." When the schools finally reopened in 1959, black pupils enrolled in both Central High School and another high school, which had previously maintained a policy of admitting only white pupils.

Little Rock was not alone in its policy of massive resistance to integration through the closing of public schools. When desegregation was ordered for the Virginia cities of Norfolk, Charlottesville, and Front Royal, the governor responded by closing the schools involved. In Prince Edward County, Virginia, resistance to desegregation was so strong that the county's public schools were closed from 1959 to 1964.

In the years immediately following 1954, little desegregation of public schools was accomplished. Every September, at the beginning of the school year, one could expect the news wires to carry stories of violence directed toward black pupils. These pupils were frequently required to walk through racist mobs to get to class, and, once in the classroom, they experienced a variety of insults and physical abuse from younger racists.[7]

On the college level, desegregation was not achieved without violence. At both the University of Mississippi and the University of Alabama the admittance of blacks triggered violence by white students. In fact, the admission of one black student to the University of Mississippi in 1962 triggered violence that ended in two deaths and 100 injuries. It was finally necessary to station 12,000 federal troops on the campus to assure the attendance of this student in classes. Federalized National Guardsmen were required to escort two black students to classes at the University of Alabama in 1963.

THE CIVIL RIGHTS MOVEMENT

By 1960 desegregation of public education was proceeding at a slow pace, and in the Deep South massive resistance remained an effective answer to the Supreme Court's ruling and to the demands of blacks. Feelings of despair over the school segregation issue were widespread in the black community. The federal government assumed no responsibility for ensuring enforcement of blacks' declared constitutional rights. The responsibility for desegregating schools rested with blacks themselves, and when they sought admission for their children to desegregated schools, it was frequently a long, costly, and complicated court procedure. Segregation and discrimination were still the social norms throughout the South, and all-white southern juries continued to refuse to convict white persons responsible for lynching black people.

In February 1960 four black college students in North Carolina sought service at a lunch counter in a five-and-dime store. When they were denied service, they remained seated. The manager ordered the lunch counter closed, but they remained seated, reading their textbooks. The news of their actions quickly spread throughout the country, and within a few days the "sit-in" movement had spread to fifteen cities in five southern states. Whenever a group of black people appeared at a lunch counter, a mob of southern whites appeared to heckle and jeer them. But the actions of the students inspired many others, black and white, to support them. Because of the determined resistance to desegregation of southern whites and because of the strong determination of blacks to achieve social change in race relations, thousands of white Americans joined forces with the blacks to give birth to the civil rights movement. Black college students organized the Student Nonviolent Coordinating Committee (SNCC) to coordinate activities aimed at desegregating places of public accommodation in the South. Peaceful demonstrations, led by college students, occurred in every major city where racial segregation was practiced openly. Thousands of blacks and their white supporters were jailed for violating local segregation laws. The lunch counter demonstrations were accompanied by nationwide economic boycotts of stores that maintained practices of segregation. Within a period of one-and-a-half years it was reported that at least 70,000 people, both black and white, participated in the sit-in movement. More than 3,600 were arrested, and some 141 students and 58 faculty members were expelled by college authorities for their activities. Altogether, one or more establishments in each of 108 southern and border cities had been desegregated because of the sit-ins.[8]

The combined effects of these demonstrations and boycotts forced several of the larger chain stores to abandon practices of segregation in service and discrimination in employment. The example then spread to other areas: "Wade-ins" were held at segregated public beaches, and "kneel-ins" were attempted in segregated churches. Always these demonstrations were peaceful, in keeping with the philosophy of nonviolent direct action. However, in virtually all cases there was violence by white people determined to maintain white supremacy at all costs.

The Interstate Commerce Commission had ruled in 1955 that racial segregation of passengers in buses, waiting rooms, and travel coaches involved in interstate travel violated these passengers' constitutional rights. Nevertheless, individual bus drivers and local law enforcement personnel continued to require blacks to sit separated from white passengers. In February 1961 the director of the Congress of Racial Equality (CORE) announced that members of the organization would test the effectiveness of this ruling by staging a series of "freedom rides" throughout the South. Other civil rights organizations joined this effort, and in May a group of black and white activists started their journey from Washington, DC, to New Orleans, Louisiana. When the bus reached Anniston, Alabama, it was bombed and burned by a mob of local whites, and the group of freedom riders was beaten. In Montgomery, Alabama, the presence of the freedom riders was met with such hostility that it was necessary to dispatch 400 U.S. marshals to keep order.

The freedom riders were jailed, beaten, or both in Alabama, Louisiana, and Mississippi. There were more than a dozen freedom rides in the South, and these rides combined the efforts of the four major civil rights organizations. In addition to CORE and SNCC, the National Association for the Advancement of Colored People (NAACP) and the Southern Christian Leadership Conference (SCLC) participated. The freedom rides involved more than one thousand persons, and the legal expenses they incurred exceeded $300,000.[9] As a result of these activities, the Interstate Commerce Commission issued an order outlawing segregation on all buses and in all terminal facilities.

The civil rights movement appealed to increasingly large numbers of white Americans. Demonstrations protesting all forms of segregation and discrimination were conducted throughout the United States, especially in the South. There were attacks on legally imposed segregation in the South and *de facto* segregation elsewhere and on discriminatory practices throughout the country. There were demonstrations at public libraries, swimming pools, public parks, and seats of municipal government throughout the Deep South and the Border South. Discrimination against black people in voting became a special target for civil rights activists, based on the assumption that once armed with the franchise, blacks would be in a position to elect public officials sympathetic to their demands. The Civil Rights Act of 1960 provided for the appointment of federal voting referees to receive applications to qualify voters if it could be proved that a person had been denied the right to vote because of race. Throughout the South voter registration schools were set up in churches. The response of many white southerners was characteristic of their resistance to change in existing practices. Black churches were bombed and burned. Churches had traditionally been exempt from the tyranny that southern blacks encountered daily, and now it appeared that blacks were not safe even in their houses of worship. Appeals to federal officials were in vain, and the reign of terror continued unabated. Arrests for these activities were rare, for local police officers often supported such activities. Black people and their white supporters remained nonviolent despite daily provocations and beatings.[10]

On occasion one city was selected to be a major target of civil rights demonstrations. SNCC selected Greenwood, Mississippi, as the site of its emancipation centennial campaign, in response to an attempt to assassinate one of its field workers. They organized a massive voter registration campaign and were met by heavily armed police officers with police dogs. When they attempted to escort local Mississippi blacks to register to vote, they were attacked by the police and their dogs.[11] The late Martin Luther King, Jr., selected Birmingham, Alabama, as SCLC's major site of antisegregation demonstrations during the centennial year. Birmingham was one of the most rigidly segregated larger cities in the South, and it was believed that if segregation barriers there could be penetrated, it would make for less difficulty elsewhere. The demonstrators were met in Birmingham by a force of police and firefighters led by a well-known segregationist. Police and firefighters were ordered to use a variety of techniques to curb the demonstrations, including fire hoses, cattle prods, and police dogs. For several days the demonstrators met greater brutality from law enforcement personnel than they had ever encountered previously, and the police and firefighters were supported in their acts by an injunction from a local judge prohibiting protest marches. When the demonstrators defied this injunction, hundreds of them were jailed. The constitutional right of citizens to petition peacefully for redress of grievances was violated, and the Department of Justice issued a statement that it was watching the situation but that it was powerless to act. It was decided by the leaders of the demonstrations that schoolchildren should participate along with adults. They, too, were met by police clubs, dogs, and fire hoses. The pictures of the repressive measures used by the police and firefighters alerted the nation and the world to the extremes that segregationists would resort to in order to maintain white supremacy.

A turning point was reached in Birmingham when following a meeting of the Ku Klux Klan, the home of the brother of the late Martin Luther King, Jr., and the motel that had served as King's headquarters and residence were bombed. Thousands of black demonstrators abandoned the philosophy of nonviolence and took to the streets with bottles and stones. They burned houses and stores and stoned police and passing cars. Before the uprising ended, they had burned a nine-block area of the city. When the demonstrators had requested federal protection from police dogs, fire hoses, and police clubs, the president had announced that no federal agency could act. However, when the blacks stoned white police officers and other citizens, federal troops were dispatched to Alabama within hours. Apparently the latter constituted acts of violence, while the former did not.

Demonstrations in many other southern and border cities followed those in Birmingham. Danville, Virginia, and Cambridge, Maryland, were among the most prominent. During the summer of 1963 some 35 homes and churches were bombed or burned, at least 10 people were killed, and more than 20,000 demonstrators were arrested. Thousands of others were shocked by cattle prods, set upon with high-pressure fire hoses, bitten by police dogs, and beaten by police. The summer demonstrations culminated in August, when 250,000 blacks and their white supporters participated in the March on Washington, the largest civil rights demonstration in history. As a direct outgrowth of these demonstrations Congress enacted the Civil Rights Act of 1964. The major provisions of this act are as follows: (1) Sixth-grade education was established as a presumption of literacy for voting purposes; (2) segregation and discrimination in places of public accommodation were outlawed; (3) public facilities (parks, playgrounds, libraries, and so on) were desegregated; (4) the attorney general was authorized to file school desegregation suits; (5) discrimination was outlawed in all federally assisted activities; (6) discrimination by employers or unions with 100 or more employees or members was outlawed; (7) the attorney general was authorized to intervene in private suits in which persons alleged denial of equal protection of the laws under the Fourteenth Amendment.

The leaders of several civil rights organizations, after achieving the victory that this act signaled, decided to concentrate their activities on voter registration and education. They had been urged by the Department of Justice to concentrate on these activities instead of street demonstrations. Consequently, in 1964 the Mississippi Summer Project was organized. Thousands of black and white activists journeyed to Mississippi to engage in activities aimed at improving the status of that state's nearly one million blacks. They concentrated on voter education and registration and on "freedom schools."[12] The activists were subjected to a serious initial setback when three of their volunteers were abducted and murdered by a mob of local racists.[13] Throughout the summer they were subjected to a variety of harassments and abuse. The casualty list was high: By October 21 at least 3 persons had been killed, 80 were beaten, 3 were wounded by gunfire in 35 shootings, more than 35 churches were burned, 35 homes and other buildings were bombed, and more than 1,000 persons had been arrested. In addition, several unsolved murders of local blacks were recorded.[14]

The Civil Rights Act of 1964 contained a provision ensuring blacks the right to vote in all elections. However, when they attempted to register, a variety of techniques, especially intimidation, kept them from exercising this right. Consequently, the major effort for 1965 was the campaign to ensure the right to vote. Resistance to black voting rights was strong. Several civil rights organizations decided to focus their attention on Alabama, which had been one of the most intransigent in this regard. Attempts to register blacks failed, and a march from Selma to Montgomery was planned to dramatize the plight of that state's black citizens. Thousands of black activists and their white supporters gathered in Selma for the march. Several attempts to march were thwarted by the police, under orders from a local sheriff. Acts of excessive use of force by police were widespread, and these acts motivated additional thousands of citizens, including many members of the clergy, from all over the United States to join the activists in Selma. The march finally materialized but not without violence. Two white activists and one black were killed and scores of others were injured.

The Selma-to-Montgomery march stimulated the Voting Rights Act of 1965, which made it possible for southern blacks to register and vote with little difficulty. It was also the last mass demonstration of the civil rights movement. During the years of peak activity, the civil rights movement enlisted the support of thousands of Americans, both black and white. Its nonviolent, direct-action approach was responsible for many of the changes affecting the status of southern blacks. But its goals and methods were hardly applicable to the problems facing the many blacks in urban slums throughout the country. Thousands of blacks and their white supporters had combined for what was felt to be the most significant movement for social change in the United States.[15] The issues were clear, and although there were differences on means toward achieving the goals, a coalition of many groups had united to work for a common end: the eradication of segregation and discrimination in American life. To a significant degree they were successful in achieving greater civil rights for blacks, but black Americans remained basically an oppressed underclass of citizens.

DESPAIR IN THE SLUMS

By 1965 approximately half of all the blacks in the United States lived outside what is generally regarded as the South (see chapter 3), primarily in the slums of urban areas. For the most part, the lives of those in nonsouthern urban areas had not been affected by the gains of the civil rights movement. A majority (three-fifths) of those remaining in the South were also crowded into the slums of urban areas, and although their lives had in some ways been affected by the civil rights movement, they too suffered from the gap between promise and performance. A vast majority of blacks, then, lived under conditions of hopelessness and despair. Little hope for change in their depressed status was apparent in 1965. At a time when the economy of the country was experiencing continued expansion, the median family income of black people was only slightly more than one-half (54 percent) of the median white family income. Eleven years after the Supreme Court outlawed segregation in public education, schools in the United States as a whole were more segregated than ever before. The unemployment rate for black people remained chronically high. Vast sums that had been allocated for public low-income housing had been diverted into middle-income housing that slum dwellers could not afford. At least 36 murders of civil rights workers in the South had been recorded, only three of which led to convictions, with no sentence of more than 10 years' imprisonment.

Many of the millions of recent black migrants from the South were from farms. Mechanization of agriculture and racist terror forced them to leave the cotton fields. They packed their bags and boarded buses headed for New York City, Chicago, Detroit, Los Angeles, and other large cities. Many thought that these moves were into less hostile territory. Upon their arrival, however, they found themselves forced into slums in the centers of these cities. They arrived poorly educated and lacking in skills. They were in many ways similar to the great waves of European immigrants who entered the United States during the last decades of the nineteenth century and the first decades of the twentieth century. However, no provision was made to ease the transition for these migrants, as had been done for white European refugees. As one observer commented:

> Had Northern cities received hundreds of thousands of immigrants from Europe in the past few decades, no doubt all sorts of emergency provisions would have been made to help settle the newcomers, make them welcome, provide food, clothing, and shelter for them, and enable them to find work. Southern Negroes obtained no such courtesy, and what recognition they did get was calculated to remind them that white Americans may fight among themselves but in the clutch know how to stand together as a race.[16]

These migrants quickly learned that outside as well as within the South, their place in the society had been clearly designated for them.

Federal measures ostensibly aimed at improving the standard of living for urban blacks have either been inadequate or have not been enacted by Congress. Many of the appropriations under the Economic Opportunity Act of 1964 never reached the persons they were designed to assist. In some cases as much as half the money in antipoverty programs was utilized for administrative purposes. The congressional elections of 1966 saw conservatives elected in many states, and the administration virtually abandoned many of its civil rights proposals in response to what was interpreted as an upsurge of antiblack feeling among the electorate. Several cities had experienced violent black demonstrations in 1964 and 1965, and conservatives seeking public office based much of their campaign on curbing "crime in the streets" (i.e., black uprisings). In such a climate either proposed legislation was defeated (e.g., the rat-control bill) or the requested appropriation was significantly reduced (e.g., the model-cities bill). In the end, politics took precedence over the welfare of poor people, a significant proportion of whom are black.

The powerlessness of black Americans is clear. The communities in which they live are not significantly different from colonial territories in the underdeveloped world. They have no control over the institutions in their communities that are technically responsible to them. Virtually all black communities are among the major depressed areas in the country. The chief support for the communities comes from outside sources; the economy is dominated by people who do not and would not live in these communities. The inadequately maintained houses are often owned by affluent (and often politically powerful) suburban residents. The schools are staffed and controlled by outsiders. Law and order are maintained by suspicious and frightened police, who frequently resort to the excessive use of force on the slightest provocation. When these residents are able to secure employment, they provide a cheap labor supply for the white community. Yet they are forced to pay prices far in excess of those paid by affluent suburban citizens for inferior products available in stores in slum neighborhoods. In many ways, then, the black community in the 1960s represented what might be called a form of internal colonialism. As one social scientist has written: "The dark ghetto's invisible walls have been erected by the white society, by those who have power, both to confine those who have *no* power and to perpetuate their powerlessness. The dark ghettos are social, political, and—above all—economic colonies. Their inhabitants are subject peoples, victims of the greed, cruelty, insensitivity, guilt, and fear of their masters."[17] Most white citizens are unaware of the conditions in these communities until the residents, as a result of their feelings of hopelessness and despair, rebel against conditions through what became traditional summer uprisings.

One of the most articulate and perceptive leaders to address himself to the millions of poor blacks in the slums was Malcolm X. He was a product of slum life and had experienced virtually all aspects of destitution so common to poor black people in the United States.[18] Because of his abilities, he achieved an international reputation as a spokesman for the aspirations of poor black people. Malcolm X was feared and admired by both black and white Americans, and frequently the same individual shared both sentiments. He was often misunderstood, although his speeches were clear. He urged black people to consolidate their efforts and to link their struggle with that of their African brothers as a means of achieving political, economic, and social equality. He did not believe that integration into the larger society was either likely or necessary in the near future. Therefore he advocated a policy of group solidarity. As a means of achieving this solidarity, he constantly advocated positive identification (i.e., pride in blackness). Malcolm X urged white Americans who sympathized with the aspirations of black people to organize themselves and work within the white community in an effort to rid it of its racist practices. He did not advocate the initiation of violence, but he was a strong proponent of armed self-defense as a means of meeting violent attacks by racists. Few leaders have been so misunderstood as Malcolm X. As a social critic, his exegesis of American society was severe but meticulous. In many ways he was the inaugurator of the Black Power movement.

BLACK POWER

For all practical purposes the civil rights movement ended in 1965. The following year civil rights organizations appeared to be searching for some cause around which to rally as a means of continuing their protest activities. Although implementation was lagging, they had won important victories: the Civil Rights Act of 1964, the Voting Rights Act of 1965, and perhaps most important of all, the recognition by Americans that the low status of black people posed a serious social problem in a world in which oppressed people were fighting for freedom and self-determination. The question, Where do we go from here? was asked by the leaders of the major civil rights organizations. In June 1966 James Meredith was shot as he started his freedom march through Mississippi. Immediately thereafter the leaders of several civil rights organizations gathered in Memphis, Tennessee, and made plans to turn the aborted march into a major civil rights campaign. During this march Stokely Carmichael, the chairman of SNCC, introduced a new and controversial slogan into the nomenclature of the movement to achieve greater civil rights for blacks. The concept of Black Power was first used in this context when the marchers reached Greenwood, Mississippi.[19] Field workers from SNCC had worked in this community, and, at a mass rally, when Carmichael proclaimed, "What we need is black power," he was cheered by the crowd of poor Mississippians.

The introduction of the concept of Black Power was debated by the leaders of CORE, SCLC, and SNCC. Martin Luther King and his associates from SCLC disapproved of its use, but the leaders of CORE and SNCC supported its use. A compromise was reached—that the concept was not to be used as the official slogan of the march—but it gained worldwide usage and generated a heated debate among the major black organizations.

Somehow the combination of the words *black* and *power* seemed to offend and frighten white Americans, especially some "liberal" white persons who had contributed time and money to the civil rights movement. To them the concept implied black supremacy (or reverse racism) and black violence. Consequently, they resigned from membership and withheld financial support from the more militant organizations. Similarly, the more moderate civil rights organizations, such as the

NAACP and the National Urban League, expressed their disapproval of Black Power. The organizations that had led the civil rights movement and that had cooperated in the major campaigns and demonstrations in the South were divided along ideological lines.

Those leaders advocating Black Power had attempted to define the concept, but such attempts were usually lost in the growing debate in the mass media of communications. To Stokely Carmichael of SNCC the concept spoke to the needs of black people at the time. It was a call to black Americans to liberate themselves from oppression by assuming control over their lives economically, politically, and socially. He said:

> Black Power means black people coming together to form a political force and either electing representatives or forcing their representatives to speak to their needs. It's an economic and physical bloc that can exercise its strength in the black community instead of letting the job go to the Democratic or Republican parties or a white-controlled black man set up as a puppet to represent black people. *We* pick the brother and make sure he fulfills *our* needs. Black Power doesn't mean antiwhite, violence, separatism, or any other racist things the press says it means. It's saying, "Look, buddy, we're not laying a vote on you unless you lay so many schools, hospitals, playgrounds, and jobs on us."[20]

Later he and Charles Hamilton elaborated on the concept of Black Power:

> It is a call for black people in this country to unite, to recognize their heritage, to build a sense of community. It is a call for black people to begin to define their own goals, to lead their own organizations, and to support those organizations. It is a call to reject the racist institutions and values of this society.
>
> The concept of Black Power rests on a fundamental premise: *Before a group can enter the open society, it must first close ranks.* By this we mean that group solidarity is necessary before a group can operate effectively from a bargaining position of strength in a pluralistic society.[21]

Floyd McKissick of CORE saw the following as elements of Black Power: increased political and economic power for blacks; improved self-image; the development of young, militant black leadership; the development of black consumer power; and strong resistance to police brutality in black communities.[22]

Although Martin Luther King, Jr., opposed the use of the concept of Black Power for a variety of reasons, he acknowledged that it had what he called a "positive meaning."[23] He saw it as a "cry of disappointment" and of despair with the present state of black–white relations. He also interpreted it as ". . . a call to black people to amass the political and economic strength to achieve their legitimate goals." Finally, he saw Black Power as "a psychological call to manhood." Despite its many positive features, King felt that the concept had too many negative values for it to serve as the basic strategy with which to meet the problems faced by black people at that time.[24] He believed that it embodied a philosophy of hopelessness about achieving basic changes in the structure of American society. In addition, as an integrationist, King saw the Black Power movement as one based on separation of the races in the United

States. He rejected the notion that any group within the larger society could achieve equality through separation. Finally, as the foremost exponent of nonviolence, he believed that the concept was often a call for retaliatory violence, which, he maintained, could only serve to impede progress in race relations.

The more moderate leaders of civil rights organizations opposed the concept of Black Power from its inception. The leaders of the NAACP and the Urban League joined five other prominent black spokespersons and responded to the militant organization by placing an advertisement entitled "Crisis and Commitment" in numerous newspapers.[25] In response to the advocates of Black Power, they enumerated what they considered to be the "principles upon which the civil rights movement rests." They included four points: (1) a commitment to the principle of racial justice through the democratic process, (2) the repudiation of violence, (3) a commitment to the principle of integration, and (4) a commitment to the principle that the task of bringing about integration is the common responsibility of all Americans, both black and white.

Some of the leading critics of Black Power rejected the concept in favor of coalition politics. They believed that the concept was harmful to the movement for greater civil rights for America's blacks because "it diverts the movement from a meaningful debate over strategy and tactics, it isolates the Negro community, and it encourages the growth of anti-Negro forces." As an alternative to Black Power, they advocated a "liberal–labor–civil rights coalition which would work to make the Democratic Party truly responsive to the aspirations of the poor, and which would develop support for programs (specifically those outlined in A. Philip Randolph's $100 billion Freedom Budget) aimed at the reconstruction of American society in the interests of greater social justice."[26]

Supporters of Black Power rejected the notion of forming coalitions with predominantly white liberal, labor, and religious organizations. They insisted that those who advocated such coalitions were proceeding on the basis of three fallacious assumptions: (1) that the interests of black Americans were identical with the interests of these groups, (2) that a viable coalition could be established between groups with power and powerless blacks, and (3) that it was possible to sustain political coalitions on a "moral, friendly, sentimental basis; by appeals to conscience."[27]

The debate over Black Power continued. The more militant organizations, CORE and SNCC, were its chief proponents; the more moderate organizations, the NAACP and the Urban League, were strongly opposed; and SCLC adopted a middle position. In keeping with their position that Black Power means black consciousness and solidarity, the militant organizations urged their white supporters to form parallel organizations and to work with the white community to rid it of the racism endemic to American life. A coalition between black and white Americans was seen as unworkable. The major impediment to equality for black people was seen as the resistance of the white community. Consequently, CORE and SNCC urged their white supporters to work within their own communities.

Less than one year after the concept was first introduced, it had gained widespread prominence. In July 1967 the first National Conference on Black Power was held in Newark, New Jersey. This conference was attended by more than one thousand black delegates from 42 cities in 36 states. They represented a broad cross section of black leaders, ranging from the militant black nationalists to employees of government agencies. One of the most significant aspects of the conference was that it brought together for the first time a wide assembly of black people who met in workshop sessions to define the concept of Black Power and who agreed to implement its components. When the conference ended, a series of resolutions had been passed, covering the following issues, among others: (1) the establishment of black financial institutions such as credit unions and nonprofit cooperatives, (2) the establishment of black universities, (3) selective purchasing and boycotting of white merchants in black communities, (4) the demand for a guaranteed annual income for all people, (5) a boycott by black athletes of international Olympic competition and professional boxing, in response to the stripping of the world heavyweight boxing title from Muhammad Ali, (6) boycotts of black churches that were not committed to the "black revolution," and (7) boycotts of black publications accepting advertisements for hair straighteners and bleaching creams.

Meanwhile, Black Power gained wider acceptance among more radical white Americans. In November 1966 students at Oberlin College, in Oberlin, Ohio, held an intercollegiate conference entitled Black Power in the Urban Ghetto, in an effort to "eliminate the emotionalism which clouds the debate on Black Power and to try to point out the basic issues involved." At its annual meeting in August 1967, the National Student Association, the largest organization of college students in the United States, resolved to support the implementation of the concept of Black Power "through any means necessary." In September the delegates attending the National Conference for New Politics in Chicago voted by a margin of more than two to one to support all resolutions of the Newark Black Power Conference and to support "black control of the political, economic, and social institutions in black communities."

Interest in the concept of Black Power was perhaps too recent in its origin to gain wide acceptance on the basis of its relevance to the problems faced by blacks. It had emotional implications that white Americans feared, but stripped of its emotional connotations, it meant the amassing by black people of the economic, political, and social power necessary to deal effectively with the problems they face as a powerless people relegated to a life of poverty in an affluent society. Furthermore, it was a call to black people to reject the social values (especially racism) that are responsible for their low status in the United States and to replace them with an ideology that embraces dignity and pride in blackness. Black solidarity was seen as a precondition to the achievement of these ends. Integration, it was felt, was much more likely to be achieved from a position of strength than from one of weakness.

The concept of ethnic power is not alien to American society. Historically, many ethnic groups have improved their status through the process of organizing themselves into power blocs. Indeed, ethnic solidarity has been a fundamental aspect of American minority relations. One writer, David Danzig, defended Black Power as follows:

... to the extent that "Black Power" expresses a determination to build a Negro Community which would be something more than euphemisms for the ghetto, it is a valid and necessary cry; to the extent that it expresses a despair of the one-by-one absorption of "deserving" Negroes into the general society and puts its faith instead in collective action aimed at dealing with collective fate, it is an intelligent response to the reality of American life.[28]

Danzig saw the attempts to establish group loyalty among blacks, which was a fundamental aspect of Black Power, as an essential means of dealing with a basically hostile society. Although other minority groups have effectively organized themselves along religious and ethnic lines into political and economic power blocs as a means of improving their status, once this goal has been achieved, they have effectively combined forces and joined what blacks call the white power structure, which serves to perpetuate the low status of blacks. They may be of Irish, Italian, Jewish, or Polish extraction, but in encounters with blacks, racial homogeneity solidifies them. In short, black subordination was achieved and has been maintained by the unabashed use of "white power."

Another writer, Joyce Ladner, who saw Black Power as "the acquisition of power by Negroes for their own use, both offensively and defensively," defended the concept, especially its emphasis on black nationalism and black consciousness, as follows:

It is important to establish a positive black identity in a great many sectors of the black communities, both North and South, rural and urban, lower and middle class. Indeed, it is both important and legitimate to teach black people (or any other ethnic minority) about their history, placing special emphasis upon the positive contributions of other black people. This black consciousness has the potential to create unity and solidarity among black people and to give them hope and self-confidence.[29]

Ladner reported that Black Power achieved success among Mississippi blacks because attempts at racial integration in that state had failed.

The use of black political power to achieve black rights was not new. In 1941 black leaders effectively forced the president to issue an executive order banning discrimination in employment in industries doing business with the federal government. Such organizations as the Negro American Labor Council of the American Federation of Labor–Congress of Industrial Organizations and the all-black organizations within urban police departments exist to protect the interests of their members. The idea underlying the concept of Black Power, then, was not new. It gained new strength in the last half of the 1960s. In 1967 a nationwide organization of elected black public officials was formed to develop methods of utilizing their combined power to improve the status of black citizens. A nationwide group of black ministers met in November 1967 in an effort to make Black Power a force in American Protestant church policies. They were organizing to serve as a pressure group within the National Council of Churches in an effort to increase the number of blacks in policy-making positions and to "bring the resources of white churches into urban ghettos in such a way as to enhance Negro leadership."[30]

The civil rights movement was basically reformist, aimed at changing some aspects of the structure of American society insofar as black people were denied some of the rights guaranteed citizens in the Constitution. It was directed toward establishing the principle of legal equality as public policy and toward the responsibility of the federal government in protecting the constitutional rights of citizens. To a degree these goals have been achieved, or at least accepted as a matter of principle. The Black Power movement, on the other hand, went beyond social reform. If the demands for political, economic, and social control by black people over the institutions that are responsible to them, along with the other changes necessary for the liberation of American blacks were achieved, American society would have undergone revolutionary changes. The civil rights movement did not address itself to the complex, deeply rooted problems facing black people in the slums of the United States. The Black Power movement did. In this sense, the Black Power movement might be said to have been the logical extension of the civil rights movement. Where the civil rights movement ended, the Black Power movement commenced; the demise of the civil rights movement gave birth to the black liberation movement.

THE CONSEQUENCES

The passage of the Civil Rights Act of 1964 and the Voting Rights Act of 1965, both of which resulted from massive civil rights campaigns conducted by black and white Americans in such places as Birmingham and Selma, Alabama, brought about a measure of change in the lives of southern blacks. The daily indignities that had characterized their lives for centuries had been somewhat ameliorated. To a degree they could share public facilities—libraries, restaurants, parks, and hotels—with white Americans. To a lesser degree they could exercise their constitutional right to vote. Many white Americans rejoiced that significant progress had been achieved in these realms, and to them the civil rights " revolution" was accomplished. They had demonstrated, marched, and suffered with their black brothers and sisters, and they had won. With this sense of accomplishment, they abandoned the civil rights movement. As long as black people were marching and singing "We Shall Overcome," they were eager to lend support. But they were unaware that the eradication of overt practices of racial segregation in public places and discrimination at the polls signaled only the first step toward equality for black people. Rather, they saw it as an end. Black people, on the other hand, were aware that the lives of few blacks outside the South had been affected by these changes. The southern black was beginning to achieve the token degree of equality that his or her counterpart outside the South had already achieved.

Collectively black people represent a vast underclass of citizens in the United States, and little attempt has been made to deal with their many long-standing problems—poverty, discrimination in employment, inadequate housing, and the like. Because of the expense involved, proposed remedies for these problems have not been taken seriously by many who have worked in the civil rights movement. Little expense had been incurred in accomplishing the modest gains of the civil rights movement, but to alter significantly the status of black people in the United States in a fundamental sense would be expensive, both in money and in psychological readjustment. It would no doubt cost billions of dollars, and white Americans would be forced to abandon one of America's longest-standing cultural myths—that of racial inferiority of the black person. Taken collectively, the price is too high for a vast majority of America's privileged class. Therefore the civil rights movement reached a deadlock: Black Americans demanded equality, while most white Americans continued to cling to the ideology of white supremacy. This resistance to change resulted from the refusal of white Americans to relinquish their position of dominance, which afforded them a variety of privileges denied to blacks.

The status of black people in the United States in 2000 indicates how much remains to be accomplished before black Americans will have achieved equality. Earnings and employment rates for blacks lag far behind those of white Americans. The average black earns approximately one-half of what the average white American earns, and the rate of unemployment among blacks is two-and-a-half times as high as among white Americans. Furthermore, when unemployed, they are likely to remain in that state twice as long as white workers. A vast majority (three-fourths) of blacks hold menial jobs. They continue to do the low-paying, unskilled jobs essential for contemporary society. At least one-half of all black people live in substandard (slum) housing, for which they are forced to pay more than their white counterparts who enjoy better-quality housing. These conditions contribute to low standards of health. For example, the infant mortality rate is twice as high for blacks as for white Americans. In education, most blacks continue to attend segregated public schools with inferior facilities. Consequently their achievement level lags behind that of white pupils.

Significant changes have been recorded in the lives of black Americans during the past two decades, but they have affected mostly only the small middle class. Today many blacks are employed in positions that heretofore had been reserved for white persons. However, the lives of the black masses in the urban slums remain unaffected. The appointment of a black to the Supreme Court or as chief administrative officer of Washington, DC, hardly affects people living substandard lives in the many cities throughout the country. Such appointments symbolize a remote opportunity that mocks the plight of the members of the underclass and reinforces their despair. It is among the black people living in urban slums that despair is most pronounced. They became acutely aware that officials of the federal government were willing to commit annually 10 times as much of the nation's resources to a war in Asia as to programs ostensibly designed to eradicate poverty at home. Similarly, they are aware that, proportionately, twice as many blacks as whites were killed in action in Vietnam. These factors, coupled with the lack of change in race relations, have contributed to the feelings of hopelessness that pervade black slums throughout the United States. Peaceful petition for redress of grievances has resulted in token change in the overt practices of segregation and discrimination. It has not secured effective action regarding the more fundamental problems that a vast majority of black people face.

One result of this lack of change in race relations was the massive uprisings in black communities that for several years came to be a regular summer feature in the United States. Each summer hundreds of black people struck at the structure of society through these uprisings. In the summers of 1963 through 1967 these phenomena occurred in hundreds of cities throughout the country, often taking on the character of urban guerrilla warfare, with the oppressed slum dwellers opposing helmeted federal troops and local law enforcement personnel. Federal, state, and local officials were generally insensitive to the real meaning of these uprisings, charging that they had been led by small bands of "extremists" directed from Havana or Peking. But for a significant proportion of black people, leaders as well as rank and file, the disturbances had a more positive than negative impact. For example, approximately one-third (34 percent) of a sample of blacks indicated that they felt that "riots" had helped their cause. Among a sample of leaders more than two-fifths (41 percent) gave a similar response. One-fifth of both categories of individuals (20 percent of rank and file and 19 percent of leaders) indicated their belief that the "riots" had hurt the cause of civil rights.[31]

The first of the major uprisings occurred in Watts, the black section of Los Angeles, in August 1965.[32] In 1966 it was Cleveland, Ohio, and in 1967, Newark, New Jersey,[33] and Detroit, Michigan.[34] In 1967 alone these uprisings occurred in some 56 cities in 31 states, resulting in at least 84 deaths, 3,828 injuries, 9,550 arrests, and hundreds of millions of dollars in property damage.[35]

The uprising in Watts lasted for five days. Thirty-four persons were killed, more than 1,000 were injured, some 4,000 arrests were made, and the estimated property damage was $40 million. More than 200 buildings were destroyed by fire, and another 400 were damaged. Of those persons killed, coroner's inquests indicated that 16 of the deaths of blacks had been caused by the Los Angeles Police Department and 7 had been caused by the National Guardsmen.[36] After the uprising many public officials appeared to be more concerned about the property losses than about the loss of human lives.

The Watts uprising signaled the end of the monopoly previously held by the advocates of nonviolence as a method of protest among blacks. At the peak of the uprising 10,000 black people took to the streets, and for more than five days fought against a force of 15,500 police and National Guardsmen. The police seized more than 850 weapons from the demonstrators, and the uprising was finally suppressed.

Another major uprising occurred in Newark in July 1967. Twenty-six people were killed, more than 1,100 were injured, and more than 1,600 were jailed. Property damage was estimated at $15 million. The black community was occupied for several days by a force of 3,000 National Guardsmen, 1,400 local police, and 500 state troopers. A majority of the deaths resulted from gunfire from Newark police who have been described as racists. It was reported that 100 black-owned stores were destroyed by the police.[37]

Immediately after the Newark uprising, Detroit experienced the bloodiest racial uprising in modern America. Forty-three people were killed, more than 2,000 were injured, and more than 5,000 were arrested. Property damage exceeded $500 million. The black residents of Detroit engaged in a form of urban guerrilla warfare with heavily armed police and soldiers. Altogether 7,000 National Guardsmen and 4,700 paratroopers supplemented the 2,500 members of the city and state police forces. With the use of tanks and machine guns the uprising was finally brought to an end after seven days of fighting. As with preceding urban uprisings, there were evidences of police brutality motivated by racism. It is reported that three young black men were executed by white policemen who found them with three white women in a motel room several blocks from the scene of the fighting.[38] Other blacks present insisted that the three men were unarmed and that the police were motivated by antiblack prejudice.

Each of these uprisings—Watts, Newark, and Detroit—was immediately triggered by what the black people involved considered unfair police action. Black people are often apprehended for minor infractions of the law for which white people are rarely punished in similar circumstances. The police are seen as the society's enforcers of unfair standards of justice and as occupying forces, and many slum residents reject this legal authority. During uprisings police frequently shoot black people of all ages for such infractions of the law as looting stores. The assumption that property rights are more sacred than human life prevails. Black people, on the other hand, interpret the looting as a means of sharing in the material rewards of a society that has, through a variety of techniques, denied them their rightful share. Although seemingly trivial incidents involving law enforcement kindle slum uprisings, these are not the underlying cause of such phenomena. In urban slums black people are forced to live in poverty and deprivation. They utilize the uprisings as a means of bringing their economic plight (unemployment and low earnings) maintained by white racism to the attention of public officials, who have generally been insensitive to their status.[39] It is through the destruction caused by these uprisings that public officials in a highly materialistic society are made aware of the hopelessness and despair of these citizens.

The conditions under which black people live have improved somewhat in the last three decades, but these changes have heightened their feelings of relative deprivation in relation to the status of white Americans. This feeling of relative deprivation has led to the crisis in race relations, which more than 30 years ago brought American society to the point at which, as the National Advisory Commission on Civil Disorders (the so-called Kerner Commission) concluded, "Our nation is moving toward two societies, one black, one white—separate and unequal."[40] The commission, which investigated the black uprisings of 1967, reported that these disorders were caused by the attitudes of white Americans toward black Americans: "White racism is essentially responsible for the explosive mixture which has been accumulating in our cities since the end of World War II."[41] Elsewhere the commission reported: "What white Americans have never fully understood—but what the Negro can never forget—is that white society is deeply implicated in the ghetto.

White institutions created it, white institutions maintain it, and white society condones it."[42] Sociological studies of causes of present black militance generally attribute this phenomenon to the feeling of relative deprivation of black people when compared with white Americans.[43]

White Americans frequently compare the socioeconomic status of black Americans with that of people living outside the United States. Such comparisons are invalid because it is the relative status of black and white Americans that has precipitated the present crisis. Black people in the United States may enjoy a higher standard of living than do citizens of the so-called underdeveloped nations, but the gap between black and white Americans continues to be vast.

It is frequently maintained that the uprisings that swept American cities impeded the cause of black equality. Such phenomena may have increased antiblack prejudice, but at the same time their long-term effect may have improved the status of blacks insofar as decreased discrimination was concerned. In short, a reduction in discrimination is more important to the cause of black equality than an increase in prejudice. The so-called "riots" of 1967 resulted in the far-reaching report by the National Advisory Commission on Civil Disorders. If the recommendations of this report had been put into effect, the result would have been widespread change in the status of black people in the United States.

In the meantime, recent developments among black people are likely to alter the character of American race relations. One such development is the increasing political awareness of black college students. Since 1962 black students at the major colleges and universities throughout the United States have organized themselves into all-black clubs and are challenging established practices.[44] They question the content of courses and the hiring practices of these institutions, and reject integration into the white, middle-class social life of these schools. They read the works of black writers, most of whom rarely appear on reading lists for regular courses. They conduct discussions on topics such as black identity and publish newspapers and magazines. In short, they introduce the concept of Black Power on the college campus.

Students were among the earliest participants in the civil rights movement in the South, but black students at predominantly white colleges and universities outside the South were often more involved in fraternities, sororities, and other social activities than in questions of equality for black slum dwellers. In the South they were made aware of their status daily through the practice of rigid segregation, while outside the South the few black students could easily be absorbed into the life of the school or effectively isolated. Frequently their lives were such that they could forget that they were black while they remained on campus. The transition from school to work, difficult at best, became increasingly so for black college students. They were not being prepared for the reality of what they would face as professionals in a racist society.

The response of black students to this situation has been an attempt to organize themselves. The first of these organizations outside the South was the Students' Afro-American Society at Columbia University. It was followed by Harvard University's African and Afro-American Students group, Yale University's Black Students' Alliance, Princeton University's Association of Black Collegians, Dartmouth College's Afro-American Society, the University of California at Berkeley's Afro-American Student Union, Hunter College's Kubanbanya, City College's Onyx, and other similar organizations at colleges throughout the United States. In December 1966, a northeastern regional conference, attended by 300 delegates from 30 schools, met at Columbia University. In 1985, this conference was held at Cornell University.

One of the primary functions of these organizations is to stress black consciousness and black pride. Through them, students identify with each other and with their less fortunate fellow blacks. Frequently the students spend their free time working with black slum dwellers, especially in tutorial programs and other educational projects. This action provides a link between the politically sophisticated students and the powerless slum dwellers. Furthermore, these students are more likely than others to understand the nature and functioning of the society in which they live. Consequently, they provide an important source of black leadership at a crucial time.

Another development in the black movement is the attempt among leaders of the more militant organizations to link the movement for black equality in the United States with the movements of other oppressed peoples throughout the world, especially those in Africa, Asia, and Latin America. One of the first black leaders in years to see the struggle of black Americans in international terms was Malcolm X, who traveled and consulted extensively in Africa and Asia.[45] An attempt to link the struggle of black people in the United States and that of Africans led Malcolm X to establish the Organization of Afro-American Unity. Since his death several other black leaders have made contacts with revolutionary individuals and organizations throughout the world.

These leaders see the struggles of black Americans as similar to those of other oppressed peoples, and they increasingly turn to the third world for support. In 1967 Stokely Carmichael was the guest of honor and a delegate at the meeting in Havana, Cuba, of the Organization of Latin American Solidarity, an organization of the leaders of revolutionary movements in Latin America. In his address to the conference he said:

> We greet you as comrades because it becomes increasingly clear to us each day that we share with you a common struggle; we have a common enemy. Our enemy is white Western imperialist society; and our struggle is to overthrow the system which feeds itself and expands itself through the economic and cultural exploitation of nonwhite, non-Western peoples. We speak to you, comrades, because we wish to make clear that we understand that our destinies are intertwined. We do not view our struggle as being contained within the boundaries of the United States, as they are defined by present-day maps.[46]

At the first meeting of the National Conference for New Politics in Chicago in September 1967, black delegates insisted that the conference adopt a resolution pledging total and unquestionable support to all wars of national liberation in Africa, Latin America, and particularly Vietnam.

According to one reporter, "Negroes increasingly see Black Power as not confined to ghetto rebellions, but rather as part of a general fight of the oppressed against the oppressor all over the world."[47] He cited several instances in which black leaders in the United States had met with leaders of revolutionary movements around the world. Floyd McKissick of CORE joined a team of other Americans who traveled to Cambodia to investigate the claims by the U.S. Department of Defense that the area of Cambodia that borders on South Vietnam was used by the North Vietnamese forces as a sanctuary. While there, he reportedly conferred with the chief of state on "peace and racism." A black lawyer and other leaders went to North Vietnam to gather evidence for the International War Crimes Tribunal organized by Bertrand Russell, and representatives of SNCC served as judges on this tribunal. In addition, SNCC maintained an international affairs department through which contact was made with other revolutionary movements, principally in Africa. When the United Nations sponsored a seminar on racial discrimination and colonialism in South Africa in the summer of 1967, both CORE and SNCC were represented.

Increasingly, the more militant black leaders attempted to internationalize the movement for equality. Such events as the assassination of Patrice Lumumba in the Congo and that of Malcolm X in New York at a time when he was establishing contacts with African leaders, and also the implication of the Central Intelligence Agency in counterrevolutionary acts outside the United States, forced some of the black leaders to see their fight for equality in global terms.

By the end of 1972 the status of the black American remained a domestic problem of considerable magnitude. Although greater changes had occurred in the previous 10 years than during the nearly one hundred years since Reconstruction, blacks remained a large underclass of citizens. The movement responsible for these changes appeared to have suffered an irreparable split over the introduction of the concept of Black Power. The militant leaders who favored the concept talked in terms of black liberation, while the more moderate leaders who opposed it clung to a belief in racial justice through the democratic process. In the meantime, black people throughout the United States were becoming increasingly politically aware of the society in which they lived.

This increasing political awareness was manifested by the widespread support in black communities throughout the United States for a black state legislator from Georgia who was denied his seat because of his outspoken opposition to the war in Vietnam; by the support accorded the world's heavyweight champion when he was stripped of his title for refusing to permit himself to be inducted into the armed forces (again because of opposition to the war in Vietnam); and by the nationwide solidarity expressed by black people when a congressman from New York, one of the most powerful elected black officials in American history, was denied his committee chairmanship and his seat in Congress. Such incidents as these were rather widely interpreted by blacks as a continuing refusal on the part of white Americans to permit blacks to share power in the society. That is, white persons in positions of power appeared willing to resort to whatever tactics were necessary to perpetuate the low status of black people in the society. The 1967 mayoral elections in Cleveland, Ohio, and Gary, Indiana, illustrated the point. In both these cities black mayors were elected, primarily because of the heavy turnout of black voters. In both cities at least 90 percent of the traditionally Democratic white voters switched parties and cast their ballots for the white Republican candidates rather than vote for blacks.[48]

In addition to increased political awareness, blacks in 1972 were more aware of their own history and of the history of the United States than at any previous time. A continuous series of past injustices and the refusal of white Americans to discontinue such practices had increased impatience and bitterness throughout the black community. For their part, white Americans generally appeared to be incapable of understanding this mood. Therefore, with few exceptions, there was little dialogue between the growing number of black militants and white Americans. Large numbers of black people were demanding control over the institutions in their communities as a means of dealing with the problems they faced. Although the Black Power militants were in a minority, an increasingly large number of blacks rejected integration as necessary for the achievement of equality. Integration, they felt, failed to solve these problems. White Americans, for the most part, rejected this notion and expressed satisfaction with the pace of civil rights in the United States. The result was that relations between black and white Americans reached a point of greater strain than at any other time in the twentieth century.

Finally, the strain in race relations in the United States was intensified by systematic attempts to curb black militancy. Black Americans had learned through the years that increased militance in pursuing their goal of liberation was likely to be met by attempts to preserve white supremacy at all costs. At no time had this been more evident. Attempts to control the pace of the movement frequently took the form of silencing the more militant leaders, either by assassinating them (e.g., Medgar Evers, Martin Luther King, Jr., Malcolm X) or by jailing them (e.g., H. Rap Brown, Eldridge Cleaver, Amiri Baraka [LeRoi Jones]). Black Americans saw such acts as further manifestations of the racism that pervaded the fabric of the society.

For the black community the murder of Martin Luther King, Jr., on April 4, 1968, clearly indicated the extent to which white bigots were willing to go to preserve the low status of blacks in the society. Although the bullet that killed King may have been fired by a single individual, that individual did not exist in isolation. His act must be understood within the larger context of the racism that has become institutionalized in American society.

Until his death, King remained the most widely respected leader in the black community. Although many of the militants disapproved of his goals and tactics, his dedication and courage were unchallenged. He steadfastly maintained a faith in nonviolence as a means of achieving the liberation of black Americans. With his assassination many black people who shared his belief became disillusioned, as the widespread disorders that followed his murder showed.

In black communities throughout the United States the response to his assassination was immediate and angry. Altogether 125 cities were affected; serious outbursts occurred in Baltimore; Chicago; Kansas City; Missouri; Pittsburgh; and Washington, DC. A total of 46 persons were killed, 2,600 were injured, and nearly 22,000 arrested. The rage of these black people was manifested by rioting, looting, and destroying buildings and other property. After nearly 10 days, 55,000 federal troops, working with local police, were able to restore order.

White Americans responded to the murder of Martin Luther King, Jr., with a massive outpouring of both genuine sentiment and sentimentality, and many of the individuals who had been the strongest opponents of his goals were among those most dramatic in their mourning. The results: one of the longest periods of mourning and one of the largest funerals in American history. For many in the black community the message of the assassination was clear: Any serious attempt to fundamentally alter the existing pattern of race relations in the United States would be met with whatever measures were necessary to curb it.

The assassination of Martin Luther King, Jr., removed from the scene one of the great reformist leaders in the history of the United States. The "dream" he envisioned at the March on Washington in 1963 has continued to remain a dream for black people, although the administration of Lyndon B. Johnson attempted, through the "Great Society" programs, to alleviate some of the poverty of the black community and provide its inhabitants with some measure of control over their lives. Johnson's mistake, however, was the misguided notion that America's domestic problems could be solved while waging one of the most brutal wars of genocide in human history. Because of his stubborn insistence on accelerating the war of aggression in Indochina, he was finally hounded out of office by opposition to this war policy. In the meantime, Richard M. Nixon was elected president after campaigning on a platform that promised, in many subtle and not so subtle ways, to reverse whatever gains blacks had managed to make during the height of the civil rights movement.

One of the more revolutionary groups to develop during the civil rights movement was the Black Panther party. The party was organized by two young militants, Huey P. Newton and Bobby Seale, in Oakland, California, in the fall of 1966. In February 1968, the party entered into a merger with SNCC, but the merger was short-lived because of bitter disputes between Panther and SNCC officials. The major point of disagreement was the Panthers' opposition to SNCC alliances with white groups.[49]

The ideology of the Black Panther party embraced some aspects of other revolutionary groups and ideologies, particularly Marxism-Leninism, but black unity and autonomy were at the core of its platform and program. Together Newton and Seale developed the program of the party, whose full name was the Black Panther Party for Self Defense. The panther had been the symbol of the Lowndes County Freedom Organization in Alabama in 1965. SNCC selected the black panther as the emblem of its organization, and the Black Panther party chose the name because the black panther is reputed to be an animal that never makes an unprovoked attack but will defend itself vehemently when attacked.[50]

Police brutality was one of the main grievances of Oakland's residents, and point seven of the program that Newton and Seale developed stated "We want an immediate end to POLICE BRUTALITY and MURDER of black people." The party insisted that the Second Amendment gave them the right to bear arms. And on the morning of May 2, 1967, a caravan of cars carrying 29 Panthers, 20 of them armed, journeyed to Sacramento, the state capital. The trip to Sacramento was widely reported in the media throughout the world, and the Black Panther party became well known. New chapters were established in several large cities, and hundreds (perhaps thousands) of angry young men from the streets were attracted to the party.

Because of its militance, the Black Panther party was considered a threat by law enforcement agencies throughout the country, including the Federal Bureau of Investigation (FBI). The FBI's director, J. Edgar Hoover, initiated a wave of repression by declaring the Black Panther party "the greatest threat to the internal security of the United States." In the meantime the party had begun providing services to the black communities in which it operated, including free breakfasts for children, free health clinics, free clothing distribution centers, and liberation schools. Furthermore, Black Panther parties were established in England, France, and Israel. At home, Chicanos, Chinese-Americans, Puerto Ricans, and poor whites emulated the Panthers by forming parallel organizations.

The nationwide campaign of repression, coupled with internal strife, served eventually to weaken and virtually destroy the Black Panther party. Perhaps the greatest threat to the Panthers and other black groups was the FBI's counterintelligence program (COINTELPRO), which was directed specifically against "Black nationalist hate groups."[51] One of the groups highest on its list of targets was the Black Panther party, and through various means, including murder, it played a major role in the destruction of the party.

•   •   •

Through the black revolt, which culminated in the civil rights movement, black people managed through intensive struggle to gain the rights of citizenship *in principle*. But they soon learned that legal equality in principle did not lead to justice in practice. The next several chapters deal with the immediate results of the peculiar history of black people in the United States.

SELECTED BIBLIOGRAPHY

BARBOUR, FLOYD B., ed. *The Black Power Revolt*. Boston: Porter Sargent, 1968.
BATES, DAISY. *The Long Shadow of Little Rock*. New York: David McKay Co., 1962.
BELFRAGE, SALLY. *Freedom Summer*. New York: Viking Press, 1965.
BENNETT, LERONE. *Before the Mayflower*. Baltimore: Penguin Books, 1966.

BURNS, W. HAYWOOD. *The Voices of Negro Protest in America.* New York: Oxford University Press, 1963.

CAGIN, SETH, and PHILIP DRAY. *We Are Not Afraid: The Story of Goodman, Schwerner and Chaney.* New York: Macmillan, 1988.

CLARK, KENNETH. *Dark Ghetto.* New York: Harper & Row, Publishers, 1965.

CLEAVER, ELDRIDGE. "Open Letter to Stokeley Carmichael," *Ramparts,* September 1969, pp. 31–32.

COLES, ROBERT. *Children of Crisis: A Study of Courage and Fear.* Boston: Atlantic Monthly Press, 1967.

CONOT, ROBERT. *Rivers of Blood, Years of Darkness.* New York: Bantam Books, 1967.

CRUSE, HAROLD. *The Crisis of the Negro Intellectual.* New York: William Morrow & Co., 1967.

FAGER, CHARLES E. *White Reflections on Black Power.* Grand Rapids, MI: Wm. B. Erdmans Publishing Co., 1967.

FORMAN, JAMES. *The Making of Black Revolutionaries.* New York: Macmillan Co., 1972.

GRIER, WILLIAM H., and PRICE M. COBBS. *Black Rage.* New York: Basic Books, 1968.

HAYDEN, TOM. *Rebellion in Newark.* New York: Random House, 1967.

HERSEY, JOHN. *The Algiers Motel Incident.* New York: Bantam Books, 1968.

HINDS, LENNOX. Foreword to Assata Shakur's Autobiography, *Assata.* Westport, CT: Lawrence Hill & Company, 1987.

HOLT, LEN. *The Summer That Didn't End.* New York: William Morrow & Co., 1965.

HUGHES, LANGSTON. *Fight for Freedom: The Story of the NAACP.* New York: Berkley Publishing Corp., 1962.

HUIE, WILLIAM BRADFORD. *Three Lives for Mississippi.* New York: Trident Press, 1965.

JONES, LE ROI. *Home: Social Essays.* New York: William Morrow & Co., 1966.

KILLENS, JOHN O. *Black Man's Burden.* New York: Trident Press, 1965.

KILLIAN, LEWIS M. *The Impossible Revolution? Black Power and the American Dream.* New York: Random House, 1968.

————and CHARLES GRIGG. *Racial Crisis in America: Leadership in Conflict.* Englewood Cliffs, NJ: Prentice Hall, 1964.

KING, MARTIN LUTHER, JR. *Stride Toward Freedom.* New York: Harper & Brothers, 1958.

————. *Where Do We Go From Here: Chaos or Community?* New York: Harper & Row, Publishers, 1967.

KUGLER, RICHARD. *Simple Justice: The History of Brown v. Board of Education and Black America's Struggle for Equality.* New York: Random House, 1975.

LEWIS, ANTHONY. *Portrait of a Decade.* New York: Random House, 1965.

LOMAX, LOUIS. *The Negro Revolt.* New York: Harper & Row, Publishers, 1962.

MALCOLM X. *The Autobiography of Malcolm X.* New York: Grove Press, 1964.

MORGAN, CHARLES. *A Time to Speak.* New York: Harper & Row, Publishers, 1964.

MUHAMMAD, ELIJAH. *Message to the Black Man in America.* Chicago: Muhammad Mosque of Islam No. 2, 1965.

PINKNEY, ALPHONSO. *The Committed: White Activists in the Civil Rights Movement.* New Haven, CT: College and University Press, 1968.

————. *The American Way of Violence.* New York: Random House, 1972.

————. *Red, Black and Green: Black Nationalism in the United States.* New York: Cambridge University Press, 1976.

POWLEDGE, FRED. *Black Power, White Resistance: Notes on the New Civil War.* Cleveland: World Publishing Co., 1967.

————. *Free at Last? The Civil Rights Movement and the People Who Made It.* Boston: Little, Brown, 1992.

Report of the National Advisory Commission on Civil Disorders. New York: Bantam Books, 1968.

WILKINSON, J. HARVIE III. *From Brown to Bakke: The Supreme Court and School Integration, 1954–1978.* New York: Oxford University Press, 1979.

WILLIAMS, ROBERT F. *Negroes with Guns.* New York: Marzani & Munzell, 1962.

WRIGHT, NATHAN. *Black Power and Urban Unrest.* New York: Hawthorn Books, 1967.

ZINN, HOWARD. *SNCC: The New Abolitionists.* Boston: Beacon Press, 1964.

NOTES

1. See Anthony Lewis, *Portrait of a Decade* (New York: Random House, 1965), chap. 3.

2. See Martin Luther King, Jr., *Stride Toward Freedom* (New York: Harper, 1958).

3. See Louis Lomax, *The Negro Revolt* (New York: Harper, 1962), pp. 81–100.

4. King, *Stride Toward Freedom*, pp. 102–7.

5. Charles Morgan, *A Time to Speak* (New York: Harper & Row, 1964), pp. 38–39.

6. Lewis, *Portrait of a Decade*, pp. 46–69.

7. See Daisy Bates, *The Long Shadow of Little Rock* (New York: McKay, 1962); Robert Coles, *Children of Crisis: A Study of Courage and Fear* (Boston: Atlantic Monthly, 1967).

8. Lerone Bennett, Jr., *Before the Mayflower* (Baltimore: Penguin, 1966), p. 407.

9. Lomax, *Negro Revolt*, pp. 132–46.

10. See Alphonso Pinkney, *The Committed: White Activists in the Civil Rights Movement* (New Haven, CT: College and University Press, 1968); Howard Zinn, *SNCC: The New Abolitionists* (Boston: Beacon Press, 1964).

11. Bennett, *Before the Mayflower*, pp. 329–40.

12. See Sally Belfrage, *Freedom Summer* (New York: Viking, 1965); Pinkney, *The Committed*; Elizabeth Sutherland, *Letters from Mississippi* (New York: McGraw-Hill, 1965).

13. Seth Cagin and Philip Dray, *We Are Not Afraid* (New York: Macmillan, 1988); William Bradford Huie, *Three Lives for Mississippi* (New York: Trident Press, 1965).

14. John Herbers, "Communique from the Mississippi Front," *New York Times Magazine*, November 8, 1964, p. 34.

15. See Pinkney, *The Committed*, chap. 5.

16. Robert Coles, "When the Southern Negro Moves North," *New York Times Magazine*, September 17, 1967, p. 25.

17. Kenneth Clark, *Dark Ghetto* (New York: Harper & Row, 1965), p. 11.

18. Malcolm X, *The Autobiography of Malcolm X* (New York: Grove Press, 1964).

19. Martin Luther King, Jr., *Where Do We Go From Here?* (New York: Harper & Row, 1967), pp. 23–32.

20. Quoted in Gordon Parks, "Stokely Carmichael: Young Man Behind an Angry Message," *Life*, May 19, 1967, p. 82.

21. Stokely Carmichael and Charles V. Hamilton, *Black Power: The Politics of Liberation in America* (New York: Random House, Inc., copyright 1967), p. 44.

22. See Fred C. Shapiro, "The Successor to Floyd McKissick May Not Be So Reasonable," *New York Times Magazine*, October 1, 1967, p. 102.

23. King, *Where Do We Go From Here?*, pp. 32–34.

24. Ibid., pp. 44–63.

25. *New York Times*, October 14, 1966, p. 35.

26. See " 'Black Power' and Coalition Politics," *Commentary*, September 1966, pp. 35–40.

27. Carmichael and Hamilton, *Black Power*, chap. 3.

28. David Danzig, "In Defense of 'Black Power,' "*Commentary*, September 1966, p. 46. Reprinted from *Commentary*, by permission; copyright © 1966, by the American Jewish Committee.

29. Joyce Ladner, "What 'Black Power' Means to Negroes in Mississippi," *Transaction* 5 (November 1967), 14.

30. Edward B. Fiske, "Black Power Bloc Formed by Protestant Clerics," *New York Times*, November 2, 1967, p. 52.

31. William Brink and Louis Harris, *Black and White* (New York: Simon & Schuster, 1967), p. 67.

32. See Robert Conot, *Rivers of Blood, Years of Darkness* (New York: Bantam, 1967); R. J. Murphy and James Watson, *The Structure of Discontent* (Los Angeles: Institute of Government and Public Affairs, University of California, 1967); T. M. Tomlinson and D. L. TenHouten, *Los Angeles Riot Study Method: Negro Reaction Survey* (Los Angeles: Institute of Government and Public Affairs, University of California, 1967).

33. Tom Hayden, *Rebellion in Newark* (New York: Random House, 1967); report of the New Jersey Select Commission on Civil Disorder, *New York Times*, February 11, 1968, p. 1.

34. See Tom Parmenter, "Breakdown of Law and Order," *Transaction* 9 (September 1967), 13–22.

35. Figures compiled from news reports in the *New York Times* during August 1967.

36. *Violence in the City—An End or a Beginning?* (Los Angeles: Governor's Commission on the Los Angeles Riots, 1965).

37. Hayden, *Rebellion in Newark*, p. 38; *New York Times,* February 11, 1968, p. 1.

38. Parmenter, "Breakdown of Law and Order," pp. 15–16; John Hersey, *The Algiers Motel Incident* (New York: Bantam, 1968); Alphonso Pinkney, *The American Way of Violence* (New York: Random House, 1972), pp. 126–30.

39. See Stanley Lieberson and Arnold R. Silverman, "The Precipitants and Underlying Conditions of Race Riots," *American Sociological Review* 30 (December 1965), 887–98.

40. *Report of the National Advisory Commission on Civil Disorders* (New York: Bantam, 1968), p. 1.

41. Ibid., p. 203.

42. Ibid., p. 2.

43. James A. Geschwender, "Social Structure and the Negro Revolt: An Examination of Some Hypotheses," *Social Forces* 43 (December 1964), 248–56; Ruth Searles and J. Allen Williams, Jr., "Negro College Students' Participation in Sit-Ins," *Social Forces* 40 (March 1962), 215–20.

44. Ernest Dunbar, "The Black Revolt Hits the White Campus," *Look*, October 1967, pp. 27–31.

45. Malcolm X, *Autobiography of Malcolm X*, especially chaps. 17–19.

46. Reported in John Gerassi, "Havana: A New International is Born," *Monthly Review* 19 (October 1967), 27.

47. William Worthy, "The American Negro is Dead," *Esquire*, November 1967, p. 126.

48. Jeffrey K. Hadden, Louis H. Masotti, and Victor Thiessen, "The Making of the Negro Mayors, 1967," *Transaction* 5 (January–February 1968), 21–30.

49. Eldridge Cleaver, "Open Letter to Stokley Carmichael," *Ramparts*, September 1969, pp. 31–32.

50. Alphonso Pinkney, *Red, Black and Green: Black Nationalism in the United States*, New York: Cambridge University Press, 1976, pp. 99–100.

51. Lennox Hinds' Forward to Assata Shakur's Autobiography. *Assata*: Westport, CT, 1987.

CHAPTER THREE

Characteristics of the Population

The peculiar history of black Americans is, in part, responsible for their present status. Black Americans, as a group, differ from white Americans in many ways. These differences invariably stem from the low status to which black Americans have been relegated in society. In no instance are these differences more pronounced than in population characteristics. In the United States there are several fundamental differences between black and white population characteristics. When black and white Americans share similar socioeconomic status positions in society, they are remarkably similar in fertility and mortality rates, for example, but the overrepresentation of black people in the lowest status category serves to make for significant group differences between them and their white fellow citizens on population characteristics.

SIZE AND GROWTH

In 1996 black people made up 13.0 percent of the American population. Their total population of 33 million is exceeded on the world scene by only 28 of the more than 180 independent nation-states and self-governing territories. Only 5 of the more than 40 independent African states have total populations that exceed the number of blacks in the United States. Within the United States, blacks are the largest visible minority group. They constitute approximately 90 percent of the "nonwhite" population of the country. The size of the black population is frequently cited as a factor influencing its integration into American society. Since black Americans have been kept in a subordinate position, and since they are responded to as a group, the very magnitude of their numbers may be considered both a handicap and an asset to their advancement in the United States.

At the time of the first population census in 1790, nearly 1 out of every 5 (19.3 percent) Americans was black. Slightly more than 750,000 blacks were enumerated by that census. With each following census the number increased to the point that two hundred years later, 33 million blacks reside in the United States. The pattern of growth has been consistent, with the percentage of increase being greatest in the earlier years. During the decade from 1800 to 1810, for example, the black population increased by 37.5 percent. The decade with the lowest percentage of increase (6.5 percent) was from 1910 to 1920. The greatest single historical contributor to the increase in the black population has been the excess of births over deaths (natural increase). Since the first census, immigration has been an insignificant element in black population growth.

The proportion of black people in the total population of the United States remained relatively stable up through the census of 1810, when there was a gradual decline that persisted up through the census of 1930. This decline in the proportion of black people in the population resulted mainly from two factors: the decline and ultimate cessation in the importation of slaves and the increase in the number of white immigrants to the United States. In the decade from 1930 to 1940, there was a gradual increase in the proportion of black people in the population. In 1930 they comprised 9.7 percent of the population, and by 1990 the proportion was approximately 13 percent. (See Figure 3-1.)

The growth pattern of the black population may be attributed to two major factors: (1) a consistent increase in numbers from the first census until the present time and (2) fluctuation as regards proportion of the total population. The proportion was reasonably steady between 1790 and 1830, decreased moderately from 1830 to 1930, and has increased gradually since 1930. The Bureau of the Census projects that by 2050, the black population will have increased significantly while the white population will have decreased significantly (see Figure 3-2).

FERTILITY

The black population of the United States is increasing at a more rapid pace than the white population. The major element in the black population growth rate is the increase in births over deaths. Throughout the present century, the birthrate among blacks has remained consistently higher than the white birthrate. In 1994 the birthrate among black women of childbearing age was 77 (per 1,000 women 15 to 44 years of age), higher than that reported for white women (65).[1]

In the general population, the birthrate for black women was higher than that for white women in 1994. Black women had a birthrate of 19.5 per 1,000 population, compared with 14.4 for white women. The birthrate for black women is significantly higher than that of white women, as is the plural birth ratio (see Table 3-1). That is a decrease in the birthrate for both groups from 1980, when the figures were 21.3 and 15.1, respectively. The highest birthrate was among women 25 to 29 years of age; the next highest rate was among those between 20 and 24.[2] (See Table 3-1.)

The average number of people per household was 2.65 in 1996. In that year there were a total of 5,434,000 black families with children under the age of 18, and

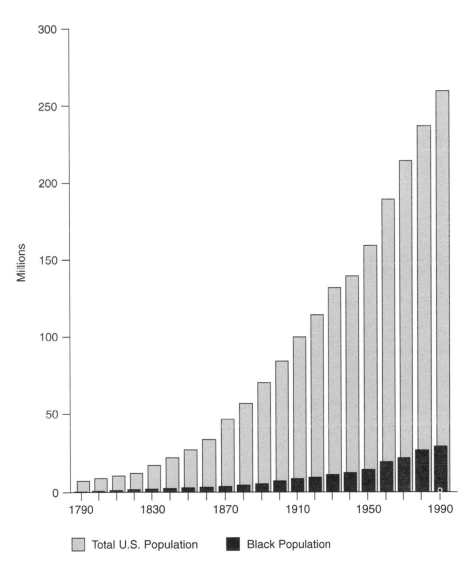

FIGURE 3-1   Total U.S. and Black Population, 1790–1990

Sources: U.S. Bureau of the Census, *Statistical Abstract of the United States: 1991* (Washington, DC, 1991); and U.S. Bureau of the Census, Current Population Reports, Series P-20, *The Black Population in the United States: March 1990 and 1989* (Washington, DC, 1991).

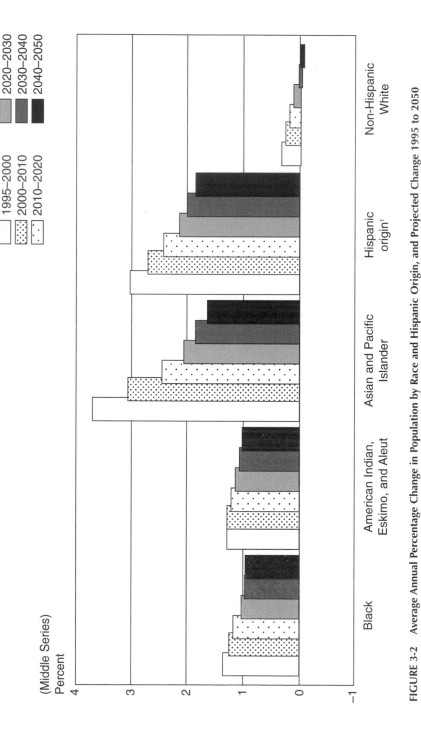

FIGURE 3-2 Average Annual Percentage Change in Population by Race and Hispanic Origin, and Projected Change 1995 to 2050

[1]Persons of Hispanic origin may be of any race. The information on the total and Hispanic population shown in this report was collected in the 50 States and the District of Columbia and, therefore, does not include residents of Puerto Rico.

Source: U.S. Bureau of the Census, *Current Population Reports,* P-23–182 (Washington, DC, 1992).

29,937,000 white families in the same circumstances. Of these, 36 percent of black family groups contained two parents, compared with 74 percent of white families. On the other hand, 64 percent of blacks in this category lived in one-parent households, compared with 26 percent for white families in the same circumstances. Among blacks, 58 percent of families were maintained by the mother and 6 percent by the father. Among white family groups, 21 percent were maintained by the mother and 5 percent by the father.[3]

MORTALITY

Reliable statistics on the death rate of black people were not available until about 1900. Although blacks have had a higher death rate than whites, the situation has gradually changed. In 1900 the death rate for blacks was 25 per 1,000 population, while for whites it was 17. Since that time the gap has narrowed to the point that in 1995, blacks had a lower death rate than whites. The rate for blacks was 8.6 per thousand, compared with 9.1 for whites.[4]

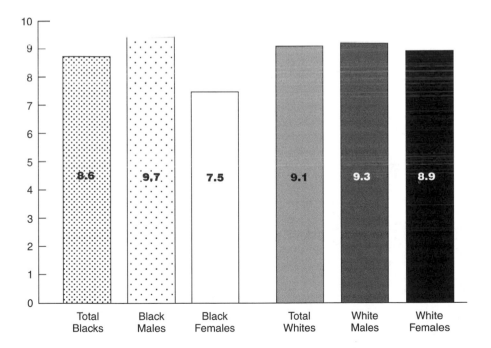

FIGURE 3-3   Death Rates per 1,000 Population, by Race and Sex, 1995

Source: U.S. Bureau of the Census, *Statistical Abstract of the United States: 1997,* Washington, DC, 1997.

TABLE 3-1 Births and Birth Rates, 1980 to 1994

Births in thousands. Births by race of child. Excludes births to nonresidents of the United States

ITEM	1980	1985	1986	1987	1988	1989	1990	1991	1992	1993	1994
Live Births[1]	**3,612**	**3,761**	**3,757**	**3,809**	**3,910**	**4,041**	**4,158**	**4,111**	**4,065**	**4,000**	**3,953**
White	2,936	3,038	3,019	3,044	3,102	3,192	3,290	3,241	3,202	3,150	3,121
Black	568	582	593	611	639	673	684	683	674	659	636
American Indian	29	34	34	35	37	39	39	39	39	39	38
Asian or Pacific Islander	74	105	108	117	129	133	142	145	150	153	158
Male	1,853	1,928	1,925	1,951	2,002	2,069	2,129	2,102	2,082	2,049	2,023
Female	1,760	1,833	1,832	1,858	1,907	1,971	2,029	2,009	1,983	1,951	1,930
Males per 100 females	105	105	105	105	105	105	105	105	105	105	105
Age of mother:											
Under 20 years old	562	478	472	473	489	518	533	532	518	501	518
20 to 24 years old	1,226	1,141	1,102	1,076	1,067	1,078	1,094	1,090	1,070	1,038	1,001
25 to 29 years old	1,108	1,201	1,200	1,216	1,239	1,263	1,277	1,220	1,179	1,129	1,089
30 to 34 years old	550	696	721	761	804	842	886	885	895	901	906
35 to 39 years old	141	214	230	248	270	294	318	331	345	357	372
40 years old or more	24	29	31	36	41	46	50	54	58	61	66
Birth rate per 1,000 population	**15.9**	**15.8**	**15.6**	**15.7**	**16.0**	**16.4**	**16.7**	**16.3**	**15.9**	**15.5**	**15.2**
White	15.1	15.0	14.8	14.9	15.0	15.4	15.8	15.4	15.0	14.7	14.4
Black	21.3	20.4	20.5	20.8	21.5	22.3	22.4	21.9	21.3	20.5	19.5
American Indian	20.7	19.8	19.2	19.1	19.3	19.7	18.9	18.3	18.4	17.8	17.1
Asian or Pacific Islander	19.9	18.7	18.0	18.4	19.2	18.7	19.0	18.2	18.0	17.7	17.5
Male	16.8	16.7	16.5	16.5	16.8	17.2	17.6	17.1	16.7	(NA)	(NA)
Female	15.1	15.0	14.9	14.9	15.2	15.6	15.9	15.6	15.2	(NA)	(NA)
Plural birth ratio[2]	**19.3**	**21.0**	**21.6**	**22.0**	**22.4**	**23.0**	**23.3**	**23.9**	**24.4**	**25.2**	**25.7**
White	18.5	20.4	21.2	21.6	22.0	22.5	22.9	23.4	24.0	24.9	25.5
Black	24.1	25.3	24.9	25.4	25.8	26.9	27.0	27.8	28.2	28.7	29.4

Fertility rate per 1,000 women[3]	68.4	66.2	65.4	65.7	67.2	69.2	70.9	69.6	68.9	67.6	66.7
White[3]	64.8	64.1	63.1	63.3	64.5	56.4	68.3	67.0	66.5	65.4	64.9
Black[3]	84.7	78.8	78.9	80.1	82.6	86.2	86.8	85.2	83.2	80.5	76.9
American Indian[3]	82.7	78.6	75.9	75.6	76.8	79.0	76.2	75.1	75.4	73.4	70.9
Asian or Pacific Islander[3]	73.2	68.4	66.0	67.1	70.2	68.2	69.6	67.6	67.2	66.7	66.8
Age of mother:											
10 to 14 years old	1.1	1.2	1.3	1.3	1.3	1.4	1.4	1.4	1.4	1.4	1.4
15 to 19 years old	53.0	51.0	50.2	50.6	53.0	57.3	59.9	62.1	60.7	59.6	58.9
20 to 24 years old	115.1	108.3	107.4	107.9	110.2	113.8	116.5	115.7	114.6	112.6	111.1
25 to 29 years old	112.9	111.0	109.8	111.6	114.4	117.6	120.2	118.2	117.4	115.5	113.9
30 to 34 years old	61.9	69.1	70.1	72.1	74.8	77.4	80.8	79.5	80.2	80.8	81.5
35 to 39 years old	19.8	24.0	24.4	26.3	28.1	29.9	31.7	32.0	32.5	32.9	33.7
40 to 44 years old	3.9	4.0	4.1	4.4	4.8	5.2	5.5	5.5	5.9	6.1	6.4
45 to 49 years old	0.2	0.2	0.2	0.2	0.2	0.2	0.2	0.2	0.3	0.3	0.3

NA = Not available.

[1]Includes other races not shown separately.

[2]Number of multiple births per 1,000 live births.

[3]Per 1,000 women, 15 to 44 years old in specified group. The rate for age of mother 45 to 49 years old computed by relating births to mothers 45 years old and over to women 45 to 49 years old.

Source: U.S. National Center for Health Statistics. *Vital Statistics of the United States*, annual; *Monthly Vital Statistics Report*; and unpublished data.

Black mothers die at a higher rate than white mothers from complications associated with birth. In 1994 the infant mortality rate for blacks was 15.8 per 1,000 live births, while for whites it was 6.6. In 1992 the maternal death rate for white women was 5.0, while for black women it was 20.8. In terms of fetal deaths in 1992, the rate for blacks and other minorities was 11.7 percent, whereas for whites it was about half that rate at 6.3. For neonatal deaths, the rate for blacks in 1996 was 10.8 or more than twice the rate for whites.[5] (See Table 3-2).

A reasonably accurate measure of the health and living standards of a people is life expectancy. In this regard, black Americans have always fared worse than white Americans. In 1900 life expectancy at birth for blacks was 33 years, while for whites it was 47.6 years. By 1995 life expectancy for both blacks and whites had increased substantially. For blacks it was 69.8—74.0 for black women and 65.4 for black men. For whites in 1995 the total was 76.5—79.6 for white females and 73.4 for white males. Females, both black and white, have always had longer expectations of life than males. It is projected by the National Center for Health Statistics that in the year 2010 the differences are likely to persist, although all groups are expected to show increases in life expectancy.[6] (See Table 3-3.)

AGE AND SEX COMPOSITION

The median age of the black population, like that of the white population, increased steadily until 1950. In 1850 the median age of blacks in the country was 17.3; by 1950 it had increased to 26.1 years. Between 1950 and 1980 the median age decreased steadily, but in 1990 it had increased to 28 years.[7] By 1996 the median age for blacks was 28.6, with black females having a median age of 30.2 and black males 26.7. For whites it was 36.2—37.2 for white females and 35.1 for white males.[8] Both black females and white females are older as a group than their male counterparts.

The increase in the median age for blacks since 1980 resulted from an increase in the average length of life and a gradual decrease of children in the population. The decrease between 1950 and 1980 resulted from declining fertility and the aging of the baby boom cohort (persons born between 1946 and 1964).

The recent increase in the median age for blacks is paralleled by a similar trend among white Americans. The black population, however, is younger than the white population. There are relatively more young people and fewer older people among blacks. For example, in 1996, 8.0 percent of white persons were in the age category 65–74 years, while among blacks 5.0 percent were in that age category.[9]

In 1970, nearly 3 million (61 percent) of approximately 5 million black families had their own children by birth under 18 years of age. This compared with 55 percent of the 46 million white families. The proportions of families with children have declined for both the black and the white populations. But in 1993, a larger proportion of black (58 percent) than white (46 percent) families included their own by birth children. In 1970, nearly 2 million black families were childless; by 1993 this

Deaths per 1,000 live births, except as noted. Excludes deaths of nonresidents of U.S. Race for live births tabulated according to race of mother, for infant and neonatal mortality rates. Beginning 1989, race for live births tabulated according to race of mother, for maternal mortality rates and mortality rates.

ITEM	1980	1983	1984	1985	1986	1987	1988	1989	1990	1991	1992	1993	1994
Infant deaths[1]	**12.6**	**11.2**	**10.8**	**10.6**	**10.4**	**10.1**	**10.0**	**9.8**	**9.2**	**8.9**	**8.5**	**8.4**	**8.0**
White	10.9	9.6	9.3	9.2	8.8	3.5	8.4	8.1	7.6	7.3	6.9	6.8	6.6
Black and other	20.2	17.8	17.1	16.8	16.7	15.5	16.1	16.3	15.5	15.1	14.4	14.1	13.5
Black	22.2	20.0	19.2	19.0	18.9	13.8	18.5	18.6	18.0	17.6	16.8	16.5	15.8
Maternal deaths[2]	**9.2**	**8.0**	**7.8**	**7.8**	**7.2**	**6.6**	**8.4**	**7.9**	**8.2**	**7.9**	**7.8**	**(NA)**	**(NA)**
White	6.7	5.9	5.4	5.2	4.9	5.1	5.9	5.6	5.4	5.8	5.0	(NA)	(NA)
Black and other	19.8	16.3	16.9	18.1	16.0	12.0	17.4	16.5	19.1	15.6	18.2	(NA)	(NA)
Black	21.5	18.3	19.7	20.4	18.8	14.2	19.5	18.4	22.4	18.3	20.8	(NA)	(NA)
Fetal deaths[3]	**9.2**	**8.5**	**8.2**	**7.9**	**7.7**	**7.7**	**7.5**	**7.5**	**7.5**	**7.3**	**7.4**	**(NA)**	**(NA)**
White	8.2	7.5	7.4	7.0	6.8	6.7	6.4	6.4	6.4	6.2	6.3	(NA)	(NA)
Black and other	13.4	12.4	11.5	11.3	11.2	11.5	11.4	11.7	11.9	11.4	11.7	(NA)	(NA)
Neonatal deaths[4]	**8.5**	**7.3**	**7.0**	**7.0**	**6.7**	**6.5**	**6.3**	**6.2**	**5.8**	**5.6**	**5.4**	**5.3**	**5.1**
White	7.4	6.3	6.1	6.0	5.7	5.4	5.3	5.1	4.3	4.5	4.3	4.3	4.2
Black and other	13.2	11.4	10.9	11.0	10.8	10.7	10.3	10.3	9.9	9.5	9.2	9.0	8.6
Black	14.6	12.9	12.3	12.6	12.3	12.3	12.1	11.9	11.6	11.2	10.8	10.7	10.2

NA = Not available.

[1] Represents deaths of infants under 1 year old, exclusive of fetal deaths.

[2] Per 100,000 live births from deliveries and complications of pregnancy, childbirth, and the puerperum. Beginning 1979, deaths are classified according to the ninth revision of the International Classification of Diseases; earlier years classified according to the revision in use at the time.

[3] Includes only those deaths with stated or presumed period of gestation of 20 weeks or more.

[4] Represents deaths of infants under 28 days old, exclusive of fetal deaths.

Source: Except as noted, U.S. National Center for Health Statistics, Vital Statistics of the United States, annual, and Monthly Vital Statistics Reports.

TABLE 3-3 Expectation of Life at Birth, 1970 to 1995, and Projections, 1995 to 2010

In years. Excludes deaths of nonresidents of the United States.

YEAR	TOTAL			WHITE			BLACK AND OTHER			BLACK		
	TOTAL	MALE	FEMALE	TOTAL	MALE	FEMALE	TOTAL	MALE	FEMALE	TOTAL	MALE	FEMALE
1970	70.8	67.1	74.7	71.7	68.0	75.6	65.3	61.3	69.4	64.1	60.0	68.3
1975	72.6	68.8	76.6	73.4	69.5	77.3	68.0	63.7	72.4	66.8	62.4	71.3
1980	73.7	70.0	77.4	74.4	70.7	78.1	69.5	65.3	73.6	68.1	63.8	72.5
1982	74.5	70.8	78.1	75.1	71.5	78.7	70.9	66.8	74.9	69.4	65.1	73.6
1983	74.6	71.0	78.1	75.2	71.6	78.7	70.9	67.0	74.7	69.4	65.2	73.5
1984	74.7	71.1	78.2	75.3	71.8	78.7	71.1	67.2	74.9	69.5	65.3	73.6
1985	74.7	71.1	78.2	75.3	71.8	78.7	71.0	67.0	74.8	69.3	65.0	73.4
1986	74.7	71.2	78.2	75.4	71.9	78.8	70.9	66.8	74.9	69.1	64.8	73.4
1987	74.9	71.4	78.3	75.6	72.1	78.9	71.0	66.9	75.0	69.1	64.7	73.4
1988	74.9	71.4	78.3	75.6	72.2	78.9	70.8	66.7	74.8	68.9	64.4	73.2
1989	75.1	71.7	78.5	75.9	72.5	79.2	70.9	66.7	74.9	69.1	64.3	73.3
1990	75.4	71.8	78.8	76.1	72.7	79.4	71.2	67.0	75.2	69.1	64.5	73.6
1991	75.5	72.0	78.9	76.3	72.9	79.6	71.5	67.3	75.5	69.3	64.6	73.8
1992	75.8	72.3	79.1	76.5	73.2	79.8	71.8	67.7	75.7	69.6	65.0	73.9
1993	75.5	72.2	78.8	76.3	73.1	79.5	71.5	67.3	75.5	69.2	64.6	73.7
1994	75.7	72.3	79.0	76.4	73.2	79.6	71.7	67.5	75.8	69.6	64.9	74.1
1995	75.8	72.6	78.9	76.5	73.4	79.6	(NA)	(NA)	(NA)	69.8	65.4	74.0
Projections:[1]												
1995	(NA)	72.5	79.3	(NA)	73.6	80.1	(NA)	(NA)	(NA)	(NA)	64.8	74.5
2000	(NA)	73.0	79.7	(NA)	74.2	80.5	(NA)	(NA)	(NA)	(NA)	64.6	74.7
2005	(NA)	73.5	80.2	(NA)	74.7	81.0	(NA)	(NA)	(NA)	(NA)	64.5	75.0
2010	(NA)	74.1	80.6	(NA)	75.5	81.6	(NA)	(NA)	(NA)	(NA)	65.1	75.5

NA = Not available.

[1] Based on middle mortality assumptions; for details, see source. Source: U.S. Bureau of the Census, *Current Population Reports*, P25–1104.

*Source: Except as noted, U.S. National Center for Health Statistics, *Vital Statistics of the United States*, annual, and *Monthly Vital Statistics Reports*.*

number had increased to nearly 3 million (75 percent). Since 1970, the proportion of children living with two parents has declined for both blacks and whites. The number of children living with one parent increased from 32 percent in 1970 to 58 percent in 1993, an 82 percent increase. At the same time, the white proportion grew by 9 percent to 21 percent, a 141 percent increase. Black children were almost three times more likely than white children to have an absent parent (64 percent versus 21 percent).[10] (See Table 3-4.)

Many children live with grandparents. Since 1970, the proportion of children living with grandparents has increased, from 3 percent to 12 percent for blacks, and from 1 percent to 4 percent for whites. In 1993, higher proportion of black children (53 percent) lived in grandparent households. For white children it was 46 percent. In many of these households, the mother of the children also lived in the household of her parents. Grandparent households tend to be concentrated inside central cities of metropolitan areas (62 percent).[11]

In a report of children at risk, the Bureau of the Census lists the following risk factors for America's children: poverty, welfare dependence, both parents absent, one-parent families, unwed mothers, and parents who have not graduated from high school.[12]

DISTRIBUTION

Black Americans differ from white Americans in their regional and rural–urban distribution in the United States.

South–Non-South

Throughout most of American history black people have been heavily concentrated in the agricultural South. At the end of the Civil War, more than 92 percent of blacks lived in the South. At the turn of the century (1900), 9 out of 10 blacks in the United States were still in the South. There has been a gradual reduction of black people in the South since that time. Throughout the present century, blacks have migrated from the South to other regions, principally the Northeast and Midwest. So widespread was this migration that by 1990 only about half (53 percent) of blacks remained in the South.

In recent years there has been a trend in the opposite direction, with blacks moving to the South from other regions in record numbers. In this regard, they are reversing a half-century exodus from the South. In the first half of the 1990s, the South gained 368,800 black residents, while the Northeast lost 233,600 blacks; the Midwest lost 106,500; and the West lost 28,700. These figures were revealed in a study by the Population Reference Bureau in Washington. According to a sociologist, "Black professionals and blue-collar workers, as well as blacks who have retired, are reversing decades of migration from the South by moving to the South's economically vibrant rural and urban areas."[13]

Table 3-4   Family Groups with Children under 18 Years Old, by Race and Hispanic Origin, 1980 to 1996

As of March. Family groups comprise family households, related subfamilies, and unrelated subfamilies. Excludes members of Armed Forces except those living off post or with their families on post. Based on Current Population Survey.

RACE AND HISPANIC ORIGIN OF HOUSEHOLDER OR REFERENCE PERSON	NUMBER (PER 1,000)				PERCENT DISTRIBUTION			
	1980	1990	1995	1996	1980	1990	1995	1996
All races, total[1]	**32,150**	**34,670**	**37,168**	**37,077**	**100**	**100**	**100**	**100**
Two-parent family groups	25,231	24,921	25,640	25,361	79	72	69	68
One-parent family groups	6,920	9,749	11,528	11,717	22	28	31	32
Maintained by mother	6,230	8,398	9,834	9,855	19	24	26	27
Maintained by father	690	1,351	1,694	1,862	2	4	5	5
White, total	**27,294**	**28,294**	**29,846**	**29,947**	**100**	**100**	**100**	**100**
Two-parent family groups	22,628	21,905	22,320	22,178	83	77	75	74
One-parent family groups	4,664	6,389	7,525	7,769	17	23	25	26
Maintained by mother	4,122	5,310	6,239	6,329	15	19	21	21
Maintained by father	542	1,079	1,286	1,440	2	4	4	5
Black, total	**4,074**	**5,087**	**5,491**	**5,434**	**100**	**100**	**100**	**100**
Two-parent family groups	1,961	2,006	1,962	1,942	48	39	36	36
One-parent family groups	2,114	3,081	3,529	3,493	52	61	64	64
Maintained by mother	1,984	2,860	3,197	3,171	49	56	58	58
Maintained by father	129	221	332	322	3	4	6	6
Hispanic, total[2]	**2,194**	**3,429**	**4,527**	**4,560**	**100**	**100**	**100**	**100**
Two-parent family groups	1,626	2,289	2,879	2,858	74	67	64	63
One-parent family groups	568	1,140	1,647	1,702	26	33	36	37
Maintained by mother	526	1,003	1,404	1,483	24	29	31	32
Maintained by father	42	138	243	219	2	4	5	5

[1]Includes other races, not shown separately.
[2]Hispanic persons may be of any race.
Source: U.S. Bureau of the Census, *Current Population Reports,* P20–488, and earlier reports; and unpublished data.

In addition to the South's improving economy, there is also a more hospitable racial climate. "The black out-migration between 1910 and the late 1960s was largely a result of the South's hostile racial climate, coupled with the economic pull of northern cities," the sociologist said. The South's population grew faster than that of any other region from 1990 to 1996, registering 46 percent of the nation's total growth. In that period, 65 percent of the nation's black population growth occurred in the South.[14]

In March 1996, the black population of the United States was distributed regionally as follows: more than one-half (54.9 percent) in the South, 18.1 percent in the Northeast, 18.2 percent in the Midwest, and 8.9 percent in the West. (See Table 3-5.)[15]

Central City–Metropolitan Area

In the United States blacks tend to be urban dwellers. While 80.4 percent of all Americans lived in metropolitan areas in 1996, 86.0 percent of blacks lived in such areas as compared with 77.4 percent of whites. Thirty percent of all Americans lived in central cities, with 54.5 percent of blacks and only 22.4 percent of whites living in those areas. The enclaves inside metropolitan areas but outside central cities (the suburbs) were home to 50.4 percent of all Americans; 31.5 percent of blacks lived in such suburbs, compared with 55 percent of whites. Finally, nonmetropolitan (rural) areas were home to 19.6 percent of all Americans, with 14.0 percent of blacks and 22.6 percent of whites living in such areas. (See Table 3-6.)[16]

An equal proportion (86 percent) of black males and black females live in metropolitan areas. This compares with 77 percent of both white males and females. Nearly one-third of black males (31.9 percent) and females (31.3 percent) live in the suburbs, compared with 55.2 percent of white males and 54.9 percent of white females. About equal percentages of black males and black females live in the various areas, and the same is true of whites. That is, the sex composition of both blacks and whites in each of these areas is roughly the same.[17] Many cities have a majority black population, as is indicated by Table 3-7.

Black people constituted roughly 13 percent of the American population in 1996. Within the United States, however, they are not just a random group of 33.5 million people out of a total of 265.2 million people. Rather, they form a minority group that in comparison with the larger white population occupies one of the lowest statuses in the society. They have been relegated to a harsh environment, not unlike that of people in the so-called developing (third world) nations. In many ways they are a nation apart from white Americans. The similarities between blacks in the United States and people of the developing nations, in demographic characteristics, are striking. For example, both have high birthrates and declining death rates. Infant mortality among black Americans is especially high (compared with white Americans), and life expectancy is lower. Black people continue to die at a disproportionately high rate from diseases that can easily be controlled by modern medical technology. A high proportion of the black population falls within the dependent-aged and dependent-children categories. They are clustered together in the central sections of the largest cities in the country. In many regards, then, black Americans resemble the people of Africa, Asia, and Latin America. This resemblance has impli-

TABLE 3-5 Distribution of the Population, by Region, Sex, and Race, March 1996

REGION AND SEX	NUMBER			PERCENT DISTRIBUTION		
	ALL RACES	BLACK	WHITE, NOT HISPANIC	ALL RACES	BLACK	WHITE, NOT HISPANIC
REGION						
Total, all persons	264,314	33,889	191,271	100.0	100.0	100.0
South	92,225	18,599	62,419	34.9	54.9	32.6
North and West	172,089	15,290	128,852	65.1	45.1	67.4
Northeast	51,534	6,130	39,722	19.5	18.1	20.8
Midwest	61,923	6,160	52,440	23.4	18.2	27.4
West	58,632	3,000	36,689	22.2	8.9	19.2
Male	129,143	15,824	93,712	100.0	100.0	100.0
South	44,649	8,534	30,493	34.6	53.9	32.5
North and West	84,494	7,290	63,219	65.4	46.1	67.5
Northeast	24,979	2,771	19,383	19.3	17.5	20.7
Midwest	30,184	2,988	25,571	23.4	18.9	27.3
West	29,331	1,531	18,265	22.7	9.7	19.5
Female	135,171	18,065	97,559	100.0	100.0	100.0
South	47,576	10,065	31,926	35.2	55.7	32.7
North and West	87,595	8,000	65,633	64.8	44.3	67.3
Northeast	26,555	3,359	20,339	19.6	18.6	20.8
Midwest	31,740	3,173	26,869	23.5	17.6	27.5
West	29,300	1,469	18,425	21.7	8.1	18.9

Source: U.S. Bureau of the Census, Current Population Survey, *The Black Population in the United States: March 1996* (Update), 1997.

TABLE 3-6 Distribution of the Population, by Residence, Sex, and Race, March 1996

(Numbers in thousands)

RESIDENCE AND SEX	NUMBER			PERCENT DISTRIBUTION		
	ALL RACES	BLACK	WHITE, NOT HISPANIC	ALL RACES	BLACK	WHITE, NOT HISPANIC
RESIDENCE						
United States						
Total, all persons	264,314	33,889	191,271	100.0	100.0	100.0
All metropolitan areas	212,454	29,151	148,093	80.4	86.0	77.4
Inside central cities	79,242	18,460	42,825	30.0	54.5	22.4
Outside central cities	133,212	10,691	105,268	50.4	31.5	55.0
Nonmetropolitan areas	51,860	4,738	43,178	19.6	14.0	22.6
Male	129,143	15,824	93,712	100.0	100.0	100.0
All metropolitan areas	103,698	13,558	72,536	80.3	85.7	77.4
Inside central cities	38,352	8,513	20,851	29.7	53.8	22.3
Outside central cities	65,346	5,045	51,685	50.6	31.9	55.2
Nonmetropolitan areas	25,445	2,266	21,176	19.7	14.3	22.6
Female	135,171	18,065	97,559	100.0	100.0	100.0
All metropolitan areas	108,756	15,593	75,557	80.5	86.3	77.4
Inside central cities	40,890	9,947	21,974	30.3	55.1	22.5
Outside central cities	67,866	5,647	53,583	50.2	31.3	54.9
Nonmetropolitan areas	26,415	2,472	22,002	19.5	13.7	22.6

Source: U.S. Bureau of the Census. Current Population Survey, *The Black Population in the United States: March 1996* (Update), 1997.

TABLE 3-7   Cities with at Least 50 Percent Black Population, 1996

CITY	PERCENTAGE OF BLACK RESIDENTS	RANK
Atlanta, GA	67.1	3
Baltimore, MD	59.2	7
Birmingham, AL	63.3	5
Detroit, MI	75.7	2
Gary, IN	80.6	1
Inglewood, CA	51.9	13
Jackson, MS	55.7	9
Macon, GA	52.2	12
Memphis, TN	54.8	11
Newark, NJ	58.5	8
New Orleans, LA	61.9	6
Richmond, VA	55.2	10
Savannah, GA	51.3	14
Washington, DC	65.8	4

Source: U.S. Bureau of the Census, *Statistical Abstract of the United States: 1997* (Washington, DC, 1997).

cations for protest movements and other expressions of discontent found among people of color throughout the world.

This is the plight of African-Americans in a country with the wealth and technology to make racial justice possible. Yet opponents of affirmative action refer to the United States as a colorblind society, one in which blacks and whites enjoy a level playing field.

SELECTED BIBLIOGRAPHY

BOGUE, DONALD. *The Population of the United States*. New York: The Free Press, 1959.

FRAZIER, E. FRANKLIN. *The Negro in the United States*. New York: Macmillan, 1957.

LEMANN, NICHOLAS. *The Promised Land: The Great Black Migration and How It Changed America*. New York: Alfred Knopf, 1991.

LIEBERSON, STANLEY. *Ethnic Patterns in American Cities*. New York: The Free Press, 1963.

TAEUBER, KARL E., and ALMA F. TAEUBER. *Negroes in Cities*. Chicago: Aldine, 1965.

U.S. BUREAU OF THE CENSUS. *Statistical Abstract of the United States: 1997*. Washington, DC, 1997.

U.S. BUREAU OF THE CENSUS. *The Black Population in the United States: March 1996 (Update)*. Washington, DC, 1997.

U.S. BUREAU OF THE CENSUS. Current Population Reports, Series P-20. *The Black Population in the United States: March 1994 and 1993*. Washington, DC, 1995.

U.S. BUREAU OF THE CENSUS. *Fertility of American Women: June 1990*. Washington, DC, 1991.

NOTES

1. U.S. Bureau of the Census, Current Population Reports, Series P-20, *Fertility of American Women: June 1990* (Washington, DC, 1991).

2. U.S. Bureau of the Census, *Statistical Abstract of the United States: 1997* (Washington, DC, 1997), p. 61.

3. Ibid., p. 55.

4. Ibid., p. 90.

5. Ibid., p. 92.

6. Ibid., p. 88.

7. U.S Bureau of the Census, Current Population Reports, Series P-20, *The Black Population in the United States: March 1990 and 1989* (Washington, DC, 1991).

8. U.S. Bureau of the Census, *The Black Population in the United States: March 1996 (Update)* (Washington, DC, 1997), p. 5.

9. U.S. Bureau of the Census, *Statistical Abstract of the United States: 1997*, p. 24.

10. U.S. Bureau of the Census, *The Black Population of the United States. March 1994 and 1993* (Washington, DC, 1995).

11. Ibid., pp. 13–15.

12. U.S. Bureau of the Census, "Census Brief: America's Children at Risk" (Washington, DC, 1997), p. 1.

13. "In a Reversal, More Blacks Are Moving to the South," *New York Times*, February 1, 1998, p. 14.

14. Ibid.

15. U.S. Bureau of the Census, *The Black Population in the United States: March 1996 (Update)*, p. 11.

16. Ibid., p. 11.

17. Ibid.

CHAPTER FOUR

Socioeconomic Status

Compared with most of the other countries in the world at the present time, the United States is essentially a middle-class society. In 1996, 34 percent of adults had at least a bachelor's degree; in the same year more than four-fifths of all workers were employed in white-collar and blue-collar occupational categories; and the median family income was $40,611. Furthermore, the middle class sets standards of behavior that people of lesser status emulate. Within this middle-class society, however, black Americans as a group are generally relegated to a lower-class position. They differ significantly from white Americans on all status indicators. Some black citizens have attained high status in the United States, but they are the exceptions. The majority of black Americans occupy the lowest status positions in the society. Through the practice of racism, American society has succeeded in relegating a significant segment of its population to a subordinate position.

Education, occupation, and income are three of the most reliable indicators of status in American society. These three variables are usually interrelated, and they reinforce one another. However, they may be usefully distinguished for purposes of analysis.

EDUCATION

In a highly industrialized nation such as the United States, formal education is a key factor in social mobility. Generations of immigrants have improved their status after reaching the United States through the acquisition of formal education. The situation of blacks has, to some extent, been affected by increasing formal education. Unlike many immigrant groups, however, their advancement has been hampered by the widespread practices of segregation and discrimination that have either denied them access to formal education or relegated them to inferior and inadequate schools. This situation changed somewhat in the 1970s.

78

Quantity of Education

At the time of emancipation a vast majority (90 percent) of the black people in the United States were illiterate.[1] During slavery times it was virtually impossible for blacks to acquire even the most fundamental tools of reading and writing. During the 1860s, however, blacks made significant strides; by 1870 the illiteracy rate had dropped to 80 percent. In each decade following the Civil War, the illiteracy rate among the blacks declined further. Yet the differential between blacks and whites has persisted. For example, in 1940 the illiteracy rate among blacks was comparable to the rate among white Americans in 1870. In 1980 the illiteracy rate among blacks was 1.6 percent; among whites it was 0.4 percent.[2] Today the rate is virtually the same for blacks and whites.

The extent of literacy among black people is a direct result of their enrollment and length of stay in school. In the decade following the Civil War, when most blacks lived on farms, few of their children were enrolled in school. Those who were enrolled attended for only short periods. The schools were overcrowded and the buildings dilapidated; the teachers were most often incompetent, rarely possessing as much as a high school education. This situation improved little with the turn of the century. It is reported that only 58 percent of black children between the ages of 6 and 14 were enrolled in school as late as 1912. Significant progress has been made in the twentieth century, and the gap between black and white school attendance has continued to narrow. By 1990, 99 percent of black and white children between 7 and 13 years of age were enrolled in school.[3]

The rates of literacy and school attendance have increased substantially in recent decades. Similarly, the median number of years of school completed for blacks has increased, and the gap between blacks and whites in this regard has gradually narrowed. By 1990 the median number of years of school completed for both blacks and whites was 12.9 years. And both black and white females have the same median number of years of school completed as males.[4] Black and white females have the same median number of years of school completed as black and white males.

The lack of a gap between blacks and whites in median number of years of school completed, however, fails to indicate the real difference in educational attainment by these two groups. For example, 65.8 percent of black males and 66.5 percent of black females in the United States in 1990 reported having completed high school, whereas 79.1 percent of white males and 79.0 percent of white females had completed high school (Figure 4-1). At the college level the gap widens still further. In 1996 nearly two-thirds (25.9%) of white Americans had completed four or more years of college, compared with less than one half of blacks (Figure 4-2).[5]

Quality of Education

Data on the extent of literacy, the proportion of school-age children attending school, and the median number of years of school completed indicate that the quantitative differences in education between black and white Americans have narrowed in recent years. However, they indicate little about the differences in the quality of education received by blacks and whites. At the time of the *Brown v. Board of Edu-*

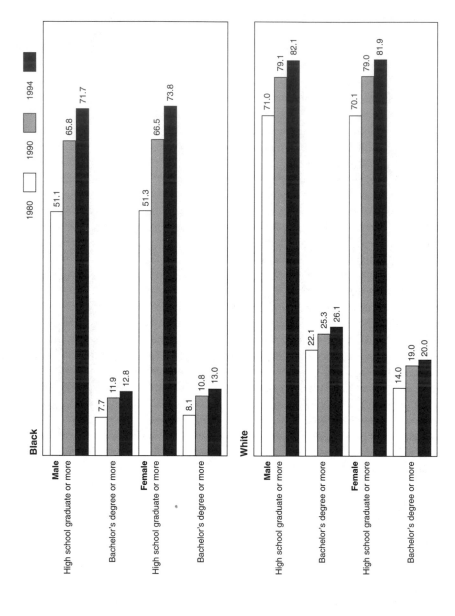

FIGURE 4-1 Educational Attainment of Persons 25 Years Old and Over, by Race and Sex, 1980, 1990, and 1994

Source: Claudette Bennett, *The Black Population in the United States: March 1994 and 1993* (U.S. Bureau of the Census, Washington, DC, 1995), p. 10.

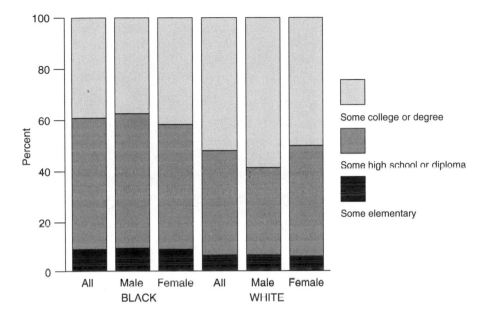

FIGURE 4-2   Educational Attainment of Persons 25 Years Old and Over: Sex by Race by School Level (March, 1996)

Source: U.S. Bureau of the Census, *Statistical Abstract of the United States: 1997* (Washington, DC, 1997).

cation decision of the Supreme Court in 1954, in which the Court declared segregation in public education unconstitutional, 68 percent of all blacks still lived in states that maintained segregated schools. Seventeen states and the District of Columbia required segregated schools by law, and four states permitted segregated schools. In many of the remaining states, black pupils attended segregated schools. These schools were inferior to those attended by white pupils in expenditure per pupil, capital outlay per pupil for schools, length of school year, training of classroom teachers, and number of books in school libraries.

In 1952, for example, southern states spent an average of $164.83 for the education of one white pupil, compared with $115.08, or 70 percent of that amount, for the education of each black child.[6] The amount of money spent per black pupil varied anywhere from 30 percent of what was spent per white pupil in Mississippi to 85 percent in North Carolina. In the same year the capital outlay per pupil for black schools in southern states was $29.58, or 82 percent of the $36.25 per white pupil.[7]

In 1950 the average number of days in the school year for black pupils in the South was 176, compared with 178 for white pupils. The average number of years of college training attained by black teachers was 3.3, compared with 3.6 for white teachers. The average number of books in school libraries per black pupil enrolled in five southern states was 1.8, compared with 4.7 per white pupil.[8]

These comparative figures serve to indicate the gap in the quality of public elementary and secondary education received by black and white pupils in the South before the 1954 decision of the Supreme Court. It should also be added that prior to the late 1940s and early 1950s the gap between the quality of black education and the education received by white pupils was even greater. With increasing pressures for the desegregation of public education, southern states attempted to forestall this eventuality by increasing the support made available for the education of blacks. In the large urban centers where a vast majority of northern blacks were concentrated, the situation differed little insofar as the quality of education was concerned.

Schools in which black children predominate are more likely to be characterized by inadequate facilities.[9] In 1966, for example, 43 percent of black elementary-school pupils in the Northeast attended schools that were at least 40 years old, compared with 18 percent of white pupils. In the United States as a whole, there were an average of 32 black pupils per room, compared with 29 white pupils. Twenty-seven percent of all black elementary-school pupils in the United States attended schools without auditoriums, compared with 19 percent of white pupils. Thirty percent of black elementary pupils attended schools without full-time librarians, compared with 22 percent of white pupils of the same level. For black students in secondary schools, the differential facilities between their schools and those attended by white pupils were as pronounced as on the elementary level. For example, 80 percent of black secondary-school pupils attended schools equipped with physics laboratories, compared with 94 percent of white secondary pupils.

Since the data on the quality of black education in the South predate the Supreme Court decision of 1954, it might be suspected that the status of black education has changed substantially since that time. However, 46 years after the desegregation decision, the changes have not completely altered the patterns of segregated education. A substantial proportion of black pupils continue to attend segregated (and inferior) schools. There has been one significant change, however: In the country as a whole, the South is "the most integrated region, even though it has a higher proportion of black students than the North and the West. The Northeast and Midwest have less than one-half as high a proportion of black students and the West has less than one-fourth."[10] The South has moved from having the most segregated schools in the country to having those that are the most integrated.

It is in the central cities and suburbs of the Northeast, Midwest, and West that minority students increasingly attend schools that are separate and unequal. Nationally, one-third (32 percent) of black students attend schools that are 90–100 percent minority. Regionally, the proportions are 24 percent in the South, 29 percent in the West, 42 percent in the Midwest, and 48 percent in the Northeast.[11]

In Kansas, Oklahoma, and Virginia, more than half of all black students attend schools that are more than 50 percent white, and more than two-fifths of black students in Alabama, Florida, and Georgia attend such schools. On the other hand, in California, Michigan, and New Jersey, less than one-fourth of black students attend schools that are more than 50 percent white (Table 4-1).

For blacks, school integration has remained relatively unchanged since the 1970s, but for Hispanics schools have become more segregated. For both groups there has been little desegregation of schools in central cities. By 1986, for example, the 25 largest central city school districts in the country had 27 percent of all black

TABLE 4-1   Percentage of Black Students in Schools More than 50 Percent White by State, by Declining Enrollment, and Change in Concentration in Predominantly Minority Schools

STATE	BLACK ENROLLMENT 1988	PERCENT OF BLACK STUDENTS IN PREDOMINANTLY WHITE SCHOOLS			CHANGE
		1980	1986	1988	1980–1988
Georgia	33.7	39.9	40.7	42.5	+2.6
Texas	13.2	36.0	36.7	32.1	−3.9
Florida	24.9	60.4	54.9	47.3	−13.1
California	8.2	24.7	23.4	21.3	−3.4
Louisiana	44.9	34.2	38.4	35.8	+1.6
Virginia	32.9	42.3	50.5	53.8	+11.5
Alabama	32.8	44.3	36.2	42.1	−2.2
Michigan	13.6	18.1	23.3	15.4	−2.7
Maryland	36.2	32.8	27.7	23.9	−8.9
New Jersey	15.3	23.3	27.2	20.4	−2.9
Missouri	16.5	36.4	39.0	36.4	0.0
Indiana	11.1	38.1	53.2	49.7	+11.6
Arkansas	21.4	42.1	46.2	38.0	−4.1
Oklahoma	10.2	65.1	59.2	62.8	−2.3
Massachusetts	6.5	44.0	41.5	41.7	−2.3
Connecticut	13.3	42.1	39.8	34.1	−8.0
Kansas	11.4	71.0	68.0	65.8	−5.2
Washington	3.4	76.4	70.4	70.6	−5.8

Source: Gary Orfield and Franklin Monfort, *Status of School Desegregation: The Next Generation* (Alexandria, VA: National School Boards Association, 1992), p. 9.

students and 30 percent of Hispanics, but only 3 percent of whites.[12] It seems unlikely that desegregation will come to these school districts.

Civil rights laws and court decisions of the 1960s and early 1970s transformed southern schools. As late as 1963 southern public schools were almost totally segregated. Rigorous enforcement of desegregation by the federal government began in 1965, and the Supreme Court provided strong leadership until 1973. A 1974 Supreme Court decision (*Miliken v. Bradley*) impeded the pace of school desegregation by placing suburban schools out of the reach of minority students. This decision had a negative impact on city–suburban school desegregation plans that many had considered necessary to achieve desegregation. There has been no progress in the integration of black students since that time.[13]

The 1992 *Freeman v. Pitts* decision of the Supreme Court in the DeKalb County, Georgia, case has been considered by many to be the most important desegregation decision since *Brown* in 1954. The DeKalb county school board petitioned the Court asking for an end to federal court supervision of its integration program. The decision of the Court on March 31 freed the school district from judicial control in matters of school integration. Prior to that time federal courts had retained oversight control of local school boards in desegregation cases. The 1992 decision was called "unworthy" by the *New York Times,* and one "that threatens to undermine that 1954 landmark [*Brown*]."[14]

Although the increasing number of black students attending integrated schools in the South indicates substantial progress, many virtually all-white private schools have sprung up throughout the region in order to avoid court-ordered desegregation of public schools. Data show that there has been a gradual increase in segregated schools in the largest cities of the country, but overall the integration of black students has changed little since the 1970s, despite the efforts of hostile administrations in Washington, and an antagonistic Supreme Court.

At the college level the quality of black education parallels that on the elementary and secondary levels. Most black college students attend predominantly white schools, and as the number of blacks attending college has increased, the number of historically black colleges has decreased, especially the black state-supported colleges in the South. Some have become predominantly white; others have merged with neighboring white schools; and still others have been abolished.[15]

Title VI of the Civil Rights Act of 1964 protects individuals from discrimination based on race, color, or national origin in programs or activities receiving federal financial assistance. This provision was enacted because there had been little desegregation in state-supported colleges and universities in the South following the 1954 *Brown* decision that rejected the "separate but equal" doctrine in public schools. At the time of the Civil Rights Act of 1964, 19 states were operating racially segregated systems of higher education.[16]

In 1990 there were 107 historically black colleges and universities with more than 228,000 students enrolled. Fifty-six of these schools were private and 51 were public. The public institutions accounted for more than two-thirds of students in historically black institutions. Most (87) of the institutions were four-year colleges or universities, and 20 were two-year institutions. In the past, more than 80 percent of all black college graduates were trained at these historically black colleges and universities. In 1990, although these schools enrolled 20 percent of black undergraduates, they awarded 40 percent of baccalaureate degrees earned by black college students.[17]

The accomplishments of the historically black colleges and universities are many.[18] More than 80 percent of all black Americans who received degrees in medicine and dentistry were trained at two of these schools—Howard University and Meharry Medical College. Three-fourths of all black persons holding doctorate degrees and four-fifths of all black federal judges received undergraduate training at historically black colleges and universities. These schools are leading institutions in awarding baccalaureate degrees to black students in life sciences, physical sciences, mathematics, and engineering. And half of the black faculty in major research universities in the country received undergraduate degrees at historically black colleges and universities.

OCCUPATIONAL STATUS

The occupational gap between black and white Americans in the first hundred years since emancipation has remained wide. At the end of the Civil War, a vast majority of blacks were employed as either farm laborers or domestic service workers. By

1890, when data on black occupational status were first collected, nearly 90 percent of black workers were still concentrated in agriculture and domestic service occupations. Sixty percent of white workers were so employed.[19] Since the beginning of the twentieth century, there has been a steady shift among black people away from these occupations, but the shift of white workers has been even greater; thus, the occupational gap between black and white workers has persisted and in some cases widened. For example, in 1992 almost twice as many blacks as whites were employed as service workers (Figure 4-3). And half as many black men as white men work in managerial and professional specialties.

Although there has been a shift from farm employment for both black and white workers, more white workers than black workers have moved into higher-status occupations. Black workers continue to be concentrated in the lowest-status positions in industry, government, and service occupations.

The greatest change in the occupational status of black people occurred between 1940 and 1970, when federal, state, and municipal governments enacted laws forbidding the traditional discriminatory employment practices against blacks. As a result of increasing employment opportunities, significantly greater numbers of blacks were in technical, sales, and administrative support positions. This is especially true for black females. Data show that there are sex and race differences in occupational distribution.

The occupational distribution of black males and females differs, although both continue to be concentrated in nonprofessional and nonmanagerial occupational groups. One-third (31.3 percent) of black males, compared with 12.0 percent of black females, were employed as operators, fabricators, and laborers in 1992; and 14.8 percent of black males, compared with 2.1 percent of black females, were employed in precision production, craft, and repair type occupations. This reflects the general male dominance in these occupations. In contrast, 38.2 percent of black females, compared with 17.3 percent of black males, were employed in technical, sales, and administrative support positions; and 27.9 percent of black females, compared with 19.0 percent of black males, were employed in service occupations. There was also a larger proportion of black females (19.5 percent) in managerial and professional specialty type occupations than black males (14.1 percent) in 1992. (See Table 4-2.)

The occupational distribution of employed black men in 1992 differed from that of white men. For example, black men (31.3 percent) were more likely to be employed as operators, fabricators, and laborers than in any other occupational group. White men, however, were more likely to be employed in managerial and professional specialty occupations.

Both black and white women were more likely to be employed in technical, sales, and administrative support occupations than in any other occupational group (38.2 percent and 44.6 percent, respectively). Differences also existed between the occupational distribution of employed black and white women. For example, black women were almost twice as likely as white women to be employed in service occupations. Over one-fourth (28.5 percent) of white women were employed in managerial and professional occupations, compared with about one-fifth (19.5 percent) of black women.

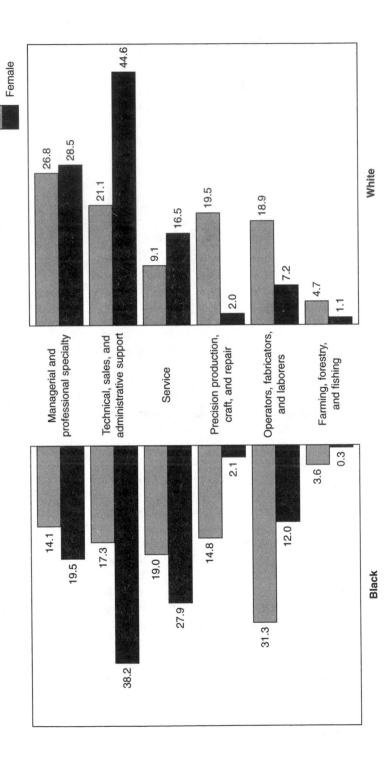

Black

Managerial and professional specialty

Technical, sales, and administrative support

Service

Precision production, craft, and repair

Operators, fabricators, and laborers

Farming, forestry, and fishing

14.1
19.5
17.3
38.2
19.0
27.9
14.8
2.1
31.3
12.0
3.6
0.3

White

Male
Female

26.8
28.5
21.1
44.6
9.1
16.5
19.5
2.0
18.9
7.2
4.7
1.1

FIGURE 4-3   Occupational Distribution of the Employed Civilian Labor Force, by Sex and Race, 1992 (annual averages)

Source: U.S. Bureau of the Census, The Black Population in the United States: March 1992 (Washington, DC, 1993).

Several federal laws, including the Civil Rights Acts of 1964, 1968, and 1991, not only prohibit discrimination in public and private employment based on race, religion, sex, or national origin, but also require that employers take positive steps to ensure that any continuing effects of past discrimination are remedied.[20] Although these laws were initially effective, they suffered a severe blow in 1989 when the Supreme Court either invalidated or diluted several laws against job discrimination.

Members of Congress charged that a hostile Supreme Court had misinterpreted these laws and initiated a drive to enact corrective legislation. But the administration of George Bush insisted that the corrective legislation created job quotas for minorities and women, and for two years whenever Congress passed new civil rights legislation, it was vetoed. However, this corrective legislation, known as the Civil Rights Act of 1991, was enacted when President Bush capitulated because it became clear that if he vetoed this bill, Congress would override his veto.[21]

Finally, one sociologist predicts a grim future for all black workers in the United States.[22] He sees the black rebellions of the 1960s as a result of the transformation from industrialization to automation in the mid-1950s. This shift, according to his theory, has rendered the black population irrelevant to the American economy, for machines have diminished the need for cheap black labor. Since white America no longer needs the labor of blacks, he feels that black genocide is a possibility. The response of blacks to automation, he maintains, has been to rebel against a society that has cast them aside and in the process stripped them of feelings of self-worth. However, in the 20 years since this prognosis was made, black workers appear to be holding fast, however precariously.

Unemployment among Black People

In addition to being employed in the lowest-status jobs in government and industry, black Americans are much more likely than white Americans to be unemployed. The unemployment rate among blacks has remained at least twice that for whites since World War II. Furthermore, if the unemployment rate that has persisted for blacks held for the labor force as a whole, the United States would have been in a state of depression since the end of that war. The rate of unemployment for blacks has not dropped below 6.4 percent since 1954. During this period white Americans have frequently enjoyed "unparalleled prosperity," depending upon the business cycle. As noted by one economist, "What is recession for the white (say, an unemployment rate of 6 percent) is prosperity for the nonwhite. He last saw an unemployment rate below 7.5 percent in 1953."[23] Even in years of peak employment, the unemployment rate for black persons remains high.

Among black workers the unemployment rate varies by age and sex. Black males are sometimes more likely to be unemployed than black females. The pattern is different for white Americans: Females are always more likely to be unemployed than males. Among both blacks and whites, younger workers are more likely to be unemployed than older ones. However, all black workers—young or old, male or female—maintain rates of unemployment that at least double those of white work-

TABLE 4-2 Employment, by Industry, 1970 to 1996

In thousands, except percent. Data from 1985 to 1990, and also beginning 1995, not strictly comparable with other years due to changes in industrial classification.

INDUSTRY	1970	1980	1990	1995	1996			
					TOTAL	PERCENT		
						FEMALE	BLACK	HISPANIC[1]
Total employed	**78,678**	**99,303**	**118,793**	**124,900**	**126,708**	**46.2**	**10.7**	**9.2**
Agriculture	3,463	3,364	3,223	3,440	3,443	25.3	2.9	17.7
Mining	516	979	724	627	569	13.2	4.6	6.6
Construction	4,818	6,215	7,764	7,668	7,943	10.0	6.6	10.4
Manufacturing	20,746	21,942	21,346	20,493	20,518	32.0	10.5	10.1
Transportation, communication, and other public utilities	5,320	6,525	8,168	8,709	8,817	28.6	14.6	8.2
Wholesale and retail trade	15,008	20,191	24,622	26,071	26,497	47.2	8.8	10.1
Wholesale trade	2,672	3,920	4,669	4,986	4,956	29.8	6.8	9.8
Retail trade	12,336	16,270	19,953	21,086	21,541	51.2	9.3	10.2
Finance, insurance, real estate	3,945	5,993	8,051	7,983	8,076	58.4	9.1	7.0
Services[2]	20,385	28,752	39,267	43,953	45,043	61.9	12.1	8.3
Business and repair services[2]	1,403	3,848	7,485	7,526	8,087	36.8	11.0	10.8
Advertising	147	191	277	267	276	55.1	4.1	6.1
Services to dwellings and buildings	(NA)	370	827	829	871	47.9	17.6	21.3
Personnel supply services	(NA)	235	710	853	866	58.4	19.6	11.1
Computer and data processing	(NA)	221	805	1,136	1,340	33.0	7.6	4.2
Detective/protective services	(NA)	213	378	506	540	22.7	22.6	8.2
Automobile services	600	952	1,457	1,459	1,630	14.5	9.3	15.3
Personal services[2]	4,276	3,839	4,733	4,375	4,358	68.7	14.3	16.0
Private households	1,782	1,257	1,036	971	936	89.1	17.8	25.2
Hotels and lodging places	979	1,149	1,818	1,495	1,504	54.4	15.5	17.0

Entertainment and recreation	717	1,047	1,526	2,238	2,386	44.0	8.7	9.8
Professional and related services[2]	12,904	19,853	25,351	29,651	30,?85	69.2	12.3	6.5
Hospitals	2,843	4,036	4,700	4,951	5,?41	76.1	16.5	6.7
Health services, except hospitals	1,628	3,345	4,673	5,957	6,158	79.2	13.8	6.4
Elementary, secondary schools	6,126	5,550	5,994	6,653	6,711	74.9	11.8	7.5
Colleges and universities	(³)	2,108	2,637	2,768	2,787	52.2	10.7	6.0
Social services	828	1,590	2,239	2,979	3,102	80.7	17.3	8.6
Legal services	429	776	1,215	1,335	1,303	56.0	4.9	4.9
Public administration[4]	4,476	5,342	5,627	5,957	5,302	44.4	16.5	6.6

NA = Not available.

[1]Persons of Hispanic origin may be of any race.

[2]Includes industries not shown separately.

[3]Included with elementary/secondary schools.

[4]Includes workers involved in uniquely governmental activities, e.g., judicial and legislative.

Source: U.S. Bureau of Labor Statistics, Employment and Earnings, monthly, January issues; U.S. Bureau of the Census, Statistical Abstract of the United States: 1997 (Washington, DC, 1997, p. 415.

ers. Indeed, the unemployment rate among black teenagers, which virtually always exceeds 20 percent, reached a peak of 48 percent in 1982, a year in which the rate for white teenagers was 20.4 percent and the general rate for whites was 8.6 percent.[24] In 1996 the unemployment rate for white teenagers was 14 percent; it was more than twice as high for blacks (37 percent).[25]

In 1996 the unemployment rate for blacks, at 12.4 percent, was at least double the rate for whites (6.0 percent). Blacks constituted 11 percent of the labor force in 1990, but they accounted for 22 percent of the unemployed.[26]

The disproportionately high rates of black unemployment have been explained as a function of blacks' unfavorable position in the occupational structure; that is, they are likely to occupy positions that are becoming obsolete. This explanation is no doubt valid in some cases, but it does not explain the disproportionately high rates of unemployment among blacks at all occupational levels. The higher unemployment rate among blacks, and their tendency to be unemployed for longer periods than white workers, more than anything else reflects the continuing practice of discrimination against blacks. In 1998 the unemployment rate was at least twice for blacks as it was for whites. This includes teenagers and adults.

Black People in Business

The historical development of business enterprise among black people began with the free blacks before the Civil War. However, their business ventures have played an insignificant role in the economy of the United States and have not been commensurate with their achievements in other aspects of American life.[27] Historically, black business ventures have generally been small, single proprietorships and have catered to the segregated black market. With the decline in segregation, the black businessperson has felt the brunt of changing patterns of race relations. For example, between 1950 and

	TEENAGERS 16–19	BLACK	HISPANIC	WHITE	EDUCATION
	Black	*Men 20 and older*			*Less than high school*
March 1998	29.1%	7.8%	6.3%	3.4%	7.2%
March 1997	32.1%	8.9%	7.0%	3.8%	8.4%
	White	*Women 20 and older*			*High school diploma only*
March 1998	12.8%	8.2%	7.2%	3.7%	4.2%
March 1997	14.1%	9.2%	8.7%	3.9%	4.4%
	All races	*All men and women over 16*			
March 1998	15.0%	9.2%	6.9%	4.1%	
March 1997	16.5%	10.5%	8.3%	4.4%	

FIGURE 4-4   **The Slack in a Tight Labor Market**

Unemployment rates are beginning to decline for teenagers, blacks, Hispanic people and people with less than a high school education, but are still far above the March national average of 4.7 percent

Source: New York Times, April 6, 1998, p. A18.

TABLE 4-3   Unemployed Workers—Summary, 1980 to 1996

In thousands, except as indicated. For civilian noninstitutional population 16 years old and over. Annual averages of monthly figures.

AGE, SEX, RACE, HISPANIC ORIGIN	1980	1985	1990	1992	1993	1994	1995	1996
Total[1]	**7,637**	**8,312**	**7,047**	**9,613**	**8,940**	**7,996**	**7,404**	**7,236**
16 to 19 years old	1,669	1,468	1,212	1,427	1,365	1,320	1,346	1,306
20 to 24 years old	1,835	1,738	1,299	1,649	1,514	1,373	1,244	1,239
25 to 44 years old	2,964	3,681	3,323	4,678	4,291	3,694	3,390	3,262
45 to 64 years old	1,075	1,331	1,109	1,727	1,662	1,456	1,269	1,289
65 years and over	94	93	105	132	108	153	153	149
Male	4,267	4,521	3,906	5,523	5,055	4,367	3,983	3,880
16 to 19 years old	913	806	667	806	768	740	744	733
20 to 24 years old	1,076	944	715	951	865	768	673	675
25 to 44 years old	1,619	1,950	1,803	2,647	2,387	1,968	1,776	1,689
45 to 64 years old	600	766	662	1,053	972	803	697	707
65 years and over	58	55	59	67	64	88	94	76
Female	3,370	3,791	3,140	4,090	3,885	3,629	3,421	3,356
16 to 19 years	755	661	544	621	597	580	602	573
20 to 24 years old	760	794	584	698	648	605	571	564
25 to 44 years old	1,345	1,732	1,519	2,031	1,905	1,726	1,615	1,574
45 to 64 years old	473	566	447	673	690	653	574	582
65 years and over	36	39	46	66	45	66	60	63
White[2]	5,884	6,191	5,186	7,169	6,655	5,892	5,459	5,300
16 to 19 years old	1,291	1,074	903	1,037	992	960	952	939
20 to 24 years old	1,364	1,235	899	1,156	1,057	952	866	854
Black[2]	1,553	1,864	1,565	2,011	1,844	1,666	1,538	1,592
16 to 19 years old	343	357	268	324	313	300	325	310
20 to 24 years old	426	455	349	421	387	351	311	327
Hispanic[2,3]	620	811	876	1,311	1,248	1,187	1,140	1,132
16 to 19 years	145	141	161	219	201	198	205	199
20 to 24 years old	138	171	167	240	237	220	209	217
Full-time workers	6,269	6,793	5,677	7,923	7,305	6,513	5,909	5,803
Part-time workers	1,369	1,519	1,369	1,690	1,635	1,483	1,495	1,433

UNEMPLOYMENT RATE (percent)[4]

	1980	1985	1990	1992	1993	1994	1995	1996
Total[1]	**7.1**	**7.2**	**5.6**	**7.5**	**6.9**	**6.1**	**5.6**	**5.4**
16 to 19 years old	17.8	18.6	15.5	20.1	19.0	17.6	17.3	16.7
20 to 24 years old	11.5	11.1	8.8	11.4	10.5	9.7	9.1	9.3
25 to 44 years old	6.0	6.2	4.9	6.8	6.2	5.3	4.8	4.6
45 to 64 years old	3.7	4.5	3.5	5.1	4.8	4.0	3.4	3.3
65 years and over	3.1	3.2	3.0	3.8	3.2	4.0	4.0	3.6
Male	6.9	7.0	5.7	7.9	7.2	6.2	5.6	5.4
16 to 19 years old	18.3	19.5	16.3	21.5	20.4	19.0	18.4	18.1
20 to 24 years old	12.5	11.4	9.1	12.2	11.3	10.2	9.2	9.5
25 to 44 years old	5.6	5.9	4.8	7.0	6.3	5.2	4.7	4.4
45 to 64 years old	3.5	4.5	3.7	5.7	5.1	4.1	3.5	3.4
65 years and over	3.1	3.1	3.0	3.3	3.2	4.0	4.3	3.4

TABLE 4-3   (*continued*)

AGE, SEX, RACE, HISPANIC ORIGIN	1980	1985	1990	1992	1993	1994	1995	1996
Female	7.4	7.4	5.5	7.0	6.6	6.0	5.6	5.4
16 to 19 years old	17.2	17.6	14.7	18.6	17.5	16.2	16.1	15.2
20 to 24 years old	10.4	10.7	8.5	10.3	9.7	9.2	9.0	9.0
25 to 44 years old	6.4	6.6	4.9	6.5	6.1	5.4	5.0	4.9
45 to 64 years old	4.0	4.6	3.2	4.4	4.4	3.9	3.3	3.3
65 years and over	3.1	3.3	3.1	4.5	3.1	4.0	3.7	4.0
White[2]	6.3	6.2	4.8	6.6	6.1	5.3	4.9	4.7
16 to 19 years old	15.5	15.7	13.5	17.2	16.2	15.1	14.5	14.2
20 to 24 years old	9.9	9.2	7.3	9.5	8.8	8.1	7.7	7.8
Black[2]	14.3	15.1	11.4	14.2	13.0	11.5	10.4	10.5
16 to 19 years old	38.5	40.2	30.9	39.7	38.8	35.2	35.7	33.6
20 to 24 years old	23.6	24.5	19.9	23.8	21.9	19.5	17.7	18.8
Hispanic [3 4]	10.1	10.5	8.2	11.6	10.8	9.9	9.3	8.9
16 to 19 years old	22.5	24.3	19.5	27.5	26.1	24.5	24.1	23.6
20 to 24 years old	12.1	12.6	9.1	13.2	13.1	11.8	11.5	11.8
Experienced workers[5]	6.9	6.8	5.3	7.2	6.6	5.9	5.4	5.2
Women maintaining families[1]	9.2	10.4	8.3	10.0	9.7	8.9	8.0	8.2
White	7.3	8.1	6.3	7.9	7.8	(NA)	(NA)	(NA)
Black	14.0	16.4	13.2	14.8	13.9	(NA)	(NA)	(NA)
Married men, wife present[1]	4.2	4.3	3.4	5.1	4.4	3.7	3.3	3.0
White	3.9	4.0	3.1	4.7	4.1	3.4	3.0	2.8
Black	7.4	8.0	6.2	8.3	7.2	6.0	5.0	4.9
Percent without work for— Fewer than								
5 weeks	43.2	42.1	46.3	35.1	36.5	34.1	36.5	36.4
5 to 10 weeks	23.4	22.2	23.5	20.9	20.6	20.6	22.0	21.8
11 to 14 weeks	9.0	8.0	8.5	8.5	8.3	9.5	9.6	9.8
15 to 26 weeks	13.8	12.3	11.7	15.1	14.5	15.5	14.6	14.6
27 weeks and over	10.7	15.4	10.0	20.3	20.1	20.3	17.3	17.4
Unemployment duration, average (weeks)	11.9	15.6	12.0	17.7	18.0	18.8	16.6	16.7

NA = Not available.
[1]Includes other races, not shown separately.
[2]Includes other ages, not shown separately.
[3]Persons of Hispanic origin may be of any race.
[4]Unemployed as percent of civilian labor force in specified group.
[5]Wage and salary workers.

Source: U.S. Bureau of Labor Statistics, *Employment and Earnings,* monthly, January issues; and unpublished data.

1960 the total number of black businesspeople declined by nearly one-fourth, from 42,500 to 32,400. The number of black-owned restaurants declined by one-third, and other retail outlets experienced an even greater decline. In addition, there was a decline in the number of black funeral directors and barbers.[28] The gradual decrease in the number of black small-business enterprises reflects, in addition to decreased segregation, a general economic trend in the larger society. Corporations experience greater rates of return than independent business organizations.

Today the black business sector remains small and fragile. However, some progress has been noted. For example, in a list of the top black businesses in 1990 published by *Black Enterprise* magazine, most of the businesses appearing on the list did not exist in 1968.[29] Much of the impetus for the development of the black business sector in the 1970s came from the federal government, but government officials in the 1980s provided little assistance and indicated that they were determined to end many of the programs that had played key roles in building an independent black business sector.

In a major setback for black business development, the Supreme Court ruled in *City of Richmond v. J. A. Croson* (1991) that a Richmond, Virginia, ordinance (similar to those in 36 states and 200 localities) requiring the city to channel 30 percent of public works funds to minority-owned construction companies violated the constitutional rights of white construction contractors to equal protection of the law.

This ruling had the effect of forcing states and municipalities to suspend or at least review thousands of minority set-aside programs. Since most of the business of the minority community comes from government programs, the legislation meant that black-owned businesses were hit hard. For example, the *New York Times* reported that in Philadelphia, black entrepreneurs saw their share of city contracts decrease from 25 percent in 1990 to 3.5 percent in 1991. This was a direct result of the *Croson* decision.[30] In that same period, the value of contracts that Philadelphia awarded to minority companies declined from $65 million to $21.3 million.

These affirmative action programs had had a significant impact on black business development. For example, the number of such businesses increased by 38 percent, from 380,000 to 424,000, between 1982 and 1987, and they saw a 100 percent increase in gross receipts, from $10 billion to $20 billion.[31] The programs were designed to atone for over 200 years of discrimination against minorities, especially blacks.

In 1997 there were some 40,000 smaller black businesses with paid employees in addition to the major ones compiled by *Black Enterprise*. They cover the spectrum from food preparation to communications, to entertainment, to automobile dealerships and computer software.

The leading black-owned industrial/service business in 1997 was TLC Beatrice International Holdings, a food products processing and distribution company. This New York City–based company had a staff of 4,500 employees and sales of $1.4 billion in 1997. This is the only black-owned business to exceed $1 billion in sales, and the first to be listed in *Fortune* magazine's list of the 500 leading businesses in the country. Altogether, black industrial/service companies had sales of $7.64 billion and more than 31,000 employees in 1997.

Automobile dealerships have been especially lucrative for black entrepreneurs (see Figure 4-5). Their sales amounted to $5.5 billion in 1997. The largest of these, the Mel Farr Automotive Group of Oak Park, Michigan, had $573 million in sales in 1997. Of the three auto manufacturers, Ford had the greatest representation among black dealers, with 54 percent, followed by General Motors (30 percent), and Chrysler (19 percent). Sixteen of the dealerships on the *Black Enterprise* list sold imported cars in 1997, a significant increase since 1990.

Figure 4-6 gives 1998 sales and staff for industrial/service and automobile dealerships.

The cosmetics business has always been one of the biggest for black people, and most of the major black companies that have made the greatest gains are those that sell products to black customers. However, in recent years high-technology has been among the fastest-growing black businesses. And in 1997 media businesses experienced strong sales growth. Similarly, construction companies and retail food and beverage concerns have performed well. However, the most striking gains in recent years have been automobile dealerships, which accounted for more than 42 percent of all sales reported by black-owned businesses. Regionally, the largest black businesses were located in the Midwest and the South.

Black-owned financial institutions comprise an important segment of the black business sector, not only because they employ people and earn income, but also because they form depositories for savings, and their investment decisions are important in black economic development. Black banks and savings and loan asso-

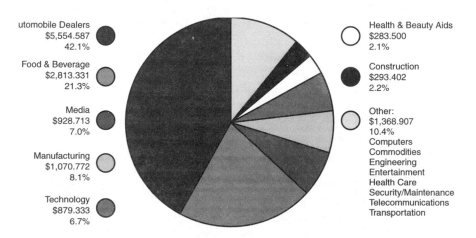

FIGURE 4-5   The 100 Largest Black-Owned Businesses (Sales by Industry)

Source: Black Enterprise, June 1998. The Earl Graves Publishing Co., Inc., 130 Fifth Avenue, New York, NY 10011. All rights reserved.

	1996	1997	DIFFERENCE	PERCENT CHANGE
Total Sales*	$14,107.600	$13,192.545	−915.055	−6.49%
Total Staff	55,242	57,116	1,874	3.39%
	1998 B.E. INDUSTRIAL/SERVICE 100			
Total Sales*	$8,182.356	$7,637.958	−544.398	−6.65%
Total Staff	46,034	48,005	1,971	4.28%
	1998 B.E. AUTO DEALER 100			
Total Sales*	$5,925.244	$5,554.587	−370.657	−6.26%
Total Staff	9,208	9,111	−97	−1.05%

*In millions of dollars, to the nearest thousand. Prepared by B. E. Research. Reviewed by Mitchell & Titus L.L.P.

FIGURE 4-6   1998 Black Enterprise 100s

Source: Black Enterprise, June 1998. The Earl Graves Publishing Co., Inc., 130 Fifth Avenue, New York, NY 10011. All rights reserved.

ciations (S&Ls) are crucial to the communities in which they operate. However, they control a very small fraction of the assets of such organizations in the United States, and they have had a troubled history, as is indicated by their numbers, assets, and failures.

To a greater extent than some other businesses, black commercial banks, S&Ls, and insurance companies depend upon the economic viability of the communities in which they operate.

Black Enterprise magazine compiled a list of the top 25 black-owned banks in 1997. These banks and other black-owned banks (total number: 38) had assets of $5.01 trillion in 1997, an increase of 9.5 percent from their total assets of $4.36 billion in 1996. Total deposits in 1997 increased to $2.98 billion from 2.79 billion the preceding year. Total loans for 1997 increased to $2.16 billion from $2.10 billion in 1996. Total capital for 1997 was $305 million, up from $271 million in 1996.

The country's largest black-owned bank in 1997 was Carver Bancorp of New York City, with $416 million in assets. Black-owned banks, with just a fraction of the assets in other banks, have gained with the robust American economy. According to *Black Enterprise*, small black-owned banks are growing at their fastest rate since the recession of the early 1990s. Figure 4-7 gives the distribution of black businesses by state, and Figure 4-8 gives a summary of the 25 black-owned banks.

Black-owned insurance companies have existed for more than 100 years. They have always served the black community, although in 1975 there were 39 black-owned insurance companies whereas by 1997 there were only 10. The 10 remaining insurance companies are located mainly in the South.

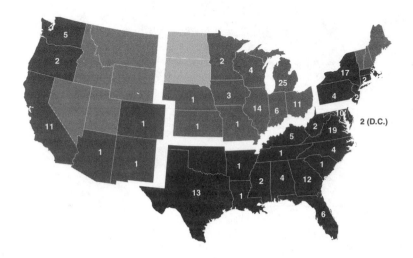

FIGURE 4-7   1998 Black Enterprise 100s by State

The largest black-owned insurance company is North Carolina Mutual Life Insurance, with headquarters in Durham, North Carolina. It opened for business in 1898, and in 1997 it had a staff of 468. In 1996, this insurance company had offices in 11 states and the District of Columbia.

In recent years black-owned insurance companies have been stagnant. For example, premium income from these banks dropped from $161 million in 1995 to $143 million in 1997, and the value of these companies dropped significantly. Figure 4-9 presents data on the 10 largest black-owned insurance companies, while Figure 4-10 lists the top ten black-owned businesses, including location, number of employees, and sales.

BLACK-OWNED BANKS	1996	1997	PERCENT CHANGE
Number of employees	1,941	2,030	4.59%
Assets*	$3,296.405	$3,572.372	8.37%
Capital*	$271.329	$304.684	12.29%
Deposits*	$2,794.481	$2,981.158	6.68%
Loans*	$2,103.249	$2,158.828	2.64%

*In millions of dollars, to the nearest thousand. Prepared by B. E. Research. Reviewed by Mitchell & Titus L.L.P.

FIGURE 4-8   1998 Top 25 Banks Summary

BLACK-OWNED INSURANCE COMPANIES	1996	1997	PERCENT CHANGE
Number of employees	2,217	1,995	−10.01%
Assets*	$680.020	$688.683	1.27%
Statutory reserves*	$494.293	$490.603	−0.75%
Insurance in force*	$18,703.293	$17,860.684	−4.51%
Premium income*	$150.112	$143.091	−4.68%
Net investment income*	$41.656	$46.592	11.85%

*In millions of dollars, to the nearest thousand. Prepared by B. E. Research. Reviewed by Mitchell & Titus L.L.P.

FIGURE 4-9   1990 Top 10 Insurance Companies Summary

Source: Black Enterprise, June 1998. The Earl Graves Publishing Co., Inc., 130 Fifth Avenue, New York, NY 10011. All rights reserved.

INCOME

The continuing pattern of employment discrimination against black people, resulting in their being relegated to the lowest-status occupations, coupled with their low and inferior educational status, is reflected in their low earnings. Black family incomes have been and continue to be significantly lower than those of white families. Little attention was focused on differential family incomes for blacks and whites prior to World War II, as is reflected in the absence of such data before 1939. Since then, however, black family income has ranged anywhere from 51 to 64 percent of white fam-

COMPANY	LOCATION	EMPLOYEES	1997 SALES*	EMPLOYEE-TO-SALES RATIO**
TLC Beatrice International Holdings Inc.	New York, NY	4,500	1400.00	1:311
Johnson Publishing Co. Inc.	Chicago, IL	2,677	361.112	1:135
La-Van Hawkins Urban City Foods L.L.C.	Baltimore, MD	2,643	86.422	1:33
V & J Foods Inc.	Milwaukee, WI	2,400	70.000	1:29
H.J. Russell & Co.	Atlanta, GA	1,862	155.300	1:83
Lundy Enterprises LLC./Pizza Hut	New Orleans, LA	1,710	26.000	1:15
The Bartech Group	Livonia, MI	1,640	62.000	1:38
Active Transportation	Louisville, KY	1,600	250.000	1:156
Barden Companies Inc.	Detroit, MI	1,600	110.000	1:69
Philadelphia Coca-Cola Bottling Co. Inc.	New York, NY	1,500	357.000	1:238

*In millions of dollars, to the nearest thousand.
**In thousands of dollars, as of December 31, 1997.
Prepared by B.E. Research. Reviewed by Mitchell & Titus L.L.P.

FIGURE 4-10   Top Ten Employment Leaders

Source: Black Enterprise, June 1998. The Earl Graves Publishing Co., Inc., 130 Fifth Avenue, New York, NY 10011. All rights reserved.

ily income. As recently as 1963 black families earned only 53 percent of what white families earned. Although the differential has fluctuated since 1950, the greatest persistent decline in the differential occurred between 1952 and 1955.[32] Since that time the gap has generally widened; blacks did not reach three-fifths of median white family income until 1966, and by 1994 the gap remained the same.

The earnings of black families vary with the region of the country in which they live. The gap between black and white families has usually been greater in the South than elsewhere in the United States. But in 1990 the median family income for whites in the South was $32,939; for blacks it was $19,029, or 58 percent of the median white family income. In the Midwest black families earned 52 percent of what white families earned; in the Northeast it was 58 percent; and in the West it was 76 percent.[33] Figure 4-11 shows that of all groups in the society, black household income was the lowest.

The differential income between black and white persons also exists between the sexes. In 1990, for example, black males earned 60 percent of what white males earned, and black females earned 80 percent of the median income of white females. On the other hand, black females earned 62 percent of the median income of black males, while white females earned only 47 percent of what white males earned.

Education is, of course, positively associated with one's earning power. In 1989, the median earnings of year-round, full-time black workers 25 years old and over with a high school education was $18,390; over half (56.5 percent) of them had earnings below $20,000. In contrast, the median earnings of year-round, full-time black workers with four or more years of college was $29,480 (60 percent higher than high-school earnings), and only about 21 percent of them earned less than $20,000. These differences held for black male and female full-time workers 25 years old and over. The median earnings for college-educated black males was $31,380, about 55 percent higher than the median for those with only high school education ($20,280), while the median earnings for black females with college education was 63 percent higher than for those with a high school education.[34]

In general, the median earnings across all educational categories of year-round, full-time workers are higher for males than for females, and for whites than for blacks. The median earnings for black females with a high school education ($16,440) was 81 percent of the earnings of their black male counterparts ($20,280). Black female college graduates earned 85 percent of the earnings of their male counterparts. The median earnings of black males with a high school education were 77 percent of the median earnings of comparable white males, while the black-male-to-white-male earnings ratio for those with four or more years of college was 76 percent. Although the data suggest that the median earnings of black females are approaching those of white females, black females are doing so by working longer hours each week and more weeks each year, and by virtue of having been in the labor force longer than white women.

There are, of course, blacks in sports and entertainment (especially music) who earn millions of dollars each year. For example, *Fortune* magazine estimates that by 1998, Michael Jordan, the basketball player, had added $10 billion to the

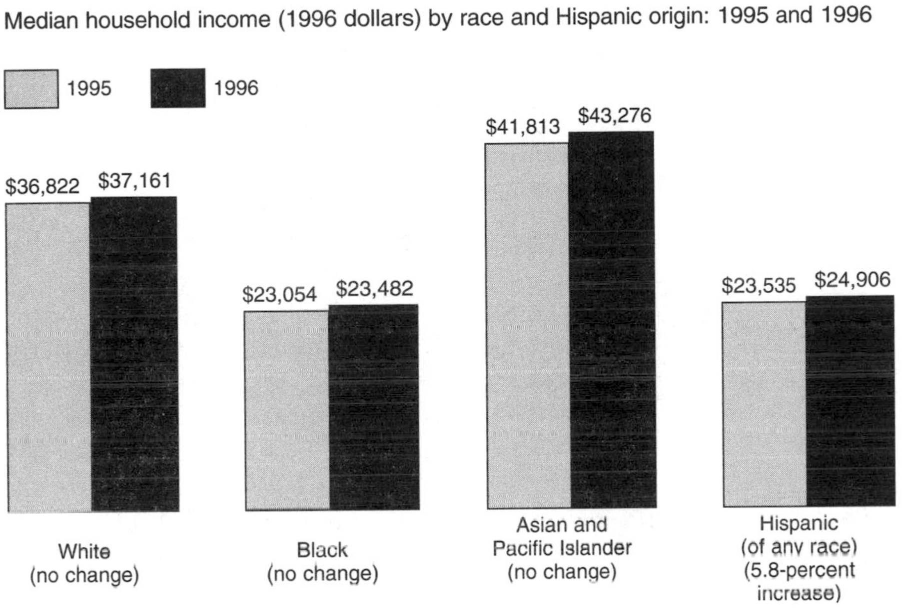

Median household income (1996 dollars) by race and Hispanic origin: 1995 and 1996

FIGURE 4-11   **Household Income Up for Hispanics, No Change for Other Groups**

Source: U.S. Census Bureau, Department of Commerce, *Money Income in the United States: 1996,* Series P60–197.

American economy.[35] Needless to say, this is the exception for any athlete in history, black or white.

The New York Times estimates that "about 95 percent of black families own no stock or pension funds." Furthermore, the *Times* laments black–white inequalities in income: "Black and Hispanic families are further behind whites today than they were 20 years ago. The yawning gaps between rich and poor and between blacks and whites are not going away anytime soon." It is reported that the typical black household had a net worth only one-tenth that of the white household.

"Poverty among black children fell last year to its lowest level in decades," adds the *Times.* "But at 40 percent, the level remains horribly high."

A Note on Race and Poverty

In 1991 the Bureau of the Census issued a comprehensive report on poverty in the United States for 1989.[36] The poverty thresholds used in this report are updated each year to reflect changes in the consumer price index. At that time the average poverty threshold for a family of four was $12,675. Average poverty thresholds varied from $6,311 for a person living alone to $25,480 for a family of nine or more members.

According to the Bureau of the Census, in 1995, 13.8 percent of Americans lived below the poverty level. For blacks the figure was 29.3 percent; for whites it was 11.2 percent. Thus, there are three times as many blacks in poverty as whites (see Table 4-4).

TABLE 4-4 Persons Below Poverty Level and Below 125 Percent of Poverty Level, 1960 to 1995

Persons as of March of the following year. Based on Current Population Survey.

YEAR	NUMBER BELOW POVERTY LEVEL (1,000) ALL RACES[1]	WHITE	BLACK	HISPANIC[2]	PERCENT BELOW POVERTY LEVEL ALL RACES[1]	WHITE	BLACK	HISPANIC[2]	BELOW 125 PERCENT OF POVERTY LEVEL NUMBER (1,000)	PERCENT OF TOTAL POPULATION	AVERAGE INCOME CUTOFFS FOR NONFARM FAMILY OF FOUR[3] AT POVERTY LEVEL	AT 125 PERCENT OF POVERTY LEVEL
1960	39,851	28,309	(NA)	(NA)	22.2	17.8	(NA)	(NA)	54,560	30.4	3,022	3,778
1970	25,420	17,484	7,548	(NA)	12.6	9.9	33.5	(NA)	35,624	17.6	3,968	4,960
1975	25,877	17,770	7,545	2,991	12.3	9.7	31.3	23.0	37,182	17.6	5,500	6,875
1976	24,975	16,713	7,595	2,783	11.8	9.1	31.1	26.9	35,509	16.7	5,815	7,269
1977	24,720	16,416	7,726	2,700	11.6	8.9	31.3	24.7	35,659	16.7	6,191	7,739
1978	24,497	16,259	7,625	2,607	11.4	8.7	30.6	22.4	34,155	15.8	6,662	8,328
1979[4]	26,072	17,214	8,050	2,921	11.7	9.0	31.0	21.6	36,616	16.4	7,412	9,265
1980	29,272	19,699	8,579	3,491	13.0	10.2	32.5	21.8	40,658	18.1	8,414	10,518
1981	31,822	21,553	9,173	3,713	14.0	11.1	34.2	25.7	43,748	19.3	9,287	11,609
1982	34,398	23,517	9,697	4,301	15.0	12.0	35.6	26.5	46,520	20.3	9,862	12,328
1983[5]	35,303	23,984	9,882	4,633	15.2	12.1	35.7	29.9	47,150	20.3	10,178	12,723
1984	33,700	22,955	9,490	4,806	14.4	11.5	33.8	28.0	45,288	19.4	10,609	13,261
1985	33,064	22,860	8,926	5,236	14.0	11.4	31.3	28.4	44,166	18.7	10,989	13,736
1986	32,370	22,183	8,983	5,117	13.6	11.0	31.1	29.0	43,486	18.2	11,203	14,004
1987[6]	32,221	21,195	9,520	5,422	13.4	10.4	32.4	27.3	43,032	17.9	11,611	14,514
1988	31,745	20,715	9,356	5,357	13.0	10.1	31.3	28.0	42,551	17.5	12,092	15,115
1989	31,528	20,785	9,302	5,430	12.8	10.0	30.7	26.7	42,653	17.3	12,674	15,843

Year												
1990	33,585	22,326	9,837	6,006	13.5	10.7	31.9	26.2	44,837	18.0	13,359	16,699
1991	35,708	23,747	10,242	6,339	14.2	11.3	32.7	28.1	47,527	18.9	13,924	17,405
1992⁷	38,014	25,259	10,827	7,592	14.8	11.9	33.4	29.6	50,592	19.7	14,335	17,919
1993	39,265	26,226	10,877	8,126	15.1	12.2	33.1	30.6	51,801	20.0	14,763	(NA)
1994	38,059	25,379	10,196	8,416	14.5	11.7	30.6	30.7	50,401	19.3	15,141	18,926
1995	36,425	24,423	9,872	8,574	13.8	11.2	29.3	30.3	48,761	18.5	15,569	19,461

NA = Not available.

[1]Includes other races not shown separately.

[2]Persons of Hispanic origin may be of any race.

[3]Beginning 1981, income cutoffs for nonfarm families are applied to all families, both farm and nonfarm.

[4]Population controls based on 1980 census.

[5]Beginning 1983, data based on revised Hispanic population controls and not directly comparable with prior years.

[6]Beginning 1987, data based on revised processing procedures and not directly comparable with prior years.

[7]Beginning 1992, based on 1990 population controls.

Source: U.S. Bureau of the Census, *Current Population Reports,* P60-194.

The number of Americans living below the poverty level in 1996 was about 36.5 million, representing 13.7 percent of the population. The poverty rate for people living in central cities declined by one percentage point between 1995 and 1996.[37]

Poverty varies by age. In 1996 the poverty rate for people under 18 years of age was 20.5 percent. The poverty rate for people 18 to 64 years of age was 11.4 percent. For those 65 and over the rate was 10.8 percent. The proportion of the elderly in the poverty population is less than that in the population as a whole. In 1996, people 65 and over were 12 percent of the population, but only 9 percent of the poor.

People under 18 years of age represent a large segment of the poor (40 percent), and in 1996 the overall rate for children under 6 years of age was 22.7 percent. Children under age 6 living in families with a female householder and no spouse present were the poorest, with 58.8 percent living below the poverty level.

In 1996, the poverty rate was 11.2 for all whites; 28.4 percent for blacks; 14.5 percent for Asians and Pacific Islanders. For persons of Hispanic origin the rate was 29.4 percent, slightly higher than for blacks. Even though the poverty rate for whites was the lowest of all groups, the majority of poor people in 1996 were white.

Among individuals, poverty is greatest among black females and children living in a household with husband/father absent. The poorest black families in the country are those in which the householder (the person in whose name the home is owned or rented) is female and young (15 to 24 years old), has little formal schooling and lives in the South. This, of course, includes children in these households.

•   •   •

As the data in this chapter show, the socioeconomic status of black people in the United States has improved in the second half of the twentieth century, but in some respects the gap between black and white Americans in education, occupation, and income remains a wide one, and in some areas it is widening rather than narrowing. Observers of the status of black citizens are eager to point out that government statistics show that about one-third of black families in the United States are now "middle class," but there is little to celebrate when the other two-thirds represent some of the most disadvantaged people in the world, including the one-third who live below the government's poverty threshold. A significant number of these people are children who see no prospect for a better life.

The ascent of conservatism in this country in the 1980s had a serious negative impact on black people. There are those who maintain that America is now a color-blind society and that affirmative action programs in education and employment represent reverse discrimination. They maintain that advancement in education and employment must be based on individual merit, not on racial "quotas." But black people have been denied full citizenship in the society not as individuals but as a group. To deny this historical reality is to engage in a massive act of self-deception.

Some observers maintain that race has become virtually insignificant in American life, and that it has been supplanted by economic class as a basis for inequality. But race has historically been structured into the institutions of this society, giving preference and privilege to whites. Although class is an important variable, it pales in significance when race is involved.

SELECTED BIBLIOGRAPHY

ASHMORE, HARRY S. *The Negro and the Schools.* Chapel Hill: University of North Carolina Press, 1954.

BALLARD, ALLEN B. *The Education of Black Folk.* New York: Harper & Row, 1973.

BATES, TIMOTHY. *The Role of Black Enterprise in Urban Economic Development.* Washington, DC: Joint Center for Political and Economic Studies, 1990.

DRAKE, ST. CLAIR, and HORACE CLAYTON. *Black Metropolis.* New York: Harcourt, Brace and Co., 1945.

FRAZIER, E. FRANKLIN. *The Negro in the United States.* New York: Macmillan, 1957.

HACKER, ANDREW. *Two Nations: Black and White, Separate, Hostile, Unequal.* New York: Charles Scribner's Sons, 1992.

KOZOL, JONATHAN. *Death at an Early Age.* Boston: Houghton Mifflin, 1967.

———. *Savage Inequalities: Children in American Schools.* New York: Crown, 1991.

ORFIELD, GARY. *Turning a Blind Eye: The Reagan Administration's Abandonment of Civil Rights Enforcement in Higher Education.* Washington, DC: Joint Center for Political and Economic Studies, 1990.

——— and FRANKLIN MONFORT. *Status of School Desegregation: The Next Generation.* Alexandria, VA: National School Boards Association, 1992.

PINKNEY, ALPHONSO. *The Myth of Black Progress.* New York: Cambridge University Press, 1984.

SIMMS, MARGARET. *Black Educational Trends: A Fact Book.* Washington, DC: Joint Center for Political and Economic Studies, 1990.

TABB, WILLIAM. *The Political Economy of the Black Ghetto.* New York: W.W. Norton Co., 1970.

U.S. BUREAU OF THE CENSUS, Current Population Reports, Series P-20. *The Black Population in the United States: March 1990 and 1989.* Washington, DC, 1991.

WILLHELM, SIDNEY. *Who Needs the Negro?* Cambridge, MA: Schenkman, 1970.

NOTES

1. U.S. Department of Labor, Bureau of Labor Statistics, "A Century of Change: Negroes in the U.S. Economy, 1860–1960," *Monthly Labor Review* (December 1962), p. 1361.
2. U.S. Bureau of the Census, *Statistical Abstract of the United States, 1982–83* (Washington, DC, 1983), p. 145.
3. *Statistical Abstract,* 1997, p. 157.
4. U.S. Bureau of the Census, Current Population Reports, Series P-20, *The Black Population in the United States: March 1990 and 1989* (Washington, DC, 1991), p. 6.
5. U.S. Bureau of the Census, *The Black Population of the United States: March 1996* (Update) (Washington, DC, 1997), p. 26.
6. Harry S. Ashmore, *The Negro and the Schools* (Chapel Hill: University of North Carolina Press, 1954), p. 13.
7. Ibid., p. 156.
8. Ibid., pp. 157–60.
9. U.S. Department of Health, Education and Welfare, Office of Education, *Equality of Educational Opportunity* (Washington, DC, 1966), pp. 10–13. These are the most recent data.
10. Gary Orfield and Franklin Monfort, *Status of School Desegregation: The Next Generation* (Alexandria, VA: National School Boards Association, 1992), p. 14.
11. Ibid., p. 8.

12. Ibid., p. 1.

13. Ibid., p. 13.

14. From an editorial in the *New York Times* entitled "Loss of Zeal for School Desegregation." April 3, 1992, p. A28.

15. Paul Delany, "Black State Colleges Are Found Periled; Integration a Factor," *New York Times,* November 26, 1971, p. 1.

16. U.S. Department of Education, Office of Civil Rights, *Historically Black Colleges and Universities and Higher Education Desegregation* (Washington, DC, 1991), p. 5.

17. Ibid., p. 8.

18. Ibid, p. 7.

19. U.S. Department of Labor, "A Century of Change," p. 1360.

20. U.S. Commission on Civil Rights, *Equal Employment Opportunity Under Federal Law* (Washington, DC, 1971).

21. From an editorial in the *New York Times* entitled "The Death of an Ugly Slogan," October 27, 1991, sec. 4, p. 14.

22. Sidney Wellhelm, *Who Needs the Negro?* (Cambridge, MA: Schenkman, 1970).

23. Rashi Fein, "An Economic and Social Profile of the Negro American," in *The Negro American*, ed. Talcott Parsons and Kenneth Clark (Boston: Houghton Mifflin, 1966), p. 114.

24. U.S. Bureau of the Census, *America's Black Population: 1970 to 1982: A Statistical View* (Washington, DC, 1983), p. 11.

25. *Statistical Abstracts, 1991,* p. 392.

26. U.S. Bureau of the Census, Current Population Reports, Series P-23, *Population Profile of the United States 1991* (Washington, DC, 1991), p. 14.

27. E. Franklin Frazier, *The Negro in the United States* (New York: Macmillan, 1957), pp. 387–93; Gunnar Myrdal, *An American Dilemma* (New York: Harper, 1944), pp. 307–14.

28. *The Negro Handbook* (Chicago: Johnson Publishing, 1966), pp. 214–15.

29. "The *Black Enterprise* 19th Annual Report on Black Business," *Black Enterprise,* June 1991, pp. 89–342.

30. Michael deCourcy Hinds, "Minority Business Set Back Sharply by Court's Rulings," *New York Times,* December 23, 1991, p. A15.

31. Ibid.

32. "The *Black Enterprise* Annual Report on Black Business," *Black Enterprise*, June 1998.

33. *The Black Population in the United States: March 1990 and 1989,* p. 97.

34. Ibid., pp. 11–12.

35. *Time,* June 22, 1998, p. 58.

36. The data in this section are from U.S. Bureau of the Census, Current Population Reports, Series P-60, *Poverty in the United States: 1988 and 1989* (Washington, DC, 1991) and are supplemented by information from *The Black Population in the United States: March 1990 and 1989.*

37. *New York Times*, February 17, 1988, p. A18.

CHAPTER FIVE

Social Institutions

The institutional life of the black community in the United States emerged and developed as a result of the peculiar interaction of black and white Americans through the years. Few aspects of institutional life in Africa survived the transfer of slaves to North America. With few exceptions, the distinctive features of black life in the United States today stem from the historical, social, and economic forces that black people have encountered since their arrival in North America. Their social institutions are a reflection of life in a racist society.

This chapter focuses on three social institutions: family life, politics, and religion. Other distinctive social institutions are discussed in appropriate sections of other chapters.

THE FAMILY

The organization and behavior patterns of the black family in the United States result mainly from economic and social conditions that blacks have encountered. Few survivals of the original African family system remain. From the breakup of the African family during slavery to the overwhelming urbanization of black people in the 1990s, family life has been in a constant process of change, adapting to economic and social forces emanating from the larger society.

Developmental Processes

The family system that developed among black people during slavery times was one with few of the characteristics that were normal to the white American family of the time. The very nature of slavery as an economic institution, as well as the attitudes that led to the institutionalization of African-American slavery, militated against black family stability. Associations between male and female slaves were frequently for the sole purpose of satisfying sexual desires. Slaveholders could, and often did, mate their slaves to produce additional property. Male slaves were frequently used as stallions; in such cases, no bonds of affection were likely to develop between them and female slaves. Furthermore, since slaves were the property of slaveholders, any family relationships that might develop could be, and frequently were, dissolved through the sale of one of the parties. Any offspring of such a union usually remained with the mother, while the father continued his sexual exploits on a new plantation.

Slave mothers frequently were affectionate and devoted to their offspring, but both the separation of the father and the presence of the slaveholder as a promiscuous role model led to the matricentric family, a development that has to some extent persisted to the present time. Children rarely saw their fathers, and mothers assumed responsibility for parental affection and care. When separated from her children, the slave mother often visited them at night. The mother, then, was the dominant and important figure in the black slave family.

Because of the precariousness of their status—economically, socially, and legally—and because of their slave heritage, with its disregard for stable family life, blacks who were free before the Civil War were unable to develop stable family relations.[1] Family disorganization, including sexual promiscuity, was widespread. However, many of the mulatto children born to black women were kept and cared for by their mothers despite severe hardships. Among the more economically secure free blacks, family relations attained a high degree of stability. Many of the prosperous mulattoes patterned their families after the middle- and upper-class white families.

The Civil War and emancipation had a disrupting effect on whatever degree of stability slave families had achieved. Marriage as a formal and legal relationship between males and females was not allowed to become a part of the mores among most slaves; however, during slavery times some stable families of husband, wife, and children did develop. With the complete uprooting of the social order in the South following the Civil War, family instability was but one element in the widespread social disorganization among the ex-slaves. In the exodus from the plantations and in the general aimless wandering that accompanied freedom, many black mothers left their children behind. Yet many others refused to part from their children, and reports testify to the sacrifices that many of them made to keep their children.[2]

Promiscuous sexual relations and frequent changing of partners became the rule among ex-slaves, especially among those who experienced difficulties adjusting in an era largely characterized by anomie. Religious leaders, state legislatures, military authorities, the Freedmen's Bureau, missionary schools, and the mass media all joined the effort to impose institutional marriage and family norms on the freedmen.[3] These efforts succeeded in some cases, but in others official monogamous marriage and stable family relations required a difficult form of self-discipline. Nevertheless, by the end of Reconstruction, blacks had come to accept many of the family patterns of the larger society.

The restoration of white supremacy in the South following Reconstruction imposed economic and social hardships on black people. It became virtually impossible for the black man to assume a position of dominance or equality with the black female. Economic exploitation, unemployment, and social subordination of black males in the larger society served to render them ineffectual as husbands and fathers. The appearance of Jim Crow laws toward the end of the nineteenth century further humiliated the black male; to a great extent these laws were geared toward keeping him "in his place" (i.e., away from the white female). Furthermore, with the widespread urbanization of blacks after 1900, family life was again disrupted. The social norms that made for family stability in the rural South were without force in the urban slums. Among the lower-income blacks, social disorganization was manifested in broken families and children born out of wedlock. On the other hand, a growing middle class among urban blacks was characterized by stable family relations and rigid adherence to the norms governing white, middle-class families.

The Family in the 1990s: Demographic Characteristics

As of March 1990 there were approximately 7.47 million black families in the United States, an increase of 1.3 million or about 8 percent in 10 years. Of these families 50 percent were married-couple families, 44 percent were headed by females with no husband present, and 6 percent were headed by fathers with no wife present.[4] Of the 56.59 million white families in the country at that time, 83 percent were married-couple families; 13 percent were headed by females with no husband present; and 4 percent were headed by males with no wife present. For black families the proportion with husband and wife present has steadily decreased in recent years. In 1970, 68 percent of all black families were husband–wife families; in 1980, 55 percent; and in 1990, 50 percent (Table 5-1). This represents a decrease of 18 percent in 20 years. The decrease for white families during this period was 6 percent.

The decrease in the proportion of married-couple families is accompanied by an increase in the proportion of families maintained by one parent, usually the

TABLE 5-1   Selected Characteristics of Families, by Race, March 1990, 1980, and 1970 (numbers in thousands)

	1990		1980		1970	
CHARACTERISTIC	BLACK	WHITE	BLACK	WHITE	BLACK	WHITE
Type of family						
All families	7,470	56,590	6,184	52,243	4,856	46,166
Percent	100.0	100.0	100.0	100.00	100.0	100.0
Married-couple families	50.2	83.0	55.5	85.7	68.3	88.9
Female householder, no husband present	43.8	12.9	40.3	11.6	28.0	8.9
Male householder, no wife present	6.0	4.1	4.1	2.8	3.7	2.2
Children under 18 years by presence of parents[a]						
Children in families	10,018	51,390	9,375	52,242	9,422	58,790
Percent living with						
Both parents	37.7	79.0	42.2	82.7	58.5	89.5
Mother only	51.2	16.2	43.9	13.5	29.5	7.8
Father only	3.5	3.0	1.9	1.6	2.3	0.9
Neither parent	7.5	1.8	12.0	2.2	9.7	1.8

[a]Excludes persons under 18 years old who were maintaining households or family groups.

Source: U.S. Bureau of the Census, Current Population Reports, Series P-20, *The Black Population in the United States: March 1990 and 1989* (Washington, DC, 1991).

mother. Between 1970 and 1990 black families maintained by the mother with no spouse present rose from 28 to 44 percent.

Between 1970 and 1990 the proportion of children under 18 years of age living in one-parent families increased for both blacks and whites, but the increase was greater for blacks. In 1970 about one-third (32 percent) of black children lived in families with one parent (usually the mother); by 1980 the proportion had increased to 46 percent, and by 1990 it was 55 percent. The increase of comparable white families in that period was from 9 percent to 15 percent to 19 percent. It is significant that in 1990, more black children lived in single-parent families (55 percent) than with both parents, and that 7.5 percent, or more than 700,000, lived with neither parent.

A significant number of black children live with grandparents. In 1989, 5 percent of all children (under 18) lived with grandparents—13 percent of all black children, compared with 3 percent of white children. In more than half (56 percent) of these families, the mother (but not the father) of the children was present, but for nearly two-fifths (38 percent) neither parent was present.[5]

Married-couple families differ from those headed by females with no husband present in several ways. For example, black married-couple families have median family incomes of $30,600, while those with female heads, with no husband present, earn $11,600. The householders in families headed by females tend to be younger than those in married-couple families. In black families with female heads, about two-fifths (42 percent) of householders are under 35 years of age, compared with slightly more than one-fourth (27 percent) of household heads in married-couple families. Furthermore, these single-parent households have more children than married-couple households. While four-fifths (80 percent) of female-headed households have children, about one-half (52 percent) of married-couple families have no children.[6] And 7 percent of the former have four or more children, compared with about 4 percent for the latter.

Nearly one-half (49 percent) of black families headed by females with no husband present lived below the government's poverty threshold in 1989 ($12,675 for a family of four).[7] Less than one-third (28 percent) of comparable white families lived in similar circumstances. In black female-headed households with children under 18 years, more than one-half (54 percent) lived below the poverty level.

A greater proportion of black families in rural areas live below the poverty threshold than those living in metropolitan areas. Outside the South, however, few black people live in nonmetropolitan areas. Within metropolitan areas, in all regions of the country, black families in central cities (where most of them live) are more likely to live below the poverty level than those in the suburbs. For example, in the Midwest, 21 percent of black families in suburbs live below the poverty threshold, compared with 36 percent in central cities.[8]

Black families are less likely than white families to own their own homes. In 1987, 43 percent of all black families owned their homes, compared with 67 percent of white families.[9] Furthermore, the median value of homes owned by black families was $50,000, compared with $72,000 for all homes in the country.

Because black families earn less than white families, they are required to spend a larger percentage of their earnings for basic needs—food, shelter, and clothing. And the housing in which they live is more congested than that of white families. Whether they own or rent their places of residence, black families are more likely than white families to live in housing units lacking complete plumbing facilities.[10]

Problems and Prospects

The black family in the United States has long been required to adapt to various societal changes and has managed to survive, sometimes precariously. In the 1990s the black family faces challenges that are arguably as difficult as any in the twentieth century. The immense resilience for which the black family has been noted throughout its history in the United States requires renewed efforts to cope with contemporary problems.

One of the foremost among these problems is the increase in households headed by women, where no husband is present, coupled with the growing number of children born to unmarried women, especially adolescents. Although these topics have been discussed elsewhere, they require further elaboration. In a society in which the state assumes little or inadequate responsibility for the well-being of families and children (unlike most of the industrialized world) but requires much of them, the responsibility is left to families and individuals. All too often these circumstances are not considered in sexual relations and family-planning decisions.

Between 1950 and 1990, the number of black households headed by women increased from 17 to 56 percent, a 39 percent increase. During the same 40 years, the number of white households headed by women increased from 5.3 percent to 17 percent, an increase of 12 percent. Although the proportion of black families headed by females has always been greater than that for white families, the ratio has remained constant at about three times greater for blacks than for whites.[11] It should also be noted that the change for both groups reflects trends in the society as a whole, and that these trends are relatively recent.

Black families are much more likely than white families to approach the extended family pattern.[12] Nevertheless, many of the female heads of household lack the maturity and income to provide for healthy families. In a significant proportion of black households headed by women, the mother is an adolescent. Adolescent pregnancy and childbearing have increased rapidly in the United States (see chapter 7). For example, the adolescent pregnancy rate (number of pregnancies per 1,000 teenagers) in the United States is the highest in the industrialized world. The rate for black teenagers is 186, double the rate for whites (93).[13]

Although the abortion rate is higher among black adolescents than among whites, the birthrate is at least four times greater. At present about 64 percent of all black births occur outside of marriage, a significant proportion of them to adolescents. Although the rate of black births outside marriage is more than four times greater than the white rate, the white rate of increase is greater than the black rate.

Compounding the problems black families face is the declining number of black males eligible for marriage. For example, research has shown that in 1989 one-fourth of all black men in the country in their twenties were in prison, on probation, or on parole. This is a significantly greater proportion than are enrolled in colleges and universities. A similar study in New York State a year later corroborated these findings. And a later study in Washington, DC, found that some 42 percent of black men between 18 and 25 were enmeshed in the criminal justice system on any given day in 1991.[14] Of the 53,377 young black men in the city, some 21,800 were involved with the criminal justice system on an average day. Of those, 7,800 were in jail or prison, 6,000 were on local probation, 3,700 were on local parole, and 1,300 were on federal probation or parole. Another 3,000 were awaiting trial on bond or being pursued on arrest warrants.

As we will see in chapter 6, homicide is the leading cause of death for young black males, and more than 90 percent of black murder victims are slain by other blacks, a situation that has been called "self-inflicted genocide."[15] Some communities have become war zones, places where poverty and neglect have bred frustration that has generated widespread violent crime. Human life is no longer sacred for many, and the taking of a life generates no feelings of remorse. One such community is Brooklyn's East New York section, where two adolescents were murdered in a crowded hall of Thomas Jefferson High School in 1992. An adolescent from this community said that most teenagers there do not consider the moral or practical implications of killing: "They are so fed up that they get to a point they just don't care anymore."[16]

Further compounding the problems facing black families, especially those in urban areas, was the introduction of crack cocaine in the mid-1980s (see chapter 7). In recent years the number of children living in zero-parent families has mushroomed, giving rise to what has come to be called "America's new orphans," and creating a call for a return to the orphanage system of the nineteenth and early twentieth centuries.[17] In the inner cities throughout the country, thousands of children are without parents, having been abandoned to other relatives, foster homes, or institutions. Their parents are dead or incarcerated or have disappeared. Poor black families, already fragile, are hardest hit. For example, at a junior high school in Oakland, California, at least two-thirds of the 750 pupils in the school are new orphans. They tend to be distrustful of adults, greedy for attention, and convinced that they are worthless because they do not have parents.[18]

When crack cocaine replaced heroin as the drug of choice in the inner city, women became more prone to drug addiction than before. As a result there has been a sharp increase in the number of infants abandoned in hospitals. Others are born addicted to drugs and with other abnormalities, and still others have been killed by drug-addicted parents. In New York City the Human Resources Administration reported that cases of child abuse and neglect in which parents were involved with drugs (mainly crack) more than tripled in the two years between 1986 and 1988. During 1986 a study of the cases of children killed as a result of neglect and abuse showed that 73 percent of these deaths resulted from drug abuse, up from 11 percent in 1985.[19] It appears that a significant number of the poorest black families are crumbling under the influence of crack.

Patterns of Family Life

In many ways black family life in the United States differs from white family life. It is often maintained that in the black family, dominance is vested in the female, while in white families dominance is vested in the male or is shared by the husband and wife. But in the vast majority of black families, as in white families, dominance is shared between the mother and the father (egalitarian pattern) or is vested in the father (patriarchal pattern).[20]

One of the chief societal functions of the family is the socialization of offspring. In the case of black parents this role becomes more difficult, for theirs is not simply a task of instilling skills, knowledge, attitudes, and values; they must also socialize their offspring into the peculiar status of being black in a racist society. Child-rearing practices constitute crucial aspects of the socialization process. In the 1940s Davis and Havighurst conducted a study of racial and class differences in child-rearing practices. They reported that few differences existed when black and white families occupied similar social class positions.[21] Subsequent studies report findings inconsistent with these.[22] One similar study, however, reports that black mothers are less likely to expose themselves to child-rearing literature than are white mothers, regardless of social class position, but that black mothers who are so exposed express more favorable attitudes toward child-rearing than do white mothers.[23] Although contradictory findings are reported, considerable evidence indicates that middle-class black parents are more like middle-class white parents in their child-rearing practices than they are like lower-class black parents.

In an effort to counteract the proliferation of books characterizing the black family as pathological, several black social scientists have published studies that attempt to present the black family as an institution characterized by both strengths and weaknesses.[24] In general, these studies posit that an examination of the strengths of black families is a necessary antidote to past and present preoccupation with their weaknesses. Historically, the black family has been presented in American scholarship as a "matriarchal" institution so unstable that it is responsible for many of the problems faced by blacks in the United States.

Robert Hill has enumerated some of the strengths of black families.[25] He sees certain characteristics of black families that contribute to their survival, development, and stability: strong kinship bonds, strong work orientation, adaptability of family roles, strong achievement orientation, and strong religious orientation. In black families kinship relations are strong, minors and the elderly are absorbed in the family, and informal adoption is relatively commonplace. Contrary to popular stereotypes, black families place a strong emphasis on work, as is evidenced by the number of families with two or more wage earners. When blacks refuse to work, it is because they are relegated to the lowest-paid jobs.

Although most black families are two-parent families in which decision making is shared, it is often necessary for each member of the family to temporarily assume the roles of others, as when both parents work or when a key member is absent for some unexpected reason. Another of the strengths of black families is their high achievement orientation, even among the poor. Indeed, black parents maintain higher aspirations for their children than white parents do, and black youths have higher educational and occupational aspirations than their white counterparts.[26] Finally, a strong religious orientation has served as a survival mechanism for black families throughout a long and difficult history.

Any social institution in a society with as many contradictions, inconsistencies, and prejudices as exist in the United States is likely to face problems. And the black family has its share of these problems. In a period of rapid social change, as is characteristic of American society, much can be learned from the black family, an institution that has maintained a reasonable degree of stability through a long series of crises.

POLITICS

With rare exceptions, black Americans have played a minor role in the political life of the United States, both in the electoral process and in public office. Historically, black people have been heavily concentrated in the South, where various techniques have been used to keep them from voting. Except during the period of Radical Reconstruction, the South succeeded in virtually disfranchising its many blacks. In 1898, for example, a senator from South Carolina boldly declared from the floor of the Senate that his state had virtually eliminated black people from voting: "We have done our best. We have scratched our heads to find out how we could eliminate the last one of them. We stuffed ballot boxes. We shot them. We are not ashamed of it."[27] Because of increasing pressure for greater civil rights, and because of additional civil rights legislation ensuring their voting rights, black people are becoming more active in American political life.

Historical Trends

Black people have been active in varying degrees in the political life of the United States since the beginning of the Radical Reconstruction. On the national level, three blacks served in the 41st Congress (1869–1871), two in the House of Representatives and one in the Senate.[28] With the exception of the 50th Congress (1887–1889), blacks served in every U.S. Congress from 1869 to 1901. The largest number—seven—served in the 43rd and 44th Congresses. All these congressmen represented southern states, and by the turn of the twentieth century, blacks had been effectively disfranchised in that region.

No blacks served in the national Congress from the 57th Congress (1901–1903) through the 71st Congress (1929–1931), but the widespread migration of black people northward and the availability of the franchise to them resulted in the election to the 72nd Congress of the first black from the North. Since that time one or more blacks have served in every Congress. With the concentration of black people in large urban centers, as a result of residential segregation, the number of blacks in Congress has gradually increased. The first black senator since 1881 was elected to the 93rd Congress (1973–1974) representing Massachusetts.

Although black Americans have frequently constituted a majority in the population of several political subdivisions in the South, since Reconstruction they have held little, if any, political power. On the state and local level, blacks held important offices during Reconstruction. During this period they were elected or appointed to such public offices as supreme court justice, lieutenant governor, secretary of state, state treasurer, superintendent of public instruction, and virtually every other public office except that of governor. In the state constitutional conventions, blacks were well represented, especially in South Carolina, Louisiana, Florida, and Virginia. At no time, however, can it be said that they effectively controlled the affairs of any state.

Beginning with the elections for the constitutional conventions in 1867, black people in the South voted in large numbers. At that time the total black vote exceeded the vote of white southerners.[29] Throughout the Radical Reconstruction period blacks actively exercised the franchise. With the restoration of white supremacy in 1877, the gains registered in this period gradually disappeared. The Populist movement in the 1890s witnessed a resurgence of black voting, but it was short-lived. By the turn of the twentieth century, through a series of devices, some legal and some illegal, the South had effectively disfranchised most of its black citizens.[30] At that time so few black people lived outside the South that their voting strength was insignificant.

With the wholesale disfranchisement of black people in the South after 1900, they were hardly represented in public office in that region during the first half of the twentieth century. With increased voting guarantees, especially the Voting Rights Act of 1965, blacks have been elected to public office at various levels—from state senator to local boards of education and, in several cases, to county sheriff—since the rise of the civil rights movement.

In the North the concentration of black people in urban areas is a relatively recent development. In the second half of the twentieth century, increasingly large numbers of blacks have held elective and appointive offices at various levels, from state senator to mayor to judges of various levels, including the U.S. Supreme Court.

With the internal redistribution of black people in the twentieth century, northern cities became the center of black political behavior. Black voters are frequently cultivated by white politicians because in certain "decisive" states black voters hold the balance of power—their votes have determined the outcome of elections.[31] In the South, especially since the passage of the Civil Rights Act of 1964 and the Voting Rights Act of 1965, black people have been registered and are voting in increasing numbers. This increased participation in elections was made evident by the election returns in 1984, when black people were elected to state legislatures and local offices throughout the South, although still not nearly in proportion to their numbers in the population.

Voting Rights

The right to vote is one of the basic civil rights guaranteed to citizens by the Constitution of the United States. Yet hardly any aspect of black people's quest for equality has met with greater resistance in the South than the right to vote. Several judicial decrees and legislative acts have been required to translate this constitutional guarantee into a reality for millions of black citizens of the United States.[32] With emancipation, two amendments, the Fourteenth and Fifteenth, were written into the Constitution especially to protect the voting rights of the newly freed slaves. These amendments specifically directed states to guarantee voting rights to black citizens.

Three civil rights acts were enacted between 1866 and 1875 as a means of assuring equality of treatment (including the right to vote) to America's blacks. These acts—the Civil Rights Act of 1866, the Civil Rights Act of 1870, and the Civil Rights Act of 1875—together with constitutional guarantees, served to permit black people in the South to exercise the right to vote with relative ease during Reconstruction. After Reconstruction, however, several states adopted so-called grandfather clauses, which restricted registration and voting to persons who had voted prior to emancipation. This practice was finally declared unconstitutional by the Supreme Court in 1915.[33] With this defeat southerners adopted the "white primary," in which the Democratic party prohibited blacks from participating in primary elections in nine states. When the white primary was outlawed, many southern states resorted to the gerrymander as a means of disfranchising blacks. In a long series of cases the Supreme Court eventually curbed this practice also.

In addition to these techniques, the poll tax, property, educational, and "character" requirements were used to keep black citizens from voting. Perhaps the most effective means of disfranchising blacks, however, were those of intimidation and violence.[34]

Because of the difficulties encountered by black people attempting to vote in the South, special legislation was again enacted in the 1950s and 1960s. The Civil Rights Act of 1957 attempted to guarantee that any black so desiring could vote. The federal government, through the Justice Department, was empowered to institute lawsuits to ensure blacks the right to vote. The Civil Rights Act of 1960 empowered the attorney general ultimately to certify blacks as qualified voters in areas where they had been kept from voting through discrimination. And the Civil Rights Act of 1964 included voting rights guarantees. One important aspect of this act is the provision that a sixth-grade education is a presumption of literacy for voting purposes.

In spite of the Constitution, the nineteenth-century civil rights acts, the judicial ruling of the Supreme Court, and the twentieth-century civil rights acts, black Americans continued to experience difficulties in voting throughout the Deep South. After the Civil Rights Act of 1964, civil rights organizations were urged to discontinue direct-action protests and to concentrate on voter registration among black people. It was believed that the most effective means of achieving their goals was through registering blacks to vote. When large-scale attempts were made to register black people in the South, however, voting registrars again utilized various techniques to keep them from voting. Acts of violence (so characteristic in the South) met voter-registration workers and black people attempting to vote. Civil rights workers and the leaders of civil rights organizations urged the enactment of new legislation to guarantee southern blacks the right to vote. As a result of these pressures, the Voting Rights Act of 1965 was enacted by Congress and signed into law on August 6. This act contains many provisions designed to assure black people that devices previously employed to disfranchise them would no longer serve this purpose. For example, literacy as a qualification for voting was suspended, and voter registration may be supervised by federal officials in political subdivisions where a pattern of discrimination is discerned.

Although intimidation and threats will no doubt continue to deter many eligible black voters, a long series of legislative acts and judicial rulings, over a period of more than one hundred years, has finally established, in principle, the right of black people to vote. It is reported that some subtle techniques—restricted registration times or places, employers' denying workers time off to register or vote, and the purging of registration rolls—still make it difficult for black people to register and vote.

Political Organization and Behavior

The second half of the twentieth century has seen the growth of greater cohesiveness in the black community than has existed since emancipation, as a direct result of an increasing sense of identity among black people and the demand for greater civil rights. No black community represents a completely unified force, however. Clearly some communities are better organized than others. The Atlanta, Georgia, black subcommunity, for example, is described by Hunter as a community with a high degree of social organization.[35] The black leadership of Atlanta followed the pattern of leadership in the larger community. However, the black community exerted less influence on policy decisions in the larger community than did other associational groupings, such as organized labor or the Jewish subcommunity. Other subcommunities were represented on policy-making committees in the larger community, but the black subcommunity was not represented: ". . . the [black] subcommunity . . . stands alone in its isolation from the sources of power as no other unit within the metropolitan area. Its channels of communication in most of its power relations with the larger community are partially blocked, if not totally closed." Because of the larger number of blacks, and because of the relatively high proportion of middle-class blacks, there was a high degree of civic participation among Atlanta's blacks. Even there, however, they were powerless to influence basic community decisions.[36] This study was made prior to the civil rights legislation of the

1960s. Since 1973 all mayors of Atlanta have been black, and a black person is one of the city's representatives in Congress.

In the past black people have relied on the courts and direct-action demonstrations rather than conventional political behavior to gain political ends. There are several reasons for this lack of conventional political behavior. Blacks are overrepresented in the lower class, and lower-class people are less likely to participate in political activities. In addition, their lives are such that personal problems of employment and maintenance are so pervasive as to rule out political involvement. Within the black community there has been a tendency for middle-class people to avoid association with the lower class.[37] Since the middle class characteristically assumes positions of political leadership in the community, the antipathy that middle-class blacks maintain toward the lower class renders cooperation difficult. Also, few individuals in the black community possess the requisite wealth for large-scale political undertakings, and political campaigns are expensive. The middle class is usually made up of professionals, and few black businesses are of such magnitude as to provide their owners with the wealth required for political leadership. Even civic and civil rights organizations in the black community are usually lacking in membership and funds. Rarely are they maintained by the residents of the community.

There is some evidence of a trend toward conventional political behavior on the part of blacks.[38] There is increasing recognition that the problems confronting them—in employment, in education, and in housing—are of such a magnitude that it is unlikely that they can be solved simply by achieving full constitutional rights.

Voter turnout in the United States rarely exceeds 50 percent of those eligible. For example, although 62 percent of eligible voters were registered in 1990, only 45 percent of those who were registered actually voted. In recent years black citizens have registered to vote in increasing numbers in the South, and they have elected blacks to political office throughout the country. The Bureau of the Census reported, for example, that 59 percent of black persons were registered in 1990 and that 39 percent of those registered voted.[39] This represents a decline from 64 percent registered and 43 percent voting in 1986.

Regionally, blacks in the Midwest were more likely to register (66 percent) and vote (43 percent) in 1990, and least likely to register (49 percent) and vote (33 percent) in the Northeast.[40] Proportionately fewer blacks than whites registered and voted, but the difference was not significant. In some states (Illinois, Ohio, South Carolina, and Tennessee), blacks were more likely than whites to register and vote, and in some others (Arkansas, California, and Mississippi), they were more likely to register, but less likely to vote.

Blacks living outside metropolitan areas (i.e., in rural areas) are most likely to register and vote, but it is mainly in the South that blacks live outside metropolitan areas. Within metropolitan areas, blacks living in central cities were slightly more likely to register and vote than those in the suburbs.[41] Among both blacks and whites, the higher the educational level and occupational status, the greater the likelihood of registering and voting in 1990. And, like citizens at large, older adults are more likely to vote than those who are younger.

Public Officials

In 1984, Jesse Jackson, a black man running for the Democratic presidential nomination, collected 21 percent of the primary and caucus votes, a total of 3.5 million popular votes. In an initial field of eight candidates, he received more votes than five of his white opponents. By the time of the next presidential primary (in 1988), Jackson received some 7 million popular votes, second only to the Democratic nominee.[42] His total included 12 percent of whites who voted, three times the number he received in 1984. He placed first in 14 primaries, including those in Maine and Minnesota, both of which are overwhelmingly white states. Jackson went to the Democratic National Convention that year with 1,200 delegates, over a quarter of the total.

When the 101st Congress convened in January 1990, its 24 black members represented the largest number of black Americans in Congress since Reconstruction. Many other blacks held elective or appointive offices on the national level. In 1990 there were 7,335 black elected officials in the United States, a 68 percent increase over 1980. In addition to those in Congress, these elected positions included state, county, and municipal officials.[43] Also, black judges were serving on the U. S. Court of Appeals, the Customs Court, U. S. District Courts, and the U.S. Supreme Court. Several dozen blacks were serving as ambassadors and Foreign Service officers. For the first time in history a black man was elected governor of a state (Virginia), and a black general was appointed chairman of the Joint Chiefs of Staff, giving him responsibility for the nation's military establishment.

In 1990 blacks held elective positions in every state except Idaho, Montana, and North Dakota. The numbers varied anywhere from one each in Hawaii and Utah to 669 in Mississippi and 705 in Alabama. More than three-fifths (61 percent) of black elected officials served in county and municipal government (county commissioners and council persons, mayors, vice mayors, alderpersons, and regional representatives), followed by education (23 percent—members of state education agencies, college boards, and school boards), law enforcement (10 percent—judges, magistrates, constables, marshals, sheriffs, and justices of the peace), and U. S. and state legislatures (6 percent, including elected state administrators).

Regionally the South, with 4,955 (67 percent) black elected officials, leads the country. There were 1,294 (18 percent) black officials in the Midwest, 725 (10 percent) in the Northeast, and 361 (5 percent) in the West. There were about twice as many black elected officials in the state of Alabama as in all the states in the West and the Northeast. States in the South led the country in the number of black elected officials in 1990, although there were no black elected officials prior to the mid-1960s, and few blacks in that region voted prior to that time.

There was only one black in the U.S. Senate in 1993; the first black to serve since Reconstruction had left office in 1980. Twenty-three of the 24 black members of the House of Representatives were Democrats. The lone Republican represented a district in Oklahoma. (See Table 5-2.)

In Congress blacks chaired six standing committees: District of Columbia, Education and Labor, Government Operations, Post Office and Civil Service, Committee on Hunger, and the Narcotics Abuse and Control Committee. On the municipal level, many of the largest cities in the country had black mayors in 1990, including Los Angeles; Philadelphia; Detroit; Washington, DC; Atlanta; New Orleans; Oakland, California; Richmond, Virginia; Birmingham, Alabama; Denver, Colorado; and Newark, New Jersey. These black mayors usually succeeded white politicians, and the cities were plagued with a variety of problems. And with the complex nature of relations between municipal and state governments and the federal government, the tasks confronting newly elected black mayors have been formidable.

Education and law enforcement are areas in which blacks are frequently appointed or elected to office. Inasmuch as data show that black students predominate in public schools in many large school districts, many such districts are headed by blacks. Data also show that blacks are disproportionately arrested for crime; that is one of the reasons that blacks in several large cities have been appointed chiefs of police.

TABLE 5-2   Members of Congress, 1981–1995

	BLACK	WHITE	ALL RACES
House of Representatives			
97th Congress, 1981	17	415	435
98th Congress, 1983	21	411	"
99th Congress, 1985	20	412	"
100th Congress, 1987	23	408	"
101st Congress, 1989	24	406	"
102nd Congress, 1991	25	407	"
103rd Congress, 1993	38	393	"
104th Congress, 1995	40	391	"
Senate			
97th Congress, 1981	0	97	100
98th Congress, 1983	0	98	"
99th Congress, 1985	0	98	"
100th Congress, 1987	0	98	"
101st Congress, 1989	0	98	"
102nd Congress, 1991	0	98	"
103rd Congress, 1993	1	97	"
104th Congress, 1995	1	97	"

Notes: "All Races" includes other races not shown separately.
Units: Number of members of the House and Senate respectively, as shown.

Source: U.S. Bureau of the Census, *Statistical Abstract of the United States, 1995,* p. 281, table 444 (data from Congressional Quarterly, Inc.). C 3.134:995

In general, black Americans hold disproportionately few elective and appointive offices—about 2 percent of the nation's total. The pattern varies with region of the country, and in recent years the greatest political activity has taken place in the South. In that region black political activity has had a significant impact, especially in decreasing the extent of routine violence against blacks characteristic of the South. Although such transfers of power from whites to blacks are not likely to alter the status of blacks, they do contribute to the spread of black pride.

RELIGION

Religion has traditionally played an important role in the lives of black Americans. The character of their religion is a reflection of their precarious status in the larger society. Denied the opportunity to participate as equals in the religious life and other institutions of the larger society, black people organized their own religious denominations as a means of coping with the social isolation they encountered. Although their religious institutions contain the same basic elements as white Protestantism, it is especially in their religion that some elements of their African heritage are to be found.[44]

Developmental History

The first black people to settle permanently in what is now the United States were systematically stripped of their traditional culture, including their religious practices. In contrast to those who settled in the Caribbean and South America, the slaves did not establish their traditional cults in North America. Slaveholders succeeded in forcing slaves to abandon the outward manifestations of their "heathen" religions. Few of the slaves had been converted to Christianity before their arrival in North America, and throughout much of the slavery era many slave holders opposed religious instruction for slaves. African slaves had been baptized since their first importation, but ". . . it was not until the opening of the eighteenth century that a systematic attempt was made on the part of the Church of England to Christianize Negroes in America."[45] These efforts were carried out by the Society for the Propagation of the Gospel in Foreign Parts, which was chartered in England in 1701. Soon afterward, white Baptist and Methodist ministers and missionaries began proselytizing among the slaves. The slaves responded considerably more enthusiastically to these efforts than they had to those from ministers and missionaries of the Church of England. Frazier sees the uneducated and emotional appeals of the Baptists and Methodists as fulfilling a special need of the slaves.[46]

On many plantations slaves were allowed to worship in white churches, often seated in the gallery but sometimes in a separate section on the main floor. In such cases the services were invariably conducted by white ministers, but there were occasionally black ministers among the slaves. Black ministers were viewed by slaveholders with distrust, especially after the rebellion of Nat Turner, who was himself a minister. But black ministers were tolerated as long as they confined themselves to sermons in which they instilled in the slaves acceptance of their status. As Myrdal has written, "Undoubtedly the great bulk of the Southern Negro preachers advocated complete acceptance of slave status."[47] By the time of emancipation a significant proportion of the slaves had been converted to Christianity, and their religious practices provided an outlet for the frustration resulting from their status. Furthermore, religion gave them a basis of social cohesion for the first time since their arrival in the New World.

The religious life of the free blacks during the slavery era differed from that of the slaves. At first black people in the North and South attended services along with white worshipers. And in both regions black ministers served mixed black–white congregations as well as all-black congregations. Several black ministers achieved widespread distinction as orators and preached to predominantly white congregations. The separate black church was established in the 1770s because of increasing tension resulting from blacks' attendance at predominantly white churches.[48] By the turn of the nineteenth century, free blacks had established both Methodist and Protestant Episcopal churches. Baptist churches, independent of white churches, were also organized during this time. In the North the churches of the free blacks assisted their counterparts in the South in two ways: Northern black churches were frequently centers of Abolitionist activity, and they aided runaway slaves by serving as stations on the Underground Railroad.

During Reconstruction the black church provided a source of social organization and social control in a time of social disruption for the newly freed slaves. There were initial conflicts between the freedmen and those blacks who had been free before the Civil War, but these were short-lived. Perhaps the most important role of the black church in this period was played in political life.[49] Since blacks in the South enjoyed civil rights on a wide scale, many of the politicians of this period were recruited from among religious leaders. They served in state legislatures, in the Freedmen's Bureau, and in many federal appointive positions. Two of the twenty blacks elected to the federal House of Representatives between 1869 and 1901 were ministers, as was one of the two senators.

The restoration of white supremacy in the South served to strip these leaders of their political power in the larger community, and many of them became leaders in education and other community institutions serving black people. The black church as a separate institution was the primary source of social life among black people. The ministry was the main source of leadership, and it was through the ministry that the black community maintained contact with the larger community. As Myrdal has written,

> In practically all rural areas, and in many urban ones, the preacher stood out as the acknowledged local leader of the Negroes. His function became to transmit the whites' wishes to the Negroes and to beg the whites for favors for his people. He became—in our terminology—the typical accommodating Negro leader. To this degree the Negro church perpetuated the traditions of slavery.[50]

The frustrations inherent in the lives of black Americans made some form of outlet essential. The character of black religion (concerned with otherworldly matters) meant that it posed no serious threat to established patterns of white supremacy. Therefore, religious activity among blacks was not only tolerated but encouraged. The minister could be trusted, and the church contained the black masses.

In the North, where white supremacy was less well institutionalized, the black church remained somewhat more independent. Unlike their southern counterparts, northern black ministers were more responsive to the needs of their followers than to the white community. Therefore, they were more likely to become involved in the politics of the larger community and frequently became leaders in opposition to segregation and discrimination against blacks. Furthermore, within the black community they engaged in social service work. On the whole, however, the black church in the North was not a militant force for social change.

With the widespread urbanization of black people that began in the second decade of the twentieth century, the focus of black life shifted from the rural South to the cities in the South and elsewhere. This radical change, like that brought about by emancipation, had a disrupting effect on the lives of black people. The uprooted masses flocked to cities, and again the church provided a basis for social organization. But within the urban environment the black church, like religious institutions in the larger society, addressed itself to problems facing its members and deemphasized its otherworldly outlook. At the same time the established urban black church gradually became less emotional in its services. Because of the widespread social disorganization accompanying the urbanization of blacks, many of them continued to feel the need for outlets from the frustrations they faced. Therefore they sought refuge in "storefront" churches, many of which were peripherally affiliated with the more institutional denominations, or in the many cults that developed.[51] The black church continued to be the primary source of social cohesion, but it did not play an important role in the endeavors of black people to achieve greater civil rights during the first half of the twentieth century.

With the greater emphasis on civil rights at midcentury, the black church became one of the prime agencies advocating social change in race relations. Black ministers became leaders in the civil rights movement, and the movement has to a large extent continued to have a religious base. Since religion had always been the only well-organized institution within the black community, such a development was inevitable.

Religious Affiliation

The lack of participation by blacks in the organized religious life of American society in general reflects their lack of acceptance by the larger society. In some respects the Christian church is one of America's most segregated institutions. The major black churches are undergoing some transformation, however, and black people are now being accepted into membership in predominantly white churches. It is impossible to specify the exact membership of any religious organization at any time because the census does not collect this information at its regular enumerations.

Therefore, it is necessary to rely on data provided by the religious organizations, and these data are frequently inflated. It is estimated that more than half of the black population are church members. Although there are some 30 different black denominations of the Christian religion alone, seven out of every eight black church members are either Baptists or Methodists.[52] Black Christians are concentrated in seven predominantly black denominations, each having more than 1 million members. Baptist denominations claimed more members than all others combined. Of these, the National Baptist Convention, U. S. A., claiming 7.5 million members, is the largest. Its membership is distributed among 30,000 churches. The National Baptist Convention of America, the second largest, had 3.5 million members in 1991; the National Missionary Baptist Convention of America had 3.2 million; and the Progressive National Baptist Convention had 1.2 million.

There are three Methodist denominations with at least 1 million members each: the African Methodist Episcopal Church with 3.5 million members is the largest, followed by the African Methodist Episcopal Zion Church with 1.2 million, and the Christian Methodist Episcopal Church with 1 million. There were more than 8 million black Pentecostal/Apostolic, Holiness, and Deliverance denominations. Two of them—the Church of God in Christ and the United House of Prayer for All People–Church on the Rock of the Apostolic Faith—claimed 4 million members each.

Other black Christian religious organizations include the Catholic Church, the Churches of Christ, nondenominational churches (including Father Divine's "Kingdom" and Peace Mission), Orthodox churches (such as the African Orthodox Church, the Ethiopian Orthodox Church in the United States of America, and the Ethiopian Orthodox Church of North America), Pan-African Orthodox (including the Shrine of the Black Madonna), Presbyterian, and Spiritualist.

Although most blacks are Christians, others adhere to Hebrew denominations (including Church of God–Black Jews, House of Judah, Nation of Yahweh, the Original Hebrew Israelite Nation, and Rastafarians). Others belong to Islamic groups (e.g., the American Muslim Mission, Ahmadiyya Movement in Islam, Moorish Science Temple Divine). There are also three different branches of the former Nation of Islam (Black Muslims): the Nation of Islam (Farrakhan), Nation of islam (John Muhammad), and Nation of Islam (the Caliph). There are several other non-Christian groups such as the Afro-American Vodun movement, the First Church of Voodoo, and Yoruba Village of Oyotunji.

Finally, all the major predominantly white religious denominations (e.g., Episcopal, Lutheran, Methodist, Presbyterian, Reformed, and Unitarian Universalist) have black members and sometimes black caucuses. Others, such as the Seventh-Day Adventists and the Jehovah's Witnesses, include large black followings.

Structure and Patterns

Since black religion in America, like other aspects of black life, is highly segregated, it might be expected to differ in some regards from religion in the larger society. The black church runs the gamut from the separationist sects and cults in large urban centers, which appeal to the poor and use emotionalism as an important part of the services, to the upper-class Protestant churches represented by the Congregationalist, Episcopal, and Presbyterian denominations, which are totally devoid of emotionalism in their services. Regardless of the type of service, black people are more likely to be affiliated with some form of church than are white Americans. Myrdal reports that in the 1930s, 44 percent of the black population were members of churches, compared with 42 percent of the white population.[53] This figure probably represented an underenumeration among blacks, because they are more likely than whites to attend services at storefront churches and to be members of small religious cults and sects whose memberships are rarely reported in church statistics.

The black community is noted for the number of churches it includes. Drake and Cayton enumerated some 500 churches in Chicago that served some 200,000 members. These churches represented more than 30 denominations. Seventy-five percent of these churches were storefront churches or "house churches" with an average membership of fewer than 25 persons.[54] A study of central Harlem in the 1960s enumerated 418 church buildings. Of this number only 122 were housed in conventional church buildings; 232 were located either in storefronts or in residential buildings, the remainder were located in large meeting halls, private homes, or social agencies.[55]

Among conventional black Protestants, religious services follow a pattern similar to that of white Protestant churches. In general, few innovations have been made in the services. The choir sings alone or is joined by the congregation in the singing of hymns; music is supplied by an organ (a piano in small churches); prayer is recited by the minister; the sermon (the center of the service) is delivered by the minister; and the collection, an essential part of the service, frequently consumes a significant proportion of the time allocated to the service.[56] In some Baptist and Methodist churches the services frequently assume a more emotional tone than in other Protestant denominations. There are frequent responses to the sermon on the part of the congregation. These responses take the form of "yes" or "Amen." Such practices are characteristic of churches that cater to the poor because middle-class Baptists and Methodists avoid outward displays of emotionalism. As Baptist and Methodist churches have altered the content of their services, some of their members have turned to storefront churches and Holiness sects:

> . . . the popular Protestant denominations (Methodist and Baptist) do not generally meet the emotional, psychological, and economic needs of traditionalists and/or submerged socioeconomic groups; consequently there has been a striking attraction of some groups who are not adjusted to religious and social change to faiths which emphasize emotion and sometimes economic provision.[57]

A small minority of blacks are members of such predominantly white denominations as the Congregational, Episcopal, and Presbyterian churches. Such black membership is drawn from the middle and upper classes. Similarly, what Frazier calls "a small intellectual fringe among middle-class Negroes" has affiliated with the

Unitarian Church. He sees these affiliations on the part of blacks as attempts to enhance their professional and social status and to lose their racial identity.[58]

The Roman Catholic Church in America is predominantly a white church. However, it has never been as segregated in its services as Protestant churches are.[59] In many areas of the South the Roman Catholic Church is the only church that black people have traditionally attended with white worshipers. Because of its rigid hierarchical structure, the Catholic Church has an advantage over Protestant churches in that integration can be imposed from the top of the organization. Catholic schools and other facilities in the South were among the first to desegregate their facilities, although not without strong resistance from Catholic laypeople. Because of its racial attitudes regarding religious services, the Catholic Church has tripled its black membership in less than three decades.[60]

The typical urban, Protestant, black church attempts to serve its members as well as God. The 11 A.M. Sunday service is usually the main event of the day, although many of the churches conduct Sunday evening services as well. Sunday school is maintained for children, and a variety of other services, such as special rallies, women's day, and children's day are conducted during the week. There are numerous men's and women's organizations associated with the church. The church building may be used for a variety of functions, including meetings for community organizations, social events, concerts, and mass meetings. In many ways the black church building serves as a community center for social and civic activities.

Rural churches in the South and the many urban sects differ somewhat. The rural church remains more conservative and other worldly than its urban counterpart. It is more emotional in its services, and the members participate more freely. Frazier describes a typical rural service as follows:

> After the congregation has assembled, someone—usually a deacon or a prominent member—"raises a hymn," that is, begins singing. The noise dies down, and, as the singer's voice grows in volume, the congregation joins in the singing. The singing is followed by a prayer by a deacon, which is approved by "Amens" on the part of the congregation. Then follow more spontaneous singing and prayer. After this comes the sermon, which is characterized by much dramatization on the part of the minister. Members of the audience express their approvals by "Amens," groans, and such expressions as "Preach it," "Yes, Lord." As a minister reaches the climax, "shouting" or a form of ecstatic dancing begins. The contagion often spreads until most of the congregation is "shouting." As the "shouting" dies down, someone—very likely the minister, who has not lost control of the services—"raises a hymn." Afterward the minister turns to such practical matters as collection and announcements concerning future services.[61]

Rural black churches in the South are usually small, wooden structures. They are unpretentious and are frequently dilapidated. Ministers lack formal religious training, and in the 1930s a vast majority had completed no more formal education than grammar school.[62] Their sermons are usually otherworldly in their content, having no relevance to the day-to-day lives of their worshipers. Nevertheless, the rural church is perhaps the outstanding social institution among rural blacks. It serves as a means of escape from the harsh lives they lead. Furthermore, it is the medium through which the community maintains its social cohesion.

Storefront churches in cities do not differ significantly in their services from the rural church. Some of the cults to which many blacks have flocked seek to "purify" Christianity by requiring their members to reject "sinful" activities, such as drinking alcoholic beverages, dancing, playing cards, and swearing. Perhaps the best known of the Holiness sects are the Father Divine Peace Mission Movement and the Unified House of Prayer for All People, founded by Bishop Charles Emanuel Grace. Other cults have rejected Christianity and are linked to the non-Christian religions of the world. These churches include the Church of God (or Black Jews), the Moorish Science Temple of America, and, more recently, the Muslim Mission. These cults represent a radical departure from Christianity, and services are frequently conducted in languages other than English, such as Hebrew and Arabic.

The Church and Civil Rights

The Montgomery Bus Boycott, originating in 1955, signaled the beginning of modern mass direct action on the part of black people to improve their status in the United States.[63] The bus boycott was organized and led by the late Martin Luther King, Jr., a Baptist minister who had become the acknowledged leader of the movement for greater civil rights for America's blacks. It is unlikely that the success of this act of mass protest could have been achieved without the involvement of the black church. Since the Civil War the black church has been the most cohesive social institution in the black community. Therefore it was inevitable that the church would play a dominant role in any emerging movement for greater civil rights. Historically, the black church played an insignificant role in matters pertaining to civil rights, concentrating rather on otherworldly matters in adherence to the norm of the larger society—that the church should not involve itself in politics. Radical social action is not alien to black religion, however. Three of the most famous of the slave insurrections were led by black ministers: Gabriel Prosser, Nat Turner, and Denmark Vesey. But the discrepancy between Christian teachings and American social practices thrust the black church into the forefront of the black rebellion against segregation and discrimination.

Since the Montgomery Bus Boycott, the civil rights movement has changed strategy on occasion, but it has remained an essentially religious movement. Moreover, it has belatedly involved white religious leaders and laypeople as well as blacks. Initially the civil rights movement was strongly tied to such Christian precepts as love of one's adversary and nonviolent resistance. Response on the part of many white Americans, especially in the South, has led many black people to question the wisdom of these techniques. Although until his assassination in April 1968 Martin Luther King remained the undisputed leader of the black protest movement, his strategy had been questioned.[64] For example, during the summer of 1964, in Mississippi alone, white Christians bombed or burned 34 black churches. These churches had long been sanctuaries in which blacks could be immune from outside intrusion. These and hundreds of similar acts of violence, including the murder of ministers, have led black people to question the notion that nonviolence and love disarm one's adversary.

Civil rights protest meetings, voter registration drives, mass-action demonstrations, and "freedom schools" were held in churches, and black ministers continued to play a dominant role in civil rights activities. The role of the black church in the protest movement has accounted for much of the movement's early success in breaking down barriers of segregation in the South. The protest movement had its origins in religion.[65] Black ministers continue to occupy leadership positions in civil rights activities. Furthermore, because of its religious orientation, thousands of white religious leaders and laypeople were impelled to align themselves with the black protest movement.[66] Hundreds of white clergypeople were arrested in civil rights demonstrations, and during the civil rights march from Selma to Montgomery, Alabama, in March 1965, leaders of each of the major religious organizations were either present or represented, as a means of demonstrating their support. In recent years the leaders of each of the national organizations representing the three major religious groups in the United States—Protestants, Catholics, and Jews—have appealed to their followers to discontinue practices of segregation and discrimination in religious worship, education, employment, and housing and to adopt attitudes of love and brotherhood toward blacks.

For his civil rights leadership and accomplishments, Martin Luther King became an internationally known and respected personality, receiving the Nobel Prize for Peace in 1964. In the United States his birthday became a national holiday in 1985. One of his associates, the Reverend Jesse Jackson, became the first viable black presidential candidate, running for the Democratic nomination in 1984 and 1988. Jackson has since become an important figure in international affairs and is considered to be the most important black political leader in the United States.

Both the role of the black church in civil rights protest activities and the religiousness of black people have been noted. The question of the link between these two elements might be raised. That is, does religion serve as a deterrent or motivation for civil rights activities? In a nationwide survey of black people, an attempt was made to answer this question.[67] In general it was found that greater religious involvement was accompanied by diminished militancy in civil rights. Furthermore, blacks who were members of predominantly black denominations, such as Baptists and Methodists, were less militant about civil rights than those who were members of predominantly white denominations, such as Episcopalians, members of the United Church of Christ, Presbyterians, and Catholics. The members of the various religious sects and cults were the least militant. The conclusion: "Until such time as religion loosens its hold over these people or comes to embody to a greater extent the belief that man as well as God can bring about secular change, and focuses more on the here and now, religious involvement may be seen as an important factor working against the radicalization of the Negro public."[68] Nevertheless, the church has been the focal point of organizing for protest, and a small minority of militant ministers have been powerful catalysts without which the movement might never have achieved the success it has.

Since the ascendancy of black nationalist ideology beginning in the second half of the 1960s, black Christian religious leaders and laypeople have attempted to make Christianity serve the cause of black liberation through the empowerment of blacks, especially those in predominantly white churches. Within traditional Protestant denominations and Catholic churches, all-black caucuses and other organizations have developed to demand a greater degree of decision-making authority in these churches. In addition, several black clergymen have advocated what is generally called a black theology of liberation.[69] They maintain that if Christianity is to survive in the black community, it must align itself with the oppressed and concern itself more with the correction of present injustices than with otherworldly matters. Other religious leaders have built a theology based on the notion that Christ was black.[70] This position holds that the black church must be in the forefront of the movement for black liberation.

Black nationalist sentiment has made its impact on black religion. Although the vast majority of black churches no doubt continue to remain aloof from the movement for black liberation, focusing instead on otherworldly matters, increasing numbers of black theologians and rank-and-file members have embraced the thrust of black nationalism.

•   •   •

Three of the primary social institutions in the black community are the family, politics, and religion. Each of these institutions generally parallels its counterpart in the larger society, but each has its distinct elements. The differences result from a long history of oppression. There is some evidence that urbanization and improvements in standard of living are minimizing the differences, especially in family patterns and religious practices. The likelihood is, however, that because of the racist nature of American society, and because of increasing black consciousness, the distinctive aspects of the institutions will persist.

Politics is perhaps the institution in which the greatest changes have taken place in recent years. Armed with the vote, black people are turning to politics as a means of forcing the society to address itself to the needs of their communities.

SELECTED BIBLIOGRAPHY

AMAKER, NORMAN C. *Civil Rights and the Reagan Administration.* Washington, DC: The Urban Institute Press, 1988.

BERNARD, JESSIE. *Marriage and the Family among Negroes.* Englewood Cliffs, NJ: Prentice Hall, 1966.

BILLINGSLEY, ANDREW. *Black Families in White America.* Englewood Cliffs, NJ: Prentice Hall, 1968.

BLOOD, ROBERT A., JR., and DONALD M. WOLFE. *Husbands and Wives.* Glencoe, IL: Free Press, 1960.

BROGAN, D. W. *Politics in America.* New York: Harper & Brothers, 1954.

CLEAGE, ALBERT B., JR. *Black Christian Nationalism.* New York: William Morrow & Co., 1972.

————. *The Black Messiah.* New York: Sheed & Ward, 1969.

CONE, JAMES H. *A Black Theology of Liberation.* Philadelphia: J. B. Lippincott Co., 1970.

DU BOIS, W. E. B. *Black Reconstruction.* New York: Harcourt, Brace & Co., 1935.

FRAZIER, E. FRANKLIN. *Black Bourgeoise.* Glencoe, IL: Free Press, 1957.

————. *The Negro Church in America.* New York: Schocken Books, 1964.

————. *The Negro Family in the United States.* Chicago: University of Chicago Press, 1966.

HACKER, ANDREW. *Two Nations: Black and White, Separate, Hostile, Unequal.* New York: Charles Scribner's Sons, 1992.

HAMILTON, CHARLES V. *The Black Preacher in America.* New York: William Morrow & Co., 1972.

HILL, ROBERT. *The Strengths of Black Families.* New York: Emerson Hall Publishers, 1972.

HUNTER, FLOYD. *Community Power Structure.* Chapel Hill: University of North Carolina Press, 1953.

KING, MARTIN LUTHER, JR. *Stride Toward Freedom.* New York: Harper & Brothers, 1958.

LADNER, JOYCE. *Tomorrow's Tomorrow: The Black Woman.* New York: Doubleday & Co., 1971.

LECKY, ROBERT S., and H. E. WRIGHT, eds. *Black Manifesto: Religion, Racism, and Reparations.* New York: Sheed & Ward, 1969.

LEVY, MARK R., and MICHAEL S. KRAMER. *The Ethnic Factor.* New York: Simon & Schuster, 1972.

LEWISON, PAUL. *Race, Class, and Party.* New York: Oxford University Press, 1932.

MARX, GARY. *Protest and Prejudice.* New York: Harper & Row, 1969.

MATTHEWS, DONALD R., and JAMES W. PROTHRO. *Negroes in the New Southern Politics.* New York: Harcourt, Brace & World, 1966.

MAYS, BENJAMIN E., and JOSEPH W. NICHOLSON. *The Negro's Church.* New York: Institute of Social and Religious Research, 1933.

MYRDAL, GUNNAR. *An American Dilemma: The Negro Probiem and Modern Democracy.* New York: Harper & Brothers, 1944.

The Negro Handbook. Chicago: Johnson Publishing Co., 1966.

PETTIGREW, THOMAS F. *A Profile of the Negro American.* Princeton, NJ: D. Van Nostrand Co., 1964.

RAINWATER, LEE, and WILLIAM Y. LANCEY, eds. *The Moynihan Report and the Politics of Controversy.* Cambridge, MA: MIT Press, 1967.

STAPLES, ROBERT, ed. *The Black Family: Essays and Studies.* Belmont, CA: Wadsworth Publishing Co., 1971.

STONE, CHUCK. *Black Political Power in America.* New York: Bobbs-Merrill Co., 1968.

U.S. DEPARTMENT OF LABOR, OFFICE OF POLICY PLANNING AND RESEARCH. *The Negro Family: The Case for National Action.* Washington, DC, 1964.

WILLIE, CHARLES V., ed. *The Family Life of Black People.* Columbus, OH: Charles E. Merrill Co., 1970.

WILMORE, GAYRAUD S. *Black Religion and Black Radicalism.* New York: Doubleday & Co., 1972.

NOTES

1. See E. Franklin Frazier, *The Negro Family in the United States* (Chicago: University of Chicago Press, 1966), especially chap. 10.

2. See, e.g., ibid., chap. 5.

3. Jessie Bernard, *Marriage and the Family among Negroes* (Englewood Cliffs, NJ: Prentice Hall, 1966), pp. 10–13.

4. U.S. Bureau of the Census, Current Population Reports, Series P-20, *The Black Population in the United States: March 1990 and 1989* (Washington, DC, 1991).

5. U.S. Bureau of the Census, Current Population Reports, Series P-20, *Marital Status and Living Arrangements: March 1989* (Washington, DC, 1990), p. 4.

6. Ibid., p. 26.

7. U.S. Bureau of the Census, Current Population Reports, Series P-60, *Poverty in the United States: 1988 and 1989* (Washington, DC, 1991), p. 12.

8. Ibid., p. 146.

9. U.S. Bureau of the Census, *Statistical Abstract of the United States: 1991* (Washington, DC, 1991), p. 726.

10. U.S. Bureau of the Census, *1980 Census of Housing: General Housing Characteristics, United States Summary* (Washington, DC, 1983), tables 6, 7.

11. Andrew Hacker, *Two Nations: Black and White, Separate, Hostile, Unequal* (New York: Charles Scribner's Sons, 1992), p. 68.

12. See Elmer P. Martin and Joanne M. Martin, *The Extended Black Family* (Chicago: University of Chicago Press, 1978); and Carol B. Stack, *All Our Kin: Strategies for Survival in a Black Community* (New York: Harper & Row, 1974).

13. Hacker, *Two Nations,* p. 76.

14. Jason DeParle, "42% of Black Men Are In Capital's Court System," *New York Times,* April 18, 1992, p. 1.

15. Hacker, *Two Nations,* p. 188.

16. Michel Marriott, "A World Defined by Dread," *New York Times,* April 27, 1992, p. B1.

17. Jane Gross, "Collapse of Inner-City Families Creates America's New Orphans," *New York Times,* March 29, 1992, p. 1.

18. Ibid.

19. Peter Kerr, "Addiction's Hidden Toll: Poor Families in Turmoil," *New York Times,* June 23, 1988, p. A1.

20. See Russell Middleton and Snell Putney, "Dominance in Decisions in the Family: Race and Class Differences," *American Journal of Sociology* 65 (May 1960), 605–9. However, in a study of black and white families in the Detroit, Michigan, area and in southeastern Michigan, it was reported that whereas the majority of white families were egalitarian (54 percent), the largest percentage of black families were dominated by the wife. The husband was found to be dominant in 19 percent of the black families; the wife was dominant in 44 percent; and 38 percent were egalitarian. See Robert A. Blood, Jr., and Donald M. Wolfe, *Husbands and Wives* (Glencoe, IL: Free Press, 1960), pp. 34–36.

21. Allison Davis and Robert J. Havighurst, "Social Class and Color Differences in Child Rearing," *American Sociological Review* 11 (December 1946), 698–710.

22. See, e.g., Martha S. White, "Social Class, Child Rearing Practices, and Child Behavior," *American Sociological Review* 22 (December 1957), 704–12.

23. Zena S. Blau, "Exposure to Child-Rearing Experts: A Structural Interpretation," *American Journal of Sociology* 69 (May 1964), 596–608.

24. See, e.g., Andrew Billingsley, *Black Families in White America;* Hill, *Strengths of Black Families;* Ladner, *Tomorrow's Tomorrow;* Robert Staples, ed., *The Black Family: Essays and Studies* (Belmont, CA: Wadsworth, 1971); Charles V. Willie, ed., *The Family Life of Black People* (Columbus, OH: Merrill, 1970).

25. Hill, *Strengths of Black Families,* p. 4.

26. See Arthur Cosby, "Black–White Differences in Aspirations among Deep South High School Students," *Journal of Negro Education* 40 (Winter 1971), 17–21; Edward Harris, "Personal and Parental Influences in College Attendance," *Journal of Negro Education* 39 (Fall 1970), 305–13; Bernard Rosen, "Race, Ethnicity, and the Achievement Syndrome," *American Sociological Review* 24 (February 1959), 47–60.

27. Cited in Rayford W. Logan, *The Negro in the United States* (Princeton, NJ: Van Nostrand, 1957), p. 51.

28. These data are reported in *The Negro Handbook* (Chicago: Johnson, 1966), pp. 271–74.

29. W. E. B. Du Bois, *Black Reconstruction* (New York: Harcourt, Brace, 1935), p. 371.

30. See, e.g., Gunnar Myrdal, *An American Dilemma* (New York: Harper, 1944), pp. 479–86.

31. See D. W. Brogan, *Politics in America* (New York: Harper, 1954), pp. 116ff. See also Oscar Glantz, "The Negro Voter in Northern Industrial Cities," *Western Political Quarterly* 13 (December 1960), 999–1010.

32. For a review of these acts and rulings see Norman C. Amaker, *Civil Rights and the Reagan Administration* (Washington, DC: The Urban Institute Press, 1988).

33. Ibid.
34. See Paul Lewison, *Race, Class, and Party* (New York: Oxford University Press, 1932); Myrdal, *An American Dilemma,* pp. 485–86.
35. Floyd Hunter, *Community Power Structure* (Chapel Hill: University of North Carolina Press, 1953), chap. 5.
36. Ibid., p. 184.
37. E. Franklin Frazier, *Black Bourgeoise* (Glencoe, IL: Free Press, 1957), pp. 224–29.
38. See Donald R. Matthews and James W. Prothro, *Negroes and the New Southern Politics* (New York: Harcourt Brace, 1966).
39. U.S. Bureau of the Census, Current Population Reports, Series P–20, *Voting and Registration in the Election of November 1990* (Washington, DC, 1991), p. 4.
40. Ibid., pp. 19–25.
41. Ibid., p. 39.
42. Marshall Frady, "Profiles: Jesse Jackson," *The New Yorker* (February 3, 1992), pp. 36–37.
43. *Statistical Abstracts: 1991,* p. 266.
44. See Melville Herskovits, *The Myth of the Negro Past* (New York: Harper, 1941), especially chap. 7: "The Contemporary Scene: Africanisms in Religious Life."
45. E. Franklin Frazier, *The Negro Church in America* (New York: Schocken Books, 1964), p. 6.
46. Ibid., p. 8.
47. Myrdal, *American Dilemma,* p. 860.
48. Benjamin E. Mays and Joseph W. Nicholson, *The Negro's Church* (New York: Institute of Social and Religious Research, 1933), pp. 29–33.
49. Frazier, *Negro Church in America,* pp. 42–44.
50. Myrdal, *American Dilemma,* p. 861.
51. Frazier, *Negro Church in America,* pp. 55–57.
52. These data and those that follow are derived from Wardell J. Payne, ed., *Directory of African American Religious Bodies* (Washington, DC: Howard University, 1991), and *Statistical Abstracts,* 1991.
53. Myrdal, *American Dilemma,* p. 864.
54. St. Clair Drake and Horace Cayton, *Black Metropolis* (New York: Harcourt, Brace, 1945), pp. 412–16.
55. *Youth in the Ghetto* (New York: Harlem Youth Opportunities Unlimited, 1964), p. 111.
56. Myrdal, *American Dilemma,* pp. 866–67.
57. Ruby F. Johnston, *The Development of Negro Religion* (New York: Philosophical Library, 1954), pp. 129–30.
58. Frazier, *Negro Church in America,* pp. 76–81.
59. See Joseph H. Fichter, "American Religion and the Negro," in *Negro American,* eds. Parsons and Clark, pp. 401–22.
60. *The Negro Handbook* (Chicago, IL: Johnson Publishing Co., 1966), p. 307.
61. E. Franklin Frazier, *The Negro in the United States* (New York: Macmillan, 1957), p. 351.
62. Mays and Nicholson, *The Negro's Church,* pp. 238–41.
63. Martin Luther King, Jr., *Stride Toward Freedom* (New York: Harper, 1958).
64. See Kenneth Clark, "The Civil Rights Movement: Momentum and Organization," in *Negro Americans,* eds. Parsons and Clark, pp. 595–625.
65. Carleton L. Lee, "Religious Roots of the Negro Protest," in *Assuring Freedom to the Free,* ed. Arnold M. Rose (Detroit, Mich.: Wayne State University Press, 1964), pp. 45–71.
66. Fichter, "American Religion and the Negro," pp. 401–22.
67. Gary T. Marx, *Protest and Prejudice* (New York: Harper & Row, 1969), pp. 94–105.
68. Ibid., p. 105.
69. See James H. Cone, *A Black Theology of Liberation* (Philadelphia: Lippincott, 1970).
70. See Albert B. Cleage, Jr., *Black Christian Nationalism* (New York: Morrow, 1972).

CHAPTER SIX

The Health
of Black People

Freedom from disease and other ailments is a universal cultural value and has been throughout human history. To a large extent the well-being of a society can be measured by the health of its citizens, and the health status of any group is an important determinant of its status in the larger society. For black Americans, their low health status is mirrored by their generally low status in the society.

In the twentieth century the United States has achieved a high level of medical technology, but the benefits of this technology are not shared equally by all groups in the society. Whether or not citizens maintain adequate standards of health depends on economic and other social factors, not the least of which are ethnicity and race. Certain groups in the society share unequally in the availability of health care and other social rewards, and this has characterized black citizens historically. For example, it was not until the passage of the Civil Rights Act of 1964 that blacks in the South were permitted to receive medical care in hospitals and other facilities (public or private) on a nonsegregated basis. Throughout much of American history, it was not uncommon for black citizens to be routinely denied medical care, frequently resulting in preventable deaths.

The seriousness of the disparity in the health status of minority and white citizens was recognized in 1984 with the formation of the Secretary's Task Force on Black and Minority Health in the Department of Health and Human Services (HHS). In its 1985 report, the task force identified six health problem areas that account for more than 80 percent of excess deaths (those that would not have occurred had mortality rates for minorities been as low as for whites). The six identified areas were cancer; cardiovascular disease and stroke; chemical dependency; diabetes; homicide, suicide, and unintentional injuries; and infant mortality.[1] Acquired immune deficiency syndrome (AIDS) was later added to the list when it was discovered that minorities represent over 40 percent of people with AIDS in the United States. The Office of Minority Health (OMH) was created in 1985 to stimulate the development of programs in an effort to ensure the implementation of the task force's recommendations.

In January 1990 Congress enacted the Disadvantaged Minority Health Improvement Act of 1990. At that time Congress found that "the health status of individuals from disadvantaged backgrounds, including racial and ethnic minorities, in the United States is significantly lower than the health status of the general population of the United States," and that "minorities suffer disproportionately high rates of cancer, stroke, heart diseases, diabetes, substance abuse, acquired immune deficiency syndrome, and other diseases and disorders." Congress also found that the incidence of infant mortality among blacks and other minorities "is almost double that for the general population."[2] This act is an amendment to the Public Health Service Act and aims to improve the health of members of minority groups by increasing funding for the OMH, providing special services for occupants of public housing, and providing scholarships and student loans for minority group members.

There have been several studies of excess or preventable deaths (those preventable by medical intervention) among the black population. One study that attracted national attention found that because of excess mortality in the late 1970s and early 1980s "black men in Harlem are less likely to reach the age of 65 than men in Bangladesh," one of the poorest countries of the third world.[3] Furthermore, the death rate from all causes in Harlem was more than double that for whites in the country and 50 percent higher than that of the black population of the country. The overall cause of the discrepancy between mortality in Harlem and the rest of New York City and the nation is widespread poverty and lack of basic health care.

In a nationwide study of 8,806 adults, blacks had differentially higher mortality rates than whites, varying anywhere from 149 percent for persons between 35 and 44 years old to 97 percent for those between 45 and 55 years old.[4] While controlling for well-established risk factors such as cholesterol level, alcohol intake, diabetes, and smoking, it was concluded that low income accounts for at least 54 percent of the excess mortality for blacks.

Finally, the Bureau of the Census reports that the expectation of life at birth in 1995 was 74.1 for black females and 64.9 for black males. This compares with 79.6 for white females and 73.4 for white males.[5] Blacks in 1995 actually had lower death rates than whites. Whites had a death rate of 9.1 per 1,000 population, while blacks had a death rate of 8.6 per 1,000 population.[6] While the death rate gap between blacks and whites has closed somewhat in recent years, blacks still die at more than four times the rate of whites from heart disease, pneumonia, cancer, asthma, and tuberculosis. (More on the specific causes of deaths later.)

The Council on Ethical and Judicial Affairs of the American Medical Association issued a report in 1990 on black–white disparities in health care.[7] It noted that substantial differences between blacks and whites exist in the quality of health care in the United States. These differences were manifested not only in higher infant mortality rates and shorter life expectancies than whites, but also throughout the health care system. For example, black men under 45 years of age had a 45 percent higher rate of lung cancer and 10 times the likelihood of dying from hypertension than white men in the same age category. Although blacks have greater health care needs, they are less likely than whites to receive health care services. Even when differences in income and severity of disease are taken into account, studies show that surgery was recommended for whites more often than for blacks; and even among those for whom surgery was recommended, whites were more likely to have the surgery performed. Black patients with kidney disease were less likely than white patients to receive long-term dialysis or kidney transplants. Even black patients who received dialysis were less likely than similar white patients to receive kidney transplants.

Racial disparities exist in treatment decisions in internal medicine. In a large-scale study of patients hospitalized for pneumonia, blacks, regardless of income, were less likely than whites to receive medical services, especially intensive care.[8] In a study of hospital admissions from the emergency department, researchers found that blacks were more likely to be classified as ward patients and whites as private patients, even when ability to pay was comparable. Ward patients were less likely to be admitted to the hospital than private patients, even when clinical characteristics were similar.[9]

We now turn to acquired immune deficiency syndrome (AIDS), a disease that has reached epidemic proportions in the past decade and a half. Blacks have higher morbidity and mortality rates from AIDS in the United States than do whites.

ACQUIRED IMMUNE DEFICIENCY SYNDROME (AIDS)

What Is AIDS?

Acquired immune deficiency syndrome, commonly known by the acronym AIDS, was first reported in the United States in 1981. It is a disease caused by the human immunodeficiency virus (HIV), which is transmitted by blood, semen, and vaginal secretions of infected persons. AIDS weakens the body's immune system, leaving its victims susceptible to opportunistic infections that do not normally attack a healthy body.

Some of the most common diseases resulting from the HIV infection are *Pneumocystis carinii* pneumonia, a form of pneumonia that is the most prevalent infection in people with AIDS; cytomegalovirus, which can cause blindness and brain and colon infections; cryptococcal meningitis, which affects both the brain and the lungs; Kaposi's sarcoma, a form of cancer; and mycobacterium avium complex, an infection of the gastrointestinal tract.[10] It is one of these diseases that eventually kills the person who has AIDS.

The virus that causes AIDS has an incubation period (the time between initial transmission and the development of disease symptoms) of from 3 to 10 years or more.[11] When the symptoms develop, however, they invariably lead to full-blown AIDS and death. In the time since the disease has been diagnosed in the United States, it has become a public health problem of major proportions and it is spreading at a rapid rate.

The Demographic Context

The AIDS epidemic is worldwide, and some countries in Africa and Asia are especially hard hit. The World Health Organization of the United Nations reported at the end of 1998 that 30.6 million people were living with HIV/AIDS, and that by the year 2000, some 40 million people will be living with HIV. Furthermore, it reported that 16,000 people become infected with HIV every day. Of those infected with HIV worldwide, 1.1 million are children under the age of 15. And HIV-associated illnesses caused the deaths of approximately 2.3 million people during 1997, including 460,000 children. Since the epidemic is concentrated in the developing world, it is estimated that there are over 27 million people in the world today who do not know they are infected.[12]

Of the more than 30 million people infected with HIV/AIDS, 90 percent live in developing nations. Two-thirds of them live in the poorest countries of sub-Sahara Africa, especially countries like Zambia, Zimbabwe, and Malawi.[13]

Worldwide more than 40 percent of AIDS cases are among women; 9 million women are infected with HIV. And AIDS is the third leading cause of death among women aged 25 to 44. In the United States AIDS is now the leading cause of death for black women, and the fifth leading cause for white women. And in 1996 women accounted for 20 percent of newly reported AIDS cases.

The Public Health Service estimates that 2,000 babies are born yearly in the United States with HIV. As of December 1996, 7,629 American children under the age of 13 had been diagnosed with AIDS. Of these children 58 percent were black, 23 percent were Hispanic, and 18 percent were white. Approximately 90 percent of children living with AIDS were infected through perinatal (mother-to-child) transmission.[14]

On the national level, 641,086 AIDS cases were reported in the United States at the end of 1997 and 390,692 had died of AIDS. The CDC reports that at this time between 650,000 and 900,000 Americans were living with HIV, with one person infected every 13 minutes.[15]

Although blacks account for 13 percent of the U.S. population, they accounted for 57 percent of all new infections in 1997. The annual AIDS rate among black women is 16 times that of white women. The contrast between black men and white men is not so great, but the CDC reports that one out of 50 of the nation's black men is believed to be infected with HIV. Although there has been a drop in AIDS death rates since 1995, white deaths have dropped by almost 70 percent while black death rates have fallen only 58 percent.[16]

The incidence of AIDS differs sharply for sex and age categories in the United States in 1996. Males account for 80 percent of all cases. Adults and adolescents (over 13 years old) account for 98 percent of all AIDS cases. Pediatric cases (under 13 years old) account for only 2 percent of the total. (See Table 6-1.)

Although the rate of infection among women is increasing rapidly, AIDS affects males far more often than females; the rate of infection among men is six times as great. Studies show that the virus passes from men to women much more easily than from women to men.[17] It has been reported that the "transmission of HIV from females to males through sexual intercourse is rare." Although the majority of men acquired the disease through homosexual contact, women with AIDS were more likely to have been IV drug users or their sexual partners.

In recent years AIDS has been spreading more rapidly among heterosexuals than homosexuals. By the end of September 1991, 42 percent of all persons in New York State and Connecticut who had been diagnosed with AIDS contracted the disease through IV drug use; in New Jersey 55 percent had become infected in this manner. A minority of cases in those states resulted from homosexual and bisexual contact.[18]

These differentials result from the nature of the disease and how it is acquired. Up to 1996, more than 40 percent were diagnosed among men who reported having sex with other men. The transmission of the virus has not been reported among female homosexuals. A minority of cases resulted from heterosexual transmission, and these cases are increasing slowly. The differences between minority and white males can be attributed to the higher incidence of drug use among minorities, which includes sharing unsterilized needles, syringes, and other equipment. The disproportionately higher incidence among white males is a function of greater homosexual activity among them.

Only 7 percent of white males were exposed to the AIDS virus through IV drug use, while 36 percent of blacks and 39 percent of Hispanics with the disease were in this exposure category. Among white males, homosexual transmission accounted for four-fifths (80 percent) of all AIDS cases, while among black males it was 44 percent and among Hispanic males 46 percent. Since AIDS is a sexually transmitted disease, the rate among children is low except for children of infected mothers.

Black and Hispanic women account for nearly two-thirds (66 percent) of all females diagnosed with AIDS through September 1996. Indeed, black women accounted for more than one-half (52 percent) of all female AIDS cases. Although the proportion of all women with AIDS is increasing at a rapid rate, the increase is much greater for minority women than for white women. More than one-half (56 percent) of all black women who have contracted AIDS were exposed through IV drug use, compared with 42 percent of white women. For Hispanic women the rate is between that of blacks and whites (50 percent). White women are slightly less likely to have contracted the disease through heterosexual contact.

Because of the nature of the transmission of HIV, AIDS cases tend to be concentrated in young adults and middle-aged persons. For example, a plurality of both black and white men and women (46 percent for men and 43 percent for women) were between 30 and 39 years of age when first diagnosed with AIDS.

Since AIDS is primarily a sexually transmitted disease, the incidence among children, although increasing, remained small up through 1991, some 3,312 cases. However, pediatric AIDS is spreading most rapidly among minority children. Hundreds of children are born with HIV each year, most to mothers who were infected either by IV drug use or by sexual partners who were users. Of all pediatric AIDS cases up through 1991, 84 percent were infected in this manner, while 5 percent were infected through blood transfusions for hemophilia or other reasons.

TABLE 6-1 AIDS Cases Reported, by Patient Characteristic, 1981 to 1996

CHARACTERISTIC	1981–1996 TOTAL	1990	1992	1993	1994	1995	1996
Total	**562,549**	**41,595**	**45,789**	**102,287**	**77,268**	**71,150**	**66,886**
Age:							
Under 5 years old	5,743	585	610	673	750	556	485
5 to 12 years old	1,521	139	139	198	220	193	175
13 to 19 years old	2,633	173	148	561	399	386	381
20 to 29 years old	99,137	8,077	7,888	18,391	12,636	11,114	9,778
30 to 39 years old	255,260	18,815	20,615	46,509	35,006	31,925	29,990
40 to 49 years old	140,718	9,651	11,540	26,137	20,359	19,470	18,891
50 to 59 years old	41,761	2,926	3,405	7,284	5,848	5,586	5,321
Over 60 years old	15,776	1,229	1,444	2,534	2,049	1,920	1,865
Sex:							
Male	477,518	36,726	39,457	85,881	63,447	57,686	53,293
Female	85,031	4,869	6,332	16,406	13,821	13,464	13,593
Race/ethnic group:							
Non-Hispanic White	268,746	22,302	22,446	47,597	32,808	29,500	26,324
Non-Hispanic Black	203,025	13,205	16,052	38,025	30,972	29,195	28,764
Hispanic	84,443	5,672	6,766	15,443	12,577	11,569	10,865
Other/unknown	6,335	416	525	1,222	911	886	933
Transmission category:							
Males, 13 years and over	473,770	36,335	39,082	85,452	62,972	57,323	52,958
Men who have sex with men	284,410	23,843	24,482	49,651	35,296	30,857	26,937
Injecting drug use	99,698	6,956	8,040	20,077	15,145	13,250	11,491
Men who have sex with men and injecting drug use	35,825	2,793	3,144	7,116	4,328	3,648	2,874
Hemophilia/coagulation disorder	4,220	332	324	1,047	478	418	297
Heterosexual contact[1]	9,279	260	611	1,806	1,854	1,840	2,168
Heterosexual contact with injecting drug user	6,121	460	627	1,180	919	889	792
Transfusion[2]	4,435	452	347	606	384	347	275

Undetermined[3]	29,782	1,239	1,507	3,969	4,568	6,074	8,124
Females, 13 years and over	81,515	4,536	5,958	15,964	13,325	13,078	13,268
Injecting drug use	37,027	2,325	2,966	7,996	5,853	5,209	4,534
Hemophilia/coagulation disorder	170	15	10	32	27	23	16
Heterosexual contact[1]	16,539	503	963	3,289	3,381	3,434	3,401
Heterosexual contact with injecting drug user	13,916	1,037	1,320	2,774	2,014	1,873	1,744
Transfusion[2]	3,234	336	258	494	316	279	263
Undetermined[3]	10,629	320	441	1,379	1,734	2,260	3,310

[1]Includes persons who have had heterosexual contact with a person with human immunodeficiency virus (HIV) infection or at risk of HIV infection.

[2]Receipt of blood transfusion, blood components, or tissue

[3]Includes persons for whom risk information is incomplete because of death, refusal to be interviewed, or loss to follow-up), persons still under investigation, men reported only to have had heterosexual contact with prostitutes, and interviewed persons for whom no specific risk is identified.

Source: U.S. Centers for Disease Control and Prevention, Atlanta, GA, HIV/AIDS Surveillance Reports, semiannual.

Black and Hispanic children accounted for more than three-fourths (77.5 percent) of AIDS cases through 1991. For both groups the disease was contracted through infected mothers. More white children were infected through blood transfusions.

Although AIDS is found throughout the country, the rate is highest in urban areas, and minorities are more concentrated in those areas. For example, the AIDS rate (number of cases per 100,000 population) up through 1991 was highest in metropolitan areas with populations exceeding 500,000 (34.4), followed by a rate of about 10 in metropolitan areas with populations between 50,000 and 500,000, and about 5 in nonmetropolitan areas.

The average AIDS rate in the United States is 17 per 100,000 population, but there are several large cities with rates in excess of 50: San Francisco (129.1), Miami (91.4), New York City (80.4), Jersey City (72.7), Fort Lauderdale (67.4), and San Juan, Puerto Rico (65.7). More than one-half (55 percent) of all persons who had contracted AIDS by 1991 lived in cities in the populous states of New York, California, Florida, and Texas.

Deaths from AIDS

Since there is no cure for AIDS and no vaccine for the virus, the death rate is necessarily high. By the end of September 1997 the CDC reported that 379,258 Americans had died of AIDS. This represents 62 percent of all adult and adolescent AIDS cases ever diagnosed in the United States. About 20,000 are infected with the virus.[19]

According to 1990 data, some 90 percent of all AIDS-related deaths have occurred among males. The majority (59 percent) of these deaths have been among men who were infected through sex with other men (identified as either homosexuals or bisexuals) who were not IV drug users, while 28 percent were IV drug users. Among IV drug users who died, the vast majority were heterosexual men and

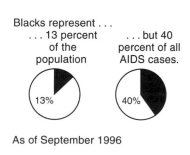
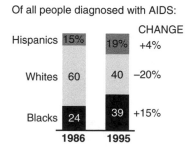

FIGURE 6-1   AIDS and Race: An Imbalance

AIDS is now the leading cause of death among blacks aged 25 to 44. Here is a look at how the disease is affecting blacks nationwide.

Source: Centers for Disease Control; *New York Times,* December 1, 1996, Sec. 13, p. 8.

women. Of all deaths, nearly three-fourths (73 percent) occurred among those between 25 and 44 years of age, almost equally divided between 25–34 year olds and 35–44 year olds.

From 1982 through 1988 deaths from AIDS increased among whites from 49 percent to 59 percent, while for minorities (black and Hispanics) the percentage of deaths declined from 51 percent to 41 percent. The percentages of deaths for both minority and white adult and adolescent males and females remained relatively constant during these years, but for minority children under 13, the increase was rapid.

Studies show that HIV progresses to AIDS more rapidly in infants and young children because their immune systems have not yet formed antibodies against common infectious organisms. Research indicates that 82 percent of infants with AIDS developed the disease before the age of three. With the increase in the spread of AIDS among heterosexuals and IV drug users, the rate of death from the disease for minority children will increase.

According to physicians at the CDC, AIDS cases are occurring nearly three times more frequently among black and Hispanic men than among white men and even more rapidly among women and children in these groups than among whites. Given the high death rate among AIDS victims, deaths from the disease among blacks and Hispanics are certain to accelerate.

Although there is no cure for the disease, medical science has made important progress against it. The virus that causes AIDS has been identified. Reliable tests have been developed to detect the presence of the virus in blood, thereby minimizing the risk of transmission through transfusions. Drugs have been developed to slow the growth of the virus in the body and delay the onset of symptoms. In addition, drugs that treat the complications of the disease have been developed. Finally, a set of rules has been established that, if rigidly followed, could end the spread of AIDS.

There is now some hope for people with HIV and AIDS. For example, the Centers for Disease Control and Prevention reported in 1998: "The rate at which people are being infected with HIV, the virus that causes AIDS, is relatively stable, but new drug treatments are slowing the increase in AIDS cases." It is reported by the Centers that "Data from some states that have been tracking both HIV infection and AIDS from 1994 to mid-1997 showed that the number of people with a new diagnosis of HIV infection each year was constant, at about 20,000 per year." In addition, the Centers reported that from 1995 to 1996, HIV diagnoses declined about 3 percent among men, to 10,395 from 10,762, but rose about 3 percent among women, to 4,253 from 4,126.[20]

In addition, "Diagnoses of HIV infection fell about 3 percent among blacks, to 8,300 from 8,569, and about 2 percent among whites, to 4,966 from 5,093. It rose 10 percent among Hispanic people, to 1,070 from 971."[21] However, there is an increase in infection for younger people. "Of the 7,200 people 13 to 24 years old whose HIV infections were reported from January 1994 to June 1997, 44 percent were female, 63 percent were black and 5 percent were Hispanic." Finally, the Centers reported that as of mid-1997, 612,078 AIDS cases had been reported to the Center and 379,258 people had died of AIDS.[22]

AIDS in Prisons

Studies of AIDS infection in the criminal justice system in the United States reveal that the disease and the virus that causes it are widespread among prison and jail inmates. The New York state prison system had 9,500 HIV positive inmates. That is the equivalent of 1 percent of all AIDS infected Americans in 1997.[23]

In a study of nearly 11,000 men and women entering 10 correctional systems in the United States from June 27, 1988, through March 14, 1989, it was reported that 471 persons, or 4.3 percent of those involved, tested positive for the virus that causes AIDS.[24] The mean age of infected persons was 29 years, and the infection rates were higher for women than for men (5.2 percent versus 2.3 percent), and higher for nonwhites (4.8 percent) than for whites (2.5 percent).

The New York City Correctional System provides further insight into AIDS infection among inmates. This system admitted over 12,000 inmates in 1989; about 90 percent were black and Hispanic. The vast majority (93 percent) of those admitted were men, two-thirds of whom were between 16 and 30 years old. After the intake process, inmates were sent to 20 different facilities, where the average daily census totals about 18,000.

For one week in 1989, all inmates entering the correctional system were surveyed.[25] Altogether 2,236 of them had their blood samples tested for HIV-1. Of that number 413 or 18.5 percent were HIV positive. The infection rate for women (26 percent) was significantly higher than for men (16 percent).

The rates for women were higher in every age and race/ethnic group. Rates for Hispanics and whites were higher than for blacks, and the rates increased with age (nearly one-third of those 35 and over tested positive). The highest rates were found for those who admitted having used heroin intravenously, and a higher proportion of women (21 percent) than men (13 percent) admitted intravenous heroin use. Among jail and prison inmates, then, AIDS is largely a heterosexual disease.

Social Factors and AIDS

There are several social factors associated with the spread of AIDS that account for the differentially high incidence of the disease among blacks and Hispanics. Poverty appears to be a major contributing factor to AIDS. Much of the high-risk behavior (IV drug use and unprotected sex) is characteristic of the poor, who frequently resort to such practices because of the stress brought on by economic conditions. In addition, poverty contributes to inadequate health care. Many low-income racial/ethnic minorities lack health insurance coverage. They tend to seek health care for acute symptoms and to have no regular sources of medical care. Because of late diagnosis and the expense of health care, the survival period for minority persons infected with HIV is shorter than for whites.

Some studies show that blacks and Hispanics know less about AIDS than whites, and that misconceptions are more common.[26] For example, many minority members have concluded, because of television reporting, that AIDS is a disease limited to white homosexual males. To some extent the lack of knowledge about the disease is associated with lower levels of general education.

Although homosexual/bisexual transmission has been significantly lower among minorities, IV drug use is much higher. Drug users often frequent communal settings (abandoned houses, public parks, vacant lots) where drugs are sold, and frequently sex is exchanged for drugs in such places, thereby enhancing the possibility of spreading the HIV virus.

Like so many other social problems, the AIDS epidemic is most destructive to those members of society who are most vulnerable because it is part of a pattern of poverty and social neglect.

AIDS and Other "Conspiracies"

There is a widespread belief among blacks that the virus that causes AIDS was created in the laboratory and that the disease was invented by racist conspirators to kill black people. This is but one of many conspiracy theories held by significant numbers of blacks (and others as well). Growing numbers of black people explain some of the problems confronting the black community in terms of racial conspiracy theories. For example, a *New York Times*/CBS-TV News poll of New Yorkers conducted in 1990 revealed that such theories are prevalent and that blacks and whites differ significantly on the extent to which these beliefs are held.[27]

When asked whether the AIDS virus was "deliberately created in a laboratory in order to infect black people," 10 percent of blacks said they believed it was true and another 19 percent said they believed it "might possibly be true." Altogether, then, nearly one-third (29 percent) did not reject the theory. For whites, only 5 percent did not reject the theory.

More than one-half (60 percent) of blacks, compared with 16 percent of whites, said they thought it was true or possibly true that "the government deliberately makes sure that drugs are easily available in poor black neighborhoods in order to harm black people." Finally, more than three-fourths (77 percent) of blacks, compared with one-third (34 percent) of whites, responded that they believed it was true or possibly true that "the government deliberately singles out and investigates black elected officials in order to discredit them in a way it doesn't do with white officials."

To some extent the sentiments expressed in these findings stem from the notorious 1932 Tuskegee Experiment in which the United States Public Health Service rounded up hundreds of poor black sharecroppers who were suffering from syphilis for an experiment in Tuskegee, Alabama. For 40 years these men were never told what had stricken them, while medical doctors simply observed the destructiveness of the disease, ranging from blindness to paralysis, dementia, and sudden death.[28]

Even after penicillin had proven to be effective in treating syphilis, these men were neither treated nor told about the medicine. They thought they were being treated for an illness, but they were subjects in one of history's most sinister human experiments. It is not surprising that black Americans are suspicious of a medical establishment that perpetrated such a deliberate act of racist victimization.

In 1991 a medical conference was held to discuss the ethical questions raised by the Tuskegee Experiment.[29] Because of the spread of AIDS and the advances in medical technology, especially in organ and tissue transplant surgery, medical personnel have been discussing the possibility of segregating by race such procedures as organ transplants and blood transfusions in order to achieve better matches between donors and recipients. With the AIDS epidemic raging throughout the country, concern has been heightened about such procedures, and about protecting patients from exploitation.

MAJOR CHRONIC DISEASES: MORIDITY AND MORTALITY

We now turn to four major chronic disease conditions in the United States: malignant neoplasms (cancer), diabetes, heart disease, and cerebrovascular disease (stroke). Blacks have significantly higher rates of morbidity and mortality than whites for some of these conditions.*

Cancer (Malignant Neoplasms)

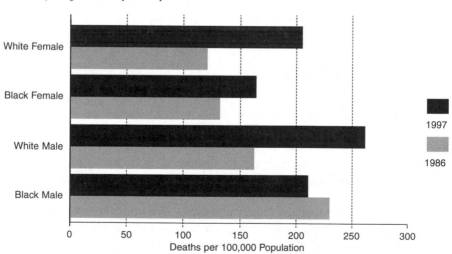

FIGURE 6-2   Deaths and Death Rates for Cancer—Rates per 100,000 Population in Specific Group

Source: Monthly Vital Statistics Report, Vol. 45, No. 11, September 2, 1997.

*According to the National Center for Health Statistics, blacks suffer disproportionately high rates of several other chronic conditions: anemia, asthma, epilepsy, gout, and mental retardation.

Diabetes Mellitus

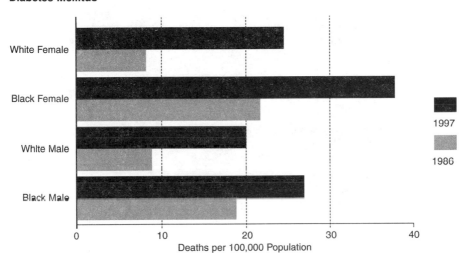

FIGURE 6-3 Deaths and Death Rates for Diabetes Mellitus—Rates per 100,000 Population in Specified Group

Source: *Monthly Vital Statistics Report*, Vol. 45, No. 11, September 2, 1997.

Diseases of the Heart

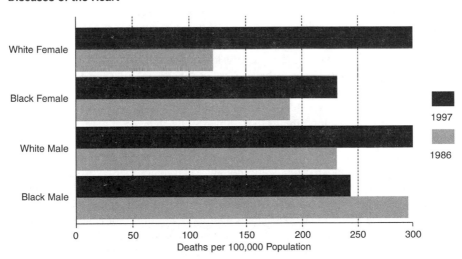

FIGURE 6-4 Deaths and Death Rates for Diseases of the Heart—Rates per 100,000 Population in Specified Group

Source: *Monthly Vital Statistics Report*, Vol. 45, No. 11, September 2, 1997.

Stroke (Cerebrovascular Disease)

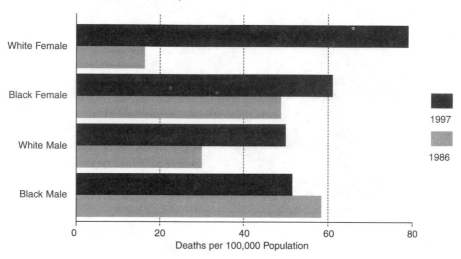

FIGURE 6-5   Deaths and Death Rates for Stroke—Rates per 100,000 Population in Specified Group

Source: Monthly Vital Statistics Report, Vol. 45, No. 11, September 2, 1997.

Cancer

Although cancer is a leading cause of death in the United States, it hits blacks and other minorities especially hard. However, in recent years the gap in death rates from cancer has closed, and in 1997 the rate of deaths from cancer per 100,000 population was slightly higher for white men (257.6) than for black men (209.5) (see Figure 6-2). Black women have generally lower rates (158.2) than white women (202.1). Black men are likely to have a greater incidence of cancer of the lung, esophagus, prostate, and stomach than white men. Black women experience higher rates of cancer of the cervix than white women.[30]

The major risk factors (things that influence the chances of getting cancer) are tobacco, nutrition, and occupation. It has been established that smoking is a major cause of lung cancer. Diet is involved in more than one-third of all cancer deaths. Salted, smoked, and pickled foods are thought to be major causes of stomach cancer, which is high among blacks. Fatty foods have been found to cause cancer, including prostate cancer, which is high among blacks. The occupations held by blacks have been found to be contributing factors to high rates of cancer, especially in industries in which they come into contact with toxic substances such as asbestos. Also, higher cancer rates have been found among workers in the steel, dye and rubber industries.[31]

Among women, cervical cancer is a major cause of death. Studies show that from 1980 through 1987, the mortality rate for black women was consistently more than twice the rate for white women.[32] The CDC reports that virtually all cervical cancer deaths are preventable by early detection and proper therapy and follow-up. For example, from 1947 through 1984, cervical cancer mortality declined by 70 percent because of the Pap smear test.[33] But blacks have been found to have lower levels of cancer knowledge than whites. They scored lower than whites on three cancer prevention knowledge measures: diet change, mammography utilization, and stool blood test utilization.[34]

Tobacco use, particularly cigarette smoking, is the major contributor to lung cancer, one of the major forms of the disease among males—one in which the rate for black males exceeds that for white males. Nationally, black men have had a mortality rate from lung cancer 23 percent greater than that of white men. Prostate cancer mortality and deaths from pancreatic cancer are much higher in black men than in white men. It is reported that the rate of smoking among black teenagers has risen sharply.

For all forms of cancer and for both females and males, the survival rate is considerably shorter for blacks than for whites. In studies between 1980 and 1985, 46 percent of all white males survived at least five years, compared with 33 percent of black males. During that period, the survival rate for women was greater than for men; for white women it was 46 percent, compared with 44 percent for black women.[35]

Diabetes

In the United States, deaths from diabetes declined between 1960 and 1986, but for black males the death rate increased modestly while it continued to decrease for white males. For women the rate for blacks continued to be nearly three times that for whites.

Diabetes is 33 percent more common among blacks than among whites, and black women are hardest hit. In 1997 the death rate from diabetes was 357.4 for black men and 329.5 for black women. White men had a rate of 153.0 and white women had a rate of 110.9. These rates are per 100,000 population (see Figure 6-3). Black women have 50 percent more diabetes than white women and face an even greater risk if they are obese. Furthermore, complications of diabetes are also more frequent in other chronic diseases among blacks; heart disease, kidney failure, and blindness are more common among blacks with diabetes than among whites with the disease.[36] Infants born to women with diabetes are much more likely to die near the time of birth than others, and the infant mortality rate for black children whose mothers suffer from diabetes is three times higher than for white babies born to mothers with the disease.[37]

The incidence of non–insulin-dependent diabetes is significantly higher in black than in white people, and black women have the highest incidence of all.[38] Several factors contribute to diabetes: obesity, genetic predisposition, and some environmental factors. Several studies show that there are important relationships between obesity, hypertension, and diabetes.[39] Since blacks have much higher rates of all three, it appears that these factors combine to increase their mortality rate.

Diabetes is likely to lead or at least contribute to other diseases, such as kidney disease, blindness, heart disease, and also to amputations. It is estimated that 10 percent of the 80,000 kidney deaths each year are attributable to diabetes, that 5,000 people lose their sight each year as a result of diabetes, and that diabetics are two to four times more likely to suffer heart disease than the general population. And 45 percent of amputations not caused by injury result from diabetes.[40]

Heart Disease

The mortality rate from diseases of the heart in the United States declined from 286 per 100,000 deaths in 1960 to 175 in 1986. However, black males and females continued to experience slightly lower rates than whites. For example, in 1997 the heart disease mortality rate for black women was 230.2 per 100,000 population, compared with 296.1 for white women. For black men it was 239.8 compared with 297.1 for white men (see Figure 6-4).

The major risk factors in heart disease are hypertension, cholesterol, tobacco, obesity, and socioeconomic status. The hypertension prevalence rate among blacks is considerably higher than that of whites. In addition, hypertension appears earlier among blacks and has a much more malignant course.[41]

Cholesterol levels among blacks and whites are about the same. Black men tend to have higher levels of some types of cholesterol, but they are not significant. More black men than white men smoke, but the pattern is reversed among women. Obesity is more common among blacks than whites, especially among black women.[42] And the risk of hypertension (and ultimately heart disease) as a consequence of being overweight has been estimated to be as high as 70 percent.

The racial disparities in heart disease morbidity and mortality are also partially explained by treatment disparities. In one study, although hospitalization rates were similar, whites were more likely than blacks in the same income categories to undergo coronary surgery.[43]

There is no evidence that any racial difference in the hereditary pattern of distribution of hypertension accounts for the racial difference in incidence. However, environmental factors play an important role. For example, there is a strong connection between socioeconomic status and hypertension caused by "a high degree of social stress and to coping styles, education, unemployment, and underemployment."[44] Low income leads to decreased access to health care, and studies estimate that low income accounts for more than one-half of the excess deaths among blacks in the United States.[45]

Stroke (Cardiovascular Disease)

The mortality rate from stroke in the United States showed a significant decline between 1960 and 1986, from 80 per 100,000 population to 31. However, for black men the death rate from stroke remained twice as high as for white men, and it was almost twice as high for black women as for white women (see Figure 6-5). In 1997 the mortality rate for stroke in black males was 50.5 per 100,000 population; for black females, it was 59.8. For white males it was 48.6 and for white females it was 75.4.

Among blacks there is also a marked excess of hypertension, a major contributor to stroke. The higher prevalence of hypertension among blacks accounts in large part for the higher stroke incidence and mortality rates.[46] Stroke has been found to be the single greatest contributor to black–white mortality differences.[47]

Other risk factors include diabetes, excessive alcohol intake, cigarette smoking, and sickle cell disease. The combination of these factors is especially lethal, and blacks have a disproportionately high rate for most of these risk factors. Furthermore, hypertension, the most important risk factor in stroke, places blacks at even greater risk "because of higher prevalence and earlier onset, greater severity, and poorer control."[48]

BLACK MEDICAL STUDENTS AND PHYSICIANS

Blacks are underrepresented in the health professions. In 1950 some 2.1 percent of all medical doctors in the United States were black, and by 1989 the figure had increased to 3.7 percent.[49] The number of black physicians has historically determined the extent and quality of medical care for the black population because minority health professionals have tended to practice in low-income areas and to serve minorities.[50]

In the 1960s, American medical schools experienced rapid growth and expansion in response to a new national priority to increase the number of physicians in the United States. Consequently, the number of medical schools increased from 86 in the 1960–1961 academic year to 103 in 1970–1971, and the entering class size increased from 8,298 to 11,348.[51] In the following decade the growth continued, leading to a total of 126 medical schools and an entering class of 17,204 students.

In the 1990–1991 academic year, there were 64,986 students enrolled in medical schools; of them 4,215, or 6.5 percent, were black (Table 6-2). Blacks accounted for more students than any minority group except for Asians and Pacific Islanders.

For students expected to graduate in the 1990–1991 academic year, blacks made up 5.9 percent, and 56 percent of that group were black women. Among beginning students, total students, and students expected to graduate, it was only among black students that females outnumbered males.

It should be noted that in the 1990–1991 academic year, three of the predominantly black schools—Howard University in Washington, DC; Meharry Medical School in Nashville, Tennessee; and Morehouse School of Medicine in Atlanta, Georgia—admitted 16 percent of all first-year black medical students, and six other schools (Wayne State University in Detroit, University of Illinois in Chicago, University of Medicine and Dentistry of New Jersey–New Jersey Medical School in Piscataway, State University of New York at Brooklyn, University of Michigan at Ann Arbor, and Case-Western Reserve University in Cleveland, Ohio) admitted an additional 16 percent. These nine schools enrolled one-third of all first-year black students.[52]

TABLE 6-2   Racial and Ethnic Background of Medical School Enrollees, 1990–1991[a]

	NUMBER (%)					
	MEN		WOMEN		TOTAL	
First Year Student Enrollment						
Whites	7,599	(45.2)	4,421	(26.3)	12,020	(71.5)
Asians and Pacific Islanders	1,552	(9.2)	974	(5.8)	2,526	(15.0)
Blacks	567	(3.4)	701	(4.2)	1,268	(7.6)
Hispanics	541	(3.2)	373	(2.1)	914	(5.3)
Other Minority	45	(0.3)	30	(0.2)	75	(0.5)
Total	10,304	(61.3)	6,499	(38.7)	16,803	(100)
Graduates						
Whites	7,929	(51.2)	4,177	(26.9)	12,106	(78.1)
Asians and Pacific Islanders	1,035	(6.7)	597	(3.8)	1,632	(10.5)
Blacks	401	(2.6)	510	(3.3)	911	(5.91
Hispanics	521	(3.3)	286	(1.8)	807	(5.1)
Other Minority	29	(0.2)	14	(0.1)	43	(0.3)
Total	9,915	(64.0)	5,584	(36.0)	15,499	(100)
Total Enrollment						
Whites	31,327	(48.2)	17,131	(26.4)	48,525	(74.6)
Asians and Pacific Islanders	5,313	(8.2)	3,212	(4.9)	8,525	(13.1)
Blacks	1,878	(2.9)	2,337	(3.6)	4,215	(6.5)
Hispanics	2,152	(3.3)	1,364	(2.0)	3,516	(5.3)
Other Minority	152	(0.2)	120	(0.2)	272	(0.4)
Total	40,822	(62.8)	24,164	(37.2)	64,986	(100)

[a]Hahnemann University in Philadelphia and the University of Texas at Galveston did not provide enrollment information; 1989–1990 data were used for these schools.

Source: Adapted from H.S. Jones, Sylvia I. Etzel, and B. Barzansky, "Educational Programs in US Medical Schools," *Journal of The American Medical Association,* August 21, 1991, p. 918.

In 1970 the Association of American Medical Colleges (AAMC) Task Force on Expanding Educational Opportunities in Medicine for Blacks and Other Minorities proposed a long-term strategy "to achieve equality of opportunity by relieving or eliminating inequitable barriers and constraints to access to the medical profession." The short-term goal of the AAMC was to increase the proportion of minority students in medical schools from 2.8 to 12 percent by 1975 or 1976.[53]

Specifically, the aims of these programs included increasing the number of minority physicians; bringing the ethnic and racial mix of medical school classes into balance with the general population; providing physicians to treat minority populations and the poor in general; eliminating ethnic/racial barriers within the medical profession; improving upward social mobility for minorities by providing access to a prestigious profession; changing the specialty mix of medicine to meet policy objectives; and rectifying perceived geographic maldistribution of physicians.[54]

After rapid gains in the 1970s, little progress has been made. The annual number of blacks matriculated reached a plateau of 1,000 in the late 1970s, declined in the early 1980s, and has recovered slightly since then. Virtually all the enrollment gains since the early 1970s were made by black women; the number of black men who matriculated in 1971 (626) has not been equaled since.[55] Between 1971 and 1985, the number of black men who enrolled in medical schools declined until 1985, when it was 486 or 30 percent below 1971.

The decline in enrollment in medical schools by black men has been attributed to several factors: declining numbers of applicants from all groups; declining popularity of undergraduate premed majors; declining numbers of blacks attending college; higher high school dropout rates for blacks, especially males; increasing poverty among blacks; and high indices of stress among black men.[56] This decline has been paralleled by an increase in black female enrollment. In addition to the factors previously cited for the decline in male enrollment, the increase in female enrollment no doubt reflects the removal of barriers that had traditionally discouraged women from the profession of medicine.

The College of Medicine at the University of Tennessee at Memphis (UT Memphis) provides a case study of the transformation of one school in order to increase black enrollment.[57] Changes in institutional philosophy and the development of several special programs were needed.

The first black medical school in the South was established in 1876 as the Medical Department of Central Tennessee College. This school ultimately became Meharry Medical College, a school that has graduated 40 percent of black physicians practicing in the United States. By the turn of the twentieth century, seven medical schools for blacks existed, one in Washington and the others in the South. Today only two of these schools—Howard and Meharry—survive.

After a long history of excluding blacks, UT Memphis College of Medicine began accepting black students in the early 1960s and graduated its first black physician in 1964. From that year through 1978, the college graduated 2,659 physicians, only 23 (0.86 percent) of them black. In 1979 a study was undertaken to identify the reasons for the low number of black students admitted each year and the high failure rate of those admitted.

Analysis of the admission data for the period 1974–1980 revealed that the pool of black applicants was small; that black applicants tended to have lower grade point averages than others; and that the college had offered acceptance to about two-fifths of all applicants but to only about one-fifth of black applicants. In other words, the college had admitted students who appeared to be at high risk of failure but did not provide the academic and social support necessary for a reasonable chance of success. Four programs were initiated to remedy these problems. A program to increase opportunities for black and other economically or educationally disadvantaged students began in 1982. It included a learning center to provide academic support, an intensive prematriculation program for students perceived to be at risk academically, and a summer enrichment program for disadvantaged undergraduate college students and high school seniors. Such summer programs had produced successful results in Georgia and Virginia.[58]

With these programs the percentage of black students having major academic difficulties dropped from 70 percent to less than 30 percent. However, since the programs focused on college level students, the black applicant pool had not increased to the extent expected. It was clear that this resulted from the paucity of black faculty in the College of Medicine, which meant that few role models existed to assist in attracting black students; also competition from other medical schools in the country to attract talented black students had increased. Therefore, a program was started to extend the minority enrichment programs back as far as the sophomore level in high school, and in 1987–1988 virtually all (97 percent) of the participants eligible to enter college did so.

A program to provide a more competitive financial aid package for black students in the state's public and private colleges of medicine and dentistry was introduced. This program increased the number of black students from 2 to 17 in two years.

By 1986 only 10 black faculty members were employed by the college. However, programs identifying and recruiting black faculty members doubled the number in two years, and by 1988 the college, with 20 black faculty members, ranked second among predominantly white southern medical schools for the number of black faculty. These efforts at the College of Medicine of UT Memphis demonstrate that if a concerted effort is made by a school to meet its social responsibility, progress can be made.

With the increasing opposition to all forms of affirmative action in the 1980s and 1990s, it should be noted that a major study of physicians who benefitted from affirmative action programs in the United States between July 1, 1974, and June 30, 1975, reported significant health care gains.[59] The study indicated that "In general, our results should be encouraging to the advocates of affirmative action." By 1975 many more minority members had received medical degrees than was the case earlier; medical schools admitted and graduated many students who would not have attended them if conventional criteria of admission had been used; minority students, more than others, tended to choose specialties that were more in accord with the health–work force policy of the federal government to increase the number of primary-care specialists; minority students pursued graduate medical education that made them better qualified than earlier general practitioners; and minority graduates treated more patients of their own ethnic/racial background than nonminority physicians, meaning that affirmative action programs have "substantially improved access to care among minority patients."

Minority physicians from affirmative action programs "served significantly larger proportions of Medicaid patients than did their nonminority counterparts." This means that these physicians treated more poor people than did others. Minority graduates, more than nonminority graduates, tended to have their practices in health–work force shortage areas; similarly, they tended to have a wider distribution of specialty areas.[60]

The report concluded that "the data on the class of 1975 provide strong testimony that [affirmative action] objectives are being served. Minorities were not merely admitted to medical schools in much larger numbers; they also graduated, took residency training, and entered practice in much larger numbers." In addition, "they entered primary-care specialties, chose to practice in federally designated health–manpower shortage areas, and cared for ethnic minority and poor patients in greater proportion than did their nonminority counterparts. Finally, our analysis found that affirmative action in medical education made good progress toward its multiple objectives."[61]

These findings are supported by those of a study of graduates from the Medical School of the University of California, San Diego. This study concluded that affirmative action graduates "see more patients daily and practice more often in rural and inner-city areas, providing medical care for ethnic minorities from lower socioeconomic strata."[62]

What happens when black medical students become medical practitioners? What are their practice patterns? One survey questioned graduates of 49 classes of the Howard University College of Medicine, including all living male graduates with known addresses in the classes of 1940, 1945, 1950, 1955, and 1960–1980, and all living female graduates with known addresses through the class of 1980.[63] Of the respondents, 77 percent were male, 83 percent were black, 14 percent were white, and 3 percent were from other minorities.

Black respondents in the survey tended to practice primary medical care. The specialty attracting the greatest percentage of black physicians was internal medicine, with 16.6 percent. This figure is similar to that of all physicians practicing in the United States in 1988 (16.2 percent).[64] More black physicians were in general/family medicine (13.6 percent) than in the American physician population at large (11.8 percent), and proportionately more than twice as many black physicians specialized in obstetrics-gynecology (14.0 percent) than in the general medical population (5.5 percent). Psychiatry attracted proportionately more black physicians (7.7 percent) than in the physician population at large (5.8 percent), and fewer blacks specialized in general surgery (5.6 percent) than all physicians in the country (6.5 percent). This pattern also held for orthopedic surgery, with 2.6 percent of blacks in this specialty, compared with 3.1 percent for all physicians in the country. And proportionately slightly fewer blacks practiced ophthalmology (2.1 percent) compared with all physicians in the country (2.7 percent).

Black physicians in the sample were significantly more likely to specialize in radiology (5.2 percent) than doctors in the general population (1.4 percent). For both anesthesiology and pathology, black physicians differed from practitioners in the larger society (3.3 percent versus 4.1 percent for anesthesiology and 0.8 percent versus 2.8 percent for pathology).

These data indicate that black physicians, more than those at large, are engaged in primary medical care, including family medicine, obstetrics-gynecology, and general internal medicine. These specialties are more in keeping with the medical needs of black people and the poor than those of physicians in the general population. At the same time black physicians are less likely to specialize in surgery and other more glamorous and higher-paying areas. It is worth noting that when asked for factors that influenced their medical specialties, more than one-half (57 percent) of black graduates of Howard University College of Medicine listed "the desire to serve a particular group of people."

When they were asked to characterize their patients, these black physicians reported that although most of their patients were black, they served others as well: 57 percent were black, 31 percent were white, and 12 percent were Hispanic and members of other minorities. In addition, they reported that most of their patients (30 percent) worked in urban areas, with 30 percent of those in the inner city. And black physicians reported that about one-third of their patients were poor. In general, black doctors provided medical care for substantial numbers of poor blacks in urban areas. This type of patient care is in accord with government policy of providing adequate health care for the minority and poor populations of the country.

HOMICIDE: A PUBLIC HEALTH PROBLEM

Homicide (murder) is the leading cause of death among black males between the ages of 15 and 24 in the United States. This amazing reality says much about the character of American society as the twentieth century draws to a close. Although homicide is not a peculiarly American phenomenon, it has reached its zenith in the United States, compared with other industrialized countries.

A survey of homicide rates in 21 industrialized countries in the late 1980s revealed that the rate (number of homicide deaths per 100,000 population) among males 15 through 24 years of age in the United States (21.9) was 4.4 times higher than the next highest rate, in Scotland (5.0). When comparisons are made for the total population, the picture is the same: "The U.S. homicide rate (8.7 per 100,000) was still 2.6 times higher than the next highest rate in Finland (3.3 per 100,000), and four to eight times higher than the rates in most other countries."[65] Most industrialized countries have rates between 1 and 3 per 100,000. Furthermore, the rate for black males in the 15 through 24 age category is 7 times that for white males in that age category (85.6 versus 11.2).

It is because of this disparity that the U. S. Department of Health and Human Services classified homicide as a public health problem. In 1985 the Department released a report from its Task Force on Black and Minority Health that found approximately 59,000 excess deaths (fatalities that would not have occurred if the mortality rates for minorities had been the same as for whites) among minorities between 1979 and 1981.[66] The major cause of these excess deaths among young black males is the high homicide rate. In addition, "death from homicide resulted in loss of life at a younger age than death from heart disease, malignant neoplasms (cancer), or cerebrovascular diseases (stroke)."[67]

Homicides are divided into two basic types: primary (those that occur between family, friends, and acquaintances and are usually crimes of rage or passion) and secondary (those that involve strangers and usually occur during a felony). In the United States the vast majority (anywhere from 65 to 85 percent in any year) of homicides occur among family, friends, and acquaintances. It is because of this pattern, in part, that homicide is considered to be more of a public health issue than one of law enforcement.

Race and Homicide

Inasmuch as homicides usually occur among friends, families, and acquaintances, it follows that in the United States the victims and perpetrators will often be of the same race. For example, the Federal Bureau of Investigation reports that 93 percent of black murder victims were slain by other blacks, and 86 percent of white homicide victims were killed by white persons.[68] Similarly, another study found that 90 percent of black male murder victims were killed by black persons, and 87 percent of white murder victims were killed by white persons.[69] A study of homicides in the United States between 1976 and 1979 found that 80 percent of murder deaths resulted from primary homicides.[70]

The high rate of homicide for young black males varied by state, the highest being recorded in Michigan (231.6), California (155.3), and New York (135.5). The lowest rates were recorded in states in the South: North Carolina (34.2), Kentucky (34.8), and Mississippi (35.1).[71]

Although the vast majority of homicide victims are male, black females died from homicide in 1986 at a rate of 11.8 per 100,000 or three times that for white females.[72] Furthermore, 40 percent of children under three who die are black, and 24 percent of all child homicide victims are black.[73]

Homicide and Firearms

The high homicide rate in the United States is, to a large extent, a result of the widespread availability of firearms, especially handguns. Americans have a long-standing love affair with the gun.[74] In the 1980s there were 200 million civilian-owned guns in the United States, including some 60 million handguns. This adds up to more than 3 guns per family in 1985.

It is the Second Amendment to the Constitution that Americans interpret as giving them the right to be armed: *A well-regulated militia being necessary to the security of a free state, the right of the people to keep and bear arms shall not be infringed.* The Supreme Court ruled in 1939 that the Second Amendment applies to the maintenance of a militia, not to an individual's right to keep and bear arms.[75] Although the Court has not reconsidered its 1939 ruling and federal courts have adhered to it, the rich and powerful gun lobby and gun-loving citizens continue to ignore the first clause in the amendment.

The consequence is that Americans are the most heavily armed people in the industrialized world and continue to resort to the use of firearms in order to resolve domestic and international disputes. No effective gun control legislation has ever been seriously considered. Yet the relationship between homicide and the prevalence of firearms is a recognized one. In 1987, for example, when 17,859 people were murdered in the country, three-fifths (59.1 percent) were killed by firearms, and of these about three-fourths (74 percent) were killed by handguns.[76] For males between 15 and 24 years of age, 3,187, or 75 percent, of the 4,223 homicide deaths were caused by firearms in 1987.

The National Center for Health Statistics reported that nearly one-half (48 percent) of blacks between 15 and 19 years of age who died in 1988 were killed by guns. The figure for white males in that age group was 18 percent.[77] Furthermore, gun-related deaths among adolescents of all ages rose more than 40 percent between 1984 and 1988, while for black teenagers the increase was more than 100 percent.

The availability of firearms is directly related to the high rate of homicide in the United States.[78] A comparative study of Vancouver, Canada, and Seattle, Washington, sheds light on the role of handguns in homicide.[79] Although the two cities were demographically similar between 1980 and 1986, Seattle had a homicide rate nearly five times that of Vancouver. Vancouver's more stringent laws made handgun acquisition more difficult. Therefore, handguns were more easily acquired in Seattle. While other weapons of killing were as available in Vancouver as in Seattle, it appears that access to firearms is associated with the higher homicide rate.

Explaining Homicide

Many theories attempt to explain the high homicide rate in the United States. Compared with other industrialized countries, American society is an especially violent one, and many elements in the culture support the use of force as a means of resolving conflict.[80] Like many other social problems, homicide appears to stem from conditions in the social structure, especially widespread poverty and unequal access to the social rewards. Homicide is most prevalent among adolescents and young adult males. One study comparing homicidal adolescents with nonviolent delinquents who were matched by age, race, sex, socioeconomic status, and educational achievement found that adolescents who kill shared these characteristics: family milieus of violence, gang participation, alcohol abuse, and educational difficulties.[81]

Other factors contributing to the high homicide rate in the United States include substance abuse, broken families, unemployment, and the culture of violence in the community.[82] The factors contributing to homicide in general are exaggerated in the case of blacks and other minorities.

Blacks are overrepresented in poverty areas of inner cities where homicide is most prevalent. They are vastly overrepresented among the poor; consequently, they, more than whites, share the conditions related to poverty—alcohol and other forms of drug abuse, unemployment, low educational achievement, broken families. When blacks and whites share comparable or similar socioeconomic status positions, differences in homicide rates decrease substantially.[83]

•   •   •

Throughout much of American history, black people have been denied equal access to health care. Although their health status has improved in recent years, they continue to be overrepresented in both morbidity and mortality rates for the major chronic diseases. This is especially true for AIDS, a fatal disease. In this case, the proportion of blacks with the disease and the virus that causes it is more than twice that of the general population. For some diseases, the mortality and morbidity rates for blacks and other minority populations resemble (and in some cases exceed) those of the developing nations of the third world.

According to research findings, special admissions programs for black and other minority students have demonstrated the value of affirmative action. Because of affirmative action, minority students enrolled in and graduated from medical schools in larger numbers than ever before, specialized in general practice and primary care specialties more often than other students, and ultimately practiced more often in low-income areas. In short, affirmative action in medical education has been a success.

Black physicians in general, more than their white counterparts, are likely to select general practice and primary care specialties. They are considerably more likely to locate their practices in low-income areas, thereby largely serving the patient population most in need of health care: minorities and the poor.

Violence in general, and homicide in particular, is one of the most critical problems facing society. The proliferation of guns (especially handguns) is such that American society has a homicide rate several times that of any country in the industrialized world. Metal detectors have been installed in public school buildings throughout the country in response to homicides in schools. Homicide is the major cause of death for young black males, a reflection of the society in exaggerated form.

SELECTED BIBLIOGRAPHY

ALTMAN, MATTHEW. *AIDS in the Mind of America*. New York: Doubleday Anchor, 1986.

ANDERSON, JERVIS. *Guns in American Life*. New York: Random House, 1984.

DEPARTMENT OF HEALTH AND HUMAN SERVICES. *Report of the Secretary's Task Force on Black and Minority Health*. Washington, DC, 1985.

FARLEY, REYNOLDS, and WALTER, ALLEN. *The Color Line and the Quality of American Life*. New York: Russell Sage Foundation, 1987.

FETTNER, ANN, and WILLIAM CHECK. *The Truth About AIDS: Evolution of an Epidemic*. New York: Holt, Rinehart and Winston, 1984.

GRAUBARD, STEPHEN, ed. *Living with AIDS*. Cambridge, MA: MIT Press, 1990.

HAWKINS, DARNELL, ed. *Homicide Among Black Americans*. Latham, MD: University Press of America, 1986.

LIEBMAN-SMITH, RICHARD. *The Question of AIDS*. New York: New York Academy of Sciences, 1986.

NICHOLS, EVE K. *Mobilizing Against AIDS*. Cambridge, MA: Harvard University Press, 1986.

U.S. PUBLIC HEALTH SERVICE. *Health Status of the Disadvantaged: Chartbook 1990*. Washington, DC, 1990.

U.S. PUBLIC HEALTH SERVICE. *The 1990 Health Objectives for the Nation: A Midcourse Review*. Washington, DC, 1986.

NOTES

1. Department of Health and Human Services, *Report of the Secretary's Task Force on Black and Minority Health* (Washington, DC, 1985).
2. P.L. 101-527, H. R. 5702, January 23, 1990.

3. Colin McCord and Harold Freeman, "Excess Mortality in Harlem," *New England Journal of Medicine,* 322 (1990), 173–77.

4. Mac W. Otten et al., "The Effect of Known Risk Factors on the Excess Mortality of Black Adults in the United States," *Journal of the American Medical Association* 263 (February 9, 1990), 845–50.

5. U.S. Bureau of the Census, *Statistical Abstract of the United States: 1997* (Washington, DC, 1997).

6. Ibid., p. 90.

7. Eugene Schwartz et al., "Black/White Comparisons of Deaths Preventable by Medical Intervention: United States and the District of Columbia," *International Journal of Epidemiology* 19 (1990), 591–97.

8. Council on Ethical and Judicial Affairs, American Medical Association, "Black/White Disparities in Health Care," *Journal of the American Medical Association* 263 (November 17, 1990), 2344–46.

9. J. Yergan et al., "Relationship Between Patient Race and the Integrity of Hospital Services," *Medical Care* 8 (1970), 309–23.

10. George F. Lemp et al., "Projections of AIDS Morbidity and Mortality," *Journal of the American Medical Association* 263 (March 16, 1990), 1497–1501.

11. Edward C. Klatt, "Diagnostic Findings in Patients with Acquired Immune Deficiency Syndrome (AIDS)," *Journal of Acquired Immune Deficiency Syndrome* 1 (1988), 459–65.

12. These data are from the November 1998 issue of the *Gay Men's Health Crisis Newsletter HIV/AIDS Facts.* This organization collects its data on HIV/AIDS from the World Health Organization and from the Centers for Disease Control.

13. Carlos Arbodeda, "A World Apart," *The Volunteer,* July–September 1998, p. 6. *The Volunteer* is a newsletter of the Gay Men's Health Crisis.

14. *Gay Men's Health Crisis Newsletter HIV/AIDS, op. cit.*

15. Ibid.

16. David France, "Challenging the Conventional Stance on AIDS," *The New York Times,* Sec. F, p. 6, December 22, 1998.

17. See, for example, Virginia Anderson, "Understanding HIV Infection and Its Medical Impact on Children and Youths," in *Courage to Care, Responding to the AIDS Crisis of Children With AIDS* (Washington, DC: Child Welfare League of America, 1990); Stephanie Brodine et al., "HTLV-1 Among U.S. Marines Stationed in a Hyperendemic Area: Evidence for Female to Male Transmission," *Journal of Acquired Immune Deficiency Syndrome* 5 (1992), 158–62.

18. "Pulse," *New York Times,* December 9, 1991, p. B1; see also Aran Ron and David Rogers, "AIDS in New York City: The Role of Intravenous Drug Users," *Bulletin of the New York Academy of Medicine* 65 (September 1989), 787–800.

19. "HIV Infection Rate Steady, but Rate of AIDS Has Slowed," *The New York Times,* April 25, 1998, p. A9.

20. Ibid.

21. Ibid.

22. Ibid.

23. Matthew Purdy, "As AIDS Increases Behind Bars, Costs Dim Promise of New Drugs," *The New York Times,* May 26, 1997, p. A1.

24. David Valhov et al., "Prevalence of Antibody to HIV-1 Among Entrants to U.S. Correctional Facilities," *Journal of the American Medical Association* 265 (March 6, 1991), 1129–32.

25. Isaac Weisfuse et al., "HIV-1 Infection Among New York City Inmates," *AIDS* 5 (1991), 1133–38.

26. Centers for Disease Control, "HIV-Related Beliefs, Knowledge and Behaviors Among High School Students," *Mortality and Morbidity Weekly Report* 37 (1988), 717; Freya Sonnenstein et al., "Sexual Activity, Condom Use and AIDS Awareness Among Adolescent Males," *Family Planning Perspectives* 21 (1989), 152–58.

27. Jason DeParle, "Talk of Government Being Out to Get Blacks Falls on More Attentive Ears," *New York Times,* October 29, 1990, p. B17.

28. James Jones, *Bad Blood* (New York: The Free Press, 1981).

29. Isabel Wilkerson, "Medical Experiment Still Haunts Blacks," *New York Times,* June 3, 1991, p. A12.

30. National Center for Health Statistics, *Health United States*, Hyattsville, MD, 1998.

31. American Cancer Society, *Cancer Facts and Figures* (New York, 1988).

32. U.S. Public Health Service, *Health Status of the Disadvantaged*, p. 29.

33. *Journal of the American Medical Association* 263 (June 13, 1990), 3001.

34. Centers for Disease Control, "Cervical Cancer Control—Rhode Island," *Morbidity and Mortality Weekly Report* 38 (1989), 659–62.

35. Christopher Jepson et al., "Black–White Differences in Cancer Prevention Knowledge and Behavior," *American Journal of Public Health* 81 (1991), 501–4.

36. Ivor Livingston, ed., *Handbook of Black American Health* (Westport, CT: Greenwood Press, 1994).

37. U.S. Public Health Service, Office of Minority Health, *Closing the Gap: Diabetes and Minorities* (Washington, DC, 1988).

38. Janice G. Douglas, "Hypertension and Diabetes in Blacks," *Diabetes Care* 13 (1990), 1191–95.

39. P. Brechtold et al., "Epidemiology of Obesity and Hypertension," *International Journal of Obesity* 5 (1981), 1–7; E. Sims, "Mechanisms of Hypertension in the Syndromes of Obesity," *International Journal of Obesity* 5 (1981), 9–18.

40. U.S. Public Health Service, *Closing the Gap: Diabetes and Minorities*, p. 2.

41. Elijah Saunders, "Hypertension in African-Americans," *Circulation* 83 (1991), 1465–67; Daniel Savage, "Hypertensive Heart Disease in African-Americans," *Circulation* 83 (1991), 1472–74.

42. D. A. Dawson, "Ethnic Differences in Female Overweight," *American Journal of Public Health* 78 (1988), 1326–29; M. G. Kovar et al., "The Scope of Diabetes in the United States Population," *American Journal of Public Health* 77 (1987), 1549–50; S. Kumanyika, "Obesity in Black Women," *Epidemiological Review* 9 (1987), 31–50.

43. Council on Ethical and Judicial Affairs, "Black/White Disparities," pp. 2344–45.

44. Saunders, "Hypertension in African-Americans," p. 1466.

45. Otten et al., "Effect of Known Risk Factors," p. 850.

46. M. L. Dyken et al., "Risk Factors in Stroke," *Stroke* 15 (1984), 1105–11; Otten et al., "Effect of Known Risk Factors," pp. 485–50.

47. Ibid.

48. Louis Caplan, "Strokes in African-Americans," *Circulation* 83 (1991), 1469–71.

49. U.S. Bureau of the Census, *Statistical Abstract of the United States: 1991* (Washington, DC, 1991), p. 103.

50. David Janes and Robin Williams, eds., *A Common Destiny: Blacks and American Society* (Washington, DC: National Academy Press, 1989), p. 436; Davis Johnson et al., "A Second Survey of Graduates of a Traditionally Black College of Medicine," *Academic Medicine* 64 (1989), 87–94; Donna Jones, "Beating the Odds: Minorities in Medicine," *Texas Medicine* 87 (1991), 38–46; Stephen Keith et al., "Effects of Affirmative Action in Medical Schools: A Study of the Class of 1975," *New England Journal of Medicine* 313 (1985), 1519–25; Timothy Ready and Herbert Nickens, "Black Men in the Medical Pipeline: Past, Present, and Future," *Academic Medicine* 66 (1991), 181–97.

51. Harry S. Jones et al., "Educational Programs in U.S. Medical Schools," *Journal of the American Medical Association* 266 (August 21, 1991), 913–20.

52. Ibid, p. 917.

53. Keith et al., "Effects of Affirmative Action," p. 1519.

54. Ibid., p. 1523.

55. Ready and Nickens, "Black Men in the Medical Pipeline," p. 181.

56. Ibid., p. 182.

57. Robert Taylor et al., "Recruiting Black Medical Students: A Decade of Change," *Academic Medicine* 65 (1990), 279–88.

58. Kathleen Lynch and Moses Woode, "The Relationship of Minority Students' MCAT Scores and Grade Point Averages to Their Acceptance into Medical School," *Academic Medicine* 65 (1990), 480–82; Vera B. Thurmond and Antonio Mott, "Minority Students' Career Choices in Education Five Years After They Completed a Summer Enrichment Program," *Academic Medicine* 65 (1990), 478–79.

59. Keith et al., "Effects of Affirmative Action," pp. 1523–24.
60. Ibid., p. 1524.
61. Ibid.
62. Nolan E. Penn et al., "Affirmative Action at Work: A Study of Graduates of the University of California, San Diego Medical School," *American Journal of Public Health* 76 (1986), 1144.
63. Johnson et al., "Second Survey of Graduates," pp. 87–94.
64. U.S. Bureau of the Census, *Statistical Abstract,* 1991, p. 103.
65. Lois Fingerhut and Joel Kleinman, "International and Interstate Comparison of Homicides Among Young Males," *Journal of the American Medical Association* 263 (1990), 3292–95.
66. *Secretary's Task Force on Black and Minority Health,* 1985.
67. Ezra Griffin and Carl Bell, "Recent Trends in Suicide and Homicide Among Blacks," *Journal of the American Medical Association* 262 (1989), 2265–69.
68. U.S. Federal Bureau of Investigation, *Crime in the United States: Uniform Crime Reports 1990* (Washington, DC: 1991), p. 11.
69. Fingerhut and Kleinman, "International and Interstate Comparison," p. 3293.
70. Evan Stark, "Rethinking Homicide: Violence, Race, and the Politics of Gender," *International Journal of Health Services* 20 (1990), 3–26.
71. Fingerhut and Kleinman, "International and Interstate Comparison," p. 3294.
72. Griffin and Bell, "Recent Trends," p. 72.
73. Stark, "Rethinking Homicide," p. 17.
74. See, for example, Jervis Anderson., *Guns in American Life* (New York: Random House, 1984).
75. Ibid., p. 108.
76. U.S. Federal Bureau of Investigation, *Crime in the United States,* p. 10.
77. "Guns Take Ever-Higher Toll Among Young Blacks." *New York Times,* March 17, 1991, p. 31.
78. David Lester, "Firearm Availability and the Incidence of Suicide and Homicide," *Acta Psychiatrica Belgica* 88 (1988), 387–93; David Lester, "Relationship Between Firearm Availability and the Incidence of Primary and Secondary Murder," *Psychological Reports* 67 (1990), 490.
79. J. H. Sloan et al., "Handgun Regulations, Crime, Assaults, and Homicide, A Tale of Two Cities," *New England Journal of Medicine* 319 (1988), 1256–62.
80. Alphonso Pinkney, *The American Way of Violence* (New York: Random House, 1972).
81. Kenneth Busch et al., "Adolescents Who Kill," *Journal of Clinical Psychology* 46 (1990), 472–85.
82. Mark Mitchell and Stacey Daniels, "Black-on-Black Homicide: Kansas City's Response," *Public Health Reports* 104 (1989), 605–08; Stark, "Rethinking Homicide," p. 19.
83. Centers for Disease Control, *The Epidemiology of Homicide in the City of Los Angeles, 1970–1979* (Atlanta, GA, 1981).

CHAPTER SEVEN

Chronic Social Problems

Any discussion of social problems among black Americans must take into account the role of racism in American life and the persistence of inequality generated by racism. Individuals, social agencies, and social institutions responsible for the enforcement of social norms operate within a long-established framework that precludes equality of treatment for black people. And efforts to move toward equality of opportunity are strongly resisted by those who benefit from the current social arrangements.

The social structure forces people to engage in nonconforming as well as conforming behavior. Most of the social problems affecting minorities in the United States result from their low status in the society, especially the widespread poverty that accompanies this status. When individuals share a comparable socioeconomic status, they are remarkably similar in behavior (with some cultural and subcultural variations). Social problems, then, stem largely from the social structure.

This chapter focuses on three social problems that black Americans share with millions of others, often in exaggerated form and degree. These problems are homelessness, adolescent pregnancy, and drug abuse. As the twentieth century comes to a close, each of these phenomena plagues the black community to a disproportionate degree.

HOMELESSNESS

Homelessness as a social problem is not a new development in the United States, but prior to the depression of the 1930s, it affected relatively few persons. During the depression, the pervasiveness of the problem led to the first federal programs to assist the homeless, including soup kitchens and public housing. After World War II the government proclaimed a decent home and a suitable living environment for every American family as a national goal, and the National Housing Act of 1949 was passed as a means of implementing this objective. Ultimately federal aid and improved economic conditions served to end mass homelessness for nearly 30 years.[1]

In the 1970s several economic developments and public policy decisions triggered an increase in homelessness that accelerated in the 1980s and has reached massive proportions. Those individuals and groups in the society most likely to suffer as a result of those policies—the elderly, women, children, minorities, immigrants, veterans, the disabled, and the mentally ill—became homeless in disproportionately large numbers.

Perhaps the single greatest impetus to the present crisis in homelessness is the lack of affordable housing. That is, the demand for affordable housing has vastly exceeded the supply. Funds for new low-income public housing were reduced by 75 percent between 1981 and 1988.[2]

During the 1980s, with the ascent of political conservatism in the United States, funding for programs that might have ameliorated the problem of homelessness was eliminated or drastically reduced. The response of government officials has been to ignore the homeless, to denigrate them, to blame them for their plight, and even to deny their existence. For example, a former president, Ronald Reagan, declared that in the United States persons without homes were homeless by choice, and that they enjoyed their carefree existence, a notion that the *New York Times* called "silly," and one betraying a "callous indifference" to the homeless.[3]

When the problem became so pervasive that it could no longer be treated lightly, the response of the federal government was to enact, in 1987, the Stewart B. McKinney Homeless Assistance Act, legislation that has had little impact on homelessness. The act includes some 20 different programs involving some nine federal agencies. It ostensibly provides shelter, food, job training, and health care for the homeless. In addition to bureaucratic difficulties, the act has never been fully funded.

Studies conducted in the late 1980s reveal this rough portrait of America's homeless:

- Families with children (the fastest-growing segment of the homeless) account for about one-third to 40 percent of the homeless.
- Over 30 percent of homeless persons are veterans.
- About 30 percent of homeless persons suffer from mental disabilities.
- Twenty to 30 percent of the homeless are employed.
- Minorities (especially blacks and Hispanics) are vastly overrepresented among the homeless.
- The number of homeless children is increasing rapidly.
- Young adult males account for a disproportionately high number of homeless persons.

It is difficult to know how many people in the United States are homeless. Estimates by the federal government range anywhere from 250,000 to 350,000,[4] those by the National Coalition for the Homeless to more than 3 million.[5] Although the latter estimate is no doubt a more realistic figure, the nature of homelessness renders precise measurement impossible.

The difficulty in enumerating the homeless is illustrated by the 1990 census. The Bureau of the Census conducted two operations designed to include the homeless in the enumeration. In the bureau's words, "A 'shelter and street night' enumeration will take place on March 20–21, 1990, counting people in hotels and motels identified beforehand as shelters for the homeless or that cost $12 or less per night. It also includes 'emergency shelters (public or private) and open locations in the streets, parks and other areas not intended for habitation.' "[6] The shortcomings of such a procedure are obvious.

There is no clear-cut definition of homelessness; however, at the very least, the homeless are people who do not have a place of residence in the conventional sense. This includes those people who live in the streets, parks, and other public areas; those who live in public and private shelters of various sorts; those who live in abandoned buildings; and those who live doubled-up with relatives and friends. Estimates of homelessness range anywhere from one quarter million to 3 million (see Table 7-1).

Causes of Homelessness

The lack of affordable housing is a result of several factors. In addition to the sharp drop in construction of public housing beginning in the 1980s, the phenomenon of gentrification of inner-city properties, such as the conversion of rental space into condominiums and the drastic loss of low-priced hotel and rooming-house space (sometimes called single-room occupancy units), forced many of the poor onto the streets. It has been estimated that 1 million units of such housing disappeared in the 1970s and 1980s.[7]

Economic changes contributing to homelessness include high unemployment and longer periods of unemployment. For example, in 1979, 460,000 people were

TABLE 7-1   The Three Most Commonly Cited Estimates for the Number of Homeless People in the United States at a Single Point in Time

250,000–300,000
1-day estimate by HUD, 1984   *(based on projection of expert opinion in 60 randomly selected geographical areas)*
500,000–600,000
1-week estimate by the Urban Institute, 1987   *(based on projected results from systematic random sample of homeless people in cities over 100,000 population)*
2 million–3 million
1-day guess by Mitch Snyder, activist, 1983   *(no known statistical basis)*

Source: Carol L. M. Caton, *Homeless in America* (New York: Oxford University Press, 1990), p. 21.

unemployed for more than 26 weeks and by 1982 the number had more than tripled to more than 1.4 million.[8] It is difficult for homeless persons to obtain employment because they have no fixed address and no home telephone number. In addition, there has been a sharp decrease in the number of manufacturing jobs and a concurrent increase in high-technology jobs requiring greater education and skills.[9]

The deinstitutionalization of patients in state and county mental hospitals and the failure to provide residences for them in community group homes has forced hundreds of thousands of helpless people into the ranks of the homeless (see following section).

Finally, during the decade of the 1980s, the ascendancy of conservatism was accompanied by significant reductions in financial support for public programs that might have ameliorated the problem of homelessness.[10] Funding for several programs was affected:

- Billions of dollars were cut from the child nutrition program.
- The food stamps program experienced serious reductions.
- The job-training program was virtually eliminated.
- Benefits provided for Medicaid were reduced.
- The minimum wage remained unchanged for the first time since the program was established in 1938.
- The school lunch program was significantly reduced.

Health Problems

The health problems of the homeless have been well documented.[11] These may be divided into general health problems, mental health disorders, and substance abuse disorders.

Studies show that as many as 80 to 90 percent of the homeless have physical health problems, and most suffer from several conditions. A study of the homeless in Baltimore revealed that homeless women suffered an average of nine health conditions, while homeless men suffered eight.[12] Some of the most frequently diagnosed physical conditions among the homeless are orodental problems, such as missing teeth; gynecologic problems in women, such as menstrual and menopausal irregularities; dermatologic problems, such as mycoptic infections and inflammations; anemia; respiratory and neurological problems; sexually transmitted diseases, especially syphilis and AIDS; and infectious diseases, particularly tuberculosis and influenza. Hypertension is especially high among both homeless black males and females, affecting about one-third of such persons.

Complicating the lives of the homeless is the likelihood that any individual will suffer from physical, mental, and substance abuse problems. Individuals suffering from AIDS pose special problems among the homeless. It has been estimated that in 1988 there were approximately 20,000 homeless persons with AIDS nationally. Furthermore, studies report that AIDS among the homeless is growing rapidly.[13] These persons usually live in mass shelters and in the streets. In New York City, the

Human Resources Administration's Division of AIDS Services attempts to place persons with AIDS and those who are HIV-positive in nonshelter housing. This agency's caseload of persons with HIV/AIDS increased from 210 in 1986 to 7,710 in 1991.[14]

It is commonly reported that about one-third of homeless people suffer from mental problems. Both the National Coalition for the Homeless and the Partnership for the Homeless put the proportion of the homeless with serious mental problems at slightly less than one-third,[15] and the United States Conference of Mayors reports that about one-third of homeless people in cities are seriously mentally ill, and that the number increased by 7 percent in one year.[16] The *New York Times* estimates that there are 20,000 mentally ill homeless persons in New York City.[17] Most of these people live in large shelters with hundreds of cots packed into one room. They are said to range from violent psychotics, to schizophrenics who rarely communicate, to those who are able to live peacefully with others. The most common mental disorders in these shelters are said to be manic depression and schizophrenia. About 50 percent of these people are said to be addicted to crack cocaine.

In a 1992 survey of the New York City homeless shelter system, which houses 15,000 residents, it was reported that 12 percent had been hospitalized for a mental or emotional problem and that 40 percent of families had either a mental health or drug abuse problem.[18] Surveys show that depression and self-destructive behavior, including suicide, are common among homeless adolescents, who often flee their homes because of sexual and physical abuse.[19]

The deinstitutionalization of patients from mental hospitals has served to complicate the problems of homelessness. From 1950 to 1980, the number of resident patients in state and county mental hospitals in the United States decreased from 512,501 to 137,810.[20] With deinstitutionalization, mental patients were to be provided with community health facilities, including group homes. However, this part of the program was rarely accomplished, forcing thousands of mentally ill persons into the street. Those who are housed live in shelters where theft and violence are widespread. The dangerousness of shelter life is the reason most often given by homeless people who refuse such housing and continue to live in the streets.

Drug abuse is reported to be widespread among the homeless. The Partnership for the Homeless reported that about one-third (31 percent) of the homeless nationally are impaired by alcohol and other drug dependencies.[21] These figures range locally anywhere from two-thirds (66 percent) of homeless men in Atlanta, Georgia, to 8 percent of homeless women in East St. Louis, Illinois. Men are more likely than women to be impaired (42 percent versus 26 percent). It is also reported that drug abuse among homeless youth is high. For example, one study reported that 70 percent of homeless runaways reported using illegal drugs.[22]

Alcohol appears to be the most widely abused substance among the homeless, followed by cocaine, and not infrequently, crack cocaine. A survey of homeless shelters in New York City reported that in large barrackslike shelters for men, 80 percent of residents use alcohol and illicit drugs, and in smaller family shelters the proportion is 30 percent.[23]

Race/Ethnicity and Homelessness

It is difficult to identify the homeless by race/ethnicity because these data are often not enumerated. However, there is every indication that blacks and other minorities are vastly overrepresented among the homeless. For example, one study reports that "Perhaps the typical [homeless] person is in his 20s or 30s, and tends to be black or Hispanic."[24] Another reports that "The model homeless person was a black male high school graduate in his middle thirties."[25] In this study blacks and Native Americans (Indians) were found to constitute considerably more than their proportionate share of the homeless. A study of the homeless shelter population in New York City reported that 94 percent were minorities (largely blacks and Hispanics, in this case).[26] And a study of homeless people in four so-called Sun Belt cities and the state of Ohio showed that black people were overrepresented by two to three times their numbers in the population.[27] For example, black people made up 10 percent of the population of Ohio, but they accounted for 30 percent of the homeless in that state.

Writing in the *Journal of the American Medical Association* in 1985, one researcher estimated that "Minority group members make up 44 percent of the total homeless population."[28] Finally, in a study of homeless men in Baltimore, 47 percent were black compared with 39 percent of men in a survey of that city's households.[29]

It is reasonable to conclude, then, that as is the case with other social problems, minorities (especially blacks) are disproportionately represented among the homeless.

Homeless Veterans

It is estimated that about one-third of single homeless men are veterans, and the federal government estimates that 150,000–250,000 veterans are homeless on any given night.[30] One study of the homeless in Los Angeles reported that veterans comprise 50 percent of homeless males in that city.[31]

Of homeless veterans, those who served in the military during the Vietnam War are overrepresented when compared with the national population of veterans.[32] Although this finding might be a function of age, since homeless Vietnam veterans do not differ significantly in age from other homeless males, studies show that Vietnam veterans are more likely to suffer from post-traumatic stress disorder, and those who suffer this disorder are more likely to be homeless. (See Table 7-2.)

Homeless veterans are victims of problems similar to those encountered by homeless males who are not veterans; chief among them are drug and alcohol abuse and mental illness. It has been estimated that like the homeless at large, about one-third of homeless veterans have mental health problems, and alcohol and other drug abuse might be problems for at least one-half of them.[33]

It is significant, but not surprising, that blacks and Hispanics are overrepresented among homeless veterans, and that they are more likely than whites to suffer medical, psychiatric, and substance abuse problems.[34]

TABLE 7-2   Urban, Poor, African-Americans: Risk of Homelessness

	HOMELESS MEN*			URBAN POOR MEN†			
	WHITES/ OTHERS	BLACKS	PERCENT BLACKS	WHITES/ OTHERS	BLACKS	PERCENT BLACKS	ODDS RATIO‡
Total	85,159	54,541	39.0	2,695,964	818,833	23.3	2.11
Veterans	43,433	17,289	28.5	583,302	162,564	21.8	1.43
Nonveterans	41,726	37,252	47.2	2,112,662	656,269	23.7	2.87

*Data from Urban Institute survey: Burt and Cohen, "Feeding the Homeless."
†Data from U.S. Department of Commerce, *Current Population Survey* (1987); males in poverty residing in standardized metropolitan statistical areas (SMSAs).
‡If the odds ratio is above 1.0, the presence of the factor is thought to significantly increase the risk of homelessness. If the odds ratio is less than 1.0, the presence of the factor is thought to be associated with a significantly reduced risk of homelessness.
Source: Carol L. M. Caton, *Homeless in America* (New York: Oxford University Press, 1990), p. 104.

The New York City Homeless Shelter System

New York City has always had its homeless persons. In the 1950s and 1960s they were largely white males who congregated along the city's skid row—the Bowery—known for its cheap hotels and bars. Since then, however, the homeless have soared in numbers and their demographic characteristics have changed radically. Today the typical homeless person is a young black or Hispanic man and the typical homeless family consists of a young black or Hispanic woman and her children. And in both cases these people are housed in large shelters.

According to the Partnership for the Homeless, there are about 105,000 homeless people in New York City. Between 48,000 and 50,000 are single adults, with about 18,000–22,000 unaccompanied youths, and 33,000–35,000 families with children.[35]

In an effort to house these people, there is an array of shelters—small ones for people with special needs, large barracks-type structures providing beds for thousands of individuals, and family shelters. A survey of the entire system, accomplished in December 1990, reported the following characteristics of clients.[36] The number of people served increased from 3,000 in 1981 to 11,000 in 1989. In 1990 there were 8,086 men (86 percent) and 1,351 women (14 percent). The average age of residents was 39 years. The vast majority (81 percent) were unemployed, and more than one-half (53.8 percent) received some form of income, an average of $150 per month.

More than one-half (54.8 percent) of shelter residents reported having a high school diploma or equivalent. Most of the homeless people—73 percent of the women and 61 percent of the men—reported having children. Some 57 percent reported having used drugs in the past, and more than one-fifth (21 percent) reported having been hospitalized for a drug problem. Only about one-fourth (26 percent) said that they had been heavy drinkers in the past. (A study of the shelter system in 1992 reported that 80 percent of homeless men in large shelters and 30 percent of those in family shelters use alcohol or other drugs, most often cocaine.[37]) Finally, 22 percent reported having received assistance with psychological or emotional problems, and 43 percent reported having a (physical) medical problem.

It is reported that New York City spends $18,000 a year for a single man to sleep in a shelter; and for a family in a barracks-style shelter, the cost is $53,000 a year. The typical family in a shelter is headed by a young black or Hispanic woman with a very young child. In the vast majority of cases, the mothers themselves had grown up in families on welfare. One in five had been physically or sexually abused, and one in ten had spent time in foster care.[38]

In addition to the network of shelters owned and operated by the city of New York, some private social agencies also operate homeless shelters. By 1990 the Partnership for the Homeless established and coordinated 153 emergency shelters in churches and synagogues in the city. These shelters provided 1,700 beds for the homeless. Cooperating with the Partnership in this effort are nearly 400 religious institutions.[39]

Attitudes toward the Homeless

In recent years attitudes toward the plight of the homeless have fluctuated from compassion to tolerance to irritation to apathy. The federal government, especially in the 1980s, appeared to adopt the attitude that homelessness was the fault of the poor, and many municipalities enacted laws aimed at regulating their behavior. For example, New York City, Atlanta, and Santa Barbara, California, have adopted measures to restrict begging, to prohibit sleeping in public parks and other open areas, and to evict the homeless from subway trains and bus terminals.[40]

Opposition to group homes and homeless shelters in residential areas is widespread, and citizens and community groups frequently succeed in prohibiting them. In a small Connecticut town when a person attempted to permit her lakefront home to be used to shelter homeless families, she was immediately challenged in court by citizens who charged her with violating zoning regulations.[41]

In a New York City suburb, when the temperature was 7 degrees and the wind-chill factor drove it to 24 below zero, a Vietnam veteran who had lived on the streets for seven years was arrested for sleeping in an abandoned apartment house.[42] His choice was either to sleep on the floor in the building or risk dying from exposure to the cold (hypothermia), the fate of thousands of homeless people each year. The Centers for Disease Control reported that 1,010 homeless people died from hypothermia in 1985.[43]

As homeless people flood city streets throughout the country, the mood of citizens appears to have hardened, but a nationwide poll in January 1992 revealed that a vast majority of citizens (7 out of 10) say that homelessness is "something the government can do a lot about."[44]

It has been suggested that homelessness violates both the Declaration of Independence and the Constitution.[45] What is clear is that homeless people suffer serious deprivations of what most people in the industrialized world consider to be basic human rights. The impact of massive homelessness on societal values is yet to be determined.

ADOLESCENT PREGNANCY AND CHILDBEARING

- Ninety-seven percent of women and 99 percent of men aged 15–19 in the United States are unmarried.*
- Fifty percent of unmarried women and 60 percent of unmarried men aged 15–19 have had sexual intercourse.
- Levels of sexual activity increase with each year of age; 27 percent of unmarried 15-year old women and 33 percent of unmarried 15 year old men have had intercourse at least once; at age 19, 75 percent of women and 86 percent of men have had intercourse.
- Teenagers are having sex for the first time at younger ages; in 1982, 19 percent of unmarried women aged 15 had had sexual intercourse; in 1988, 27 percent. In 1979, 56 percent of unmarried men aged 17 in metropolitan areas had had sexual intercourse; in 1988, 72 percent.
- Sexual activity levels vary considerably by race/ethnicity. Among 15–19-year-old men, blacks have the highest incidence of intercourse, followed by whites and Hispanics.
- Most of the increase in female sexual activity in the 1980s was among white teenagers and those in higher-income families, narrowing the previous racial/ethnic and income differences.

As these data demonstrate, sexual activity among adolescents in the United States is widespread. And it begins at an early age. Studies show that sexual intercourse begins as early as 13 or 14 for males and 14 or 15 for females. Black adolescents, both male and female, generally initiate sexual activity earlier than whites by an average of two years.[46] By the age of 19, 96 percent of black males have had sexual intercourse, compared with 85 percent of whites and 82 percent of Hispanics (Figure 7-1).

Studies of teenage sexual behavior show that in addition to earlier sexual activity, black teenagers had more sexual partners, but fewer acts of intercourse than their white counterparts. For example, data from national surveys show that black teenage males between 15 and 19 had 8.3 partners since first intercourse, while whites had 4.3; and black teenagers had 2.4 sexual partners in one year, compared with 1.8 for whites.[47] In 1979, 51 percent of all female teenagers reported having had sex with two or more partners since first intercourse; for black females the proportion was 62 percent.

Sexual intercourse was more frequent among white teenagers than among blacks. For example, data from national samples show that 43 percent of white

---

* Unless otherwise indicated, statistical data are from *Facts in Brief: Teenage Sexual and Reproductive Behavior in the United States* (New York: The Alan Guttmacher Institute, 1991).

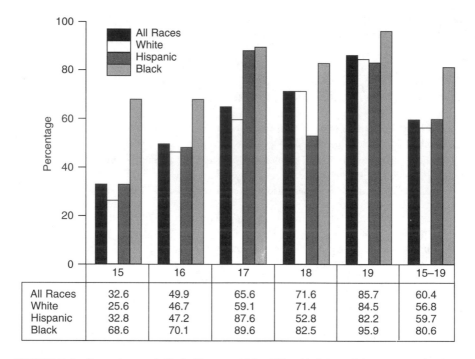

	15	16	17	18	19	15–19
All Races	32.6	49.9	65.6	71.6	85.7	60.4
White	25.6	46.7	59.1	71.4	84.5	56.8
Hispanic	32.8	47.2	87.6	52.8	82.2	59.7
Black	68.6	70.1	89.6	82.5	95.9	80.6

FIGURE 7-1   Percentages of Single Teenage Males Who Had Sexual Intercourse, by Age, According to Race/ethnicity, United States, 1988

Source: Reproduced with the permission of The Alan Guttmacher Institute from F. L. Sonenstein, Joseph H. Pleck, and Leighton C. Ku, "Sexual Activity, Condom Use and AIDS Awareness Among Adolescent Males," *Family Planning Perspectives,* Vol. 21, No. 4, July/August 1989, p. 153.

females had sexual intercourse at least once a week, compared with 32 percent of black females. Black males had intercourse less frequently than whites, but not significantly so.[48]

Contraceptive Use

- More teenage women surveyed in 1988 used contraception the first time they had intercourse than in 1982 (65 percent versus 48 percent), yet one-third used no protection the first time they had intercourse.
- Contraceptive use at first time of intercourse has increased almost entirely because of a doubling in condom use during the 1980s (from 23 percent to 47 percent).
- Seventy-nine percent of sexually active teenage women use a contraceptive method— up from 71 percent in 1982. They are more likely, however, than any other age group to be nonusers: 1 in 5 use no method.
- Fifty-seven percent of sexually active unmarried men aged 15–19 used a condom at last time of intercourse, and among those aged 17–19 in metropolitan areas, condom use more than doubled between 1979 and 1988—from 21 percent to 58 percent.

- Sixty-six percent of black, 54 percent of white, and 53 percent of Hispanic men aged 15–19 used a condom the last time they had sexual intercourse.
- In general, younger women are more likely than older women to become pregnant while using any contraceptive—11 percent of teenage birth control pill users experience contraceptive failure during the first year of use, compared with 6 percent among women aged 15–44.

Data show that black teenagers, both male and female, are more likely than their white counterparts to use contraceptives, especially condoms, during intercourse. For example, in 1988, 62 percent of black teenagers reported using condoms, compared with 56 percent of whites. Among sexually active teenage females in 1982, 7.5 percent used some form of contraception; for black females 13.5 percent used contraceptives, compared with 6.4 percent for whites.[49]

Adolescent Pregnancy

- Teenagers in the United States have one of the highest pregnancy rates in the industrialized world—twice as high as England, France, and Canada, three times as high as Sweden, and seven times as high as the Netherlands.[50]
- Each year more than 1 million teenagers (1,014,620 in 1987), 1 in 10 women aged 15–19, and 1 in 5 who are sexually active, become pregnant.
- Fifty percent of teenage pregnancies conceived in 1987 resulted in births, 36 percent in abortion, and an estimated 14 percent in miscarriage.
- In 1987 the teenage pregnancy rate (pregnancies per 1,000 women aged 15–19) was 109, and 72 among those aged 15–17.
- Minority teenagers have twice the pregnancy rate of white teenagers; in 1987 the rate was 189 and 90, respectively.
- By the age of 18, 1 in 4 (24 percent) teenagers will become pregnant at least once, and more than 4 in 10 (44 percent) will do so by the age of 20.
- Twenty-one percent of white teenagers and 40 percent of minority teenagers will become pregnant at least once by the age of 18, and 41 percent of whites and 63 percent of minorities by age 20.
- Nearly 1 in 5 teenagers who experience a premarital pregnancy become pregnant again within a year. Within 2 years, more than 31 percent will have a repeat pregnancy.
- Eight in 10 teenage pregnancies are unintended—9 in 10 among unmarried teenagers and about one-half of married teenagers.

The number of teenage pregnancies and the teenage pregnancy rate rose gradually during the 1970s but leveled off in the 1980s. In 1972 the pregnancy rate was 95; in 1980 it was 111; and by 1987 it was 109.[51] Among minority teenagers the pregnancy rate dropped to a low of 181 pregnancies per 1,000 teenagers in 1984, then rose 5 percent to 189 in 1987, while for whites in this age category, the rate declined 6 percent, from 96 to 90.

White teenagers, more than blacks, resolve premarital pregnancy through marriage. They are about six times more likely than blacks to marry before the outcome of the first premarital pregnancy.[52] Black teenage mothers lead all other racial and ethnic groups in total births (see Figure 7-2.)

Adolescent Childbearing

- The teenage childbearing rate in the United States is halfway between Canada's and Latin America's. By the age of 20, 1 in 9 women in Canada, 2 in 10 in the United States, 3 in 10 in Brazil, and 5 in 10 in Guatemala have had their first child.

- About one-half of all teenage pregnancies end in births. In 1988, teenage births in the United States totaled 488,941 (10,558 to those under age 15), and 66 percent of those were to unmarried teenagers—54 percent of all births to whites and 91 percent of all births to blacks.

- Seven in 10 births to teenagers result from unplanned pregnancies.

- The teenage birthrate (births per 1,000 women aged 15–19) in 1988 was 53.6, among whites it was 43.7, and among minorities, 95.3.

- The birthrate for teenagers aged 15–17 increased 10 percent between 1986 and 1988; the 1988 rate was the highest since 1977. The increase occurred almost entirely for blacks and Hispanics.

- For women having their first birth in 1988, 23 percent were teenagers. Among whites, 2 of 10 first births were to teenagers, and among blacks it was 4 of 10.

- Nearly one-fourth of all babies born to teenagers are not first births.

- Fewer than 10 percent of teenagers who give birth place their babies for adoption.

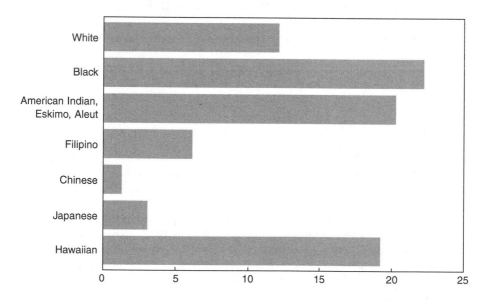

FIGURE 7-2   Births to Teenage Mothers as a Percent of Total Births, by Race, 1994

Source: Chart prepared by U.S. Bureau of the Census, *Statistical Abstract of the United States: 1997,* (Washington, DC, 1997).

• On average, 33 percent of women under 20 who give birth receive inadequate prenatal care, either because they start care late in pregnancy or because they have too few medical visits.

Among white adolescents aged 15–19, the birthrate declined between 1980 and 1987, but among blacks the rate fell from 1980 to 1984, then rose in 1987.[53]

Currently about 64 percent of all black children are born out of wedlock, many to adolescent mothers.[54] In 1980 adolescent births represented 26 percent of all births among blacks, compared to less than 14 percent among whites. The teenage birthrate for blacks (99.8 per 1,000 women aged 15–19) is more than twice that for whites (44.7). For blacks, the rate increases from 20.4 for 14 year olds to 145.7 for women 20 years of age. The comparable figures for whites are 2.7 to 81.0. Although blacks accounted for 28 percent of all adolescent births in 1980, they accounted for nearly one-half of premarital births.[55]

Abortion among Adolescents

• Four in 10 teenage pregnancies (excluding miscarriages) end in abortion.
• Twenty-six percent of all abortions in the United States each year are to women under 20 years old. In 1987 the total number of abortions in this group was 406,790.
• Every year about 4 percent of women aged 15–19 have an abortion.
• In 1987, 948,550 women aged 15–19 became pregnant. Of this number 47 percent gave birth, 40 percent had legal abortions, and an estimated 13 percent had miscarriages.
• The number of abortions in the United States has stabilized at about 1.6 million each year.
• Contrary to popular opinion, the abortion rate for black women is much higher than for white women, 2.7 times as high in 1987 (56 per 1,000 live births versus 21).

According to national data, of all women having abortions in the United States in 1987, 65 percent were white and 35 percent were minority. However, minority teenagers have higher abortion rates than do whites (78 percent and 37 percent, respectively).[56]

Although the abortion rate (number of abortions per 1,000 live births in the group) for teenagers aged 15–19 rose during the 1970s, it has remained stable after 1980. Among white teenagers the abortion rate declined from 85 in 1982 to 71 in 1987, a drop of 16 percent. Among minority teenagers, however, the abortion rate increased from 66 in 1980 to 73 in 1987, an increase of 11 percent.[57]

In the 1970s studies showed that white pregnant teenagers who were unmarried were about three times more likely than blacks to choose abortion.[58] This pattern has changed significantly in subsequent years.

Adoption versus Parenting

One of the significant differences between black and white adolescent mothers is that blacks are less likely than whites to place their babies for adoption. Studies show that 18 percent of white teenagers give up their children for adoption, but only 2 percent of blacks do.[59] In some cases, adoption was hardly considered as an option for a largely black population.[60]

Pregnant teenagers who choose to place their children for adoption rather than to parent did so because they thought the outcomes, such as their continuing in school and assuring an adequate future income, as well as the baby's development, would benefit by their choice; those who did not consider adoption felt that these outcomes would be more likely to happen if they parented, or that the outcomes would not be affected by their choice.[61] Those who elected to place their children for adoption were more advantaged economically and held more positive attitudes about adoption than the others.

The Fathers of Children Born to Teenage Mothers

Black males are the most sexually active adolescents in the United States; they initiate sexual activity earlier and have more sexual partners than do black females and Hispanic and white adolescents.

Data on the fathers of children born to adolescent mothers are not extensive. However, national data indicate that in 1984 approximately 3 percent of all live births in the United States were fathered by males under the age of 20. Of the children born to teenage mothers, 23 percent had teenage fathers.[62]

Following are characteristics of teenage fathers:[63]

- More than one-half of adolescent fathers nationally reported some involvement with the criminal justice system.
- Adolescent fathers, more than adolescent nonfathers, tend to come from single-parent families.
- Most adolescent males in the United States are not well prepared for the responsibilities of parenthood.
- One study reveals that one adolescent father in five had at least one other child by a different woman.
- One-half of teenage mothers complain about receiving little assistance from the father in raising the children. Black mothers voice this complaint more often than white mothers.
- Most teenage fathers do not support their offspring financially.
- More than four of five (84 percent) fathers of children born to adolescent mothers lived separately from the children. In 10 percent of cases the mother did not know the whereabouts of her child's father.

Studies show that adolescent fathers, compared with adolescent nonfathers, are more likely to have academic and other school problems; to engage in aggressive antisocial behavior, to use drugs, and to be involved with the criminal justice system.[64] Furthermore, they are more likely, when employed, to work at low-status occupations. They are also more likely to come from homes that are educationally and financially disadvantaged.

Data indicate that adolescent males are ill-prepared for the responsibilities of fatherhood; many voice concerns about vocational, educational, health, and family problems. In one national study, academic and drug problems as well as general conduct problems were more common among adolescent fathers than among adolescents in general.

Black teenage fathers, like teenage mothers, are younger than their white counterparts. About one-third of fathers of infants born to white mothers, compared with very few fathers of children born to black teenage mothers, had been married to the child's mother at the time of conception. In addition, black adolescent fathers are more likely than whites to be unemployed.[65]

Consequences of Teenage Childbearing

Nearly one-half of black women aged 15–17 lived with only one parent in 1982: 45 percent with their mother, and 2 percent with their father. Only 45 percent lived with both parents. By comparison, 78 percent of white adolescent women lived with both parents, and 16 percent lived with the mother only.[66]

More black adolescents than white lived in families below 100 percent of the poverty line: 41 percent of black women aged 15–21 in 1981 had family incomes below 100 percent poverty, compared with 14 percent of whites. The proportions of women 15–17 in this economic category were 44 percent for blacks and 13 percent for whites.[67]

By 1990, 73 percent of all children under 18 years of age lived with both parents: 79 percent of whites, 38 percent of blacks, and 67 percent of Hispanics. Nearly one-third (31 percent) of these children lived with parents who had never married: 19 percent for whites, 52 percent for blacks, and 33 percent for Hispanics. Twelve percent of white mothers living alone with children were under 25 years of age; 27 percent had less than a high school education; and 36 percent were unemployed. For blacks, 18 percent were under 25; 34 percent had less than a high school education; and 52 percent were unemployed. For Hispanics, the proportions were 15 percent, 55 percent, and 54 percent, respectively.

In 1990, 21.6 percent of all children under 18 years of age lived with one parent—the mother. For black children, the proportion was 51.2 percent, compared with 16.2 percent for whites, and 27. 1 percent for Hispanics.[68] Finally, studies show that because teenage mothers are emotionally immature, they place themselves and their babies at risk for medical problems.[69] In addition, school-age children who were born to adolescent parents exhibit more behavioral problems and score lower on intelligence tests than other school-age children.[70]

A basic problem of adolescent pregnancy and childbearing is poverty. Given the nature of American society, it is difficult to foresee any positive outcomes from the volume of adolescent childbirths, especially among minorities. Of all industrialized countries, the United States alone has no consistent family planning policy.

SUBSTANCE ABUSE

This section focuses on the use of both legal and illicit drugs. The legal drugs discussed include alcohol and tobacco; the illicit ones are cocaine, crack cocaine, and heroin. Crack cocaine will be discussed at some length because it is relatively new, and it is believed by many to have the most serious adverse effects of any drug on both the individuals involved and the larger society.

For each drug the most recent data available are from the 1990 National Household Survey on Drug Abuse, prepared by the National Institute on Drug Abuse of the U.S. Department of Health and Human Services.[71] These data are supplemented by information from other sources.

Alcohol

Alcohol is potentially a dangerous drug, but its sale and use are not proscribed, and it is the major drug of choice in the United States. The 1990 National Household Survey on Drug Abuse reported that some 167 million Americans, or 83 percent of persons 12 years of age and older, have used alcohol. Some 103 million people or 51 percent of the population had used the drug in the past month (at the time of the survey). Some 42 million or 21 percent of the population reported drinking frequently (once a week or more).

More males (88 percent) than females (79 percent) have used alcohol, and whites are slightly more likely than blacks and Hispanics to be frequent drinkers. Among men, however, roughly the same proportion of each group were frequent drinkers (approximately 30 percent). White women (13 percent), on the other hand, are somewhat more likely to be frequent drinkers than black (12 percent) or Hispanic (8 percent) women.

In addition to being more frequent drinkers, whites are more likely than blacks or Hispanics to drink at early and at older ages. Of all the categories, Hispanic women are the least likely to drink and white men are the most likely.

Studies show that blacks drink somewhat less than whites and are more likely to abstain from drinking.[72] Furthermore, alcohol plays a smaller role in home and family life among blacks than among whites.

A nationwide study revealed that black adolescents drink significantly less than do their white counterparts.[73] It reported that 38 percent of black adolescents abstained or drank less than once a year, compared with 27 percent of comparable whites.

Among minorities, blacks are reported to drink less than Puerto Ricans and to drink less often.[74] However, among black adults, alcohol and drug abuse are said to be causes of lower than average life expectancy among blacks.[75]

Although alcohol is legal in the United States, and its recreational use is socially acceptable, its adverse social effects are greater than those of all illicit drugs. It is said to be the direct cause of between 80,000 and 100,000 deaths annually, and is a factor in nearly one-half of murders, suicides, and accidental deaths.[76] Alcohol-related traffic deaths are the leading cause of death for adolescents.

According to the U. S. Public Health Service, alcohol is a factor in more than 10 percent of all deaths in the country and 50 percent of all homicides. Furthermore, cirrhosis of the liver kills some 30,000 people annually in the United States, and the mortality rate from the disease among blacks is double that in the white population.[77]

Fetal alcohol syndrome, another alcohol-related health problem, is diagnosed in one of every 750 live births. This disease is marked by birth defects and usually occurs in women who drink heavily during pregnancy. Alcohol passes across the placenta into the bloodstream of the fetus and reaches the same concentration as in that of the mother. The symptoms include brain damage, low birth weight, and facial and bodily abnormalities.[78]

Tobacco

According to the 1990 National Household Survey on Drug Abuse, 147 million (73 percent) Americans 12 years of age and over have used cigarettes, and 54 million had smoked in the last month (before the survey). Males are more likely to have smoked (79 percent) than females (68 percent) and to be regular smokers. Whites (76 percent) are more likely to have smoked than blacks (64 percent) or Hispanics (62 percent), and more likely to smoke regularly. Hispanic women (15 percent) are least likely to smoke, and white men are the most likely. Smoking increases with age among each of the three groups; within each group the youngest persons are more likely to use tobacco than any other drug.

Tobacco is a psychoactive substance that stimulates the central nervous system. Its addictive potential is so great that the surgeon general of the United States declared it to be as addictive as cocaine and heroin.[79]

According to the Centers for Disease Control, cigarette smoking is declining in the United States, and the annual rate of decline has been higher among men than among women. However, cigarette smoking "remains the most important preventable cause of death in our society" and is responsible for an estimated 390,000 deaths annually, or more than one in every six deaths.[80]

The Centers for Disease Control reported that in 1987 approximately one-third (33 percent) of adults in the United States used some form of tobacco regularly: 39 percent of men and 27 percent of women. Most of these persons used only cigarettes, although a small minority used cigarettes in combination with other forms of tobacco (e.g., chewing tobacco, cigars, and snuff). Overall, 29 percent of adults were said to have smoked cigarettes—31 percent of men and 27 percent of women.[81] Smoking was most prevalent among those between 25 and 44 years of age, and least prevalent among those over 75 years old.

According to the CDC, black men were more likely to smoke than white men (39 percent versus 31 percent), but the rates for black (27 percent) and white (28 percent) women were similar. According to *Statistical Abstracts,* the proportion of blacks in the population who smoke cigarettes has exceeded the proportion of whites since 1965.[82] (This report differs from that of the 1990 National Household Survey on Drug Abuse. In addition, there is some evidence that among adolescents, blacks are less likely than whites to smoke cigarettes.[83]) In addition, persons who smoked cigarettes were more likely than nonsmokers to use alcoholic beverages and to consume greater quantities of alcohol.

Cigarette smoking has been found to be a major cause of several life-threatening diseases, including emphysema, cancer of the lungs and airways, coronary heart disease, and vascular disease. It is linked to many other cancers, such as cancer of the esophagus and pancreas, and to low birth weight.[84]

Although the destructive potential of tobacco use is well established, cigarettes are one of the most heavily advertised products. The advertising usually associates smoking with a glamorous life-style, healthy activities, and social success. There is evidence that cigarette companies target their advertising campaigns to minorities, women, blue-collar workers, and teenagers, groups that make up an increasing proportion of the smoking population.[85]

•   •   •

The National Institute on Drug Abuse classifies the following drugs as illicit (meaning unlawful): cocaine, hallucinogens, heroin, inhalants, marijuana, and nonmedical use of psychotherapeutics (analgesics, sedatives, stimulants, and tranquilizers). Although most of these drugs are illegal in the United States, many of them are widely used. For example, the 1990 National Household Survey on Drug Abuse reported that 74 million (37 percent) of Americans have used illicit drugs, and some 13 million had used them in the past month (when the survey was made). Whites had used illicit drugs more than blacks and Hispanics. Males (42 percent) were more likely than females (32 percent) to have used illicit drugs and more likely to have been frequent users. (This survey included marijuana as an illicit [and dangerous] drug, but it is not included here because there is disagreement about this designation in the medical community, as well as controversy concerning marijuana's long-term effects, if any.)

Cocaine

It is reported in the 1990 National Household Survey on Drug Abuse that some 23 million Americans (11.3 percent of the population) have used cocaine (including crack cocaine) and that nearly 1 million use some form of the drug at least once a week. Males (14 percent) more than females (9 percent) are likely to have used some form of cocaine and are more likely to be frequent users (once a week or more).

In terms of race/ethnicity, whites and Hispanics (12 percent each) are more likely to have used cocaine than blacks (10 percent). Hispanic males (16 percent) are more likely than white (14 percent) and black (13 percent) males to have used cocaine and are more likely to be frequent users. White females are more likely than black or Hispanic females to have ever used cocaine and are more likely to be frequent users.

Some estimates of cocaine users exceed those of the National Institute on Drug Abuse. For example, it has been reported that anywhere between 1 and 30 million Americans use the drug in any year.[86] Another report puts the number of regular cocaine users in the United States at 5 million with 1 million in the metropolitan New York region.[87] Cocaine is said to be the most frequently used illegal stimulant in the United States.

The effects of and reactions to cocaine have been described.[88] It enters the bloodstream through the nostrils when snorted through a straw, rolled paper, or spoon. It is sometimes ingested intravenously. When inhaled it peaks in 10 to 20 minutes and lasts for one-and-one-half to two hours; injection brings forth the feeling of euphoria in much less time.

Cocaine releases adrenaline, thereby stimulating the central nervous system. It also usurps the need for food and sleep, and in high doses it produces extreme euphoria and sometimes feelings of megalomania and omnipotence.

Adverse reactions are many and serious. They may be cardiopulmonary, including chest pain, palpitations, shortness of breath, and cardiac arrest; psychiatric, including anxiety, psychosis, confusion, depression, hallucinations; neurologic, including dizziness, headache, seizure, and stroke; constitutional, including weakness, chills, fever, fatigue, and insomnia; gastrointestinal, including nausea, abdominal pain, and vomiting; as well as problems of the eyes, ears, nose, and throat, including blurred vision and nasal congestion. Multiple symptoms are usually present.

Pregnant women who use cocaine frequently experience spontaneous abortion; premature birth; low-birth-weight babies; congenital fetal malformation; and fetal irritability, tremulousness, and malnutrition. In addition, cocaine is likely to be used in combination with other drugs, and because it can cause increased libido, it has been associated with the spread of sexually transmitted diseases, especially AIDS.

Crack Cocaine

The 1990 National Household Survey on Drug Abuse reported that 2.7 million Americans, or 1.4 percent of the population 12 years of age or over, had used crack cocaine and that nearly a half million (494,000) were regular users. Males are more than twice as likely as females to be regular users. A higher proportion of blacks (3.1 percent) had used crack cocaine than Hispanics (1.6 percent) or whites (1.1 percent). Blacks were more likely to be regular users, and considerably more black females had used the drug than Hispanics and whites. Of the nearly 500,000 regular crack cocaine users, more than 200,000 were said to be black.

Cocaine hydrochloride, a white crystalline powder that is about 95 percent pure, is converted into crack cocaine by boiling it in a mixture of sodium bicarbonate (baking soda) and water. The mixture is then dried until it becomes a soaplike substance. It is then cut and placed in transparent vials resembling vitamin capsules and smoked in pipes. It is most often smoked in crack houses where participants frequently remain for several days.[89] The name *crack* comes from the sudden, sharp sound the drug makes when smoked.

Because crack cocaine is smoked, it goes directly into the lungs when inhaled and then reaches the brain in a few seconds. It produces extreme euphoria in a very brief time, and for this reason it has become the drug of choice for many. It is said to be unmatched in its ability to produce euphoria and exhilaration. People who have used other drugs for years report sensations never before experienced: instant irritability, rage, and aggression.

Crack cocaine is inexpensive, highly addictive, and easy to use; it is therefore popular among adolescents, although most users are young adults. Its use has increased rapidly, especially in poor urban areas. Although it is inexpensive, its addictive power is so great that constant users require hundreds or thousands of dollars a week to support the habit, and crime (including homicide, robbery, theft, and prostitution) is usually the source of the income.

Crack cocaine first appeared on the West Coast in the early 1980s and made its debut on the streets of New York in 1984. Scientists doing research on drug addiction report that crack cocaine is the most addictive drug in existence, and that the addiction comes more quickly and lasts longer than with any other illicit drug because the drug stimulates the pleasure center in the base of the brain.[90] But the euphoria fades quickly, leaving users depressed, anxious, and without pleasure. The biochemistry of crack cocaine addiction is such that the craving for the drug in addicts is so intense that relapse is almost inevitable, and the cravings last much longer than for other drugs.

Crack cocaine abuse is associated with the same adverse reactions as cocaine, often to a greater extent and more severely.[91] Studies show that the use of crack cocaine during pregnancy has serious effects on the fetus, including low birth weight, brain damage, and various malformations. The *New York Times* described one such child as "a mere patch of flesh with a tangerine-sized head and limbs like splinters."[92]

Crack cocaine abuse has been linked to increased child abuse and neglect. For example, the *New York Times* reported that urban child welfare agencies said in 1989 that 70 percent of the children they saw were cared for by grandmothers and other relatives because their crack-addicted parents had abandoned them. A sharp increase in the number of children killed by crack-addicted parents has been reported.[93]

Crack cocaine abuse has been associated with increased aggression, resulting in increases in violent crime and other strains on the criminal justice system. For example, one study in San Francisco reports a 560 percent increase in cocaine-related arrests of minors between 1986 and 1988, and a 218 percent increase in felony court cases related to cocaine (usually crack) possession and sales.[94] The *New York Times* reported that "In community after community crack violence has overwhelmed law enforcement."[95]

Although crack cocaine has been reported to be prevalent in the suburbs of New York and elsewhere, its damage has been greatest in poor black and Hispanic neighborhoods.[96]

One of the most destructive results of the increase of libido and impairment of judgment that result from crack cocaine addiction is its increased role in the spread of sexually transmitted diseases, especially AIDS. In crack houses where it is most often smoked, crack cocaine is frequently used in exchange for sex.[97] In some cases as many as one-half of the crack cocaine users seeking drug treatment test positive for the virus that causes AIDS.

The *New York Times* editorialized that "Crack poses a much greater threat than other drugs. It is reaching out to destroy the quality of life and life itself, at all levels of American society. Crack may be to the 80's and the 90's what the Great Depression was to the 30's or the Vietnam War was to the 60's and 70's."[98]

The following cases illustrate the grim effects of crack cocaine abuse.[99]

In 1986, a 27-year-old single mother of a young child who worked as an aide in a nursing home in Staten Island, New York, began using crack after both of her parents died. At the time her salary was adequate to maintain a modest apartment and to provide for her daughter. She was also able to deposit money in a bank account for her daughter. The enterprising young woman worked until 5 o'clock, picked up her daughter from the baby sitter, cooked dinner, checked her daughter's homework, and prepared her clothes for the next day.

When she was introduced to crack, at first it lifted her spirits. But she was unable to stop using the drug, and she soon began attending all-night crack parties. Her daughter, her relatives, and her employer noticed that she was changing. She lost weight and in three months she lost her job and was evicted from her apartment. The young woman asked her sister to keep her daughter for a week, but she did not return for her for two months. During this time she sold her daughter's bedroom furniture, the living room furniture, the rugs, the refrigerator, and the washing machine. In addition, she depleted her bank account and that of her daughter.

Homeless, she moved in with her brother and started selling crack from his apartment. Together they hired two guards with pistols to protect them and their profit of $3,000 a week. They frequently smoked crack for 24 hours a day. In a few months they were arrested when the police raided the apartment. She spent a month in jail before being placed by a judge in a drug treatment program. Of the four siblings, one sister, the only one who is not a crack addict, cares for the family's nine children.

A Harlem mother was less fortunate. She had managed to care for her children for years while addicted to heroin. However, after she became a crack addict in 1987, she disappeared into the streets where she obtained crack in exchange for sex. After a short time she died during a seizure. When identified at the morgue by a social worker, she had dried blood over her mouth and weighed only about 50 pounds.

Heroin

According to the 1990 National Household Survey on Drug Abuse, 1.6 million Americans, or 0.8 percent of the population 12 years of age and older, have ever used heroin. Men are more than twice as likely as women to have used the drug, and blacks (1.7 percent) are more likely than Hispanics (1.2 percent) and whites (0.7 percent) to have used heroin. Heroin use appears to peak at a later age than that of other illicit drugs. Regionally, heroin is used most often on the East and West coasts, followed by the Midwest, and least often in the South.

Heroin is derived from opium and is therefore a depressant drug. It induces sleep and lessens nervous tension. Of all illegal depressants, heroin is most frequently used. Like most opiates, heroin produces relief from pain, hypnosis, and euphoria. It is usually ingested intravenously with a hypodermic needle, although it may be sniffed or smoked.

The effects of heroin use have been described.[100] About 10 seconds after injection, users experience a wave of euphoric feelings, visceral sensations, and facial flushing. The euphoric feelings give the user a general feeling of well-being and an escape from reality. With one injection these feelings can last for hours. Heroin addicts are usually not violent because the drug depresses aggression; and unlike users of some other illicit drugs, those who use heroin have little or no interest in sex.

There are many side effects and withdrawal symptoms associated with the use of heroin, including respiratory arrest, anxiety, increased blood pressure, nausea, insomnia, and cardiovascular collapse. In addition, because hypodermic needles are often shared, heroin use is associated with sexually transmitted diseases such as AIDS and hepatitis. For example, it has been estimated that more than one-half (60 percent) of the approximately 200,000 heroin addicts in New York City are infected with HIV, the virus that causes AIDS.

In 1991 it was estimated that there were about 500,000 heroin addicts in the United States, with about one-half of them living in New York City alone, the distribution center for the country.[101] Minorities, especially blacks, have long been over-represented among heroin addicts. However, the use of the drug decreased with the increased use of cocaine and crack cocaine.

The use of heroin has been on the increase since 1990, according to drug enforcement officials.[102] This increase in usage is said to have resulted from several factors, including improved growing conditions for opium poppies, the raw material for heroin, in Asia and Latin America. For many years the heroin sold on the streets was said to contain only about 10 percent of the pure drug, but in recent years it has been 40–45 percent pure. This means that the drug can now be snorted like cocaine or smoked like crack cocaine, thereby avoiding the use of hypodermic needles.

According to drug treatment professionals, there is a widespread myth that heroin is not addictive and is less harmful when snorted. This myth was shattered in 1991, when several addicts died from snorting toxic heroin.[103] A new "designer" drug called "Tango and Cash" appeared on the streets of the South Bronx in New York City on February 2, 1991, and spread throughout the Northeast in a short time. By the next day 12 people had died from this drug and 200 had been hospitalized in New York, New Jersey, and Connecticut. By February 7, at least 17 persons had died.[104]

Although "Tango and Cash" was sold as heroin, laboratory tests revealed that it contained a chemical, fentanyl, which is used as a tranquilizer during surgery. According to public health officials, when mixed with heroin, fentanyl increases the potency of the drug by a factor of 27. The New York City Health Commissioner said of the new drug that "it overwhelms opiate receptors in the brain, causing the users to stop breathing."[105] Because addicts are constantly searching for a more intense euphoria, this drug was immediately popular, despite its deadly potential.

Heroin use is said to be on the increase also because newer forms are widely available that are less expensive than in the past. Diluted heroin sold in 1991 for as little as $5 or $10. Underground chemists continue to experiment, seeking to create synthetic forms of heroin that can be made inexpensively in laboratories.

• • •

Minorities in the United States, especially black Americans, are overrepresented among the homeless, among adolescents who become pregnant and bear children, and among those addicted to the most harmful drugs. Although the data on the extent of these social problems are sometimes contradictory, they are persuasive. Research on these problems reveals that, to a great degree, they result from widespread poverty, brought about by the racist nature of the society. This makes it difficult for black citizens and other minorities to conform to standards of behavior the society sets for all citizens.

SELECTED BIBLIOGRAPHY

ABADINSKY, HOWARD. *Drug Abuse: An Introduction.* Chicago: Nelson-Hall, 1989.

AGAR, MICHAEL. *Ripping and Running: A Formal Ethnography of Urban Heroin Addicts.* New York: Seminar Press, 1973.

BAUMOHL, JIM (ed.), *Homelessness in America.* Phoenix, AZ: The Oryx Press, 1996.

CATON, CAROL. *Homeless in America.* New York: Oxford University Press, 1990.

GIBBS, J. T., et al., eds. *Young, Black and Male in America: An Endangered Species.* Dover, MA: Auburn House, 1988.

HACKER, G. A., R. COLLINS, and M. JACKSON, *Marketing Booze to Blacks.* Washington, DC: Center for Science in the Public Interest, 1987.

HAYES, C. D. *Risking the Future: Adolescent Sexuality, Pregnancy and Child Bearing.* Washington, DC: National Academy Press, 1987.

HOPPER, KIM. "The New Urban Niche of Homelessness: New York City in the Late 1980s." *Bulletin of the New York Academy of Medicine* 66 (September–October 1990), 435–50.

Institute of Medicine. *Homelessness, Health and Human Needs.* Washington, DC: National Academy Press, 1988.

JONES, E. F., J. D. FORREST, and N. GOODMAN, et al. *Teenage Pregnancy in Industrialized Countries.* New Haven, CT: Yale University Press, 1986.

JONES, E. F., et al. "Teenage Pregnancy in Developed Countries: Determinants and Policy Implications." *Family Planning Perspectives* 17 (March–April 1985), 53–63.

NATIONAL COMMISSION ON MARIHUANA AND DRUG ABUSE. *Drug Use in America: Problem in Perspective.* Washington, DC, 1973.

NATIONAL INSTITUTE ON DRUG ABUSE. *AIDS and Intravenous Drug Abuse Among Minorities.* Rockville, MD, 1989.

NATIONAL INSTITUTE ON DRUG ABUSE. *National Household Survey on Drug Abuse: Population Estimates, 1990.* Washington, DC, 1991.

REYES, L. M., and L. D. WAXMAN. *The Continuing Growth of Hunger, Homelessness, and Poverty in America's Cities: 1986, A 26–City Survey.* Washington, DC: U.S. Conference of Mayors, 1986.

ROSSI, PETER. *Down and Out in America: The Causes of Homelessness.* Chicago: University of Chicago Press, 1989.

SNOW, DAVID, and LEON ANDERSON. "Identity Work Among the Homeless: The Verbal Construction and Avowal of Personal Identities." *American Journal of Sociology* 92 (May 1987), 1336–71.

SUGAR, MAX, ed. *Adolescent Parenthood.* New York: Spectrum, 1984.

WATTS, T., and R. WRIGHT, eds. *Black Alcoholism: Toward A Comprehensive Understanding.* Springfield, IL: Charles C. Thomas, 1983.

NOTES

1. Information and data in this section were provided by the National Coalition for the Homeless.
2. National Coalition for the Homeless, *Homelessness in the United States: Background and Federal Response* (New York, 1988).
3. From an editorial in the *New York Times,* January 1, 1989, Section 4, p. 10.
4. Department of Housing and Urban Development, *A Report to the Secretary on the Homeless and Emergency Shelters* (Washington, DC, 1984).
5. National Coalition for the Homeless, *Homelessness in the United States,* p. 1; Charles Marwick, "The 'Sizeable' Homeless Population: A Growing Challenge for Medicine," *Journal of the American Medical Association* 253 (June 14, 1985), 3217–25.
6. Bryant Robey, "Two Hundred Years and Counting: The 1990 Census," *Population Bulletin* 44 (April 1989), 13–14.
7. Kim Hopper, "The New Urban Niche of Homelessness: New York City in the Late 1980's," *Bulletin of the New York Academy of Medicine* 66 (September–October 1990), 435–50; Marwick, "Sizeable Homeless Population," pp. 3217–25.
8. Marwick, "Sizeable Homeless Population," pp. 3218–19.
9. Hopper, "New Urban Niche," p. 438.
10. This information is from a letter to the *New York Times* by Don Sloan, M.D.: "Health Care Suffered in Reagan Boom," February 22, 1990, p. A22.
11. William R. Breakey et al., "Health and Mental Health Problems of Homeless Men and Women in Baltimore," *Journal of the American Medical Association* 262 (September 8, 1989), 1352–57; Council on Scientific Affairs, American Medical Association, "Health Care Needs of Homeless and Runaway Youths," *Journal of the American Medical Association* 262 (September 8, 1989), 1358–61; William J. Vicic, "Homelessness," *Bulletin of the New York Academy of Medicine* 67 (January–February 1991), 49–54.
12. Breakey et al., "Health and Mental Health Problems," p. 1354.
13. Josephine Martin, "The Trauma of Homelessness," *International Journal of Mental Health* 20 (Summer 1991), 17–27.
14. *New York City Five Year Plan for Housing and Assisting Homeless Adults* (New York, Office of the Mayor, 1991).
15. Partnership for the Homeless, *Moving Forward: A National Agenda to Address Homelessness in 1990 and Beyond* (New York, 1989).
16. From AP wire service, article: "Mentally Ill Homeless Are on Rise."
17. Celia W. Dugger, "Big Shelters Hold Terrors for Mentally Ill," *New York Times,* January 12, 1992, p. 1.
18. Celia W. Dugger, "New York Report Finds Drug Abuse Rife in Shelters," *New York Times,* February 16, 1992, p. 44.
19. C. L. M. Caton, "The Homeless Experience in Adolescent Years," in *The Mental Health Needs of Homeless Persons,* ed. E. L. Bassuk (San Francisco: Jossey-Bass, 1986).
20. Marwick, "Sizeable Homeless Population," p. 3224.
21. Partnership for the Homeless, "Moving Forward," pp. 12–13.
22. Council on Scientific Affairs, AMA, p. 1159.
23. Celia W. Dugger, "New York Report Finds Drug Abuse Life in Shelters," *New York Times,* February 16, 1992, p. 44.
24. Vicic, "Homelessness," p. 50.
25. Peter H. Rossi et al., "The Urban Homeless: Estimating Composition and Size," *Science* 235 (March 13, 1987), 1337.

26. Celia W. Dugger, "New York Report Finds Drug Abuse Rife in Shelters," *New York Times,* February 16, 1992, p. 44.

27. David Snow and Leon Anderson, "Identity Work among the Homeless: A Verbal Construction and Avowal of Personal Identity," *American Journal of Sociology* 92 (May 1987), 1336–71.

28. Marwick, "Sizeable Homeless Population," p. 3218.

29. Pamela Fischer et al., "Mental Health and Social Characteristics of the Homeless: A Survey of Mission Users," *American Journal of Public Health* 76 (May 1986), 519–24.

30. Jason DeParle, "Aid for Homeless Focuses on Veterans," *New York Times,* November 11, 1991, p. 8A.

31. Richard Ropers and Richard Boyer, "Perceived Health Status Among the New Urban Homeless," *Social Science and Medicine* 24 (1987), 669–78.

32. L. Gelberg and L. S. Linn, "Mental Health, Alcohol and Drug Use and Criminal History Among Homeless Adults," *American Journal of Psychiatry* 145 (1988), 191–96; Robert Rosenheck, P. Gallup, and C. A. Leda, "Vietnam Era and Vietnam Combat Veterans Among the Homeless," *American Journal of Public Health* 81 (May 1991), 643–46.

33. DeParle, "Aid for Homeless," p. A8.

34. Rosenheck et al., "Vietnam Era and Vietnam Combat Veterans," p. 644.

35. Partnership for the Homeless, *The Ninth Year: Achievement and Initiatives* (New York, 1991).

36. *New York City Five Year Plan,* Chapter 1.

37. Celia W. Dugger, "New York Report Finds Drug Abuse Rife in Shelters," *New York Times,* February 16, 1992, p. 44.

38. Ibid.

39. Partnership for the Homeless, *The Ninth Year,* p. 3.

40. Peter Steinfels, "Apathy is Seen Greeting Agony of the Homeless," *New York Times,* January 20, 1992, p. Al.

41. Stephanie Strom, "House for the Homeless Provokes Dispute," *New York Times,* May 19, 1990, p. Bl.

42. Wayne King, "Man Trespasses To Stay Alive: Is He Justified?" *New York Times,* March 6, 1990, p. Bl.

43. From AP wire service: "Deaths From Cold Soar as Homeless Increase," *New York Times,* Dec. 25, 1988, p. 26.

44. Peter Steinfels, "Apathy is Seen Greeting Agony of the Homeless," *New York Times,* January 20, 1992, p. B7.

45. "On Homelessness and the American Way," *American Journal of Public Health* 76 (September 1986), 1084–85.

46. Cheryl Alexander et al., "Early Sexual Activity among Adolescents in Small Towns and Rural Areas," *Family Planning Perspectives* 21 (1989), 261–66; Janet B. Hardy et al., "Fathers of Children Born to Young Urban Mothers," *Family Planning Perspectives* 21 (1989), 159–63; Freya Sonenstein et al., "Levels of Sexual Activity Among Adolescent Males in the United States," *Family Planning Perspectives* 23 (1991), 162–67; Freya Sonenstein et al., "Sexual Activity, Condom Use and AIDS Awareness Among Adolescent Males," *Family Planning Perspectives* 21 (1989), 153–58; Max Sugar, "Adolescent Pregnancy in the United States: Problems and Prospects," *Adolescent and Pediatric Gynecology* 4 (1991), 171–85; L. S. Zabin et al., "Ages of Physical Maturation at First Intercourse," *Demography* 23 (1986), 595.

47. Sonenstein et al., "Sexual Activity," p. 164.

48. Ibid.

49. Hardy et al., "Fathers of Children," p. 161; Sugar, "Adolescent Pregnancy," p. 172.

50. Elsie F. Jones et al., "Teenage Pregnancy in Developed Countries: Determinants and Policy Implications," *Family Planning Perspectives* 17 (1985), 53–63.

51. Stanley Henshaw et al., "Characteristics of U. S. Women Having Abortions, 1987," *Family Planning Perspectives* 23 (1991), 75–81.

52. Melvin Zelnik and John Kantner, "The Resolution of Teenage First Pregnancies," *Family Planning Perspectives* 6 (1974), 74–80.

53. Henshaw et al., "Characteristics of U.S. Women," pp. 75–81.

54. U.S. Bureau of the Census, *Statistical Abstract of the United States: 1991* (Washington, DC, 1991), p. 67.

55. Alan Guttmacher Institute, "Information on Fertility Patterns: Focus on Black Adolescents," unpublished, no date.

56. Henshaw et al., "Characteristics of U.S. Women," pp. 75–81.

57. Ibid.

58. Zelnik and Kantner, "Resolution of Teenage First Pregnancies," pp. 74–80.

59. Ibid.; Edmund Mech, "Pregnant Adolescents: Communicating the Abortion Alternative," *Child Welfare* 65 (1986), 555–67.

60. Michael Bracken et al., "Abortion, Adoption, or Motherhood: An Empirical Study of Decision-Making During Pregnancy," *American Journal of Obstetrics and Gynecology* 130 (1978), 251–62.

61. D. Kalmuss, P B. Namerow, and L. Cushman, "Adoption Versus Parenting Among Young Pregnant Women," *Family Planning Perspectives* 23 (1991), 17–23; Michael D. Resnick et al., "Characteristics of Unmarried Adolescent Mothers: Determinants of Childrearing Versus Adoption," *American Journal of Orthopsychiatry* 60 (1990), 577–84.

62. Janet B. Hardy and Anne K. Duggan, "Teenage Fathers and the Fathers of Infants of Urban, Teenage Mothers," *American Journal of Public Health* 78 (1988), 919–22.

63. A.B. Elster, M.E. Lamb, and J. Tavoré, "Association Between Behavioral and School Problems and Fatherhood in a National Sample of Adolescent Youths," *The Journal of Pediatrics* 111 (1987), 932–36; Janet B. Hardy et al., "Fathers of Children Born to Young Urban Mothers," *Family Planning Perspectives* 21 (1989), 159–63.

64. Elster et al., "Association Between Behavioral and School Problems," pp. 932–36; Hardy and Duggen, "Teenage Fathers," pp. 919–22.

65. Elster et al., "Association Between Behavioral and School Problems," pp. 932–36.

66. Guttmacher Institute, "Information on Fertility Patterns."

67. Ibid.

68. U.S. Bureau of the Census, Current Population Reports, Series P-20, *Marital Status and Living Arrangements, March 1990* (Washington, DC, 1991).

69. Hardy et al., "Fathers of Children."

70. Janet B. Hardy et al., "Long-Range Outcome of Adolescent Pregnancy," *Clinical Obstetrics and Gynecology* 21 (1978), 1215–32; W. E. Oppel and A. B. Royston, "Teenage Births: Some Social, Psychological and Physical Sequelae," *American Journal of Public Health* 61 (1971), 751–56.

71. National Institute on Drug Abuse, *National Household Survey on Drug Abuse: Population Estimates, 1990* (Washington, DC, 1991). This report is based on a survey of the American household population aged 12 and over.

72. D. Herd, "Rethinking Black Drinking," *British Journal of Addiction* 82 (1987), 219–23; J. A. Neff, "Alcohol Consumption and Psychological Distress Among U.S. Anglos, Hispanics and Blacks," *Alcohol and Alcoholism* 21 (1986), 111–19; L. Ronan, "Alcohol Related Health Risks among Black Americans," *Alcohol Health and Research World* 11 (1987), 36–39.

73. T. C. Hartford, "Drinking Problems Among Black and Non-Black Adolescents," *Annals of the New York Academy of Sciences* 472 (1986), 130–41.

74. B. Fernandez et al., "Drinking Patterns of Inner City Blacks and Puerto Ricans," *Journal of Studies on Alcohol* 47 (1986), 156–60.

75. *Alcohol Health and Research World* 11 (1987), 39.

76. Howard Abadinsky, *Drug Abuse: An Introduction* (Chicago: Nelson-Hall, 1989), p. 3; *New York Times,* May 13, 1987, p. 27; *U.S. News and World Report,* November 30, 1987, pp. 56–63.

78. U.S. Public Health Service, Office of Minority Health, *Closing the Gap: Chemical Dependency and Minorities* (Washington, DC, 1988).

78. Ibid., p. 2.

79. *New York Times,* May 17, 1988, p. A1.

80. *Morbidity and Mortality Weekly Report* 38 (October 13, 1989), 685–87.

81. Ibid., pp. 685–87.

82. U.S. Bureau of the Census, *Statistical Abstract of the United States, 1991*, p. 123.

83. See, for example, Barbara Bettes et al., "Ethnicity and Psychological Factors in Alcohol and Tobacco Use in Adolescence," *Child Development* 61 (1990), 557–65.

84. U.S. Public Health Service, p. 3.

85. R. M. Davis, "Current Trends in Cigarette Advertising and Marketing," *New England Journal* of *Medicine* 316 (1987), 725–32; *Journal of the American Medical Association* 263 (June 6, 1990), 2872–75.

86. Abadinsky, *Drug Abuse*, p. 7; "Cocaine Update," *American Family Physician* 41 (January 1990), 247–50; Mary A. House, "Cocaine," *American Journal of Nursing* 90 (April 1990), 41–45.

87. Jane Gross, "A New, Purified Form of Cocaine Causes Alarm as Abuse Increases," *New York Times*, November 29, 1985, p. A1.

88. Abadinsky, *Drug Abuse*, pp. 80–83; Steven Brody et al., "Cocaine-Related Medical Problems: Consecutive Series of 233 Patients," *The American Journal of Medicine* 88 (April 1990), 325–31; Mark S. Gold, *800 Cocaine* (New York: Bantam Books, 1984); Deborah Hannan and Alan Adler, "Crack Abuse: Do You Know Enough About It?" *Post Graduate Medicine* 88 (July 1990), 141–47; House, "Cocaine," pp. 41–45.

89. Abadinsky, *Drug Abuse*, pp. 84–86; G. R. Gay, "Cocaine," *New York State Journal of Medicine* 89 (1989), 384–86; Hannan and Adler, "Crack Abuse," p. 141.

90. Gina Kolata, "Drug Researchers Try to Treat a Nearly Unbreakable Habit," *New York Times*, January 25, 1988, p. 1.

91. See footnote 87. Also, Robert Fullilove et al., "Risk of Sexually Transmitted Disease Among Black Adolescent Crack Users in Oakland and San Francisco, Calif.," *Journal of the American Medical Association* 263 (February 9, 1990), 851–54; T. Mieczkowski and C. J. Boyd, "Drug Use, Health, Family and Social Support in 'Crack' Cocaine Users," *Addictive Behaviors* 15, (1990), 481–85.

92. Editorial: "Crack: A Disaster of Historic Dimension, Still Growing," *New York Times*, May 28, 1989, Sec. 4, p. 14.

93. Peter Kerr, "Addiction's Hidden Toll: Poor Families in Turmoil," *New York Times*, June 23, 1988, p. A1.

94. Editorial: "Crack: A Disaster of Historic Dimension, Still Growing," *New York Times*, May 28, 1989, Sec. 4, p. 14.

95. Editorial: "Crack: A Disaster of Historic Dimension, Still Growing," *New York Times*, May 28, 1989, Sec. 4, p. 14.

96. Peter Kerr, "Addiction's Hidden Toll: Poor Families in Turmoil," *New York Times*, June 23, 1988, p. A1.

97. Fullilove et al., "Risk of Sexually Transmitted Disease," pp. 851–54; Hannan and Adler, "Crack Abuse," pp. 146–47.

98. An Advertisement from Partnership For A Drug Free America.

99. Peter Kerr, "Addiction's Hidden Toll: Poor Families in Turmoil," *New York Times*, June 23, 1988, p. A1.

100. Abadinsky, *Drug Abuse*, pp. 93–97; Michael Agar, *Ripping and Running: A Formal Ethnography of Urban Heroin Addicts* (New York: Seminar Press, 1973); Vincent Dole, "Addictive Behavior," *Scientific American* 243 (1980), 138–54.

101. Evelyn Nieves, "Toxic Heroin Has Killed 12, Officials Say," *New York Times*, February 4, 1991, p. B1.

102. Joseph B. Treaster, "A More Potent Heroin Makes a Comeback in a New Needleless Form," *New York Times*, April 28, 1991, Section 4, p. 4.

103. Evelyn Nieves, "After 6 Addicts Die, Police in Northeast Warn of Toxic Drug," *New York Times*, February 3, 1991, p. 1.

104. Joseph B. Treaster, "At a Fast and Lethal Hub of the Heroin Trade," *New York Times*, February 8, 1991, p. B1.

105. Evelyn Nieves, "After 6 Addicts Die, Police in Northeast Warn of Toxic Drug," *New York Times*, February 3, 1991, p. 1.

CHAPTER EIGHT

Crime and Justice

ADULT CRIME

Crime has become an especially difficult problem for citizens of the United States, regardless of whether they live in urban, suburban, or rural areas. Efforts to control crime vary from police department to police department. For many years crime was considered to be largely an urban problem, especially prevalent in the inner cities. But small towns and rural areas are experiencing increasingly high rates of crime.

Arrests for criminal behavior have usually been higher in minority communities than in the white community. Does this mean that people of color, because of their precarious status, are more likely to commit crimes than others? Or are they simply more likely to be arrested for crimes than whites? According to a 1996 report of the Federal Bureau of Investigation (FBI), although black people comprise 13 percent of the population, they are responsible for nearly one-third (30.7 percent) of all crimes culminating in arrests.[1]

There were, in 1996, more than 11 million arrests for crimes in the United States, with whites accounting for more than twice as many arrests as blacks. On the other hand, blacks are arrested for far more crimes than their proportion of the population. There is no way of knowing how many crimes were actually committed, because not all crimes are reported to law enforcement personnel; furthermore, there is evidence that police are more likely to arrest blacks and other minorities than whites. (This phenomenon will be discussed later in this chapter.)

The FBI utilizes data collected from local police departments, and divides the data into the most serious crimes (felonies) and those of lesser importance (misdemeanors). The 1996 FBI report was based on data from 9,661 agencies representing 189,885,000 people. The most serious crimes are murder, forcible rape, robbery, aggravated assault, burglary, larceny–theft, motor vehicle theft, and arson. (See

Table 8-1.) Blacks are reported to be arrested more often than whites for all these felonies when compared with their percentage in the population. However, in terms of total felony arrests made, blacks exceed whites in number of arrests only for murder and robbery.

When both violent crime and property crime lead to arrests, while blacks are overrepresented in both categories when compared with their percentage of the population, they are less likely to be arrested for both violent crime and property crime.

For all other offenses (mostly misdemeanors), whites exceed blacks in each category, but the only arrests for which the black arrest rate does not exceed their percentage in the population is driving under the influence. The misdemeanors for which whites exceed blacks in arrests are vandalism, sex offenses, violation of liquor laws, drunkenness, suspicion, curfew and loitering laws, and runaways. Insofar as murder is concerned, the reported rates begin to decrease with age. However, among blacks those males between the ages of 15 and 24 had the highest homicide rate in 1994.[2] Among those between 75 and 84 years of age, the figures are significantly higher for blacks (both males and females) than for whites.

Americans appear to have a love affair with guns, and the availability of such weapons is in large part responsible for the high homicide rate in the country. Even young children are increasingly carrying handguns to school, often with deadly consequences. And while there have been gun control laws enacted in the United States, the powerful National Rifle Association opposes virtually all gun control laws, even those designed to protect police officers.

The Second Amendment to the Constitution is interpreted by some Americans as giving them the right to be armed. The Supreme Court ruled in 1939 that the Second Amendment applies to the maintenance of a militia, not to the individual's right to keep and bear arms.[3]

JUVENILE CRIME

It appears that among white people, black teenagers are thought to be the group in society most responsible for serious crimes. According to the FBI, black teenagers are less likely to be arrested for crimes than black adults. White youths are responsible for 70 percent of all juvenile arrests, while black teenagers are responsible for 27 percent. (See Table 8-2.) Murder and robbery are the only serious offenses for which blacks are arrested more often than whites.

White teenagers account for one-half of all violent crime and 70 percent of all property crime. In all other crime categories except gambling, white juveniles are responsible for most arrests.

While blacks are overrepresented in virtually all categories of less serious crimes, they are underrepresented in three criminal categories: driving under the influence, violation of liquor laws, and drunkenness. White juveniles are responsible for more than 90 percent of arrests for driving under the influence and violation of liquor laws.

TABLE 8-1   Total Arrests, Distribution by Race, 1996

9,661 agencies; 1996 estimated population 189,885,000

OFFENSE CHARGED	TOTAL ARRESTS					PERCENT DISTRIBUTION				
	TOTAL	WHITE	BLACK	AMERICAN INDIAN OR ALASKAN NATIVE	ASIAN OR PACIFIC ISLANDER	TOTAL	WHITE	BLACK	AMERICAN INDIAN OR ALASKAN NATIVE	ASIAN OR PACIFIC ISLANDER
TOTAL	**11,072,832**	**7,404,170**	**3,400,338**	**139,290**	**129,034**	**100.0**	**66.9**	**30.7**	**1.3**	**1.2**
Murder and nonnegligent manslaughter	14,439	6,176	7,928	119	216	100.0	42.8	54.9	.8	1.5
Forcible rape	24,317	13,637	10,124	266	290	100.0	56.1	41.6	1.1	1.2
Robbery	121,673	48,412	70,828	651	1,782	100.0	39.8	58.2	.5	1.5
Aggravated assault	387,090	230,785	147,463	3,929	4,913	100.0	59.6	38.1	1.0	1.3
Burglary	263,774	179,063	78,473	2,853	3,385	100.0	67.9	29.8	1.1	1.3
Larceny–theft	1,094,186	709,109	351,993	13,707	19,377	100.0	64.8	32.2	1.3	1.8
Motor vehicle theft	131,892	74,618	53,022	1,579	2,673	100.0	56.6	40.2	1.2	2.0
Arson	13,739	10,175	3,297	132	135	100.0	74.1	24.0	1.0	1.0
Violent crime	547,519	299,010	236,343	4,965	7,201	100.0	54.6	43.2	.9	1.3
Property crime	1,503,591	972,965	486,785	18,271	25,570	100.0	64.7	32.4	1.2	1.7
Crime Index total	2,051,110	1,271,975	723,128	23,236	32,771	100.0	62.0	35.3	1.1	1.6
Other assaults	971,267	606,019	340,930	13,071	11,247	100.0	62.4	35.1	1.3	1.2
Forgery and counterfeiting	88,063	56,461	29,547	511	1,544	100.0	64.1	33.6	.6	1.8
Fraud	324,121	204,054	115,980	1,470	2,617	100.0	63.0	35.8	.5	.8
Embezzlement	11,434	7,216	3,985	59	174	100.0	63.1	34.9	.5	1.5
Stolen property; buying, receiving, possessing	110,834	63,893	44,647	870	1,424	100.0	57.6	40.3	.8	1.3

Vandalism	233,952	171,124	56,725	3,220	2,883	100.0	73.1	24.2	1.4	1.2
Weapons; carrying, possessing, etc.	161,016	93,430	64,534	1,152	1,900	100.0	58.0	40.1	.7	1.2
Prostitution and commercialized vice	81,022	47,809	31,065	528	1,620	100.0	59.0	38.3	.7	2.0
Sex offenses (except forcible rape and prostitution)	70,546	52,136	16,691	79	928	100.0	73.9	23.7	1.1	1.3
Drug abuse violations	1,127,114	681,008	433,352	5,600	7,154	100.0	60.4	38.4	.5	.6
Gambling	16,982	7,711	8,588	66	617	100.0	45.4	50.6	.4	3.6
Offenses against family and children	102,944	67,531	32,561	1,129	1,723	100.0	65.6	31.6	1.1	1.7
Driving under the influence	1,011,470	876,558	104,793	16,867	13,252	100.0	86.7	10.4	1.7	1.3
Liquor laws	489,219	395,689	78,178	12,007	3,345	100.0	80.9	16.0	2.5	.7
Drunkenness	522,159	423,358	84,362	12,450	1,989	100.0	81.1	16.2	2.4	.4
Disorderly conduct	625,861	390,499	223,234	8,052	4,076	100.0	62.4	35.7	1.3	.7
Vagrancy	21,719	11,800	9,416	422	81	100.0	54.3	43.4	1.9	.4
All other offenses (except traffic)	2,763,311	1,758,183	938,754	34,429	31,945	100.0	63.6	34.0	1.2	1.2
Suspicion	4,843	3,272	1,492	56	23	100.0	67.6	30.8	1.2	.5
Curfew and loitering law violations	142,135	103,664	34,756	1,655	2,060	100.0	72.9	24.5	1.2	1.4
Runaways	141,710	110,780	23,620	1,649	5,661	100.0	78.2	16.7	1.2	4.0

Source: Federal Bureau of Investigation, *Crime in the United States 1996* (Washington, DC, 1997).

TABLE 8-2   Total Teenage Arrests, Distribution by Race, 1996

OFFENSE CHARGED	ARRESTS UNDER 18					PERCENT DISTRIBUTION				
	TOTAL	WHITE	BLACK	AMERICAN INDIAN OR ALASKAN NATIVE	ASIAN OR PACIFIC ISLANDER	TOTAL	WHITE	BLACK	AMERICAN INDIAN OR ALASKAN NATIVE	ASIAN OR PACIFIC ISLANDER
TOTAL	**2,099,997**	**1,462,863**	**573,498**	**25,515**	**38,121**	**100.0**	**69.7**	**27.3**	**1.2**	**1.8**
Murder and nonnegligent manslaughter	2,171	849	1,248	14	60	100.0	39.1	57.5	.6	2.8
Forcible rape	4,123	2,279	1,772	38	34	100.0	55.3	43.0	.9	.8
Robbery	39,012	15,432	22,578	193	809	100.0	39.6	57.9	.5	2.1
Aggravated assault	56,791	32,775	22,594	576	846	100.0	57.7	39.8	1.0	1.5
Burglary	97,634	71,885	22,861	1,305	1,583	100.0	73.6	23.4	1.3	1.6
Larceny–theft	369,771	260,972	94,522	5,371	8,906	100.0	70.6	25.6	1.5	2.4
Motor vehicle theft	54,755	31,647	20,876	815	1,417	100.0	57.8	38.1	1.5	2.6
Arson	7,289	5,836	1,290	81	82	100.0	80.1	17.7	1.1	1.1
Violent crime	102,097	51,335	48,192	821	1,749	100.0	50.3	47.2	.8	1.7
Property crime	529,449	370,340	139,549	7,572	11,988	100.0	69.9	26.4	1.4	2.3
Crime Index total	631,546	421,675	187,741	8,393	13,737	100.0	66.8	29.7	1.3	2.2
Other assaults	171,111	106,615	59,906	1,942	2,648	100.0	62.3	35.0	1.1	1.5
Forgery and counterfeiting	6,225	4,829	1,242	63	91	100.0	77.6	20.0	1.0	1.5
Fraud	18,864	9,940	8,238	82	604	100.0	52.7	43.7	.4	3.2
Embezzlement	957	599	344	2	12	100.0	62.6	35.9	.2	1.3
Stolen property; buying, receiving, possessing	30,127	18,179	11,111	306	531	100.0	60.3	36.9	1.0	1.8
Vandalism	103,207	82,357	18,057	1,272	1,521	100.0	79.8	17.5	1.2	1.5
Weapons; carrying, possessing, etc.	39,331	24,877	13,480	356	618	100.0	63.3	34.3	.9	1.6

Prostitution and commercialized vice	1,104	650	412	25	17	100.0	58.9	37.3	2.3	1.5
Sex offenses (except forcible rape and prostitution)	12,644	8,812	3,589	112	131	100.0	69.7	28.4	.9	1.0
Drug abuse violations	158,161	98,396	57,221	1,093	1,451	100.0	62.2	36.2	.7	.9
Gambling	2,263	334	1,916	1	12	100.0	14.8	84.7		.5
Offenses against family and children	5,796	4,344	1,253	50	149	100.0	74.9	21.6	.9	2.6
Driving under the influence	12,775	11,651	725	251	148	100.0	91.2	5.7	2.0	1.2
Liquor laws	112,191	101,943	6,284	2,989	975	100.0	90.9	5.6	2.7	.9
Drunkenness	17,098	15,066	1,557	366	109	100.0	88.1	9.1	2.1	.6
Disorderly conduct	159,814	100,900	56,113	1,429	1,372	100.0	63.1	35.1	.9	.9
Vagrancy	2,869	1,823	1,002	21	23	100.0	63.5	34.9	.7	.8
All other offenses (except traffic)	328,465	234,209	84,564	3,450	6,242	100.0	71.3	25.7	1.1	1.9
Suspicion	1,604	1,220	367	8	9	100.0	76.1	22.9	.5	.6
Curfew and loitering law violations	142,135	103,664	34,756	1,655	2,060	100.0	72.9	24.5	1.2	1.4
Runaways	141,710	110,780	23,620	1,649	5,661	100.0	78.2	16.7	1.2	4.0

Source: Federal Bureau of Investigation, *Crime in the United States 1996* (Washington, DC, 1997).

Murder is the most serious crime on the FBI's list, and in 1996, it was reported that fully 31 percent of the total murders in the United States were committed by blacks. This compares with 70 percent by white males.[4]

Black and white females are reported to be far less likely than black and white males to commit crimes. White females are reported to have committed 2.6 percent of all murders in 1994, while black females are reported to be responsible for 12 percent of all murders.

In the age category 15 to 24, blacks were reported to be responsible for more murders than whites. Indeed, blacks in general, with few exceptions, are reported to exceed their percentage in the population in murder rates in 1994. Males commit more homicides than females, and black males between the ages of 75 and 84 are said to have high murder rates compared to others in that age category.[5]

Two of the reasons for the high murder rate in the United States are the easy availability of guns and a steady dose of deadly violence on television. In the 1980s there were said to be 200 million civilian-owned guns in the United States, including some 60 million handguns. This adds up to more than three guns per family. The United States is said to have the highest murder rate in the industrialized world. As is indicated in chapter 6, two comparable cities in the United States and Canada have different homicide rates. The homicide rate in the U.S. city is much higher, due largely to the availability of firearms in the country.[6]

According to *Time* magazine, 1 in 12 high schoolers is threatened or injured with a weapon each year. The magazine estimates that there are as many firearms in the United States as there are people—more than 235 million in 1998.[7]

In the late 1990s there have been several cases of young schoolchildren who have taken loaded handguns to school, sometimes killing fellow students and teachers. Indeed, in May 1998 a five-year-old child was charged with bringing a loaded semiautomatic to kindergarten. The child "said he wanted to shoot and kill several students, as well as the teacher who had disciplined him."[8]

During the 1997–98 school year, there were a series of widely publicized incidents in which young people (preteenagers or teenagers) took loaded weapons, including assault weapons, to school, where they shot and killed or wounded dozens of students and teachers. These incidents did not happen in the inner city, and no black students were involved. Some feel that these were copycat incidents, and all of them happened in small towns or rural areas. The most serious incidents took place in Pearl, Mississippi; West Paducah, Kentucky; Edinboro, Pennsylvania; Jonesboro, Arkansas; and Springfield, Oregon. They were so closely spaced that law enforcement officials speculated that there was an epidemic of these crimes in the United States.

Around the country, at least a dozen students and two teachers were slain, in lunchrooms, in schoolyards, at morning prayers.[9] The first incident occurred in Pearl, Mississippi, in October 1997, when a 16-year-old boy stabbed his mother to death, then fatally shot his former girlfriend and another girl and wounded several students. After Pearl came West Paducah, Kentucky, where a 14-year-old boy shot and killed three girls who were in a prayer meeting. After West Paducah came Jonesboro,

Arkansas, where an 11-year-old boy and his 13-year-old friend opened fire. Four girls and a teacher were killed, while nine students and a teacher were wounded.

In April 1998, as the carnage continued, *Time* magazine carried on its cover the picture of a young child with an assault rifle, with the heading "Armed and Dangerous."[10] As the magazine reported, these shootings were for just one school year, and there had been similar incidents in previous years. They had occurred in schools in Grayson, Kentucky; Amityville, New York; Redlands, California; Blackwell, South Carolina; Lynnville, Tennessee; Moses Lake, Washington; and Bethel, Alaska. Altogether, 13 people were killed in these shootings.

POLICE BRUTALITY AND OTHER ACTS OF CRUELTY AGAINST MINORITIES

For decades it has been known that police officers throughout the country practice various forms of brutality against people of color. Perhaps the most potent reminder of this was what happened to Rodney King, a black motorist in Los Angeles, in the early morning hours of May 3, 1991. He was savagely beaten by four police officers, while another 19 officers witnessed the incident. This case probably would not have received worldwide attention if it had not been captured on videotape by a concerned citizen. King suffered broken bones, skull fractures, a damaged eye socket, and possibly brain damage as a result of this beating. (See chapter 9.)

A grotesque act of police brutality that received considerable publicity happened in New York City in 1997.[11] In this case a Haitian immigrant, 30-year-old Abner Louima, was arrested outside a Brooklyn nightclub in the early hours of the morning. While being driven to the precinct house, he was severely beaten by four police officers. Once they reached the station house, one police officer took him to the bathroom and rammed the handle of a plunger into Louima's rectum and then into his mouth, breaking his teeth, while another officer held him down. After these acts of barbarity, Louima left his cell with his pants down around his ankles. He was later taken to a hospital, where it was found that the beating had caused severe internal injuries.

The Brooklyn district attorney appointed a member of his staff to prosecute the case, in which he said the officers should be charged with aggravated assault and sexual assault rather than attempted murder.[12] An attorney who represents victims of police brutality said "ramming a plunger up the rectum of the suspect and rupturing his intestines is an act of attempted murder because if left untreated the injuries will produce death through the loss of blood or other means."

State troopers on the New Jersey Turnpike, like members of the New York City Police Department, have long had a reputation for discriminating against people of color, especially black males. These troopers use what is called "profiling," that is, "making a stop of someone they believe to be involved in the drug trade." African-Americans give it another name—"D.W.B." or "Driving While Black."[13]

In April 1998, New Jersey state troopers pulled over four men in a van who were on their way to a college basketball clinic. Before the incident was over, the troopers had fired 11 shots into the van, wounding three of the passengers, two seriously. In the van were three young black men and one Hispanic man. A state judge in 1996 had ruled that the police were carrying out "a policy of 'selective enforcement' by targeting blacks for investigation and arrest." The judge added that "the utter failure of the state police hierarchy to monitor and control a crackdown program or to investigate the many claims of institutional discrimination manifests its indifference if not acceptance."[14]

A federal district court judge said that an officer of Filipino origin had been subjected to racial discrimination and a hostile work environment by New Jersey state troopers. And he added that a black male was stopped and was told that he could avoid a ticket "if he tap-danced on the side of the road."

In the van incident, at around 11 o'clock on the night of April 23, 1998, the police stopped the vehicle because they said it was traveling at a speed of 74 miles per hour in a 55-mile-per-hour zone, but it turned out that the troopers were not equipped with radar. The police continued to lie about what had happened. They claimed that the driver of the van had put it in reverse in an attempt to ram the troopers' vehicle. But the van's windshield was shattered by bullets, and witnesses said that the police account did not accurately describe what happened. When they read about the troopers' report, the witnesses came forth to dispute it, and to say that the troopers had fired 11 shots without provocation.

Furthermore, a black man who passed while the incident was taking place reported that the cruise control on his car was set at 60 m.p.h. Instead of the van attempting to back into the police car, this observer said, the van had lurched forward, rather than backwards as the state troopers had claimed. One driver who had stopped on the turnpike said he had seen the officers shoot at the van after it had rolled down into a ditch. Several others came forward to refute the police report.[15]

The turnpike case received widespread publicity, attracting such high-profile defense lawyers as Johnnie Cochran, Barry Scheck, and Peter Neufield, all veterans of the O. J. Simpson trial. Cochran said "We think this is an important case, not only for the state of New Jersey but for everybody in this country."[16] Along the entire length of Interstate Highway 95, from Maine to Florida, the police stop young and middle-aged minority men because they ostensibly fit the profile of drug couriers. This highway runs through the state of Maryland, where a federal lawsuit was filed by 11 black motorists, backed by the American Civil Liberties Union, charging state troopers with countless stops without provocation. Representative John Conyers, Democrat of Michigan, said: "There are virtually no African American males—including congressmen, actors, athletes and office workers—who have not been stopped at one time or another . . . driving while black."[17]

"Marshaling numbers from the state troopers' own records, the plaintiffs in the Maryland case presented dizzying facts: while 75 percent of the drivers on I-95 are white, only 23 percent of those that troopers stopped and searched from 1995 to 1997 were white; 17 percent of the drivers are black, yet 70 percent of those pulled over were black."[18]

In 1966, 21-year-old Shane Daniels, a young black man from Long Island, was leaving a nightclub when he was attacked by two white men, one a New York City police officer. One of the officers beat the young man with a metal bar outside the nightclub. When bystanders, including friends of Daniels, came to his defense, the police officer, Constantine Chronis, held them back with his gun. He resigned from the police department shortly after the incident. Shane Daniels was almost killed, and after two years he was still suffering from the effects of the beating.[19]

There have been several high-profile cases of police brutality in New York City in recent years. Bob Herbert, a columnist for the *New York Times*, listed a few of them:[20]

- A 25-year-old Navy veteran was killed on a Bronx subway platform in 1996. The victim, a black man, was killed by a shot in the back by a white police officer.
- Anthony Baez died from an illegal choke-hold by a police officer after a dispute erupted during a touch football game. The ball had accidentally hit the outside of the car in which the white police officers were sitting. (More on this important case later in this chapter.)
- Charles C. Campbell, a black man, was beaten and shot to death in a Dobbs Ferry parking lot by an off-duty policeman who did not like where Campbell had parked his car.
- There was a near-fatal attack on Lebert Folkes, a 29-year-old black man from Queens, who was dragged from his sister's car and shot in the face at point-blank range. The white police officer said he thought the car was stolen, but it was not.

The New York City Police Department released a study in which it was acknowledged that minority officers are more likely to face internal disciplinary hearings than are their white colleagues. The Police Department denied that this was a result of racial discrimination, and said that minority officers "are more likely to be involved in serious infractions, particularly while off duty."[21] The report cited such acts as failing random drug tests and taking part in illegal activity. "Of all the police officers called before a departmental trial, 16 percent of all Hispanic officers, 14.3 percent of all black officers, and 9.9 percent of all white officers were dismissed." It should be added that minorities comprise only 27 percent of the New York City police force.

Finally, on an island in Washington State that is an enclave of wealth, a 53-year-old black man, one of 300 blacks among the 21,000 residents, reports that he is often stopped by the police.[22] The man, Wayne Perryman, said he had once been stopped by police officers while walking to lunch. The officers told him, "We got a report of a black guy hanging around this office complex." Perryman's complaints are echoed by other blacks living on this island of software billionaires with mega yachts. A black man who was a janitor for the Mercer Island School District was stopped so many times that the school district gave police officers a poster bearing his picture, with the words "NOT WANTED" printed on the poster.

Referring to police departments in the United States, John Hope Franklin, the head of President Clinton's advisory panel on race relations, said in an interview, "This country cut its eye teeth on racism. And what used to be called Jim Crow is still in vigorous shape—especially in police precincts and in police cars."[23]

In recent years New York City police officers have raided and tortured minority citizens in mistaken searches for guns and drugs. Perhaps one of the most serious cases took place in Brooklyn. According to the *New York Times*, police officers in early May 1998 "broke down the doors of a Brooklyn apartment, guns drawn, tossed a stun grenade through the front hall and handcuffed everyone inside, including a mentally retarded 19-year-old girl who was taking a shower. They were looking for guns and drugs. They found only a terrified family."[24] According to the family, their mentally retarded daughter was menstruating and needed a sanitary pad. She was given one only after she was visibly bleeding.[25] The family filed a $200 million lawsuit for damages to the family and their property. This was the fourth in a series of high-profile cases that had similar consequences beginning in February and March, 1998.

In the first incident, on February 27, 1998, the police raided the home of a black man in the Bronx. The resident, who thought he was being robbed, took a gun and fired a shot. "The police then fired at least 26 bullets into the room. Again the police had raided the wrong house." The same day the police raided the apartment of an 18-year-old mother and her two children. They were given similar treatment.[26]

On March 18, 1998, the police raided the apartment of another black family in Brooklyn, only to find a grandmother watching television with her daughter and grandson. There were no drugs or guns.

Finally, in June of 1987 the police raided still another apartment in Brooklyn. The police had been told by informants that drug dealing was taking place in Apartment 2M. But there was no Apartment 2M in the building. When they raided what they thought was the correct apartment they found only a Hispanic woman and two children, ages one and six.[27] After the police broke down the door, the mother asked them if she could take the screaming baby out of the crib. The response was no.

At his weekly news conference, the police commissioner had this to say about the raid: "It's just like a number of other cases that are popping up as people line up to see if they can sue the city for big dollars with attorneys who hold press conferences rather than litigate."[28] He did not bother to apologize for all the police terror.

The New York City police get the information on which apartments to raid from underworld informants, many of whom are drug addicts and drug dealers. These so-called confidential informants are usually criminals "seeking to trade what they know for reduced charges, shorter sentences or cash."[29]

Police officers in New York City and elsewhere in the country are notorious for committing perjury, especially when they have been brutal to citizens. And when they kill citizens, as often happens, their fellow officers lie for them. This is especially true when their victims are persons of color, as in the case of Anthony Baez, mentioned earlier. In 1994 when police officer Francis Livoti strangled Anthony Baez to death with an illegal choke-hold, he was tried by a judge and acquitted of the death. But the judge called him and other officers who testified for him "a nest of perjury." Furthermore, the Civilian Complaint Review Board had informed police officials that Livoti had been guilty of brutality in nine cases before the Baez case, but he was not removed from service. The medical examiner's office found that Baez had died of asphyxiation as a result of the choke-hold.

The Baez family was upset by the judge's ruling, and the case was taken to federal court, where it was charged that Livoti had violated the civil rights of Anthony Baez. After the death, it was discovered that Livoti and the other officers on duty with him had met to plot a strategy to coordinate their lies. Among other things, the officers claimed that Baez was killed by a black man who had disappeared. Members of the jury knew the officers were lying, and convicted Livoti of violating the civil rights of Anthony Baez. As the *New York Times* editorialized: "The [police] department cannot protect the community if there is reason to question the veracity of officers on the beat and on the witness stand. A system in which officers who brutalize and kill civilians are protected by other officers destroys the public trust and erodes the ability of the force to do its job."[30]

CAPITAL PUNISHMENT

The first point to be made about capital punishment is that the United States is the only industrialized nation in the world that continues this practice. Even South Africa has abolished the death penalty. The practice is a violation of the United Nations Universal Declaration of Human Rights, which endorses "The right of every human being not to be killed and not to be subjected to torture or to cruel and degrading punishment." The United States signed that declaration, but it was not ratified by Congress.[31]

Surveys of the American people indicate that about 80 to 85 percent support the death penalty.[32] It is firmly entrenched in American life. "In state after state, year after year, and to an increasing degree, bills are filed to augment, increase and speed up and in other ways make the death penalty laws at the state level more effective."[33]

In 1976, the U.S. Supreme Court considered the constitutional question of whether the death penalty was a violation of the Eighth Amendment provision against "cruel and unusual punishment." When the Court reached its decision, all but two of the justices concluded that the death penalty was not an unconstitutional punishment.[34] In 1987, the Supreme Court ruled that although, as administered, capital punishment was more likely to be imposed in a discriminatory manner against black defendants, the death penalty was constitutional.

According to the American Civil Liberties Union, more than 13,000 people have been legally executed since colonial times, most of them in the early twentieth century. By the 1930s, as many as 150 people were executed each year.[35] In 1972, the Supreme Court invalidated hundreds of scheduled executions, declaring them "arbitrary and capricious," but as reported above, this decision was discounted and capital punishment was restored in 1976.

As of April 1, 1998, there were 3,387 prisoners on death row in the United States (see Table 8-3). Most (46 percent) of the prisoners awaiting death were white, followed by blacks (42 percent) and Hispanics (8 percent), with Native Americans and Asians accounting for less than 1 percent each. Ninety-nine percent of death row inmates were male, and there were 69 (2 percent) juveniles.

The South has the greatest number of prisoners awaiting death. Three states in that region account for more than 50 percent of all executions, led by Texas with 147 (33 percent), Virginia with 49 (11 percent), and Florida with 43 (9.5 percent).[36]

Of the fifty states and the District of Columbia, thirteen do not have capital punishment statutes. Most states with such laws utilize lethal injection on the assumption that this procedure is more "humane," but the gas chamber, electrocution, and hanging are used in some. Some states give the death row prisoner a choice of methods.

As is indicated in Table 8-4, males are more likely to be executed than females, and white men (48 percent) more often than black males (37 percent) and Hispanic men (5 percent). Whether or not one is executed depends largely on the race of the defendant

TABLE 8-3   Death Row Inmates by Race and Gender as of April 1, 1998

	NUMBER OF DEATH ROW INMATES	PERCENTAGE
Total Number: 3,387		
Race of Defendant:		
White	1,611	47.56%
Black	1,420	41.93%
Latino/Latina	265	7.82%
Native American	45	1.33%
Asian	25	.74%
Unknown at this issue	21	.62%
Gender:		
Male	3,344	98.73%
Female	43	1.27%
Juveniles:		
Male	69	2.04%

DISPOSITIONS SINCE JANUARY 1, 1973:
Executions: 451
Suicides: 51
Commutations: 76   (including those by the Governor of Texas
                                 resulting from favorable court decisions)

Died of natural causes, or killed while under death sentence: 112
Convictions/Sentences reversed: 1,642

JURISDICTIONS WITH CAPITAL PUNISHMENT STATUTES: 40

Source: NAACP Legal Defense and Educational Fund, "Death Row, U.S.A." (New York, 1998).

TABLE 8-4   Total Number of Executions Since Capital Punishment Was Reinstated in 1976, by Race and Gender

Total: 451

Gender of Defendants Executed			**Gender of Victims**		
Total number: 451			Total number: 611		
Female	3	.67%	Female	265	43.37%
Male	448	99.33%	Male	346	56.63%

Race of Defendants Executed			**Race of Victims**		
White	254	56.32%	White	505	82.65%
Black	166	36.81%	Black	76	12.44%
Latino/a	24	5.32%	Latino/a	21	3.44%
Native American	5	1.11%	Asian	9	1.47%
Asian	2	.44%			

Defendant-Victim Racial Combinations

White Defendant and		
White Victim	355	58.10%
Black Victim	8	1.31%
Asian Victim	2	.33%
Latino/a Victim	8	1.31%
Black Defendant and		
White Victim	133	21.77%
Black Victim	66	10.80%
Asian Victim	3	.49%
Latino/a Victim	2	.33%
Latino Defendant and		
White Victim	14	2.29%
Latino/a Victim	10	1.64%
Asian Victim	1	.16%
Black Victim	1	.16%
Native American and		
White Victim	5	.82%
Asian Defendant and		
Asian Victim	3	.49%

Source: NAACP Legal Defense and Educational Fund, "Death Row, U.S.A." (New York, 1998).

and the race of the victim. In most (58 percent) of those executed, both the defendant and the victim were white. Of special importance is what happens when the defendant is black and the victim is either black or white. The second highest execution rate (22 percent) is for black defendants and white victims. When the defendant and the victim are both black, 11 percent are executed, the third highest category. When the victim is black and the defendant white, there is little likelihood that the defendant will be executed. This combination accounted for only 1 percent of executions.

A 1987 study of death sentencing in New Jersey found that "prosecutors sought the death penalty in 50 percent of cases involving a black defendant and a white victim, but in only 28 percent of cases involving black defendants and black victims." And in a 1985 study in California, "six percent of those convicted of killing whites got the death penalty, compared to three percent of those convicted of killing blacks." Blacks, poor whites, and those who live in the South are most likely to face execution.[37]

Texas practices a form of frontier justice when it comes to the death penalty. As one professor noted about the town of Huntsville, Texas: "Huntsville has become a kind of laboratory for the bureaucratizion of capital punishment. An execution is not a disruptive and monumental event."[38] In the first five months of 1997, Texas executed 15 men, all but three of them white. However, in the following month (June), 11 men were executed, five of whom were black.

Executions are gruesome events. For example, all prisoners who are killed in Florida are executed in the electric chair. In 1997 when one prisoner was strapped to the electric chair, flames erupted from the top of the leather face mask the defendant wore as 2,000 volts of electricity were turned on. "It took several seconds for the flames to go out, but the state doctor said he thought the death had been painless." Earlier, in 1995, "another condemned killer let out a muffled scream as he was being executed."[39] Michael Radelet, a professor opposed to the death penalty, said after the last malfunctioning of Florida's electric chair, "The story in this case is not a malfunctioning electric chair but a malfunctioning criminal justice system. It executes people with a strong argument of innocence, strong evidence of mental disorder and against the wishes of the families of victims."[40]

One other observer of an execution described it as follows:

> The electricity hit him. His body stiffened spasmodically. A thin swirl of smoke trailed from his head. People outside the witness room could hear crackling and burning; a faint smell of burned flesh lingered in the air, mildly nauseating some people. The body remained taut. Three minutes passed, while the officials let the body cool. Immediately after the execution, I'm told, the body would be too hot to touch and would blister anyone who did.

The above case is far from unique. A study in the *Stanford University Law Review* "documents 350 capital convictions in this century, in which it was later proven that the convict had not committed the crime."[41] The American Civil Liberties Union cites several cases in which executions were anything but swift and painless. Some examples: "In Texas, there have been three botched executions since 1985. . . . In one case "it took 24 minutes to kill an individual, after the tube attached to the needle in his arm leaked and sprayed noxious chemicals toward witnesses." In another case, in 1989, one prisoner choked and heaved for several minutes before dying because the dosage of lethal drugs was too weak.

On the question of the swiftness of the death penalty, it was reported in 1966, when 376 people were on death row, that "six have been on death row for 20 years and another 107 have been there at least a decade."[42] It is reported that "most of these cases were poorly tried at the trial level." This is frequently the case for death row defendants. Lawyers for indigent prisoners are normally paid far less than most lawyers earn. A court-appointed defense lawyer may earn less than teenagers at McDonald's and less than the minimum wage. "An Alabama lawyer who spends 500 hours preparing for a death penalty trial will be paid $4 an hour."[43] In many cases these lawyers are not qualified for the task. In Houston, Texas, for example, a 72-year-old court-appointed lawyer "slept through the testimony of several witnesses." A local newspaper there declared: "His mouth kept falling open and his head lolled back on his shoulders, and then he awakened just long enough to catch himself and sit upright. Then it happened again. And again. And again."[44]

On the question of innocent people on death row, the Death Penalty Information Center reported in 1997 that since 1993, 69 prisoners were released from death row because they had been wrongly convicted.[45] Furthermore, the American Bar Association reported in 1997 that "The system for administering the death penalty in the United States is unfair and lacks adequate safeguards. The Bar Association noted that the system is getting worse, and stated that executions should be stopped until a greater degree of fairness and due process can be achieved."[46]

Prisoners sentenced to death row are not necessarily the people convicted of the most serious crimes. Rather, they are people of color and the poor. According to the American Civil Liberties Union, "the only factors seem to be race and poverty. Who gets the death penalty is largely determined, not by the severity of the crime, but by race, sex and economic class of the criminal and victim geography."[47]

Some states (12) and the District of Columbia have no capital punishment statutes, and that does not increase the number of murders in those jurisdictions. Furthermore, the theory that capital punishment is a deterrent to murder has been proven false by experiments in the abolition of capital punishment.[48] Some examples: Colorado abolished capital punishment in 1897 and returned to it in 1901. The average annual number of convictions for murder during the five years before abolition, during the abolition years, and during the five years following were 15.4, 18, and 19.

Missouri abandoned the death penalty in 1917 and brought it back in 1919. The homicide rate per 100,000 population during the years 1911–1916 averaged 9.2 a year, and during abolition it was 10.7. During the years 1920–1924, it was 11.

South Dakota reintroduced the death penalty in 1939, having abolished it in 1915. Identical average annual homicide rates were reported during the five years before and the five years after restoration.

After an exhaustive study of experiments with the abolition of capital punishment, these data can be summarized as follows: "If any conclusion can be drawn, it is that there is no evidence that the abolition of the death penalty generally causes an increase in criminal homicides or that its re-introduction is followed by a decline."[49]

•　　　•　　　•

There is no doubt that many police officers throughout the country are prejudiced against people of color. They treat minorities in ways they would never treat white people. Ours is a violent society, and police work is difficult in such a climate, but one must question the authenticity of the number of crimes police report against minorities. The police are especially prone to commit acts of brutality against people of color. They continue these practices because they are not likely to be prosecuted for their crimes against citizens they are sworn to protect. Furthermore, the United States is one of the few countries to defy the modern trend of abolishing the death penalty. Most Americans support capital punishment, and therefore lawmakers continue to ignore the worldwide trend although there is no evidence that it serves any useful purpose.

Finally, a recent study by the Death Penalty Information Center on racial disparities in death penalty cases in Philadelphia found that black defendants "are nearly four times more likely than other defendants to be sentenced to death, even when the circumstances of killings are the same." Studies in other states show the same pattern. For example, in Florida the odds of a death sentence were 4.8 times higher when victims were white; in Illinois, 4 times higher; in North Carolina, 4.4 times higher; and in Mississippi, 5.5 times higher.[50]

Even the Supreme Court has acknowledged that as practiced, capital punishment is racist, but it continues to uphold it as constitutional.

SELECTED BIBLIOGRAPHY

AMERICAN FRIENDS SERVICE COMMITTEE. *Struggle for Justice*. New York: Hill and Wang, 1971.

ANDERSON, JERVIS. *Guns in American Life*. New York: Random House, 1984.

BEDAU, HUGO (ed.) *The Death Penalty in America*. Garden City, NY: Doubleday Anchor, 1967.

EMERGENCY CIVIL LIBERTIES COMMITTEE. "The Death Penalty in America." *Bill of Rights Journal*. December 1995.

FEDERAL BUREAU OF INVESTIGATION. *Crime in the United States, 1996*. Washington, DC, 1997.

NAACP LEGAL DEFENSE AND EDUCATIONAL FUND. *Death Row, USA*. New York, Spring 1998.

PREJEAN, HELEN. *Dead Man Walking*. New York: Vintage Books, 1993.

SELLIN, THORSTEN (ed.). *Capital Punishment*. New York: Harper and Row, 1967.

U.S. BUREAU OF THE CENSUS. *Statistical Abstract of the United States: 1967*. Washington, DC, 1997.

NOTES

1. Federal Bureau of Investigation, *Crime in the United States, 1996* (Washington, DC, Government Printing Office, 1997).

2. U.S. Bureau of the Census, *Statistical Abstract of the United States: 1997* (Washington, DC, 1997), p. 102.

3. Jervis Anderson, *Guns in American Life* (New York: Random House, 1984), p. 108.

4. *Statistical Abstract of the United States: 1967*, p. 102.

5. Ibid., p. 102.

6. J. H Sloan et al., "Handgun Regulations, Crime, Assaults, and Homicide: A Tale of Two Cities," *New England Journal of Medicine*, 319 (1988), 1256–62.

7. "Still Under the Gun," *Time*, July 6, 1998, pp. 34–35.

8. *New York Times*, May 11, 1998, p. A13.

9. Rick Bragg, "Past Victims Relive Pain as Tragedy Is Repeated," *New York Times*, May 25, 1998, p. A8.

10. See *Time*, April 6, 1998, pp. 36–39.

11. Joseph P. Fried, "Papers Detail Identification of Attacker by Louima," *New York Times*, May 9, 1998.

12. Peter Noel, "Were the Cops Trying to Kill Abner Louima?" *Village Voice*, September 23, 1997, p. 47.

13. John Kifner and Daniel Herszenhorn, "Racial 'Profiling' at Crux of Inquiry into Shooting by Troopers," *New York Times*, May 8, 1998, p. B1.

14. Ibid.

15. John Kifner, "State Police Deny Claim of Racial Stops," *New York Times*, May 12, 1998, p. B4.

16. David Herszenhorn, "Lawyers Prepare Stage for Lawsuit in Turnpike Shooting," *New York Times*, May 9, 1998, p. B4.

17. Harriet Barovick, "DWB: Driving While Black," *Time*, June 15, 1998, p. 35.

18. Ibid.

19. John T. McQuiston, "Judge Merges Trials of 2 men in L.I. Racial Beating," *New York Times*, May 13, 1998, p. B6.

20. Bob Herbert, "One More Police Victim," *New York Times*, August 14, 1997, p. A31.

21. Kit R. Roane, "Police Admit Minority Officers Are Punished More Often," *New York Times*, March 14, 1998, p. B3.

22. Timothy Egan, "On Wealthy Island, Being Black Means Being a Police Suspect," *New York Times*, May 10, 1998, p. 12.

23. Nat Hentoff, "Jim Crow in Blue," *Village Voice*, September 23, 1997, p. 20.

24. Michael Cooper, "Scared Family Says Police Raided the Wrong Home," *New York Times*, May 8, 1998, p. B1.

25. Ibid.

26. Ibid.

27. Michael Cooper, "City Is Sued by a Woman Whose Home Was Raided," *New York Times*, May 14, 1998, p. B3.

28. Ibid.

29. Michael Cooper, "Raids, and Complaints, Rise as City Draws on Drug Tips," *New York Times*, May 26, 1998, p. A1.

30. *New York Times*, "The Threat of Police Perjury," June 30, 1998, p. A22.

31. Helen Prejean, *Dead Man Walking* (New York: Vintage Books, 1993), p. 103.

32. Hugo Bedau, "The Death Penalty in America," *Bill of Rights Journal*, December 1995, p. 13.

33. Ibid., p. 15.

34. Ibid.

35. American Civil Liberties Union, "Death Penalty Q & A," *Bill of Rights Journal*, December 1995, p. 31.

36. NAACP Legal Defense and Educational Fund, *Death Row, USA*, New York, Spring 1998.

37. American Civil Liberties Union, *Death Penalty Q & A*, op. cit., p. 32.

38. Sam Howe Verhovek, "As Texas Executions Mount, They Grow Routine," *New York Times*, May 25, 1997, p. 1.

39. Mireya Navarro, "Despite Fire, Electric Chair Is Defended in Florida," *New York Times*, March 27, 1997, p. A18.

40. Ibid.

41. American Civil Liberties Union, *Death Penalty Q & A*, op. cit., p. 32.

42. Jackie Hallifax and Ron Word, "Justice Isn't Swift For Killers in Florida," *Palm Beach Post*, July 9, 1996, p. 1A.

43. Bob Herbert, "Cheap Justice," *New York Times*, March 1, 1998, p. 15.

44. Ibid.

45. Bob Herbert, "No Room For Doubt," *New York Times*, July 21, 1997, p. A17.

46. Ibid.

47. American Civil Liberties Union, *Death Penalty Q & A*, op. cit., p. 32.

48. Thorsten Sellin (ed.), *Capital Punishment* (New York: Harper and Row, 1967), pp. 122–24.

49. Ibid., p. 124.

50. Fox Butterfield, "New Study Adds to Evidence of Bias in Death Sentences," *New York Times*, June 7, 1998, p. 22.

CHAPTER NINE

Assimilation into American Society

The extent to which black Americans are assimilated into the larger society is the subject of considerable debate. They were among the earliest arrivals in North America, but they were quickly stripped of their native African cultures. Their tribal organization, religion, family life, and language were systematically destroyed. It thus became necessary for them to adopt the patterns of life of the white Europeans with whom they were forced to live. The adoption of Western culture became a difficult task, for they were permitted to assimilate into the society only to the extent that their services could be utilized by their white rulers. In general, they were forced to live a dual existence: Their lives had to be structured in terms of the demands made on them by the larger society and in terms of the necessity to survive in a generally hostile environment. When formal slavery ended more than a century ago, it was replaced by a caste system, which prevented substantial alteration of the dual environment within which black people lived. A rigid system of segregation and discrimination replaced the institution of slavery, and this system continues to preclude assimilation into the larger society.

Being in the society but not a part of it has fostered a conflict among black Americans: Some strive to identify with white middle-class values while others reject all aspects of white culture. The former attitude sometimes leads to negative identification (self-hatred), while the latter frequently manifests itself in black nationalism. The majority of blacks would no doubt welcome the chance to become assimilated into the larger society. To the extent that there are forces among blacks resisting such an eventuality, these forces are a result of widespread rejection by white Americans.

There have been few systematic attempts to examine the extent to which black people are assimilated into the larger society, partly because the assimilation process has only recently been systematically analyzed. Milton Gordon sees the process of assimilation as one involving several steps or subprocesses.[1] Each step represents a "type" or "stage" in the assimilation process. He identifies seven variables by which one may gauge the degree to which members of a particular group are assimilated into the host society that surrounds them. The stages and the subprocesses follow.[2]

TYPE OR STAGE OF ASSIMILATION	SUBPROCESS OR CONDITION
Cultural or behavioral assimilation	Change of cultural patterns to those of host society
Structural assimilation	Large-scale entrance into cliques, clubs, and institutions of host society, on primary-group level
Marital assimilation	Large-scale intermarriage
Identificational assimilation	Development of a sense of peoplehood based exclusively on host society
Attitude receptional assimilation	Absence of prejudice
Behavior receptional assimilation	Absence of discrimination
Civic assimilation	Absence of value or power conflict

It is possible to apply these variables systematically to the status of black people in the United States at the present time in an attempt to determine the extent to which they have assimilated into American society.

CULTURAL ASSIMILATION

To what extent have black Americans adopted the cultural patterns of the larger society in which they find themselves? The systematic stripping from the slaves of their African cultures was detailed in chapter 1.[3] Debate persists, however, on the extent and nature of the survival of African cultures among black people in the United States. In the more than three-and-one-half centuries that black people have inhabited what is now the United States, they have adopted the culture of the larger society to the extent that it is difficult to detect any significant vestiges of their original cultures. In North America small numbers of slaves were scattered over a large area on numerous plantations and farms. Even when a sizable number of slaves were held by the same owner, they were likely to have been from a variety of cultures in Africa. Under such circumstances the retention of aspects of their original cultures was difficult. In addition, they were forbidden to speak their native languages, and their family patterns were systematically destroyed. Although it is still possible to detect survivals in religious life,[4] Christianity made significant inroads among the slaves, and their religious practices developed along the lines of those of white Christians. Indeed, ". . . the religion of the slaves was, in essence, strikingly similar to that of the poor, illiterate white men of the antebellum South."[5] In other aspects of culture as well, few survivals of African civilizations remain.

There have been frequent attempts by individual blacks and organizations to reemphasize aspects of traditional African cultures, but among the majority of blacks these attempts have been unsuccessful. Historically the most successful of these movements was the Universal Negro Improvement Association, led by Marcus Garvey.[6] The most recent is the Muslim Mission (popularly known as the Black Muslims), led originally by Elijah Muhammad and now by his son, Marith Deen Muhammad.[7] In urban areas throughout the United States, Black Nationalist groups continue to search for aspects of their past that were destroyed by the institution of slavery.

According to Gordon, the extent to which black people have adopted the cultural patterns of the host society varies by class. He sees the middle- and upper-class blacks as being totally acculturated, while "lower-class Negro life . . . is still at a considerable distance from the American cultural norm."[8] A vast majority of black Americans are poor (lower class), and in some respects their cultural patterns deviate from those of the larger society. To a large extent, however, these differences are a function of class rather than race. Gordon's analysis posits "middle-class white Protestant Americans as constituting the 'core society.' " Clearly many poor blacks deviate from the norms of this group, as do poor white Protestant Americans. In the sense that poor blacks adhere to lower-class American culture patterns, they may be said to be acculturated. Poor blacks in the rural South are not significantly different from their poor white counterparts in food habits or religious practices, for example. They eat the less expensive foods and tend to be more emotional in their religious practices, and so do poor, rural, white southerners. Blacks in nonsouthern urban areas may differ in this regard from poor whites in the same areas, but the differences are a function of their southern, not their African, heritage.

Middle- and upper-class blacks are hardly distinguishable from white Americans of comparable social-class level in many cultural patterns. There is even some evidence that they frequently overconform to middle-class standards of behavior in religious observances, in dress, in sexual behavior, and in child-rearing practices.[9] But this does not mean that black culture is a myth; Blauner has convincingly demonstrated that it is not.[10]

In recent years there have been several studies of various aspects of black life in the United States that attempt to demonstrate that a distinctive culture exists among American blacks. These studies have focused on language, patterns of family life, styles of dress, patterns of social organization, music, and other elements of culture.[11] Some maintain that the distinctive cultural patterns of the black community are primarily a result of African survivals, while others see them as resulting mainly from a life of oppression in the United States.

Inasmuch as blacks were initially denied the right to participate in the culture of the larger society, while at the same time they were not permitted to practice their original cultures, they had to create a way of life (culture) in a hostile environment. In many regards these cultural patterns differ from those of the dominant society. To maintain that significant segments of the black community have largely assimilated the culture of the larger society is not to deny that cultural (or subcultural) differences persist. Although serious scholarly research on black culture is relatively recent in its origin, black people have maintained through the years that in many respects their way of life differs from that of white Americans. It is perhaps necessary to await more definitive research in the area before concrete conclusions can be reached. However, it seems fair to say that in many respects the acculturation process is virtually complete for large segments of the black community.

STRUCTURAL ASSIMILATION

Black Americans usually maintain their own separate institutions within the black community. (See chapter 5.) Historically this situation has not resulted from voluntary isolation; rather, a caste system of segregation and discrimination against blacks has precluded their large-scale entrance into cliques, social clubs, and other social organizations and activities along with white Americans on a primary-group level. However, with increasing racial pride among black people today, voluntary racial separation is not uncommon. In the "rank order of discriminations" against blacks by white southerners, as enumerated by Gunnar Myrdal, activities specifically concerned with personal relations, such as dancing, bathing, eating, and drinking together with blacks, followed closely after intermarriage and interracial sexual relations as forbidden behavior.[12] Such practices are more characteristic of the South than elsewhere, but in general they characterize the relations between black and white people throughout the United States. The caste system, which separates blacks and whites, dictates that members of these two social categories should not associate in any relationships that imply social equality. This ban generally extends to marriage, dancing, eating together, and social visiting.

The traditional pattern of relations between black and white Americans has been slightly altered in recent years, but in general the pattern of almost total isolation of the black community from the white community persists. As black people continue to settle in the central cities of the largest urban areas, the isolation is becoming more pronounced. Studies of black–white relations in the South show the pervasiveness of rigid segregation along racial lines in the major social groups and institutions.[13] The tradition in the South is deeply rooted in the mores, and social change is slow.

Outside the South the isolation of the black community is only slightly less pronounced than in the South. Most white Americans live their lives with only the slightest awareness of the lives of their black fellow citizens except during periods of racial unrest. A vast majority of the blacks who live outside the South live in urban areas, but those who live in small towns live isolated lives compared to their urban counterparts. Two studies illustrate the dearth of interracial association between blacks and whites in small northern cities. In Elmira, New York, it was reported that the black community is so isolated that its inhabitants think of themselves not as citizens of Elmira but as citizens of the black community. Such references as "all over town" or "the prettiest girl in town" do not refer to Elmira but to the specific section in which the blacks are concentrated.[14] Given such conditions as these, it is clear that blacks have not entered into social groups and activities with their white coresidents. Social contacts between the two groups are minimal.

In a small Connecticut town it was reported: "While Negro–white neighborhood relations are friendly, they are characterized for the most part by lack of contact between the two races."[15] The blacks maintained their own church, and in public social activities sponsored by other churches, discrimination against blacks was evident. There were few adult interracial social contacts. Only two of the many formal organizations, the Chamber of Commerce and the town band, had black members. On the adolescent level a similar pattern was discerned. Social contact between black and white persons was, in this case, limited to athletic and recreational activities. The school system was found to be the only institution in which black and white citizens participated with some degree of equality.

In large cities outside the South, there is little social contact between blacks and whites. The social life of blacks tends to be centered around their own social, civic, and religious organizations.[16] Recently, however, middle- and upper-class blacks have often participated freely with whites in social groups. Nevertheless, the vast majority of blacks continue to have only superficial social contact with white persons. The maintenance of rigid residential segregation is a strong deterrent against the structural assimilation of blacks into the life of the larger society.

Structural assimilation may be subdivided into primary and secondary assimilation.[17] Those social institutions that are rooted in the black community (e.g., schools) are primary, and those either partially (e.g., schools) or totally (e.g., economic activities) located in the white community are secondary to the black community. When this dichotomy is made, it is clear that assimilation has progressed at a much more rapid pace in secondary institutions than in those that are primary. Inasmuch as primary institutions tend to be in the private sector of American life and those that are secondary tend to be public, the interest of black people has been more in secondary assimilation than in primary assimilation.

MARITAL ASSIMILATION

The United States represents a society that has attempted to curb the process of racial amalgamation through legislation forbidding the marriage of blacks and nonblacks. Historically most states have enacted laws forbidding the marriage of black and white persons. Although these laws were disregarded in some states, they were rigidly enforced in others, thereby limiting the number of black–white interracial marriages. The penalties for violating these antimiscegenation laws varied by state, ranging up to $2,000 in fines and terms of imprisonment up to 10 years.[18]

These antimiscegenation laws were gradually repealed in most nonsouthern states by the time the Supreme Court declared them unconstitutional in the case of *Loving v. Virginia* in 1967. At that time 16 states, most of them in the South, had such laws, and some of them retained these laws into the 1970s. Even in those states in which the laws had been repealed, social mores strongly forbidding intimate interpersonal association across racial lines limited the number of black–white interracial marriages. The result was that such marriages occurred infrequently in the United States.

The most comprehensive current data on interracial marriage are provided by the Bureau of the Census.[19] There were 337,000 black–white interracial married couples in 1996, 220,000 of them (65 percent) involving black males and white females and 117,000 (35 percent) involving white males and black females. (Data on interracial marriages can be found in Table 9-1.) These make up a very small fraction of all married couples in the United States. However, these marriages are increasing at a rapid pace. The number of such marriages more than tripled between 1970 and 1996, from 65,000 in 1970 to 337,000 in 1996.

These data do not present a complete picture of interracial marriage in the United States. Indeed, it has been reported that such marriages "skyrocketed" by more than 800 percent between 1960 and 1990. That means that roughly 1 in 25 married couples were interracial in 1996, and there are "at least three million children of mixed-race parentage in the United States, and this figure doesn't include the millions of Hispanic Mestizos and black Americans who have European and Indian ancestors."[20]

TABLE 9-1   Married Couples of Same or Mixed Races and Origins, 1980 to 1996

In thousands. As of March. Persons 15 years old and over. Persons of Hispanic origin may be of any race. Except as noted, based on Current Population Survey.

RACE AND ORIGIN OF SPOUSES	1980	1990	1995	1996
Married couples, total	**49,714**	**53,256**	**54,937**	**54,664**
RACE				
Same race couples	48,264	50,889	51,733	51,616
White/White	44,910	47,202	48,030	48,056
Black/Black	3,354	3,687	3,703	3,560
Interracial couples	651	964	1,392	1,260
Black/White	167	211	328	337
Black husband/White wife	122	150	206	220
White husband/Black wife	45	61	122	117
White/other race[1]	450	720	988	884
Black/other race[1]	34	33	76	39
All other couples[1]	799	1,401	1,811	1,789
HISPANIC ORIGIN				
Hispanic/Hispanic	1,906	3,085	3,857	3,888
Hispanic/other origin (not Hispanic)	891	1,193	1,434	1,464
All other couples (not of Hispanic origin)	46,917	48,979	49,646	49,312

[1]Excluding White and Black.

Source: U.S. Bureau of the Census, *Current Population Reports*, P20-488, and earlier reports; and unpublished data.

Interracial marriages vary by region of the country. White men in California, for example, were six times as likely as midwestern men to marry outside their race. Such marriages are more than twice as prevalent in California as in the rest of the country. And although black outmarriage rates have risen, they remain much lower than outmarriage rates for Hispanics and American Indians. For the 25–34 age group only 8 percent of black men marry outside their race, while fewer than 4 percent of black women do the same.

The most probable major reason for the low black outmarriage rates is the antiblack prejudice in society. Furthermore, antiblack prejudice is likely to be picked up by immigrants when it is not brought with them from their countries of origin.

In May 1997, a Knight-Ridder poll showed that while most respondents were generally comfortable with intermarriage, 3 in 10 respondents opposed marriage between blacks and whites. However, the 1990 census reports that men aged 25–34 in the military were 2.3 times as likely to marry nonwhite women as civilians. And white women in the same age group who served in the military in the 1980s were 7 times as likely as their civilian counterparts to have black husbands.

The attitudes of black people on interracial marriage differ from those of whites. When questioned in 1991, a solid majority (66 percent) of whites said that they would oppose a close relative's marrying a black person, and one-fifth said such marriages should be illegal.[21] On the other hand, black people exhibited indifference to interracial marriage, with about two-thirds saying they would neither favor nor oppose a relative's marrying someone of another race.

With the increasing number of such marriages has come greater tolerance of them. However, strong resentment is often voiced by whites, many of whom feel that even such an intimate decision should not be left to the individuals involved. As late as 1991 a white Methodist minister in Pennsylvania refused to marry a black–white interracial couple after meeting the black party to the marriage.[22] From this discussion it is clear that black–white intermarriage in the United States is still an uncommon phenomenon.

IDENTIFICATIONAL ASSIMILATION

The position of black people in the United States is unique. They form one of the largest and oldest minorities in the country. Racially distinct from the majority, they are highly visible as a minority group. They were enslaved for more than two-and-one-half centuries, and they continue to be rather widely regarded as racially inferior. Consequently, they are responded to as blacks rather than as Americans. The circumstances under which they live virtually preclude their development of a sense of peoplehood based exclusively on the host society. They are forced to think of themselves as a separate ethnic group rather than simply as Americans.

Despite the many difficulties black people have encountered, their allegiance to the United States is clear. Their interest appears to be in being accorded full citizenship. For example, in a nationwide survey conducted in 1963 an overwhelming majority of blacks (81 percent) indicated that they thought the United States was worth fighting for in a war.[23] Similarly, when asked in 1966 to rank black leaders, a nationwide sample of blacks ranked integrationist leaders such as Martin Luther King, Jr., and Roy Wilkins higher than the more militant anti-integrationist leaders such as Stokely Carmichael and Elijah Muhammad.[24] However, surveys conducted for the National Advisory Commission on Civil Disorders in 15 cities that had experienced black rebellions in the summer of 1967 reported a growing disenchantment on the part of blacks. In Detroit, of those who participated in the rebellion, 34.9 percent said the country was not worth fighting for in case of a major world war, while 15.5 percent of those who did not participate answered similarly. In Newark 52.8 percent of those who reported participating in the rebellion said they did not think the country was worth fighting for in case of a world war, while 27.8 percent of those who did not participate gave the same response.[25] In general, then, it appears that the main concern for a vast majority of America's blacks is that they be accorded the same rights of citizenship as other Americans.

When legal slavery ended in the United States, black people were not permitted to enter into the mainstream of society, as were their counterparts in Central America and the Caribbean. Rather, a situation developed in which all blacks, no matter what the extent of their achievement might have been, were regarded simply as blacks; a black could never expect to be accorded treatment comparable to that of a white American, regardless of the latter's lack of achievement. A black is not just another public official, he or she is a *black* public official: the black justice of the Supreme Court, the black mayor of Washington, DC, the black governor of Virginia, and so on. When the official's position is known, he or she is accorded a certain amount of deference regardless of race. However, if the position is not known, he or she is responded to by most Americans as "just another black" and is treated accordingly in most situations. White Americans do not see black people as individuals, distinguishable from one another; rather, they see them as an indistinguishable mass. Under such circumstances they are responded to indiscriminately. The black farm laborer and the Nobel prize winner are both simply blacks, with all that the word implies. One black respondent, in commenting on job relations with white fellow workers, said: "I don't care how a white person treats you. They have a feelin' in 'em that you're colored—I know my place, no matter where I am."[26] This respondent, in a northern city, accurately defined the general attitude of white Americans toward blacks.

Forced into the position of a self-conscious minority, the tendency of members of that group to think of themselves collectively is inevitable. When a fellow black achieves a certain distinction, it becomes a source of pride for other blacks. Conversely, when a fellow black is charged with some act that meets with social disapproval, it becomes a source of embarrassment for other blacks. In other words, to black Americans, as well as to white Americans, one is either black or white, and one responds in terms of these two categories. To a black *us* means blacks and *them* means white persons.[27]

Finally, Louis Harris and Associates conducted a national survey of black and white attitudes on several issues during the last week of December 1984 and the first week of January 1985. Interviewers asked respondents whether they agreed with the statement, "Even though we call America a melting pot of religious and racial minorities, there is still a lot of prejudice against minority groups." Fully 94 percent of blacks responded affirmatively, compared with 84 percent of whites.[28] Such views on the part of black people may be said to represent a lack of identificational assimilation among them.

Because black people have occupied an oppressed and segregated status in the United States for centuries, the likelihood of their developing a sense of "peoplehood" with white Americans seems remote. Indeed, in recent years, although they have made some gains in the area of integration, there appears to be a growing tendency for black people to develop a strong sense of identification with other blacks, an increasing pride on their part in being black. Such ingroup identification militates against the development of a sense of identification with the host society.

ATTITUDE RECEPTIONAL ASSIMILATION

Studies of prejudice among white Americans generally indicate that antiblack prejudice is widespread in the United States. Intensity of attitudes varies, depending on the region of the country, social-class level, age, religion, and other variables, but in general antiblack prejudice is the social norm among white Americans. There is some indication of change in attitudes insofar as the more impersonal dimensions of prejudice are concerned, especially in recent years,[29] but in certain realms attitudes remain firmly antiblack.

The earliest studies of prejudice indicate that white Americans maintained strongly negative attitudes toward intimate association with nonwhite persons, especially black persons. In the 1920s an overwhelming majority of white Americans indicated that they would reject blacks as relatives through marriage (98.6 percent), as personal friends in social clubs (90.9 percent), and as neighbors (88.2 percent).[30] In the 1960s the pattern still held: 84 percent of white persons reported that they would object to a close friend's or relative's marrying a black, and 51 percent said they would object to black neighbors.[31]

In more recent years, surveys have shown a decline in prejudiced attitudes toward black people. For example, a 1997 *Time*/CNN poll of 1,282 adults and 601 adolescents found that a striking number of young people (black and white) have moved beyond their parents' views on race.[32] The adolescents say that race is less important to them than it is to adults. This study reported that when asked about the impact of racism in their lives the vast majority (62 percent) of the black teenagers said that it was "a small problem" or "not a problem at all." (Data on race relations by teenagers can be found in Figure 9-1.)

Black teenagers are more reluctant than whites to believe that "failure to take advantage of available opportunities" is more a problem for blacks than discrimination. Indeed, the *Time*/CNN poll compares blacks and whites on several issues with some surprising (and rosy?) findings.

Which of the following is more of a problem for blacks today?

	TEENS	ADULTS
FAILURE TO TAKE ADVANTAGE OF AVAILABLE OPPORTUNITIES	Whites: 31% / Blacks: 58%	Whites: 52% / Blacks: 51%
DISCRIMINATION BY WHITES	Whites: 47% / Blacks: 26%	Whites: 22% / Blacks: 26%

Is racism a big problem or a small problem?

	TEENS	ADULTS
BIG PROBLEM	Whites: 58% / Blacks: 62%	Whites: 64% / Blacks: 78%
SMALL PROBLEM	Whites: 34% / Blacks: 34%	Whites: 27% / Blacks: 17%

Are the problems that most blacks face today caused primarily by whites, or don't you think this is the case?

	TEENS	ADULTS
YES	Whites: 32% / Blacks: 18%	Whites: 14% / Blacks: 29%
NOT THE CASE	Whites: 55% / Blacks: 74%	Whites: 72% / Blacks: 61%

Have you ever been a victim of discrimination because you are black?

	BLACK TEENS	BLACK ADULTS
Yes:	23%	53%
No:	77%	45%

Have you ever been a victim of discrimination because you are white?

	WHITE TEENS	WHITE ADULTS
Yes:	16%	20%
No:	83%	79%

Will race relations in this country ever get better?

	TEENS	ADULTS
YES	Whites: 76% / Blacks: 55%	Whites: 60% / Blacks: 43%

Do you favor or oppose colleges' reserving a certain number of scholarships exclusively for minorities and women?

	TEENS	ADULTS
FAVOR	Whites: 55% / Blacks: 64%	Whites: 46% / Blacks: 60%
OPPOSE	Whites: 33% / Blacks: 26%	Whites: 47% / Blacks: 34%

Do standardized tests, such as the SATs, give an unbiased measure of all applicants' qualifications, or are they biased against minority applicants?

	TEENS	ADULTS
UNBIASED	Whites: 59% / Blacks: 45%	Whites: 53% / Blacks: 28%
BIASED	Whites: 17% / Blacks: 40%	Whites: 25% / Blacks: 53%

	WHITE TEENS	BLACK TEENS
Are you likely to go to college?	Yes: 93%	Yes: 95%
Have you used illegal drugs?	Yes: 13%	Yes: 6%
Have you drunk alcohol?	Yes: 32%	Yes: 19%
Have you had sex?	Yes: 15%	Yes: 28%

FIGURE 9-1 Views on Race Relations: Teens versus Adults

From a telephone poll of 816 white adults, 374 black adults, 301 white teens and 300 black teens taken for TIME/CNN from Sept. 23 to Oct. 2 by Yankelovich Partners Inc. Margins of error are ±3.4%, 5.1%, 5.6% and 5.6% respectively

Source: Time, November 24, 1997.

A poll conducted by the Gallup Organization in January–February 1997 of 1,269 blacks and 1,680 whites found widespread pessimism among Americans on race relations, but many were more optimistic in 1997 than they had been in previous years.[33] For example, in 1972 only 25 percent of white Americans approved of marriage between blacks and whites, whereas in 1997 the figure was 61 percent. (See Figure 9-2.)

A reduction in prejudice, although important, does not necessarily indicate a change in the status of black people, for prejudice is not the sole ingredient in racism. More crucial to blacks in this regard are the institutionalized practices that maintain white dominance. That is, the racism in the institutions of the society precludes social justice for blacks. So long as these practices endure, the reduction of negative attitudes will not significantly alter the status of black people.

BEHAVIOR RECEPTIONAL ASSIMILATION

The prejudiced attitudes of white Americans are frequently translated into discriminatory behavior. Hence black Americans experience difficulty in securing employment, housing, and education; they are treated differentially in the administration of justice. In the South they experience discrimination in voting and in places of public accommodation. Indeed, discrimination against black people in the United States is institutionalized.[34] Like prejudiced attitudes, discriminatory practices vary depending on the region of the country. Outside the South black people experience little difficulty in voting or gaining access to places of public accommodation, but in housing, employment, and education, discrimination against black people is commonplace in all regions. Discriminatory practices relegate black people to an inferior status in the United States and affect each aspect of their lives. When they are forced into inferior schools, they receive inferior education, which relegates them to inferior employment, which in turn relegates them to inferior housing. The cycle is complete. Furthermore, their low status makes them "inferior," and their "inferiority" justifies acts of discrimination against them. The product of past discrimination is cited to justify continued discrimination.

Acts of discrimination are a manifestation of the legacy of slavery. Although these acts have been practiced since emancipation, they were intensified and extended in scope between 1890 and 1925. For example, Mississippi passed a statewide law requiring separate taxis for black and white persons as late as 1922.[35] Few attempts were made by the federal government to deal with antiblack discrimination until the 1950s, although executive orders had ostensibly dealt with discrimination as early as World War II. The most sweeping federal attempt to deal with these practices was the Civil Rights Act of 1964.

Perhaps the area in which discrimination against black people is most widespread is housing. Throughout much of the present century, the entry of a black family into a neighborhood inhabited by white Americans stimulated mob violence. Discrimination in housing was so widespread that virtually all black families that

Hopeful Signs

A new national survey revealed widespread pessimism among Americans on race relations, but there was cause for optimism, especially when the responses to some questions were compared with results from earlier polls.

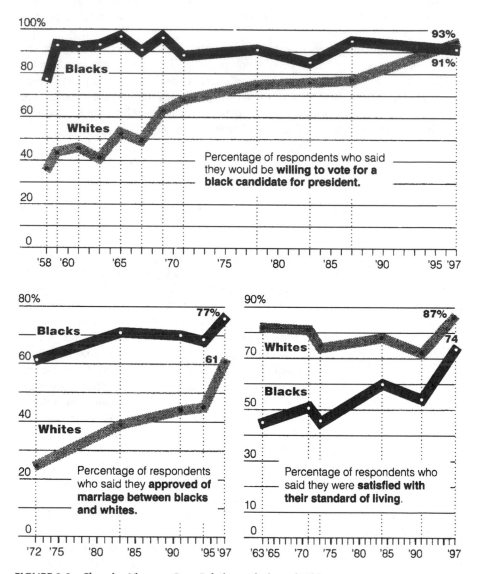

FIGURE 9-2 Changing Views on Race Relations: Blacks and Whites

Based on national polls conducted by the Gallup Organization. The most recent poll was conducted by telephone Jan. 4–Feb. 28 with 1,269 blacks and 1,680 whites.

Source: New York Times, June 15, 1997, Sec. 4, p. 4.

attempted to leave neighborhoods inhabited by blacks were likely to experience acts of discrimination related to housing.[36] Discrimination in housing is not limited to low-income blacks—wealthy athletes, opera singers, popular entertainers, judges, and educators have experienced difficulty in finding housing outside black neighborhoods of large cities. The pattern of discrimination has been nationwide. In every American city it is possible to tell the race of a citizen by his or her address. There is no large city in which blacks and whites share the same neighborhood to any great extent.[37]

Repeated attempts to prohibit discrimination in housing have met with limited success. On November 20, 1962, the president of the United States issued an executive order barring discrimination by reason of race, color, religion, or national origin in the "sale or rental of residential property and related facilities owned by the federal government or aided or assisted by it."[38] Prior to that time several states and municipalities had enacted legislation barring racial discrimination in housing, and the Supreme Court had ruled in 1948 that federal and state courts could not enforce restrictive covenants in housing. Most housing in the country is privately owned and financed, and few municipal and state laws and, prior to the Fair Housing Act of 1968, no federal laws covered such housing. Furthermore, when laws forbidding discrimination in housing have existed, enforcement has been virtually nonexistent.

The Fair Housing Act of 1968 established for the first time a comprehensive fair housing program, making it illegal to discriminate in almost all housing, public and private. What was lacking, however, was vigorous enforcement of the act. At the beginning of the administration of Ronald Reagan in 1981, the federal government moved away from enforcing fair housing laws, maintaining that voluntary compliance was the principal mechanism for fair housing.[39] Voluntary compliance meant no compliance with the law. Among the first acts of the Reagan administration was to withdraw interpretive regulations of the Fair Housing Act.

The Housing Marketing Practices Survey of the Department of Housing and Urban Development, conducted in 1977, concluded that "Discrimination in the housing market persists on a significant scale in all areas of the United States."[40] It was found that in the rental market, blacks had a 27 percent chance of encountering discrimination. Overall, in the sales market blacks had a 24 percent chance of encountering discrimination concerning the availability of housing. A black home buyer had a 15 percent chance of being the victim of discrimination if he or she visited one firm; if, however, he or she visited four firms, the chance of encountering discrimination at least once increased to 48 percent.

In the United States the ability of an individual to earn a living is largely his or her own responsibility. Federal, state, and municipal governments have, however, from time to time enacted legislation to ensure that black people would enjoy equal employment opportunities with other Americans. The first of these attempts was an executive order barring discrimination in war industries, government training programs, and government industries. It was issued by President Roosevelt in 1941, after blacks threatened a massive march on Washington to protest discrimination in the national defense program. Since that time many federal, state, and municipal laws—most recently the Civil Rights Act of 1991—ostensibly forbade racial discrimination in employment. Nevertheless, discrimination against blacks continues. Because of acts of discrimination, it is frequently difficult for black males to fulfill their potentials as husbands and fathers. They are literally the last to be hired and the first to be fired.

Discrimination exists not only in securing employment, but also in the type of employment to which black Americans are relegated. (See chapter 4.) Because of discrimination against them in employment, the median income of black families in 1990 was only slightly more than one-half the white median family income. In the same occupational category with comparable experience, black people can expect to earn anywhere from one-half to nine-tenths of what their white counterparts earn. Some of the differential in income may be attributable to lack of training on the part of blacks, but the major factor accounting for these differentials is discrimination in employment.

Discrimination in securing employment continues on a wide scale. It is most clearly reflected in differential rates of unemployment for black and white workers, and it is one of the cruelest forms of discrimination. At no time since 1954 has the unemployment rate for black workers been less than twice the rate for white workers. Some of the black unemployment must be attributed to structural changes in the economy, and black workers are likely to be less well trained than white workers, but high rates of black unemployment exist for black workers *at all levels of skill.* That is, black professional workers are just as likely to have significantly higher rates of unemployment compared with white professionals as are black unskilled workers compared with white unskilled workers. Furthermore, blacks are likely to be unemployed for longer periods than their white counterparts.

Overt discrimination in education is prevalent throughout the United States. The major factor affecting the quality of education for blacks outside the South is *de facto* segregation in public schools, which results in the overwhelming majority of black pupils attending schools that are either totally or predominantly black (see chapter 4). *De facto* segregation in public schools, of course, results from residential discrimination in most cases. In recent years public school desegregation has proceeded at a faster rate in the South than outside that region.

Discrimination in the administration of justice, at all levels of the criminal justice system, is as characteristically American as any other aspect of the culture. Probably the most prevalent form of discrimination in the criminal justice system is police misconduct, which often takes the form of excessive use of force, sometimes culminating in the death of blacks. Such police misconduct has been the stimulus for riots and uprisings in American cities. Within the context of American society, the conviction of police officers for acts of brutality is rare. It is somehow felt that violence (including murder) by law enforcement officials is invariably justified.

One of the most extraordinary cases of police brutality occurred on March 3, 1991, when a black motorist—Rodney King—was apprehended for speeding after a 15-minute high-speed chase by white police officers in Los Angeles. A total of 23 police officers appeared at the scene shortly after midnight. King was knocked to the pavement, hogtied, and savagely beaten and kicked by four police officers while 19 others stood by observing. Within a brief period of 81 seconds, King was kicked dozens of times and clubbed with batons a total of 56 times. After the beating his badly wounded body with multiple fractures and cuts was put into an ambulance and sent to a hospital.

What was unusual about this act of police brutality is that the incident was captured on videotape by George Holliday, a resident of a nearby apartment building, distributed throughout the world, viewed by millions on television, and condemned as an act of police brutality in its rawest form. Most shocking of all, however, was the not-guilty verdicts of the jury that tried the four officers for felony assault charges. The jury, which included no black people, concluded on April 29, 1992, that the policemen had broken no laws when they brutally beat Rodney King even though people the world over witnessed the beating on television. Even President George Bush said in a television interview that he was "sickened" by what he saw on the videotape. He later called the incident "revolting" and said he was "stunned" by the verdict. Yet the jurors felt that this extent of brutality was required to protect 23 armed policemen from an unarmed motorist.

Although the beating took place in multiethnic Los Angeles, the trial was moved to the city of Simi Valley in suburban, mostly white Ventura County, a city whose residents are said to "worship the police," many of whom live there.

Within hours after the jury acquitted the four policemen, angry citizens in Los Angeles took to the streets, expressing their outrage at the verdict by burning buildings and looting stores. The verdict of acquittal inspired similar protests by citizens in other cities throughout the country—Atlanta, Las Vegas, Miami, San Francisco, Seattle, and Tampa.

An even more glaring example of discrimination in the criminal justice system is demonstrated by capital punishment. The Supreme Court ruled in *McCleskey v. Kemp* (1987) that although the death penalty, as administered, discriminated against blacks, it was constitutional. Data were presented to the court demonstrating that murderers who killed white people faced a 10 times greater chance of a death sentence than murderers of blacks.[41] Even among people convicted of killing whites, blacks have a much greater chance than whites of being sentenced to death. Although admitting that the practice was discriminatory, the justices nevertheless decided that Warren McCleskey could be executed.

CIVIC ASSIMILATION

There appears to be a growing conflict between black and white people concerning some fundamental "value and power" interests in the United States. Although such conflicts are not new, only in recent years have they manifested themselves openly. Inasmuch as blacks share the same religion and other basic culture elements with the majority of white Americans, there are fewer conflicts than is the case with some other minority groups. Nevertheless, blacks constitute one of the groups that has shared less than equally in the basic rewards of society, both in goods and services. They have faced discrimination in every aspect of American life, and today they are overrepresented among the country's poor. The result of such a set of circumstances has led to serious questions about the professed cultural values of society.

The major civic conflicts between black and white Americans appear to be in two areas: (1) the disproportionate distribution of power in society, and (2) the lack of responsibility on the part of government toward citizens. The former was clearly evident in the Black Power movement and the latter in such organizations as Mothers for Adequate Welfare, the National Welfare Rights Organization, the Poor People's Campaign, and the New York Citywide Coordinating Committee of Welfare Recipients, a coalition of welfare-action groups in New York City.

The Black Power movement first gained prominence in the spring of 1966. It was a direct result of the almost total lack of control by black people of the institutions and agencies that are responsible to them. As Stokely Carmichael, the man most responsible for the interest in Black Power, viewed the concept, it referred to political, economic, and judicial control, by black people, in areas where they were in a majority. In areas where they were in a minority, it referred to a sharing of control. "It means the creation of power bases from which black people can work to change statewide and nationwide patterns of oppression through pressure from strength—instead of weakness."[42] In other words, Black Power means that blacks, like other minorities, should organize themselves into power blocs, a fundamental aspect of the pluralist pressure group process in American society.

Black Americans have always been, and continue to be, overrepresented among the nation's poor (see chapter 4); and since homelessness has become a major social problem, they are vastly overrepresented among the ranks of the homeless (see chapter 7). In the political arena, significant gains have been made since the 1960s, especially in electing black public officials, but as of 1990 blacks made up only about 2 percent of all elected officials in the country (see chapter 5). These differences are largely a function of racial discrimination.

The lack of government responsibility toward citizens is frequently demonstrated in public opinion polls showing that blacks and whites have widely different perceptions on some issues. For example, as indicated in chapter 6, significant segments of the black community expressed a lack of confidence in public officials on several issues. Three of these issues are the belief that the virus that causes AIDS was deliberately created in laboratories in order to infect black people, that the government deliberately permits addictive drugs to be easily available in the black community, and that the government deliberately singles out black elected officials for criminal investigation and prosecution.

In 1985, the Harris Survey conducted a nationwide study of blacks and whites. When respondents were asked to agree or disagree with the statement "Blacks suffer more in hard times and gain less in good times" more than three-fourths (76 percent) of blacks agreed, compared with slightly more than one-half (55 percent) of whites.[43]

The following year (1986), the Harris Survey reported that "A record of 77 percent of all blacks feel alienated and powerless."[44] In some respects, however, blacks expressed greater confidence than did whites in the leadership of Congress and of state and local governments. That such views are held by blacks in the face of all the problems they face expresses optimism that somehow things will get better.

There is some evidence, however, that black perceptions are shaped by the realities of the policies of those in positions of power. For example, when asked about how they fared under the administration of Ronald Reagan, seven times as many blacks felt that they were worse off under Reagan than better off overall. On several key dimensions—getting jobs, getting a better education for their children, having their rights protected, and getting better housing—blacks felt that black people were worse off under the administration of Ronald Reagan than under that of other presidents.[45]

In general, there appears to be a growing awareness among black people in the United States that responsibilities between citizens and government are reciprocal. That is, the government has the right to make certain demands on citizens, and citizens have similar rights to make certain demands on their government. Throughout most of American history the former idea has been accepted, but the latter has not.

Although it must be said that at the present time, there are few areas of value or power conflict between black and white Americans, there are some crucial conflicts, and in all likelihood these conflicts will intensify as demands are made by black people for greater sharing in society. As the conflicts intensify, their resolution is likely to become more difficult.

•   •   •

From the preceding analysis one must conclude that among black people, assimilation has not been accomplished in most aspects of American life. Blacks are to some extent acculturated, for they share the culture of the larger society. However, there is minimal structural, marital, and identificational assimilation, although marital assimilation is increasing rapidly. They continue to experience widespread prejudice and discrimination; therefore, in terms of attitude receptional and behavior receptional assimilation, they lag behind many other minorities. On the civic assimilation variable, the process is uneven. Few conflicts exist at present, but where there is conflict, it is fundamental, and the likelihood is that these conflicts will increase.

In a report published by the National Research Council, the authors had this to say about black assimilation in American society:

> Within desegregation settings throughout American society, blacks do not share equal authority and representation throughout an organization or institution. In major institutions with considerable numerical representation of blacks at some levels (e.g., sports and entertainment fields), blacks are conspicuously absent from decision-making positions.[46]

The prospects for the complete assimilation of black people into American life are extremely grim. Perhaps the single most important impediment to this process is the extent to which racism has become institutionalized in American life. White

Americans refuse to accept black people as equals. Black Americans, on the other hand, have endeavored through the years to achieve assimilation into the larger society through peaceful legal means. They have been constantly rebuffed. This is in large measure a function of racial privilege. White Americans resist the assimilation of blacks because this would jeopardize the privileges that they enjoy at the expense of black people. Consequently, a small but growing number of black people are now questioning the desirability of total assimilation. Thus it seems fair to say that the likelihood of complete assimilation is indeed remote.

SELECTED BIBLIOGRAPHY

ASANTE, MOLEFI. *The Afrocentric Idea.* Philadelphia: Temple University Press, 1987.

BLAUNER, ROBERT. *Black Lives, White Lives.* Berkeley: University of California Press, 1989.

————. *Racial Oppression in America.* New Yorker: Harper & Row, 1972.

BRINK, WILLIAM, and LOUIS HARRIS. *Black and White.* New York: Simon & Schuster, 1967.

————. *The Negro Revolution in America.* New York: Simon & Schuster, 1964.

CAMPBELL, ANGUS. *White Attitudes toward Black People.* Ann Arbor, MI: Institute for Social Research, 1971.

CLARK, KENNETH B. *Dark Ghetto.* New York: Harper & Row, Publishers, 1965.

CONOT, ROBERT. *Rivers of Blood, Years of Darkness.* New York: Bantam Books, 1967.

COX, OLIVER C. *Caste, Class and Race.* Garden City, NY: Doubleday & Co., 1948.

DAVIS, ALLISON, BURLEIGH GARDNER, and MARY GARDNER. *Deep South.* Chicago: University of Chicago Press, 1937.

DILLARD, J. L. *Black English: Its History and Usage in the United States.* New York: Random House, 1972.

DOLLARD, JOHN. *Caste and Class in a Southern Town.* New Haven, CT: Yale University Press, 1937.

DRAKE, ST. CLAIR, and HORACE CAYTON. *Black Metropolis.* New York: Harcourt, Brace & Co., 1945.

FRAZIER, E. FRANKLIN. *Black Bourgeoisie.* Glencoe, IL: Free Press, 1957.

————. *The Negro in the United States.* New York: Macmillan Co., 1957.

————. *A Freedom Budget For All Americans.* New York: A. Philip Randolph Institute, 1966.

GOLDSTEIN, RHODA L., ed. *Black Life and Culture in the United States.* New York: Thomas Y. Crowell & Co., 1971.

GORDON, ALBERT I. *Intermarriage: Interfaith, Interracial, Interethnic.* Boston: Beacon Press, 1964.

GORDON, MILTON M. *Assimilation in American Life.* New York: Oxford University Press, 1964.

GREENBERG, JACK. *Race Relations and American Law.* New York: Columbia University Press, 1959.

HACKER, ANDREW. *Two Nations: Black and White, Separate, Hostile, Unequal.* New York: Charles Scribner's Sons, 1992.

HANNERZ, ULF. *Soulside: Inquiries into Ghetto Culture and Community.* New York: Columbia University Press, 1969.

HERSKOVITS, MELVILLE. *The Myth of the Negro Past.* New York: Harper & Brothers, 1941.

JANES, GERALD, and ROBIN M. WILLIAMS, JR., eds. *A Common Destiny: Blacks and American Society.* Washington, DC: National Academy Press, 1989.

KNOWLES, LOUIS, and KENNETH PREWITT. *Institutional Racism in America.* Englewood Cliffs, NJ: Prentice Hall, 1969.

LAURENTI, LUIGI. *Property Values and Race: Studies in Seven Cities.* Berkeley: University of California Press, 1960.

LIEBOW, ELLIOT. *Tally's Corner: A Study of Negro Streetcorner Men.* Boston: Little, Brown, 1967.

McENTIRE, DAVIS. *Residence and Race.* Berkeley: University of California Press, 1960.

MADHUBUTI, HAKI. *Black Men: Obsolete, Single, Dangerous?* Chicago: Third World Press, 1990.

MARX, GARY. *Protest and Prejudice.* New York: Harper & Row, 1969.

MENDELSON, WALLACE. *Discrimination.* Englewood Cliffs, NJ: Prentice Hall, 1962.

MYRDAL, GUNNAR. *An American Dilemma: The Negro Problem and Modern Democracy.* New York: Harper & Brothers, 1944.

NORTHWOOD, L. K., and ERNEST BARTH. *Urban Desegregation.* Seattle: University of Washington Press, 1965.

PINKNEY, ALPHONSO. *The Myth of Black Progress.* New York and London: Cambridge University Press, 1984.

Report of the National Advisory Commission on Civil Disorders. New York: Bantam Books, 1968.

SILVER, JAMES W. *Mississippi: The Closed Society.* New York: Harcourt, Brace & World, 1964.

STEINBERG, STEPHEN. *The Ethnic Myth.* Boston: Beacon Press, 1989.

TAEUBER, KARL, and ALMA TAEUBER. *Negroes in Cities.* Chicago: Aldine, 1965.

WHITTEN, NORMAN, and JOHN F. SWED, eds. *Afro-American Anthropology: Contemporary Perspectives.* New York: Free Press, 1970.

WILLIAMS, ROBIN M., JR. *Strangers Next Door: Ethnic Relations in American Communities.* Englewood Cliffs, NJ: Prentice Hall, 1964.

WOODWARD, C. VANN. *The Strange Career of Jim Crow.* New York: Oxford University Press, 1957.

WRIGHT, BRUCE. *Black Robes White Justice.* Secaucus, NJ: Lyle Stuart, 1987.

NOTES

1. Milton M. Gordon, *Assimilation in American Life* (New York: Oxford University Press, 1964), chap. 3.

2. Ibid., p. 71.

3. See also E. Franklin Frazier, *The Negro in the United States* (New York: Macmillan, 1957), chap. 1.

4. See Melville J. Herskovits, *The Myth of the Negro Past* (New York: Harper, 1941); Frazier, *Negro in the United States,* pp. 14–19.

5. Kenneth M. Stampp, *The Peculiar Institution* (New York: Knopf, 1956), p. 377.

6. See Edmund D. Cronon, *Black Moses* (Madison: University of Wisconsin Press, 1964).

7. See E. U. Essien-Udom, *Black Nationalism* (Chicago: University of Chicago Press, 1962); C. Eric Lincoln, *The Black Muslims in America* (Boston: Beacon Press, 1961).

8. Gordon, *Assimilation in American Life,* p. 76.

9. See, for example, E. Franklin Frazier, *Black Bourgeoisie* (Glencoe, IL: Free Press, 1957).

10. Robert Blauner, "Black Culture: Myth or Reality?" in *Afro-American Anthropology: Contemporary Perspectives,* ed. Norman E. Whitten, Jr., and John F. Szwed (New York: Free Press, 1970), pp. 347–66.

11. See J. L. Dillard, *Black English: Its History and Usage in the United States* (New York: Random House, 1972); Rhoda L. Goldstein, ed., *Black Life and Culture in the United States* (New York: Crowell, 1971); Ulf Hannerz, *Soulside: Inquiries into Ghetto Culture and Community* (New York: Columbia University Press, 1969); Whitten and Szwed, *Afro-American Anthropology.*

12. Gunnar Myrdal, *An American Dilemma* (New York: Harper, 1944), p. 60.

13. See, for example, Allison Davis, Burleigh Gardner, and Mary Gardner, *Deep South* (Chicago: University of Chicago Press, 1940); John Dollard, *Caste and Class in a Southern Town* (New Haven, CT: Yale University Press, 1937); Hylan Lewis, *Blackways of Kent* (Chapel Hill: University of North Carolina Press, 1955); Hortense Powdermaker, *After Freedom* (New York: Viking, 1939)

14. Robert B. Johnson, "Negro Reactions to Minority Group Status," in *American Minorities,* ed. Milton L. Barron (New York: Knopf, 1957), pp. 192–212; Robin M. Williams, Jr., *Strangers Next Door* (Englewood Cliffs, NJ: Prentice Hall, 1964), pp. 235–43.

15. Frank F. Lee, "Race Relations Pattern in a Small Town," *American Sociological Review* 19 (1954), 138–40.

16. St. Claire Drake and Horace Cayton, *Black Metropolis* (New York: Harcourt, Brace, 1945); Kenneth B. Clark, *Dark Ghetto* (New York: Harper & Row, 1965). Research conducted in a suburban community 13 miles from Detroit, Michigan, indicates that this pattern holds there. See Stanley Weiss, "The Contextual Effect: A Mosaic of Social Class Phenomena as Reflected through Subcultural Life

within a Bi-Racial Metropolitan Community," Seminar on the Metropolitan Community (University of Michigan, 1966).

17. See E. Franklin Frazier, "The Negro Middle Class and Desegregation," *Social Problems* 4 (April 1957), 291–301; Donald L. Noel, "Minority Responses to Intergroup Situations" (Department of Sociology, Ohio State University).

18. See Brewton Berry, *Race and Ethnic Relations* (Boston: Houghton Mifflin, 1958), p. 250.

19. U.S. Bureau of the Census, *Statistical Abstract of the United States, 1997* (Washington, DC), p. 57.

20. These data and those that follow are from Michael Lind, "The Beige and the Black," *New York Times Magazine*, August 16, 1998, pp. 38–39.

21. Isabel Wilkerson, "Black–White Marriages Rise, But Couples Still Face Scorn," *New York Times,* December 2, 1991, p. A1.

22. Ibid., p. B6.

23. William Brink and Louis Harris, *The Negro Revolution in America* (New York: Simon & Schuster, 1964), p. 61.

24. William Brink and Louis Harris, *Black and White* (New York: Simon & Schuster, 1967), p. 54.

25. *Report of the National Advisory Commission on Civil Disorders* (New York: Bantam, 1968), p. 135.

26. Williams, *Strangers Next Door,* p. 246.

27. See Seymour Parker and Robert Kleiner, "Status Position, Mobility, and Ethnic Identification of the Negro," *Journal of Social Issues* 20 (April 1964), 85–102.

28. Johnson, "Negro Reactions to Minority Group Status," pp. 192–212.

29. Harris Survey, 1985.

30. See Paul B, Sheatsley, "White Attitudes toward the Negro," in *The Negro American,* ed. Talcott Parsons and Kenneth B. Clark (Boston: Houghton Mifflin, 1966), pp. 303–24.

31. Emory S. Bogardus, *Immigration and Race Attitudes* (Boston: Heath, 1928), p. 25.

32. *Time*, November 24, 1997, pp. 88–91.

33. *New York Times*, June 15, 1997, Sec. 4, p. 4.

34. See Wallace Mendelson, *Discrimination* (Englewood Cliffs, NJ: Prentice Hall, 1962).

35. See C. Vann Woodward, *The Strange Career of Jim Crow* (New York: Oxford University Press, 1957), p. 103.

36. Eunice Grier and George Grier, "Equality and Beyond: Housing Segregation in the Great Society," in *The Negro American,* ed. Parsons and Clark, pp. 525–54; Davis McEntire, *Residence and Race* (Berkeley, CA: University of California Press, 1960); L. K. Northwood and Ernest Barth, *Urban Desegregation* (Seattle: University of Washington Press, 1965).

37. U.S. Commission on Civil Rights, *A Sheltered Crisis: The State of Fair Housing in the Eighties* (Washington, DC, 1983), pp. 140–141.

38. Louis Harris, "Poll Results Contradict Claims that Prejudice Is Increasing."

39. U.S. Commission on Civil Rights, *Civil Rights '63: Report of the U.S. Commission on Civil Rights* (Washington, DC, 1963) p. 99.

40. U.S. Department of Housing and Urban Development, *Measuring Discrimination in American Housing Markets* (Washington, DC, 1979).

41. Stokeley Carmichael, "What We Want," *New York Review of Books*, September 22, 1966, p. 5.

42. Louis Harris, op. cit.

43. Louis Harris, "Blacks Still Severely Critical of Reagan Despite His Personal Appeal" (Orlando, FL: Tribune Media Services, 1986).

44. Ibid., p. 2.

45. Gerald Jaynes and Robin M. Williams (editors), *A Common Destiny: Blacks and American Society* (Washington, DC, National Academy Press, 1989, p. 103.

46. Ibid.

CHAPTER TEN

The Demise
of Affirmative Action

The term *affirmative action* was first used in 1961 by President John F. Kennedy in an effort to strengthen an existing executive order prohibiting racial discrimination by government contractors in their employment practices. The notion of affirmative action was not controversial; rather, it signaled that America was, at last, dealing with its oldest and most difficult social problem. Later the concept of affirmative action was applied beyond the Kennedy executive order "to a variety of programs, private and public, voluntary as well as legally coerced that sought to guarantee the employment—or in the case of educational institutions, the admission of qualified African-Americans."[1]

In the first 100 years since emancipation, the black population of the United States made modest gains in attaining full citizenship status, but blacks remained second-class citizens, separated from the dominant white population by castelike barriers and discriminated against in virtually all aspects of life. In the 35 years since then, the gains made by black citizens equal or exceed those of the first 100 years. The quest for full equality, however, remains an elusive one, as is demonstrated by economic and social conditions in black communities throughout the country.

During the years of the "Great Society," Lyndon Baines Johnson, the thirty-sixth president, attempted to drive the nation toward equality for black citizens through legislative means, but the war in Vietnam precluded the continuation of his many-faceted program. Johnson understood what was necessary to transform American society into one in which equality of opportunity was more than a mere slogan. After the passage of the Civil Rights Acts of 1964 and 1965, he realized that most of the legal rights of blacks had been given protection. "But these legislative victories served to illuminate the full dimensions of the American dream," he said at a commencement address at Howard University in June 1965. He added:

> You do not wipe away the scars of centuries by saying: Now you are free to go where you want and do as you desire and choose the leaders you please. You do not

take a person who for years has been hobbled by chains and liberate him, bring him to the starting line of a race, and then say you are free to compete with all others, and still just believe you have been completely fair. Thus it is not enough to open the gates of opportunity. All our citizens must have the ability to walk through those gates. This is the next and more profound state of the battle for civil rights. We seek not just freedom but opportunity. We seek not just legal equity but human ability, not just equality as a right and a theory but equality as a fact and equality as a result.[2]

Because of the continued discrimination against blacks and other people of color, Johnson issued Executive Order 11246 in 1965, setting forth affirmative action guidelines. The analogy of a running race used by President Johnson is at the heart of affirmative action. But Johnson's successor, Richard Nixon, was not only unsympathetic to blacks, he was antagonistic. For example, one of his first acts as president was to attempt to slow the pace of school integration by announcing that his administration would rely less on fund cutoffs by the Department of Health, Education and Welfare to achieve integration in the schools, and more on the courts.[3] It should be noted here, however, that President Nixon imposed the so-called Philadelphia Plan on federal building contractors in Philadelphia, thereby implementing the government's most explicit quota plan in 1969. The first official government affirmative action plan was the Philadelphia Plan, which was designed to end "racial segregation in the construction industry by making federal contracts contingent on the racial composition of the work force."[4]

Affirmative action ultimately became unpopular. This unpopularity was foreshadowed in a speech by Senator James Eastland of Mississippi when the Civil Rights Act of 1964 was introduced. "The bill would discriminate against white people. I know what will happen if the bill is passed. I know what will happen if there is a choice between hiring a white man or hiring a Negro, both having equal qualifications. I know who will get the job. It will not be the white man."[5]

Initially there was little opposition to affirmative action, a practice that India introduced after independence in 1948 and that the United States had always practiced for its military veterans. There are other examples of countries attempting to make amends for past injustices.

It is ironic that at a time when there appeared to be some major progress in improving the citizenship status of black people in the United States, and some commitment to racial equality, the national mood shifted rather abruptly to one of continued subjugation and racial oppression. Beginning with the *Brown v. Board of Education* decision of the Supreme Court in 1954 and continuing through most of the decade of the 1960s, there was reason for America's black citizens to suspect that their liberation from oppression was underway and that those citizens opposed to equality for blacks were in a small minority. And it appeared that government agencies supported their aspirations. But as is so characteristic of American society, the national mood shifted radically, and through a variety of actions at all levels, blacks found themselves with fewer allies in their quest for equality. Public support for blacks virtually disappeared, and they were again being blamed for their own plight in a society where racism has historically been an integral part of all institutions and has served to maintain and protect white privilege.

Affirmative action for people of color soon became rather widely known as "reverse discrimination," and lawsuits sprang up in many places where affirmative action was practiced. Charges of "quotas" were widespread, although the Civil Rights Act of 1964 contained a sentence explicitly disavowing quotas. White males, who had always been the beneficiaries of a form of affirmative action since the founding of the country, were determined to maintain their white male privilege.

THE CASE OF ALLAN BAKKE

The case of the *Regents of the University of California v. Allan Bakke* has been a critical one for minorities and women since 1973, when Bakke first applied to the School of Medicine at the University of California at Davis. Bakke was rejected by the school in the spring of 1973 and again in the fall of 1974, as he had been at 10 other medical schools to which he had applied.[6] After the second rejection at the University of California at Davis, Bakke learned that the medical school maintained a special admissions policy setting aside 16 of the 100 first-year positions for members of economically and educationally disadvantaged minorities. At the urging of an administrator at the school he retained a lawyer to file suit against the university, challenging the admissions policy on the grounds that it violated the equal protection clause of the Fourteenth Amendment. In other words, he charged the medical school with practicing "reverse discrimination," in that it gave preferential treatment to minorities.

The Yolo County (California) Supreme Court ruled that the university's program was invalid in that it discriminated against Bakke because of his race. However, it did not order the medical school to admit him, and both the university and Bakke appealed. Finally, the California Supreme Court held, on September 16, 1976, that the university's affirmative action program was unconstitutional because it violated the equal protection rights of white people. The school was ordered to admit Bakke in the fall of 1977, but it was permitted to retain its admissions policy until the United States Supreme Court could review the case. The review was granted in February 1977, and the decision was handed down on June 28. By a five-to-four margin the Supreme Court ruled that the admissions program at the University of California at Davis was illegal because it violated Title VII of the Civil Rights Act of 1964, not the equal protection clause of the Fourteenth Amendment.

The *Bakke* case was of such significance that six separate opinions were written by the justices. Both Justices Thurgood Marshall and Harry Blackmun wrote dissenting opinions in strong language. For example, Justice Blackmun wrote:

> I suspect that it would be impossible to arrange an affirmative action program in a racially neutral way and have it be successful. To ask that this be so is to demand the

impossible. *In order to get beyond racism, we must first take account of race.* [italics added] There is no other way. And in order to treat some persons equally, we must treat them differently.[7]

Justice Marshall wrote:

Today's judgement ignores the fact that for several hundred years Negroes have been discriminated against, not as individuals, but rather solely because of the color of their skins. It is unnecessary in 20th century America to have individual Negroes demonstrate that they have been victims of racial discrimination; the racism of our society has been so pervasive that none, regardless of wealth or position, has managed to escape its impact. I fear that we have come full circle. After the Civil War our government started several "affirmative action" programs. This Court in the *Civil Rights Cases* and *Plessey v. Ferguson* destroyed the movement toward equality. For almost a century no action was taken, and this nonaction was with the tacit approval of the courts. Then we had *Brown v. Board of Education* and the Civil Rights Acts of Congress, followed by numerous affirmative programs of the type used by the University of California.[8]

But a majority of justices concurred in the decision written by Justice Lewis F. Powell. In essence this decision invalidated the affirmative action program at the University of California at Davis and ordered Bakke admitted. The supporters of Bakke, by the positions they took, signified their belief that the long history of racial oppression in the United States (as described by Justice Marshall in his dissent) was now behind us and that minorities had achieved parity with whites. Some even maintained that affirmative action and the civil rights gains of the 1960s had now tipped the scale in favor of minorities.

The confusing decision of the Supreme Court in the Bakke case immediately had an adverse impact on affirmative action programs around the country. Indeed, even before the Court announced its decision, many organizations, fearful that the decision would be negative, cut back on affirmative action programs.[9]

- Ohio construction contractors obtained a preliminary injunction against some state projects set aside for minority contractors on the grounds that this was barred by *Bakke*.
- Some white workers at an Aramco steel plant in Ashland, Kentucky, brought suit to eliminate apprenticeship quotas set in the 1974 consent decree. The decree provided that 50 percent of new apprenticeship openings were to be filled by black, Hispanic, and female workers.
- An antibusing organization in Los Angeles took the city to court on the grounds that "excessive busing" means a quota system, prohibited by *Bakke*.
- In Richmond, Virginia, a redevelopment project utilizing one-fourth black workers was reexamined in the light of the *Bakke* decision.
- Citing the *Bakke* case as a precedent, a Los Angeles judge declared unconstitutional a recently passed federal law requiring that 10 percent of some government construction funds go to minority-owned companies. A similar ruling was rendered in Boston.
- In New Jersey, a ratio in hiring to remedy police and fire department discrimination was ruled unconstitutional by the New Jersey Supreme Court.

• A federal court declared that the use of quotas in the distribution of scholarship funds was impermissible.

THE CASE OF BRIAN WEBER

After the decision in the *Bakke* case it was assumed by many whites, especially conservatives, that the nation would return to business as usual in matters pertaining to race. In another important case, that of the *United Steelworkers of America v. Weber*, a 32-year-old white worker at the Kaiser Aluminum plant in Gramercy, Louisiana, sued the company and the union, charging reverse discrimination. The plant and the union, in 1974, had established an affirmative action program for minority and female employees. Since its opening in 1956, the company maintained, it had never discriminated against blacks. But in the region where the plant is located, the total number of blacks was only about 20 in a work force of 500.[10]

The United Steelworkers of America devised the affirmative action plan in nationwide collective bargaining with Kaiser Aluminum and Chemical Corporation. The program called for an increase in black and female participation in higher-paying and skilled jobs. To achieve this goal the plan called for admitting blacks and women until they constituted 40 percent and 5 percent of the work force, respectively. These goals were to be accomplished by admitting workers to the training program on a 50–50 basis: one minority or female to one white male.

Brian Weber applied for the special training program, but it was ruled that he had insufficient seniority to get one of the places reserved for whites.[11] However, two blacks admitted had less seniority than Weber. When he filed a grievance through the union, that too was denied. He then wrote the Equal Employment Opportunity Commission in New Orleans for a copy of the Civil Rights Act. After a visit there, he filed a formal complaint. There was never a hearing, and when he did not hear from the Commission, he filed a class action suit representing all the white workers at Kaiser. He brought suit in Federal District Court charging violation of Title VII of the Civil Rights Act of 1964.

The District Court held that the program was illegal because the black workers benefiting from the program had not themselves been victims of discrimination. The case was then appealed to the United States Court of Appeals for the Fifth Circuit, where the lower court's ruling was upheld. In December 1978 the Supreme Court of the United States agreed to hear the case. During its oral hearings, Weber's lawyer argued that Congress "meant to outlaw not discrimination in its most literal meaning, but discrimination that is invidious in the context of racial bigotry."[12]

The *Weber* case, unlike that of *Bakke*, did not involve the Fourteenth Amendment to the Constitution; in fact, it did not invoke the Constitution at all. The Supreme Court viewed the Kaiser plan as a voluntary agreement between private parties whose behavior is not regulated by the Constitution. Therefore the justices limited themselves to the question of whether Congress meant to bar this kind of voluntary action when discrimination based on race was outlawed.

On June 27, 1979, the United States Supreme Court handed down its decision in the Weber case. Two of the justices did not participate—one because he had worked for Kaiser, and the other because he had been ill and did not participate in the oral arguments. In a 5-to-2 decision, the Court held that voluntary affirmative action plans, even those with numerical quotas, did not necessarily violate Title VII of the Civil Rights Act of 1964. Writing for the majority, Justice William Brennan wrote:

> It would be ironic indeed if a law triggered by a nation's concern over centuries of racial injustice and intended to improve the lot of those who had "been excluded from the American dream for so long" constituted the first legislative prohibition of all voluntary, private, race-conscious efforts to abolish traditional patterns of racial segregation and hierarchy. . . . An interpretation that forbade all race-conscious affirmative action would bring about an end completely at variance with the purpose and must not be rejected.[13]

Chief Justice Warren Burger and Associate Justice William Rehnquist issued dissenting opinions. The Chief Justice wrote that in enacting Title VII, "Congress expressly *prohibited* the discrimination against Brian Weber the Court approves now." He accused the majority of "totally rewriting a crucial part of Title VII to reach a desirable result."[14] Justice Rehnquist wrote another angry dissenting opinion.

The *Weber* case was seen as a victory for blacks and women, for if Weber had won the case in the Supreme Court it would have served to set back affirmative action programs for decades into the future. Weber's claim that he had nothing to do with past discrimination against blacks, and consequently should not have been denied admission to the training program, was appropriately answered by an official of the Office of Federal Contract Compliance in the Department of Labor. He said: "The question is whether you give priority to a group that's been systematically deprived of opportunity while Brian Weber's parents and grandparents were not discriminated against. If someone must bear the sins of the father, surely it must be their children."

Bakke, like many other whites, elected to file a "reverse discrimination" suit. And the notion of reverse discrimination is not a valid concept where affirmative action is concerned. It is a smokescreen thrown up by those who would perpetuate the subordinate position of blacks in the United States. The cry of reverse discrimination is, in some cases, an effort to distort the meaning of affirmative action and its intent—to provide equal educational and employment opportunities. The critics of affirmative action programs insist that such programs violate the principle of meritocracy in favor of hiring "unqualified" blacks; however, proponents of the decision argued that reverse discrimination against individual white males cannot be equated with the systematic discrimination against blacks.

BLACK CONSERVATIVES AND AFFIRMATIVE ACTION

In the 1980s a small group of Americans—black conservatives—emerged as conservatism became the dominant ethos of the society, And like Booker T. Washington before them, they were opposed to affirmative action (compensatory justice) in the workplace and in education. Black conservatives maintain that race is no longer a salient factor in American life for blacks. That is, society is colorblind and white society is not responsible for the condition of black people. In other words, they blame the victims of oppression for their status in the society, asserting that blacks must rely on individual initiative and self-help rather than on government assistance.

One of the most remarkable things about this new breed of black conservatives is that most of them have been beneficiaries of affirmative action. While black conservatives have been around for centuries, it was affirmative action that caused their ranks to increase. Many of them held important positions during the administrations of Ronald Reagan and George Bush. According to the historian Julian Bond, "It's the same old story. Whites trying to tell black folks who should be their leaders."[15]

A black Republican who served in both the Nixon and Reagan administrations, and who is critical of the black conservatives, had this to say: "They merely say they are conservative, say they are opposed to affirmative action and are immediately picked up by a right-wing sponsor, such as the Hoover Institution, the Heritage Foundation, and the American Enterprise Institute, groups not known for their sensitivity to black issues."[16]

Some conservative politicians, on the other hand, generally support the traditional civil rights leaders in their quest for affirmative action and other forms of government assistance. These people include William T. Coleman, secretary of transportation in the Ford administration; Arthur Fletcher, who served in the Nixon administration; and former senator Edward W. Brooke, a Republican from Massachusetts. For example, Coleman has said, "We must go beyond mere neutrality . . . if we are ever to overcome the lasting legacy of slavery and discrimination. That requires affirmative action."[17]

Shelby Steele, a professor of English, sees affirmative action as a move away from equal opportunity, and in his discussion he appears to be concerned primarily with preferential treatment or numerical quotas. In a chapter devoted to affirmative action he writes: "I think affirmative action has shown itself to be more bad than good and that blacks . . . now stand to lose more from it than they gain."[18] He writes, "I believe affirmative action is problematic in our society because it tries to function as a social program. Rather than ask it to ensure equal opportunity we have demanded that it create parity between the races."[19]

Writing in the *New York Times Magazine*, Steele says, "The effect of preferential treatment—the lowering of normal standards to increase black representation—puts blacks at war with an expanded realm of debilitating doubt, so that the doubt itself becomes an unrecognized preoccupation that undermines their ability to perform, especially in integrated situations."[20]

Thomas Sowell, an economist with the Hoover Institution, maintains that affirmative action is at odds with equal opportunity because the former requires that individuals be judged with regard to group membership, while equal opportunity requires that people "be judged on their qualifications as individuals, without regard to race, sex, age, etc."[21]

Furthermore, Sowell feels that affirmative action does not advance the cause of civil rights. "Those who support affirmative action . . . are faced with the embarrassing fact that the economic rise of minorities has slowed noticeably as the 'equality of opportunity' policies of the 1960s metamorphosed into affirmative action quotas in the 1970s."[22]

Sowell maintains that affirmative action violates the Civil Rights Act of 1964, although its constitutionality has been upheld by the Supreme Court in several decisions. He calls the Court's rulings upholding affirmative action "bold dishonesty." He asks, "Why do courts twist words and torture logic like this?" His answer: "There is nothing like doing 'the right thing' to justify lying deception and overreaching one's authority."[23]

In a pamphlet, *Affirmative Action Reconsidered: Was it Necessary in Academia?*, Sowell answers the question in the negative. Furthermore, he enumerates several ways in which he feels that affirmative action programs hurt the academic world without benefiting minorities and women.[24]

Stephen Carter, a law professor, begins his statement of opposition to affirmative action in the first chapter of his book with the following observation: "I got into law school because I am black."[25] Carter is primarily concerned with affirmative action in colleges and universities, and although he claims to express the views of beneficiaries of affirmative action, he is clearly opposed to it. He says, "I sift the case for and against affirmative action in the professions, and propose a compromise that returns our systems of racial preference to their simpler, more defensible roots."[26]

Finally, Carter writes that racial preferences "are not the most constructive method of overcoming the barriers that keep people of color out of high-prestige positions. They are often implemented in ways that are insulting, and besides, they can carry considerable costs."[27]

Another black conservative economist, Glenn Loury, addressed the seventy-fifth annual conference of the National Urban League in 1985, and told his audience that affirmative action and other programs could "destroy the possibility of attaining 'race' equality of status for black Americans." He argues vehemently against "racial quotas" and said the black community should "shoulder the responsibility for its own problems, even if they stemmed from past discrimination."[28]

Black conservatives tend to minimize the persistence of racism in American society. For example, William Wilson maintains that "Race relations in America have undergone fundamental changes in recent years, so much so that now the life chances of individual blacks have more to do with their economic class position than with their day-to-day encounters with whites."[29]

OPPOSITION TO AFFIRMATIVE ACTION GATHERS STEAM

Although there have been many lawsuits to rid the country of affirmative action, thousands of blacks have profited from the practice. The earlier period of affirmative action might be called the second reconstruction for America's black population.

Beginning with the Supreme Court decision in *Brown v. Board of Education* in 1954, followed by the Civil Rights Act of 1964, the Voting Rights Act of 1965, and the Fair Housing Act of 1968, substantial progress was made in eliminating segregation and discrimination. And it should be noted that these rather drastic changes in race relations resulted from the protracted struggles of the black population. In addition to these acts of the legislature and the courts, the black population, especially young people, demonstrated by means of rebellions in large cities. This was especially true after the assassination of Martin Luther King in 1968. They showed that they were unwilling to suffer the oppression that had been thrust upon them by racist white Americans.

During this period there were groups in the country, mainly conservatives and racists, who held that blacks were advancing too rapidly. How was it possible for a people who had suffered severe discrimination and deprivation of their basic human rights to be advancing too rapidly? The answer to this question lies in the notion that black people were considered innately inferior to whites.

The country was rapidly becoming more conservative. Jimmy Carter, a liberal, lost the presidential election of 1980 to Ronald Reagan, an old-line conservative. Indeed, a *New York Times*/CBS poll found that white people had voted Republican, in large part, because they believed that the Democratic party had become too concerned with blacks.[30]

In California in 1995, two conservative professors led a drive to put an initiative on the state ballot in 1996 asking citizens to vote on affirmative action. In addition, candidates for the Republican nomination for president—Bob Dole, Phil Gramm, and Lamar Alexander—joined the anti–affirmative action crusade. President Bill Clinton, a strong supporter of affirmative action, gave a speech at the National Archives on the subject. Among other things, he said: "Based on the evidence, the job is not done. So, here is what I think. We should reaffirm the principle of affirmative action and fix the practices. We should have a simple slogan: Mend it but don't end it."[31] Each of his Republican predecessors had opposed affirmative action in some way. Most of the public opposition came from angry white men, who were convinced that it had stacked the deck against them.

The historian Roger Wilkins reports on a 1995 issue of *U.S. News and World Report* in which the magazine "introduced a package of articles on these issues with the question on its cover: 'Does affirmative action mean No White Men Need Apply?' " Inside, the lead story carried a painting with a white man separated from opportunity ladders easily being scaled by women and dark men. And the story yielded up the following sentence: "Affirmative action poses a conflict between two cherished American principles: The belief that all Americans deserve equal opportunities and the idea that hard work and merit, not race or religion or gender or birthright, should determine who prospers and who does not."[32]

But affirmative action was not designed to punish anyone; it was rather—as a result of a clear-eyed look at how America actually works—an attempt to enlarge opportunity for *everybody*, Wilkins writes. The many complaints about numerical guidelines or quotas are misplaced because without these practices there would be no way of knowing whether the law was being upheld. And there would be the familiar cry of not being able to find qualified blacks and women, always using the word "qualified" for blacks but never for whites.

As Wilkins writes:

> Affirmative action has done wonderful things for the United States by enlarging opportunity and developing and utilizing a far broader array of the skills available in the American population than in the past. It has not outlived its usefulness. It was never designed to be a program to eliminate poverty. It has not always been used wisely, and some of its permutations do have to be reconsidered, refined or, in some cases, abandoned. It is not a quota program.[33]

Finally, Wilkins, in making the case for affirmative action, writes:

> In a society so conceived and so dedicated, it is understandable that white males would take their preferences as a matter of natural right and consider any alteration of that as a primal offense. But a nation that operates in that way abandons its soul and its economic strength, and will remain mired in ugliness and moral squalor because so many people are excluded from the possibility of decent lives and from forming any sense of community with the rest of society.[34]

Many others in the mid-nineties strongly supported affirmative action. Lawrence Otis Graham, for example, writes about the indignities black professionals face:

> Even though I am the beneficiary of affirmative action, I can acknowledge some of its flaws—its tendency to create resentment among white men and its potential for generating a sense of "group entitlement" among minorities and women. But my experiences as a corporate lawyer, professor and black professional in a mostly white environment have shown me that work place bias in America, even today, is so intractable that it justifies affirmative action as a permanent policy.
>
> The amount of subtle bias I face as a lawyer continues to dismay me. For example, I have worked with clients or co-counsel who have become comfortable with me through phone conversations and correspondence. But upon meeting me, they are suddenly fidgety and wary of my competence.[35]

Bob Herbert, a columnist for the *New York Times*, discusses opposition to affirmative action by conservatives who think that the "biggest problem of discrimination in the United States today is bias against white men." He continues, "The arguments against affirmative action are almost always crafted in racial terms because demagogues know that race is the way to get the emotional flames roaring. . . . The United States is going through a period in which the politics of meanness is in the ascent."[36]

After reviewing several cases in which the Supreme Court approved affirmative action programs, one writer concluded that "There is nothing radical or un-American in these simple therapeutic concepts of affirmative action. However, these perfectly sound principles have been so abused by fringe politicians and pressure groups that the original purposes have been obscured and the general public has become befuddled."[37]

In support of affirmative action, Michael Kinsley writes about merit versus talent. Because of the widespread opposition to affirmative action in the United States, he writes:

> The answer must be that race is such a toxic subject in American culture that it should not enter into calculations about people's places in society—even in order to benefit racism's historic victims. That is a respectable answer. But it understandably rings hollow to many blacks, who see this sudden and ostentatious anathema on racial consciousness as a bit too convenient. Where was colorblindness when they needed it?[38]

In a 1997 *New York Times*/CBS national poll Americans expressed their views on affirmative action. (See figure 10-1.) This happened during the height of opposition to affirmative action, and the results were marked by ambivalence and tangled views.[39] When asked the question, "What is the best thing to do with affirmative action programs giving preference to some minorities?" the largest group (43 percent) replied "Change them," one-fourth (25 percent) said "Do away with them," and an equal number (24 percent) said "Leave them as they are." When the answers of blacks and whites on affirmative action were compared, the differences were striking.

Two Supreme Court decisions in 1995 served to set back affirmative action in employment. In a 5-to-4 decision, the Court ruled on June 12 against federal programs that award benefits on the basis of race. Congress had required that at least 10 percent of federal money spent on highway projects go to businesses owned by "disadvantaged individuals." In 1989 an agency solicited bids to build a section of a highway in Colorado. Writing for the Court, Justice Sandra Day O'Connor said that such programs must be subject to the most searching judicial inquiry and can sur-

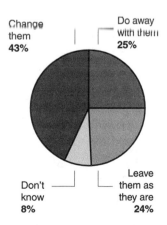

FIGURE 10-1   QUESTION: What is the best thing to do with affirmative action programs giving preference to some minorities?

Source: New York Times/CBS News Poll. *New York Times*, December 14, 1997, p. 1.

vive only if "narrowly tailored" to accomplish a compelling government interest. Justice Clarence Thomas, who opposes all forms of affirmative action, and who was one of its beneficiaries, said: "In my mind, government sponsored racial discrimination based on benign prejudice is just as noxious as discrimination inspired by malicious prejudice. In each instance it is racial discrimination, plain and simple."[40]

And on June 29, the Supreme Court upheld a challenge to Georgia's 11th District, one of the many districts created in 1992 to increase minority representation in Congress. According to the Court, the creation of congressional districts using race as a predominant factor should be presumed to be unconstitutional.[41] In an editorial, the *New York Times* wrote: "The Georgia decision joins a line of recent Supreme Court cases laying bogus to 'colorblind' Constitutional law but in fact merely blind to the still-unfilled Constitutional promise to overcome the nation's racist past."[42]

One of the most enduring facts of American life is the opposition to minority rights. It is an indication not only of racism but also of meanness.

CASES IN TEXAS AND CALIFORNIA

Affirmative action at the University of Texas School of Law provides an interesting account of the way in which many persons and organizations have attempted to resegregate the school. The state of Texas, one of the country's most populous, has had a long history of problems with blacks and the law school. In 1950 Heman Sweatt, a black person, applied to the University of Texas Law School. The policy at the time was to provide "separate but equal" facilities for blacks. At that time the university opened a law school for blacks. The school had just two students, and classes for the two blacks were held across the street from the state capitol.[43]

The U.S. Supreme Court declared this practice unconstitutional, saying the program was separate but not equal. The school began its affirmative action program in the 1970s, but graduated its first black student in 1953. In some of the following years the entering class had no black applicants. However, in the 1990s minority enrollment increased. Then in 1992 "Cheryl Hopwood and three other white law school applicants asserted that they were denied admission because affirmative action policies gave unfair preferences to less qualified minority applicants."

The three-judge panel, appointed by the United States Court of Appeals for the Fifth Circuit, in New Orleans, shook the academic world in 1996 "by ruling not only that the law school's admission policies were illegal but also that the Supreme Court's ruling in the *Bakke* reverse discrimination case was no longer valid." The Fifth Circuit's ruling said that the law school "may not use race as a factor in admissions even for the wholesome purpose of correcting perceived racial imbalance in the student body."[44]

But in a letter to state legislators in Texas, the head of the Office of Civil Rights in the U.S. Department of Education, Norma Cantu, said: "The Hopwood decision applied only to admission programs used by the school at the time the suit was filed." Cantu said that "Texas is required to continue to root out current discriminatory practices and the vestiges of past discrimination and make its campuses more accessible to minorities." The letter from the Department of Education said, in addition, that not only can race be used as a factor in admissions, but universities "have a clear and legal obligation to do so to remedy current discrimination or the effects of past discrimination." In addition, the letter "told Texas officials that they must aggressively take steps like affirmative action to attract minorities or risk losing $500 million in student scholarships, work-study programs and research grants."[45]

In the class of fall 1997 there were only 6 black students and 18 Mexican-Americans. "Last year 65 black students and 70 Mexican-Americans were admitted to the school. . . . Undergraduate acceptances at the entire University of Texas fell to 314 black and 1,568 Hispanic applicants in 1996, from 421 blacks and 1,568 Hispanics applicants in 1966."

In an effort to comply with the U.S. Department of Education, the Texas House of Representatives has passed a plan that would use "a combination of rankings of high school seniors and consideration of economic disadvantage to maintain racial and ethnic diversity."[46]

The affirmative action situation in California has had a different outcome from that in Texas. In 1996 a ballot initiative—Proposition 209—barred consideration of race, ethnicity or sex in public employment, contracting and admissions to public colleges and universities in California. Proposition 209 was cosponsored by Ward Connerly, a conservative black man, who is a regent of the University. According to Connerly, affirmative action discriminates against whites. At a round table discussion sponsored by the presidential advisory panel on race, Connerly said: "One thing that might help move this panel forward is to take the whole subject of affirmative action off their plate. Let them deal with the broader subject of race absent the issue of preferences."[47]

Later, in commenting on the decreasing number of blacks at colleges and universities in California, Connerly said that the new figures were attributable to the end of what he called a dual-track system with different standards for whites and Asians on the one hand and black, Hispanic, and other minority applicants on the other hand. He added, "They reveal beyond the shadow of a doubt that the university was discriminating against Asians and whites."[48]

Connerly is not satisfied with the end of affirmative action in California; he now wants to rid the colleges and universities of ethnic studies. According to him such programs promote self-imposed segregation.[49] Furthermore, he said he was concerned that "ethnic studies served as a divisive force, catering to members of a given ethnic group and stressing that group's differences from the rest of society." He also questioned whether the purpose of the classes was truly academic or whether they were exercises in racial and ethnic pride.

In response to Connerly, William Banks, a professor of African-American studies at the Berkeley campus, had this to say: "He has concluded that people are happy with the drop in ethnic enrollments and, hey, while the animal's bleeding, let's put another stake in its leg."

Indeed, the drop-off in applications from blacks and Hispanics has been substantial. Should the initiative remain in effect, as is likely, the projections for the freshman class of 2002 are grim, as shown in Figure 10-2.

According to data released by the University of California at Berkeley, "overall representation of non-Asians in the freshman class at the University of California at Berkeley, now the nation's most selective public university, will be 10.54 percent, compared with 21.92 percent last year (1997). The class will include 98 blacks, far fewer than the 260 black freshmen in the fall of 1997."[50]

The vice-chancellor at the University of California at Los Angeles said of the drop in minority enrollment, "The real danger—our biggest concern—is that the University of California system will become a segregated system. If this trend continues over the next five or six years, the diversity on this campus will be seriously compromised, and with it, our greatness." Across the university's eight campuses, minority representation will be down 2.4 percentage points, from 17.6 in 1997 to 15.2 for the fall of 1998 because the less prestigious campuses like Riverside, Santa Barbara, and Santa Cruz increased the number of black and Hispanic students accepted.[51]

Proposition 209 has caused significant drops in minority enrollment. Some examples: "The University campuses at Irvine, San Diego and Davis showed sharp declines in the number of black, Hispanic and American Indian students who applied when compared with last year, even as the number of ethnic minority student applications increased substantially." At the University of California, Irvine, "1,291 Hispanic students were admitted for the fall, compared with 1,412 in 1997, along with 246 blacks, compared with 303; 57 American Indians, compared with 66; 3,375 whites, compared with 3,770; and 5,309 Asian American students, compared with 5,389."[52]

Furthermore, according to Anthony Lewis, a columnist for the *New York Times*: "Abolishing affirmative action has the ironic result of excluding students who can do the work. The elite campuses of the University of California this spring (1998) rejected 800 black and Hispanic applicants with 4.0 grade point averages."[53] Enrollment of minorities decreases at major University of California branches but increases at some of the less well-known branches (see Figure 10-3).

While the State of Texas has dealt with the problem of diversity by requiring universities to accept the top 10 percent of all graduates from high schools, the University of California system has made no attempts to increase diversity on its campuses.

The *Wall Street Journal*, a newspaper known for its conservatism, editorialized in favor of some sort of preference for black Americans:

> In the broadest sense, what most people likely support is the belief that somehow, somewhere, a lot of black Americans got the short end of the stick. Whether it was slavery, the obvious pathologies of inner-city life or the crummy schools, it seems obvious

The racial breakdown of students who have been accepted by the University of California for fall 1998, post-affirmative action. Students may ultimately decide to enroll elsewhere.

ADMISSIONS TO UNIVERSITIES OF CALIFORNIA

		BLACK	ASIAN	AMERICAN INDIAN	FILIPINO*	WHITE/OTHER	HISPANIC†	DID NOT REPORT
BERKELEY	'97	598	3,866	77	—	3,831	1,411	627
	'98	255	3,861	47	—	3,635	852	1,586
	Pct. Chg.	**-57**	**+0**	**-39**	—	**-5**	**-40**	**+153**
LOS ANGELES	'97	488	4,154	81	—	3,456	1,497	569
	'98	280	4,187	46	—	3,334	1,001	1,463
	Pct. Chg.	**-43**	**+1**	**-43**	—	**+4**	**-33**	**+157**
SAN DIEGO	'97	373	4,071	105	477	5,309	1,427	1,541
	'98	203	3,928	66	472	4,790	979	2,603
	Pct. Chg.	**-46**	**-4**	**-37**	**-1**	**-10**	**-31**	**+69**
DAVIS	'97	518	3,380	122	433	6,305	1,626	692
	'98	332	3,630	100	500	5,640	1,302	1,915
	Pct. Chg.	**-36**	**+7**	**-18**	**+15**	**-11**	**-20**	**+177**
IRVINE	'97	303	4,611	66	778	3,770	1,412	442
	'98	246	4,490	57	819	3,375	1,291	1,423
	Pct. Chg.	**-19**	**-3**	**-14**	**+5**	**-10**	**-9**	**+222**
RIVERSIDE	'97	257	3,706	29	—	1,815	1,071	197
	'98	345	4,140	51	—	2,027	1,536	816
	Pct. Chg.	**+34**	**+12**	**+76**	—	**+12**	**+43**	**+314**
SANTA BARBARA	'97	438	3,075	149	—	7,933	2,215	725
	'98	375	2,871	111	—	6,433	1,701	2,060
	Pct. Chg.	**-14**	**-7**	**-26**	—	**-19**	**-23**	**+184**
SANTA CRUZ	'97	223	2,021	82	295	4,915	1,159	562
	'98	219	2,169	96	347	4,443	1,245	1,709
	Pct. Chg.	**-2**	**+7**	**-17**	**+18**	**-10**	**+7**	**+204**

FIGURE 10-2   The Freshman Class, 2002?

*Data not available at all schools.

†May be of any race.

Source: New York Times, April 1, 1998, p. B11.

The number of black, Hispanic, and American Indian students in the fall freshman class at the University of California's two most competitive campuses, Berkeley and Los Angeles, will drop sharply from the previous year. However, some of its campuses will show an increase in non-Asian minority group enrollment.

		BLACK			HISPANIC			AMERICAN INDIAN			TOTAL STUDENTS		
		ADMITTED	ENROLLING	RATE	ADMITTED	ENROLLING	RATE	ADMITTED	ENROLLING	RATE	ADMITTED	ENROLLING	RATE
BERKELEY	'97	547	260	47.5%	1,251	492	39.3%	67	24	35.8%	8,320	3,629	43.6%
	'98	224	98	43.8	635	264	41.6	29	14	48.3	8,300	3,660	44.1
LOS ANGELES	'97	518	219	42.3	1,518	603	39.7	86	40	46.5	10,657	3,951	37.1
	'98	304	131	43.1	1,010	458	45.3	49	15	30.6	10,821	4,267	39.4
SAN DIEGO	'97	374	80	21.4	1,458	381	26.1	117	28	23.9	13,338	3,508	26.3
	'98	226	61	27.0	1,035	300	29.0	68	22	32.4	13,453	3,600	26.8
DAVIS	'97	504	107	21.2	1,604	408	25.4	117	38	32.5	13,521	3,679	27.2
	'98	354	104	29.4	1,341	396	29.5	106	39	36.8	13,694	3,796	27.7
IRVINE	'97	298	55	18.5	1,399	302	21.6	66	9	13.6	11,294	3,011	26.7
	'98	283	71	25.1	1,371	365	26.6	59	22	37.3	12,177	3,326	27.3
RIVERSIDE	'97	342	88	25.7	1,334	337	25.3	33	7	21.2	8,422	2,004	23.8
	'98	372	123	33.1	1,626	500	30.8	54	14	25.9	9,416	2,369	25.2
SANTA BARBARA	'97	442	137	31.0	2,280	591	25.9	151	41	27.2	14,883	4,094	27.5
	'98	374	109	29.1	1,716	573	33.4	112	44	39.3	13,819	3,875	28.0
SANTA CRUZ	'97	277	52	18.8	1,331	280	21.0	89	20	22.5	9,439	2,257	23.9
	'98	265	61	23.0	1,393	350	25.1	99	27	27.3	10,841	2,532	23.4

FIGURE 10-3 A Shift in Enrollment

Source: University of California. Reprinted in the *New York Times*, May 21, 1998, p. 28.

that some sort of extra effort across the broad spectrum of American life would be necessary to start the cycle of upward mobility.[54]

RETHINKING AFFIRMATIVE ACTION

In recent years, especially the last half of the 1990s, many opponents are modifying their resistance to affirmative action; but there are a few who initially supported it who now oppose it. In their book *America in Black and White: One Nation Indivisible*, a Harvard professor and his wife, also a professor, who refer to themselves as former liberals have denounced affirmative action.[55]

> The cornerstone premise of the Thernstroms is that things are not so bad as they seem, that both blacks and whites are better than, and different from, their stereotypes. Whites, they argue, are mischaracterized as a racist monolith, when in fact polls show a different picture. Whites surveyed in the 1940s wanted firm separation of the races, but by 1994 a majority told pollsters they have blacks as neighbors and close friends; at least a third say they have had blacks over for dinner.[56]

The book has been severely criticized. For example, the writer Gore Vidal calls the book "bad history" and "the worst history book of the year." Among other things, Vidal writes:

> Their argument is simple. Affirmative action for minorities is wrong, particularly in the case of African Americans, because such action takes it for granted that they are by nature inferior to whites and so require more financial aid (and slacker educational standards) than canny whites or those eerily look-alike, overly numerate Asians. This is inspired. . . . Now the Therms can maintain that the true racist is one who believes in affirmative action, because he is anti-black.[57]

On the other hand, some who have steadily opposed affirmative action are beginning to change their tune. For example, the conservative James Q. Wilson "grudgingly accepts affirmative action at public colleges, but proselytizes for it in police and fire departments, arguing that these agencies must be racially representative."[58]

The Harvard sociologist Nathan Glazer, formerly an ardent opponent of affirmative action, has changed his mind. In 1975 he expressed his disdain for affirmative action in a book titled *Affirmative Discrimination*. In that book he wrote:

> I will examine in this book policies in three areas: employment, school desegregation, and residential location. I will analyze the position of those who support present policies [affirmative action] and will argue that the consensus of the middle 1960s has been broken, and that it was and remains the right policy for the United States—right for the groups that had suffered, and in some measure still suffer from prejudice and discrimination, and right for the nation as a whole.

He refers to the black community as a "tangle of pathology." He blames blacks for their condition in American society, and says that black males would rather receive welfare than work. "The gravest political consequence [of affirmative action] is undoubtedly the increasing resentment and hostility between groups that is fueled by special benefits for some."[59]

Glazer ends his book as follows: "It is now our task to work with the intellectual, judicial, and political institutions of the country and to reestablish this simple and clear understanding, that rights attach to the individual, not the group, and that public policy must be exercised without distinction of race, color, or national origin."[60]

It is true that the Civil Rights Act of 1964, the Voting Rights Act of 1965, and the Fair Housing Act of 1968 served to elevate the citizenship status of black Americans. But it is equally true that legal equality in principle does not necessarily lead to justice in practice. Laws that are not enforced are hardly worth the effort that goes into enacting them. And it is difficult to find policy recommendations in *Affirmative Discrimination* that would in any way improve the plight of the oppressed among us.

Now Glazer has had a startling change of heart on affirmative action. He has recently said that ending it would visit so much damage on the aspirations and advancement of blacks that opponents of granting preferences to qualified black college applicants should rethink their position.[61]

Recently, in an interview with a reporter from the *New York Times*, Glazer was asked why he had so radically changed his position on affirmative action. He replied: "You begin to break with orthodoxy, and then you see other challenges to it. They don't seem so outlandish or threatening as they once did."[62] (The shifting views on affirmative action may be found in Figure 10-4.)

THE LAST WORD ON AFFIRMATIVE ACTION

The most comprehensive study of affirmative action was conducted by two ex-university presidents: Derek Bok, former president of Harvard, and William G. Bowen, former president of Princeton. Their book, *The Shape of the River*, was published in September 1998 by Princeton University Press.[63]

This study, covering over 20 years at some of the nation's elite colleges, is based on the "records and experiences of tens of thousands of students." They examined "grades, test scores, choice of major, graduation rates, careers and attitudes of 45,000 students at 28 of the most selective universities." While both authors are advocates of race-conscious admissions policies, "they wanted to test the assumptions underlying such policies." After the completion of the study, the authors say it should "put to rest major objections to such policies, especially the notion that both whites and blacks are ultimately cheated by them."

The study "limits itself to the practice of race-conscious admissions in elite higher education; that is, to considering the race of the applicant to be a critical factor in whether they should be admitted—as important, say, as where they are from or extracurricular activities."

Americans reject preference in hiring and promotion . . .

Do you believe where there has been job discrimination in the past, preference in hiring and promotion should be given?

TO WOMEN — No 51%, Yes 37%
TO BLACKS — No 52%, Yes 35%

. . . but support some special efforts for minorites . . .

To make up for past discrimination, do you favor or oppose programs that make special efforts to help minorities get ahead?

Favor 55%, Oppose 39%, Don't know 7%

Do you favor or oppose employers' and colleges' using outreach programs to hire minority workers and find minority students?

Favor 60%, Oppose 27%, Don't know 10%

. . . and for the poor.

Suppose affirmative action programs to help minorities and women were ended and new programs were created to help poor people. Should preference be given to people from poor families?

Yes 53%, No 37%, Don't know 11%

WHERE WHITES AND BLACKS AGREE . . .

	TOTAL	BLACK	WHITE
Favor special educational programs to assist minorities in competing for college admissions	63	82	59
Oppose	28	11	31
Favor government financing for job training for minorities to help them get ahead in industries where they are underrepresented	69	95	64
Oppose	24	3	29
Necessary to have laws to protect minorities against discrimination in hiring and promotion	69	88	65
Not necessary	27	9	31
It is a good idea to select a person from a poor family over one from a middle-class or rich family if they all are equally qualified.	56	65	53
Not a good idea	27	20	28
As a result of affirmative action, less qualified people are hired and promoted and admitted to college:			
At least some of the time	79	67	81
Hardly ever or never	15	28	13

. . . AND WHERE THEY DISAGREE

Necessary to have affirmative action programs to make sure companies have racially diverse work forces	44	80	38
Not necessary	51	17	57

FIGURE 10-4   Views of Affirmative Action

Source: New York Times/CBS News Poll, December 14, 1997, p. 1.

Although black students at elite universities receive somewhat lower grades than whites, and graduate at a lower rate, after graduation these students achieve notable successes. "They earn advanced degrees at rates identical to those of their white classmates. They are even slightly more likely than whites from the same institutions to earn professional degrees in law, business and medicine. And they become more active than their white classmates in civic activities." Indeed, the authors call black graduates of elite institutions "the backbone of the emergent black middle class," and their influence "extends beyond the workplace." Furthermore, they say, "They can serve as strong threads in the fabric that binds their own community together and binds those communities into the larger social fabric as well."

The authors report: "A striking finding was how much an elite education served as a pathway to success for all races. Blacks graduating from elite colleges earned 70 percent to 85 percent more than did black graduates generally." Contrary to popular opinion, "blacks and whites reported fairly substantial social interaction at college, which they said helped them relate to members of different racial groups later in life." And "the more selective the college, the more likely were blacks who attended it to graduate, obtain advanced degrees and earn high salaries."

Bok and Bowen say they focused on selective universities because they illustrate an often-ignored point: "The debate over race-conscious admissions is relevant only to about 25 percent of the universities. The rest take all or nearly all people who apply." Furthermore, the authors say, other facts in the debate have been overlooked. "Until now, the issue has involved much emotion but little evidence. . . . When the Supreme Court decided *Brown v. Board of Education* in 1954, it relied heavily on social science studies. We hope our data influence the current Supreme Court when it rules on affirmative action."

The study is based on "data about students who entered college in 1976 and 1989 and on lengthy follow-up questionnaires distributed to them. . . . Eighty percent of those receiving the questionnaires responded." Bok and Bowen say in their book that "a 'race-neutral' admissions policy would be disastrous for American society, reducing black preferences at top colleges to less than 2 percent from 7 percent." As an illustration of what that would mean, they constructed "a rough profile of 700 blacks admitted in 1976 under race-conscious policies. Of the 700, 225 obtained professional degrees or doctorates; 70 are doctors, 60 are lawyers, 125 are business executives and more than 300 are civic leaders. Their average salary is $71,000."

This book is a most welcome addition to the literature on affirmative action, and it is an important one. Most of the writers who oppose affirmative action have not had as comprehensive data as did Bok and Bowen. Therefore, this study, in its comprehensiveness and rigor, stands alone. An editorial in the *New York Times*[64] had this to say about the study:

> A new study of elite colleges provides striking confirmation of the success of affirmative action in opening opportunities and creating a whole generation of black pro-

fessionals who are now leaders in their fields and their communities. No study of this magnitude has been attempted before. Its findings provide a strong rationale for opposing current efforts to demolish race-sensitive policies in colleges across the country.

The evidence collected flatly refutes many of the misimpressions of affirmative action opponents. For example, black students who were admitted to the most selective schools with S.A.T. scores that were lower than those of their white counterparts, instead of becoming more discouraged by keener competition, had higher graduation rates than blacks who had the same test scores but went to less-competitive schools.

Instead of spreading racial resentment, diversity-enhancing policies were highly valued by both blacks and whites as being important to their college experience and helpful in their jobs. Even in academic majors, the stereotype of black students is wrong. Less than 3 percent of blacks pursued a major in ethnic studies. Blacks and whites majored in engineering and the hard sciences in the same proportions.

Perhaps most impressive is how well the African-American students performed after college. . . . Forty percent of black graduates from the 1976 group obtained a professional or doctoral degree after college, compared with 37 percent of white graduates.

. . . as the data and the authors of this study argue so eloquently, merit must also be defined in light of an institution's mission. Taking race into account, as one of many factors, has allowed these colleges to choose individuals of high potential, enhance education for all students by creating diversity on campus and fulfill the broader societal need by educating a group of minority students who are becoming leaders in every walk of life.

This type of study should be used as a basis for social policy, as is the case in many European countries, rather than ignored, which is the American way. But this study is not likely to impress opponents of affirmative action because their opposition is not rationally based.

Percentage of graduates who attained a doctoral or professional degree . . .

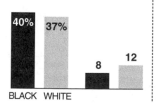

Percentage of graduates from the group of elite colleges who have led community or social service activities since college, by type of advanced degree and race.

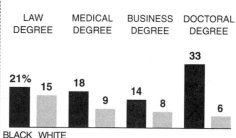

FIGURE 10-5   Affirmative Achievement

A new study of graduates from a group of 28 highly selective colleges and universities gives support to race-conscious admissions policies. Here are some of the study's findings.

Source: William G. Bowen and Derek Bok, *The Shape of the River,* New York Times, September 9, 1998, p. B10.

The former affirmative action bashers, black and white, who have changed their opinions are not likely to have much effect on race relations in the United States, because contrary to Nathan Glazer's praise for American society as a liberal democracy, the law professor Derrick Bell is probably correct in his assessment in his book, *Faces at the Bottom of the Well*, in which he sees the permanence of racism in the United States. He argues "that even those herculean efforts we hail as successful will produce no more than 'short-lived victories that slide into irrelevance as racial patterns adapt in ways that maintain white dominance.' "[65]

The shifting views on affirmative action may be found in Figure 10-4. It should be noted that blacks have different views on the subject than whites. As far as affirmative action is concerned, Americans are more sympathetic toward women than toward blacks (see Figure 10-5).

SELECTED BIBLIOGRAPHY

BELL, DERRICK. *Faces at the Bottom of the Well*. New York: Basic Books, 1993.

——. *Race, Racism and American Law*. Boston: Little, Brown,1980.

BLAUNER, ROBERT. *Racial Oppression in America*. New York: Harper & Row, 1972.

BOWEN, WILLIAM, and DEREK BOK. *The Shape of The River: Long-Term Consequences of Considering Race in College and University Admissions*. Princeton, NJ: Princeton University Press, 1998.

CARTER, STEPHEN. *Reflections of an Affirmative Action Baby*. New York: Basic Books, 1991.

COLEMAN, JONATHAN. *Long Way To Go: Black and White in America*. Boston: Atlantic Monthly Press.

EDWARDS, TAMALA. "Throwing the Book at Race." *Time*, September 8, 1987.

EZORSKY, GERTRUDE. *Racism and Justice: The Case for Affirmative Action*. Ithaca, NY: Cornell University Press, 1991.

FLEMMING, JOHN, et al. *The Case for Affirmative Action for Blacks in Higher Education*. Washington, DC: Howard University Press, 1978.

GLAZER, NATHAN. *Affirmative Discrimination: Inequality and Public Policy*. New York: Basic Books, 1975.

——. *We Are All Multiculturalists Now*. Cambridge, MA: Harvard University Press, 1998.

GUINIER, LANI. *Lift Every Voice: Turning a Civil Rights Setback into a New Vision of Civil Rights*. New York: Simon and Schuster, 1998.

HIGGINBOTHAM, A. LEON. "Breaking Thurgood Marshall's Promise." *New York Times Magazine,* January 18, 1998.

HOLMES, STEVEN. "Re-Rethinking Affirmative Action." *New York Times*, April 5, 1998, Section 4, p. 5.

JOHNSON, LYNDON BAINES. *The Vantage Point: Perspectives on the Presidency 1963–1969*. New York: Holt, Rinehart and Winston, 1971.

MITCHELL, ALISON. "Defending Affirmative Action, Clinton Urges Debate on Race." *New York Times*, June 15, 1997.

PINKNEY, ALPHONSO. *The Myth of Black Progress*. New York: Cambridge University Press, 1984.

SOWELL, THOMAS. *Civil Rights: Rhetoric or Reality?* New York: William Morrow, 1984.

——. *Pink and Brown People*. Stanford, CA: Hoover Institution's Press, 1991.

STEELE, SHELBY. *The Content of Our Character*. New York: Harper Perennial, 1990.

STEINBERG, STEPHEN. *The Ethnic Myth*. Boston: Beacon Press, 1989.

——. *Turning Back: The Retreat from Racial Justice in American Thought and Policy*. Boston: Beacon Press, 1996.

TURNER, JAMES P. "The Fairest Cure We Have." *New York Times*, April 16, 1995, Section 4, p. 11.

WILKINS, ROGER. "The Case For Affirmative Action: Racism Has Its Privileges." *The Nation*, March 27, 1995.

WILLIAMS, PATRICIA. *The Alchemy of Race and Rights*. Cambridge, MA: Harvard University Press, 1991.

NOTES

1. Nicholas Katzenbach and Burke Marshall, "Not Color Blind: Just Blind," *New York Times Magazine*, February 22, 1998, pp. 42–45.
2. Lyndon Baines Johnson, *The Vantage Point: Perspectives on the Presidency 1963–1969* (New York: Holt, Rinehart and Winston, 1971), p. 166.
3. Michael W. Miles, *The Odyssey of the American Right* (New York: Oxford University Press, 1980), pp. 318–19.
4. Michael Kinsley, "The Spoils of Victimhood: The Case Against the Case Against Affirmative Action," *The New Yorker*, March 27, 1995, p. 65.
5. Nicholas Lemann, "Taking Affirmative Action Apart," *New York Times Magazine*, June 11, 1985, p. 40.
6. Alphonso Pinkney, *The Myth of Black Progress* (New York: Cambridge University Press, 1984), p. 150.
7. *Chronicle of Higher Education*, July 10, 1978, p. 13.
8. Ibid., pp. 11–12.
9. Ibid., pp. 159–160.
10. *New York Times*, June 28, 1979, p. B12.
11. Ibid.
12. *New York Times Magazine*, February 25, 1979, p. 101.
13. Ibid.
14. John Flemming et al., *The Case for Affirmative Action for Blacks in Higher Education* (Washington, DC: Howard University Press, 1978), p. 90.
15. *New York Times*, December 22, 1991, section 4, p. 2.
16. Ibid.
17. Lee A. Daniels, "The New Black Conservatives," *New York Times Magazine*, October 4, 1981, p. 22.
18. Shelby Steele, *The Content of Our Character* (New York: Harper Perennial, 1990), p. 113.
19. Ibid.
20. Shelby Steele, "A Negative Vote on Affirmative Action," *New York Times Magazine*, May 13 1990, p. 49.
21. Thomas Sowell, *Civil Rights: Rhetoric or Reality?* (New York: William Morrow, 1984), p. 38.
22. Ibid., p. 133.
23. Thomas Sowell, *Pink and Brown People* (Stanford, CA: Hoover Institution's Press, 1981), p. 23.
24. Thomas Sowell, *Affirmative Action Reconsidered: Was it Necessary in Academia?* (Washington, DC: American Enterprise Institute, 1975), pp. 38–39.
25. Stephen Carter, *Reflections of An Affirmative Action Baby* (New York: Basic Books, 1991), p. 11.
26. Ibid., p. 3.
27. Ibid., p. 6.
28. *New York Times*, July 25, 1985, p. A16.
29. William Wilson, *The Declining Significance of Race* (Chicago: University of Chicago Press, 1978), p. 1.
30. *New York Times*, June 3, 1981, p. D8.
31. *New York Times*, July 20, 1995, p. B10.
32. Roger Wilkins, "The Case for Affirmative Action: Racism Has Its Privileges," *The Nation*, March 27, 1995, p. 409.

33. Ibid.
34. Ibid., p. 401.
35. Laurence Otis Graham, "The Case for Affirmative Action," *New York Times*, May 21, 1995, section 3, p. 13.
36. Bob Herbert, "*The* Wrong Target," *New York Times*, April 5, 1995, p. A25.
37. James P. Turner, "The Fairest Cure We Have," *New York Times*, April 16, 1995, Section 4, p. 11.
38. Kinsley, "The Spoils of Victimhood," p. 62.
39. *New York Times*, December 14, 1997, p. 1.
40. Linda Greenhouse, "Justices, 5 to 4, Cast Doubt on U.S. Programs That Give Preferences Based on Race," *New York Times*, June 13, 1995, p. A2.
41. Linda Greenhouse, "Justices in 5–4 Vote Reject Districts Drawn With Race the Predominant Factor," *New York Times*, June 30, 1995, p. Al.
42. "Gutting the Voting Rights Act," *New York Times*, June 30, 1995, p. A26.
43. Peter Applebome, "Affirmative Action Ban Changes Law School," *New York Times*, July 2, 1997, p. A14.
44. Peter Applebome, "Texas Told to Keep Affirmative Action in Universities or Risk Losing Federal Aid," *New York Times*, March 26, 1997, p. B11.
45. Ibid.
46. Peter Applebome, "Seeking New Approaches for Diversity," *New York Times*, April 23, 1997, p. B7.
47. "Excerpts from Round Table With Opponents of Racial Preferences," *New York Times*, December 22, 1997, p. A24.
48. Ethan Bronner, "Black and Hispanic Admissions Off Sharply at U. of California," *New York Times*, April 1, 1998, p. Al.
49. Frank Bruni, "California Regent's New Focus: Ethnic Studies," *New York Times*, June 18, 1998, p. A20.
50. Ethan Bonner, "Fewer Minorities Entering U. of California," *New York Times*, May 21, 1998, p. A28.
51. Ibid.
52. "Visible Shift in Admissions in California," *New York Times*, March 18, 1998, p. A19.
53. Anthony Lewis, "Turn of the Tide," *New York Times*, May 18, 1998, p. A19.
54. "Defining Affirmative Action," *Wall Street Journal*, April 20, 1998, p. A18.
55. Stephan Thernstrom and Abigail Thernstrom, *America in Black and White: One Nation Indivisible* (New York: Simon and Schuster, 1998).
56. Tamala M. Edwards, "Throwing the Book at Race," *Time*, September 8, 1997, p. 61.
57. Gore Vidal, "BAD History," *The Nation*, April 20, 1998.
58. Brent Staples, "The Quota Bashers Come in from the Cold," *New York Times*, April 12, 1998, Section 4, p. 12.
59. Nathan Glazer, *Affirmative Discrimination: Ethnic Inequality and Public Policy* (New York: Basic Books, 1975), p. 200.
60. Ibid., p. 221.
61. Steven A. Holmes, "Re-Rethinking Affirmative Action," *New York Times*, April 5, 1998, section 4, p. 5.
62. James Traub, "Nathan Glazer Changes His Mind, Again," *New York Times Magazine*, June 28, 1998, p. 25.
63. William G. Bowen and Derek Bok, *The Shape of the River: Long-term Consequences of Considering Race in College and University Admissions* (Princeton, NJ: Princeton University Press), 1998.
64. "The Facts about Affirmative Action," *New York Times*, September 14, 1998, p. A32. I quote from the study, interviews with the authors, and the editorial at some length because of their importance.
65. Richard Bernstein, "Racism Is (a) Entrenched? or (b) Fading," *New York Times*, November 8, 1997, p. B7.

CHAPTER ELEVEN

Race Relations at the Crossroads

As the twentieth century draws to a close, what can be said about the future citizenship status of African-Americans? After several centuries of slavery, the Civil War brought an end to the peculiar institution. For a few years, during the period of Reconstruction, it appeared that the country was willing to grant the former slaves full citizenship, but politicians and southern landowners soon took steps to ensure that racial inequality in the form of segregation and discrimination would face black people into the distant future. They were aided in this endeavor by the highest court in the land, the Supreme Court, which continues to play a negative role for black people.

For nearly one hundred years after emancipation, laws were passed or upheld by the Supreme Court ensuring that people of color would remain second-class citizens. From the infamous *Plessy v. Ferguson* decision of 1896 up to the *Brown v. Board of Education* decision in 1954, black people were so rigidly segregated that it was a period of virtual slavery, and white supremacy was defended by the highest officials of the country. That is to say, white supremacy became a crucial element of American life.

It is important to note that whatever progress was made by blacks was a result of the struggle by black people rather than the benevolence of whites. However, since the beginnings of the civil rights movement, two Presidents may be singled out for their contributions to blacks: Lyndon Baines Johnson and William Jefferson Clinton.

Johnson came to the presidency with a determination to improve the status of blacks in society. A skilled Texas politician, he was instrumental in the passage of such legislation as the Civil Rights Act of 1964, the Voting Rights Act of 1965, and the Fair Housing Act of 1968. He appointed the first black cabinet officer and named the first black to the Supreme Court. His interest in the enhancement of the status of people of color was both genuine and all-consuming. But any assessment of his presidency must be tempered with his ruthless conduct in pursuing the war in Vietnam.

Nevertheless, he was the first president to devote much of his energy and skills to the betterment of race relations in the modern era.

Clinton, also a southerner, came to the presidency after being governor of Arkansas, where he had devoted much of his energy to the problems of race relations in that state. He understood the problems of segregation and discrimination and was determined to eradicate them to the extent possible. He has a thorough knowledge of black history, and after becoming president, at one time he boasted that he was one of the few white persons who knew the words to the "Negro National Anthem" ("Lift Every Voice and Sing"). While he was in law school he made it a point to fraternize with black students, and he was frequently the only white student to join blacks in the dining room.

In his first year in office he appointed five blacks to cabinet posts, whereas no other administration contained more than one. And, as he proudly pointed out, they were all in nontraditional positions. He is strongly supportive of affirmative action and would like to be remembered as the president whose main achievement was the improvement of race relations in the United States.

When the independent counsel, Kenneth Starr, in charge of investigating the so-called Whitewater affair in Arkansas, released a report in September 1998 in which he charged President Clinton with sexual misconduct with a White House intern, Clinton's strongest supporters were blacks. As one black congressman said after discussing the matter with other blacks, "People would say, 'take care of the President. Take care of my man.' " He continued, "They don't want to see him resign. They don't want to see him impeached. They just want us to leave him alone because there's this deep feeling in the black community that this President has been there for us."[1] According to a *New York Times*/CBS News poll, blacks are much more likely than whites to approve of Clinton's job performance, to regard him favorably, and to oppose his resignation or impeachment. Furthermore, within the president's own party, black Democrats are significantly more supportive than their white counterparts. (See Figure 11-1.)

In interviews, the comedian Chris Rock and black leaders "cited everything from Mr. Clinton's choice of friends to his choice of musical instruments in explaining that he has connected with minorities, both politically and viscerally, in a manner never achieved by previous presidents." Many of those interviewed by the *Times* "remarked on the ease with which Mr. Clinton moves in black circles, noting that he golfs with Vernon Jordan, that he and his family seek spiritual counsel from the Reverend Jesse Jackson, and that he sings in black churches without the aid of a hymnal."

Theatrical producer George C. Wolfe had this to say: "What he has been able to project, unlike any other President in recent memory, is that he is completely and totally comfortable with black Americans. . . . It is not something that had to be negotiated or learned." The Reverend Joseph Lowry, retired president of the Southern Christian Leadership Conference, said of Clinton, "The man has soul."

"Most minorities clearly admire the President's defense of affirmative action, his appointments of black officials and judges and his eagerness to confront racism."

Despite his latest troubles, Clinton is still significantly more popular with blacks than whites. Results of polls after the State of the Union address, the grand jury testimony and the release of the Starr report:

		FEB. 19–21*		AUG. 19–20		SEPT. 12–14	
		BLACKS	WHITES	BLACKS	WHITES	BLACKS	WHITES
Clinton's job performance							
Do you approve of the way Bill Clinton is handling his job as President?	Approve	93%	63%	94%	50%	86%	58%
	Disapprove	4	31	6	36	8	38
Personal image							
Is your opinion of Bill Clinton favorable or not favorable?	Favorable	91	52	82	42	69	34
	Unfavorable	4	34	4	47	10	52
Moral values							
Does Bill Clinton share the moral values most Americans try to live by?	Agree	80	34	71	29	63	22
	Disagree	12	49	25	56	32	73
Who's to blame							
Whom do you blame more for the current scandal situation?	Clinton	5	38	24	54	27	59
	His political enemies	85	51	63	36	55	32

*The question on moral values is from a CBS News poll conducted Feb. 1. Based on nationwide telephone surveys conducted Feb. 19 to 21 with 965 whites and 96 blacks; Aug. 19 and 20 with 788 whites and 92 blacks; and Sept. 12 to 14 with 1,512 whites and 166 blacks. Within any single poll, differences between blacks and whites of 11 points or more are significant. Between any two polls, a difference among blacks in one poll and blacks in the other of 12 points or more is significant.

FIGURE 11-1 The Race Gap: Clinton Maintains Black Support

Source: *New York Times*, September 19, 1998, p. A10.

Their support is also a product of distinct cultural traits born of the black experience in the United States, including a broad distrust of prosecutors, an instinctive empathy for the persecuted and a spiritual emphasis on forgiveness and redemption, many African-Americans said.

The comedian Chris Rock even describes Clinton as "the first black President." This sentiment is shared by Nobel Prize winning author Toni Morrison. He continued, "It is very simple. Black people are used to being persecuted. Hence, they relate to Clinton." Alvin Poussaint, a black psychiatrist, had this to say: "They circulate rumors that he must have black ancestry." And a poll conducted in 1997 by the Joint Center for Political and Economic Studies, a black think tank, found that Clinton "was more popular among blacks than either Jesse Jackson or Colin Powell."

Furthermore, blacks in the study by the *New York Times* agreed with "Hillary Rodham Clinton's statement that a 'vast right wing' conspiracy had been directed against her husband," and they believe the conspirators were motivated by a desire to reverse the gains made by blacks during the Clinton administration. "You just can't help but think that some of this is race based," said Julian Bond, chairman of the NAACP. He continued: "In civil rights terms, this guy's a liberal, and there's a part of the body politic that just can't stand this. They have been determined to bring him down from the very first."

During his national career, blacks have been among Clinton's most ardent supporters. "He received an estimated 83 percent of the black vote in the 1992 Presidential election (compared with 39 percent of white votes) and 84 percent in 1996 (compared with 43 percent among whites)." Also, black people, far more than whites, approve of his handling of his job. The Reverend Calvin Butts of the Abyssinian Baptist Church in Harlem said that black people "simply are more willing to judge him by his stride than his stumble."

"Those interviewed . . . spoke of the economy's boost for black employment and homeownership. They cited the President's numerous appointments of blacks to significant jobs, a record 13 percent of political appointments." They also mentioned Clinton's approach to racial issues, including his "mend it, don't end it" prescription for affirmative action, his creation of the advisory board on race, "and his trip to Africa where he expressed regret for America's role in slavery."

Finally, a black Detroit businessman said, "African Americans are largely a religious people, and forgiveness is part of the culture. It has been a survival technique. We couldn't survive with all the pent-up hatred, hostility and fear, so we've had to forgive and move on."

THE PRESIDENT'S INITIATIVE ON RACE

In 1997 President Clinton announced the formation of the Advisory Board of the President's Initiative on Race, saying that the initiative was one of his highest priorities. The racially mixed board consisted of seven members, including religious and labor leaders, academics, and former politicians. Initially the panel members were concerned with spurring Americans to talk about race, and it was later decided that the initiative should also recommend specific race-related actions to the administration.

The board met for the first time in July 1997 and declared that it was "charged with beginning a dialogue among Americans of various ethnic and racial groups, and guiding the president in developing a major race relations initiative."[2]

The president selected the distinguished black historian John Hope Franklin to chair the initiative. Franklin knew that the advisory committee faced a daunting task. In an interview he turned to history to explain why the task was so difficult: "The real problem was the development of an ideology of white supremacy." Speaking about the Thirteenth Amendment and the early Civil Rights Act, he had this to say: "These things don't measure the depth and the tenacity of these views about race that have been injected into our civilized discourse for 300 years. You can't change that overnight."[3]

There are those who criticize the President's Initiative on Race, but his staff has begun to put the initiative into practice. In one instance, for example, a member of Clinton's staff persuaded the executives of the National Football League to permit the president to make a public service announcement during the 1998 Super Bowl. "As a result an estimated 133.4 million viewers heard Mr. Clinton say: 'As we enjoy today's Super Bowl, let's remember that Americans of all races and ethnic groups are on the same team. Working together we can win.' "[4]

The Advisory Board recommended that the administration strengthen the enforcement of federal antidiscrimination laws. The result was the following:[5]

- The budget sent to Congress proposed an increase of $86 million in financing for agencies like the Equal Employment Opportunity Commission, the Department of Housing and Urban Development, and the Justice Department's Civil Rights Division.
- The Office of Management and Budget revived the practice (canceled by Ronald Reagan's administration) of analyzing the budget's impact on civil rights. As a result, the budget has several policy initiatives on race relations and minority advancement, including an increase in housing vouchers for poor families who leave welfare, and the restoration of food-stamp benefits.
- President Clinton announced a five-year $400 million plan to increase life expectancy and health standards for minority groups.
- The administration announced an agreement with the major automobile makers to raise to 5 percent the number of contracts going to minority suppliers.
- The White House announced an increase in loan guarantees to businesses owned by blacks and Hispanics.
- For the first time, because of White House insistence, the annual report of the Council of Economic Advisers contains a separate chapter on how racial and ethnic groups are faring.
- Finally, cabinet secretaries and subcabinet officials have been a part of 140 race relations dialogues in more than 40 cities since the start of the initiative.

There is no doubt that the president is committed to improving the status of people of color, but with conservative Republicans in control of Congress, it is questionable that the measures that require congressional approval will be enacted.

The President's Initiative on Race has met some criticism. Lani Guinier, a black law professor, maintains that more than a dialogue on race is necessary to improve the lot of people of color in the United States. While she sees merit in the initiative, she feels that the issue of affirmative action to highlight inequality is missing in the approach. She feels that the race initiative is "a chance to engage Americans to brainstorm about new ways of moving forward on concrete problems. That is not easy, but when it happens, a good conversation becomes a prologue to community action, not just a showcasing or confirming of preconceived ideas."[6]

A conservative black sociologist, Orlando Patterson, says in an article that racism is not the issue the panel should be discussing. Rather, he says, the problem is economic. Furthermore, he says, "race relations between blacks and whites have never been better. What is more, the majority of African-Americans are content, even optimistic, about their interactions with European Americans."[7] He concludes his article with the following: "Martin Luther King's dream of an integrated America has not been deferred. The nation is overcoming what was once its greatest flaw, racism." One wonders how a black sociologist can be so naive about the problem of race in the United States.

THE ROLE OF BLACK CONSERVATIVES: THE CASE OF CLARENCE THOMAS

One of the most unfortunate developments in the last decade was the nomination by President George Bush of Clarence Thomas, a black man known for his extremely conservative views, to replace Thurgood Marshall on the Supreme Court. Marshall was the first black to sit on the Court, and he was widely recognized for his liberal views on race and other issues. After his nomination in 1991, Clarence Thomas was subjected to harsh criticism by all the major civil rights leaders, who opposed his nomination because, although he was a beneficiary of affirmative action when he applied to law school, he opposed it for others. Furthermore, Thomas was charged with sexual harassment by a former employee with whom he worked at the Equal Employment Opportunity Commission.

After his narrow confirmation by the Senate, he set about to vote against every measure before the Court that would enhance the status of black people. Furthermore, he maintained a policy of speaking only to conservative white groups, especially in the South. Whenever he was asked by a black group to speak, the invitation was usually later withdrawn because of his conservative, antiblack views.

However, on July 29, 1998, after several protests, he was permitted to speak before the annual convention of the National Bar Association in Memphis, Tennessee. According to a reporter for the *New York Times*, "Justice Thomas's deeply complicated and troubled relationship with his fellow black Americans was on vivid public display in his appearance before the convention of the National Bar Association, the largest group of black lawyers [an organization that opposed his confirmation to the Supreme Court]. It was an event to which he had been invited months ago, only to have a large, prominent group of members try to have the invitation rescinded."[8] It is reported that "about half of the audience applauded, while the other half remained silent."

During his speech Justice Thomas called his critics "illiterate," among other things. For example, he said he did not need anyone "telling me who I am today. This is especially true of the psychosilliness about forgetting my roots or self-hatred." He continued:

> I have come here today, not in anger or to anger, though my presence has been sufficient, obviously, to anger some. Nor have I come to defend my views, but rather to assert my right to think for myself, to refuse to have my ideas assigned to me as though I was an intellectual slave because I'm black. I come here to state that I am a man, free to think for myself and do as I please. I have come here to assert that I am a judge and I will not be consigned the unquestioned opinion of others.[9]

One of Clarence Thomas's severest critics has been Judge A. Leon Higginbotham, the former chief judge of the United States Court of Appeals for the Third Circuit in Philadelphia. After the speech Judge Higginbotham and "several hundred others went into an adjoining room to hear Justice Thomas's critics analyze his work and compare him unfavorably to the man he replaced on the Court, Justice Thurgood Marshall."[10]

At the time Justice Thomas had been invited to address the convention, Judge Higginbotham had argued that it was a mistake to have him as the keynote speaker because that would bestow an undeserved honor on someone whose rulings on the Court "have done more to turn back the clock of racial progress than any other African American public official in the history of this country."[11] This view is widely shared by most black people who know of his antiblack record on the Supreme Court.

Indeed, the *New York Times* editorialized:

> Clarence Thomas unloaded on his critics the other day, twisting the case against him just as he did seven years ago when the Senate was considering his nomination to the Supreme Court. Then he complained he was a target of a "high-tech lynching." This week he charged critics with vilifying him because he is a black who does not hold liberal views. . . . What Justice Thomas seems unable to appreciate is that the issue is not his race, but the content of his ideas. . . . It is no surprise that his staunchly conservative positions on social issues have been denounced by civil rights leaders as damaging to the welfare of minorities. . . . His instinct to turn antagonism toward his ideas into a racial matter is an odd impulse for a man who wants to be judged on his intellect and ideas alone. . . . The speech was received politely, but his impact on American law remains a bitter matter for those who see advances in social policy being steadily eroded.[12]

Given the record of Justice Thomas since he became a member of the Supreme Court, one can agree with Judge Higginbotham that he has done more to impede the cause of civil rights than any other black public official. He is just one of several black conservatives opposed to affirmative action and other civil rights measures. (See chapter 10.) This is not a new development, but the others are not public officials.

CONTINUING VIOLENCE AGAINST BLACKS

In 1972 this author published *The American Way of Violence*, one of the first books to label the United States a violent society.[13] The book was criticized by many at the time as being unfair, even un-American—but in the years that followed, many other books made the same claim. And today there appears to be a consensus that the conclusion reached was indeed correct. Since that time our society has become even more violent, making the United States one of the most violent of all industrial nations.

Nowhere has the violence of the last three decades been more pronounced than in the behavior of the police against people of color. (See chapter 8.) Every day in some part of the country minorities are the victims of police violence, much of it gratuitous. The police frequently inflict violence on minorities because they know that they will be protected by their superiors, and that they are not likely to suffer as a result. In addition, it is rare that a jury will convict a police officer, regardless of the severity of the crime.

For example, on October 29, 1984, six police officers arrived at the New York City–owned apartment of Eleanor Bumpers, a 66-year-old ailing grandmother. The police had been ordered to evict Eleanor Bumpers because she was four months late in paying the $96.85 monthly rent. When she resisted, the police pumped two blasts from a 12-gauge shotgun into her body.[14]

When the police officers arrived, Eleanor Bumpers refused to open her door to them, fearing that they were robbers. The officers then punched out the lock on the door and entered the apartment. The six officers were equipped with hard plastic shields designed to protect them against blows and knife thrusts. They were also equipped with a U-shaped restraining bar attached to a long handle that is used to pin a person, and with chemical mace.

Inside the apartment, Officer Stephen Sullivan opened fire on Mrs. Bumpers as she held a knife in her right hand. Nine pellets struck her in the chest and one struck her on the right hand, severing her fingers. Officer Sullivan then shot her again, knocking the knife out of her hand. What was left of her hand was described by the doctor who treated her in the hospital emergency room as "a bloody stump." The doctor testified that after the first shot, Eleanor Bumpers could not have used the knife because "it was anatomically impossible for this hand to hold this knife." A paid "expert witness" for the prosecution maintained that although her fingers had been severed, "there was no apparent damage to the part of the hand that controls the power grip," and that "she would have been physically able to hold a knife." Officer Sullivan was then cleared of charges that he killed Eleanor Bumpers. As is usual, the other five officers committed perjury in support of Sullivan.

Several similar hate crimes occurred in New York City during the presidency of Ronald Reagan (no friend of people of color), and during the period when Ed Koch (an enemy of minorities) was mayor of New York City. These hate crimes occurred throughout the country.

One grotesque recent case was the lynching of a black man by Ku Klux Klansmen in Texas. On June 7, 1998, a black man was lynched by three white men in the small town (8,000 residents) of Jasper, Texas. In one of the most brutal cases in history, the black man, 49-year-old James Byrd, Jr., was taken to the woods, where he was brutally beaten, then chained to the back of a truck and dragged for two miles. James Byrd's torso "was found on the edge of a paved road, his head and arm in a ditch about a mile away, according to the Jasper County District Attorney."[15]

The president of the state chapter of the National Association for the Advancement of Colored People, Gary Bledsoe, said "the eastern part of Texas, which includes Jasper, has been considered a problem area and a hotbed of Klan activity for years." He recalled that in 1993 when a public housing project in nearby Vidor, Texas, was being integrated, "a white supremacist threatened the first black residents, and teenagers dressed in sheets confronted the black newcomers."[16]

Two of James Byrd's three killers were 23 years old, and one was 31. The three had criminal records for burglary and drug possession, and had served jail time together.

The three men were held without bail, and news of the lynching quickly spread around the country. President Clinton called the killing "shocking and outrageous," and said the residents of Jasper "must join together across racial lines to demonstrate that an act of evil like this is not what this country is all about." He added, "I think we've all been touched by it, and I can only imagine that virtually everyone who lives there is in agony at this moment."[17]

While past lynchings had frequently been accompanied by picnics and other forms of entertainment, in this case the white population mourned along with the blacks. The father of one of the lynchers released a handwritten letter apologizing for his son's actions. He wrote: "It hurts me deeply to know that a boy I raised and considered to be the most loved boy I knew could find it in himself to take a life. This deed cannot be undone, but I hope we can all find it in our hearts to go forward in peace and with love for all. Let us find in our hearts love for our fellow man. Hate can only destroy."[18]

It is important to note that this is the first recorded lynching in some years. The dearth of recent lynchings in a country where they were frequent in the past, and the response of the people in Jasper, Texas, might be seen as indicating some improvement in race relations; it also illustrates the continued racial violence in the society.

While the people of Jasper, Texas, expressed outrage at the lynching, not so with a group of men in Broad Channel, Queens, New York City, including policemen and firemen. Rather, during a Labor Day parade in 1998, which was sponsored by the Broad Channel Volunteer Fire Department and Ambulance Corps, police officers and firemen displayed their racism.[19]

There was a float in the parade in which off-duty police officers and firemen wore blackface and Afro wigs, frequently threw watermelon slices from the flatbed of the truck, played basketball, and danced with boom boxes held next to their ears. "At one point, one of the participants reenacted the June lynching of a black man, James Byrd, who was dragged to his death behind a pickup truck in Jasper, Texas." The theme of the float was "Black to the Future: 2098," which according to some participants referred to the year when their community would have to accept blacks as residents. Presently the community is all white.

Broad Channel, which is near Kennedy International Airport, is just three miles from Howard Beach, where 23-year-old Michael Griffith, a black man, was chased by a group of white teenagers onto a busy highway where he was killed by a car. Ironically, the parade was held on Cross Bay Boulevard, the same highway where Michael Griffith was killed. And the citizens of Broad Channel responded to the float in much the same way Howard Beach residents had responded to the racist murder of Michael Griffith. Many of Broad Channel's residents denounced the criticisms of the parade, saying it was "unnecessary and overblown." They called the float a "joke" and said news reports were "stirring up trouble."

One Broad Channel resident said that his community "didn't have any prejudice" because it has few, if any, black residents. He referred to blacks as "the colored people," an expression that had also been used by residents of Howard Beach, and one that is generally considered racist by blacks when used in this type of context. A black woman who works in the neighborhood said that Broad Channel had long been considered hostile territory by blacks.

Broad Channel is a community of 1,600 residents, none of them black, and the parade attracted a crowd of 3,000 spectators. When a group of black people, numbering about 100, marched in Broad Channel a few days later to protest the parade, some residents showed support, greeting them with lemonade, water, and crumb cake. But the video of the parade itself showed widespread "laughing and clapping." Mayor Rudolph Giuliani, known for his hostility to blacks, called the parade "a disgusting display of racism." Furthermore, he made sure that police and firemen involved were dismissed from their jobs.

Incidents of this type are common in the United States, where many white Americans are deeply prejudiced against people of color. It does not appear that such deeply rooted prejudice will end in the near future, if ever.

DISTORTED NOTIONS ON THE STATUS OF BLACKS

There are many Americans (both black and white) of conservative persuasion who somehow feel that there has been great improvement in race relations in the United States. Some of them attribute what they feel is progress to affirmative action, and one cannot deny that affirmative action has enlarged the black middle class and permitted others to improve their status in society. But it is paradoxical that the very people who subscribe to this assumption themselves oppose affirmative action. And some of them, including some who are professors of sociology in major universities (thanks to affirmative action) are even naive enough to deny that America is still a racist society. Stephan and Abigail Thernstrom's book *America in Black and White: One Nation, Indivisible*[20] is probably one of the most confusing and dishonest books dealing with race relations. According to sociologist Stephen Steinberg, "The Thernstroms' tailoring of history to their ideological position leads them to argue that 'the gains made by African Americans in the affirmative action era have been less impressive than those that occurred before preferential policies.' "[21] Steinberg continues, "Thus to a large extent, the black middle class is the product of the very policy that the Thernstroms deplore: affirmative action. The existence of this black middle class does not signify deracialization of labor markets, but on the contrary, the application of affirmative action policies which are necessary to override entrenched racism."[22]

The research of the Thernstroms was funded by several conservative foundations. Steinberg says of the Thernstroms: "They have employed all the tools of social science, and a talent for sophistry, to deny the obvious: that our society is still deeply driven by race and that we are currently in the throes of a racial backlash that threatens to wipe out many of the gains extracted from white society through the black protest movement."[23] He concludes: "All of this specious reasoning and distortion of fact leads to the ultimate fallacy: that after two centuries of slavery and one century of Jim Crow, and persistent racism in job markets everywhere, the nation can retreat behind a facade of color blindness."[24]

One must agree with Steinberg's conclusion: "That we are currently in such a period of retrogression, there can be no doubt. However, it is of little help when scholars, especially those ensconced at elite universities, respond by taking comfort in 'progress' instead of decrying the reversal of hardwon gains."[25]

•   •   •

There is a deeply ingrained feeling among many (if not most) white Americans that people of color are somehow innately inferior to white Americans. There is some hope that some of the younger generation of whites do not maintain such attitudes. But as the foregoing chapters make clear, black Americans are presently at a crossroads. Some important gains have resulted from affirmative action, but there is widespread sentiment for its abolition, based on the belief that there is no longer a need for such programs because ours is a colorblind society. This feeling results from a combination of racism and meanness, both of which are deeply entrenched in the minds of whites. With that in mind, it is difficult to foresee any significant improvement in the citizenship status of people of color.

SELECTED BIBLIOGRAPHY

BOWEN, WILLIAM G. and DEREK BOK, *The Shape of the River: Longterm Consequences of Considering Race in College and University Admissions*. Princeton, NJ: Princeton University Press, 1998.

PINKNEY, ALPHONSO, *Lest We Forget: Howard Beach and Other Racial Atrocities*. Chicago: Third World Press, 1994.

————. *The Myth of Black Progress*. New York: Cambridge University Press, 1984.

PLATT, ANTHONY, "The Land That Never Has Been Yet: U.S. Race Relations at the Crossroads." *Social Justice*, Spring 1997.

SHIPLER, DAVID. *A Country of Strangers: Blacks and Whites in America*. New York: Alfred Knopf, 1997.

STEINBERG, STEPHEN. *Turning Back: The Retreat from Racial Justice in American Thought and Policy*. Boston: Beacon Press, 1996.

NOTES

1. Kevin Sack, "Blacks Stand by a President Who 'Has Been There For US,'" *New York Times,* September 19, 1998, pp. A1, A10. The quotations in this section are largely a result of interviews by reporters from the *Times* and the *Times*/CBS News Poll.

2. Beth Barker, "Forcing America to Keep Faith," *AARP Bulletin*, September 1977.

3. Ibid.

4. Steven A. Holmes, "Clinton Staff Starts to Put Race Policy Into Practice," *New York Times*, March 1, 1998, p. 17.

5. Ibid.

6. Lani Guinier, "Dialogue Without Depth," *New York Times,* December 16, 1997, p. A31.

7. Orlando Patterson, "Racism Is Not the Issue," *New York Times*, November 16, 1997, p. 15.

8. Neil A. Lewis, "Justice Thomas Suggests Critics' Views Are Racist," *New York Times*, July 30, 1998, p. A1.

9. "Excerpts From Speech by Justice Thomas," *New York Times*, July 30, 1998, p. A14.

10. Neil A. Lewis, op. cit.

11. Ibid.

12. "Justice Thomas Speaks," *New York Times*, July 31, 1998, p. A18.

13. New York: Random House, 1972.

14. Alphonso Pinkney, *Lest We Forget: Howard Beach and Other Racial Atrocities* (Chicago: Third World Press, 1994).

15. Carol Marie Cooper, "Black Man Fatally Dragged in a Possible Racial Killing," *New York Times*, June 10, 1998, p. A16.

16. Ibid.

17. Carol Marie Cooper, "Town Expresses Sadness and Horror Over Slaying," *New York Times*, June 11, 1998, p. A16.

18. Ibid.

19. The following accounts are from the *New York Times* of September 11, 1998, p. B1; September 12, 1998, pp. D7 and D9; September 13, 1998, p. 51; September 14, 1998, p. B1; and an editorial from the same newspaper on September 14, 1998, p. A32.

20. Stephan Thernstrom and Abigail Thernstrom, *America in Black and White: One Nation, Indivisible* (New York: Simon & Schuster, 1997).

21. Stephen Steinberg, "Up From Slavery: The Myth of Black Progress," *New Politics*, Summer 1998, p. 61.

22. Ibid.

23. Ibid., p. 60.

24. Ibid., p. 62.

25. Ibid., p. 66.

Name Index

Subject Index

B

Baez, Anthony, 195–96
Bakke decision, 227–29
Banks, black-owned, 94–95
Baptists, 119, 120, 122, 123, 125, 126
Baraka, Amiri (LeRoi Jones), 55
Behavioral receptional assimilation:
  conditions for, 206
  discriminatory acts, 215, 217–19
Behavior receptional assimilation, 215,
  217–19
Birthrate, black population, 62, 65, 66–67
Black Cabinet, 25
Black church:
  and political life, 120, 121, 125–27
  typical service, 123, 124
  See also Religion and worship
Black Codes, 17–18
Black ghetto, 41–42
  conditions of, 42
Blackmun, Harry, 227–28
Black Muslims, 122, 207
Black Panthers, 56–57
  FBI against, 57
  ideology of, 56–57
  leaders of, 56
Black population:
  educational level, 78–84
  fertility rates, 62, 65, 66–67
  grandparent households, 71
  income, 97–103
  median age of population, 68, 71
  mortality rates, 65, 68
  occupational status, 84–97
  sex composition, 68
  size/growth of, 61–65
Black Power movement, 43–48
  black opposition to, 44–45
  compared to civil rights movement, 48
  issues addressed by, 46–48
  King's reaction to, 44–45
  link to other oppressed peoples, 53–54
  and Malcolm X, 41–42
  National Conference on Black Power, 45–46
  National Student Association, 46
  split in, 54
  Student Nonviolent Coordinating Committee
    (SNCC), 43, 44, 45
  use of term, 43–44, 220
Bledsoe, Gary, 257
Bond, Julian, 252
Brennan, William, 230
Brooke, Edward W., 231
Brown, H. Rap, 55
Brown, John, 10
Brown v. Board of Education, 79, 81, 83, 226,
  233, 244, 249

Bumpers, Eleanor, 256
Bureau of Refugees, Freedman, and Abandoned
  Lands, 18
Burger, Warren, 230
Bush, George, 87, 254
Business, black-owned, 90, 93–97
  government assistance, 93
  historical view, 90, 93
  leading businesses, 93–97
Butts, Calvin, 252
Byrd, James, Jr., 257

C

Caliph, 122
Campbell, Charles C., 195
Cancer, 142, 144–45
  cervical cancer, 144–45
  lung cancer, 145
  racial comparisons, 142, 144
  risk factors, 144
  survival rate, 145
Capital punishment, 197–201
  American support for, 197
  delayed execution, 200–201
  deterrent theory, 201
  geographic variations, 198–200
  as human rights violation, 197
  innocent on death row, 201
  racial comparison, 198–99, 202, 219
Cardiovascular disease, 143, 146–47
  hypertension, 146, 147
  racial comparisons, 143
  risk factors, 146
  stroke, 146–47
Carmichael, Stokely, 212
  and Black Power movement, 43, 44, 53,
    220
Carter, Jimmy, 233
Carter, Stephen, 232
Carver Bancorp of New York City, 95
Catholic Church, 122, 124
Cervical cancer, and black women, 144–45
Children:
  AIDS victims, 134, 135, 139
  homicide victims, 153
Christian Methodist Episcopal Church, 122
Christians, black, 122
Church of England, 119
Churches of Christ, 122
Church of God, 125
Church of God-Black Jews, 122
Church of God in Christ, 122
Cigarette smoking, 175–76
  and black males, 145
  physical effects of, 176
  racial comparisons, 175